Judges and the Language of Law

"This elegantly written monograph argues persuasively that a central cause for the decades-long expansion of judicial power lies not so much in the ambition of judges as in changes of the law itself: As the specificity of laws has declined, so the power of the courts has expanded. Matthew Williams' masterful analysis, which straddles history, law and political science, causes us to rethink key theories of the judicialization of politics. His work is a tour de force that will be appreciated not only for its combination of computational text analysis with nuanced process tracing histories of judicial power, but also for its expansive ambition, covering seven decades and five jurisdictions."

—Petra Schleiter, *Professor of Comparative politics, University of Oxford, UK*

"We live in an age of data and data analytics. Analysing huge swathes of legislative text across time and jurisdictions, Matthew Williams has revealed a series of fascinating changes in language use. He clearly demonstrates that indeterminacy in the language of legislation affords considerable scope for judges and those exercising judicial determinations to exercise wide powers of interpretation. This clearly written book with its compelling narrative is an important contribution to our understanding of law and policy in the 21st century."

—Professor Sir Nigel Shadbolt, *Department of Computer Science, University of Oxford, UK*

Matthew Williams

Judges and the Language of Law

Why Governments Across the World Have Increasingly Lost in Court

palgrave
macmillan

Matthew Williams
Jesus College
University of Oxford
Oxford, UK

ISBN 978-3-030-91494-3 ISBN 978-3-030-91495-0 (eBook)
https://doi.org/10.1007/978-3-030-91495-0

This Palgrave Macmillan imprint is published by the registered company Springer Nature Switzerland AG
The registered company address is: Gewerbestrasse 11, 6330 Cham, Switzerland

For Jasper

PREFACE

At the time of writing, *The Texas Heartbeat Act 2021* (also known as SB8) has been, in effect, approved by the US Supreme Court. The law privatises anti-abortion enforcement to Texan citizens. This led US Attorney General Merrick Garland to sue the state for improper delegation of state functions (*United States v Texas*, Case No. 1:21-cv-796-RP). The aim of SB8 is to subvert Federal protections of abortion held in the cases of *Roe v. Wade*, and *Planned Parenthood v Casey*. The Supreme Court refused to issue an injunction preventing the law's enforcement, and thereby tacitly approved its constitutionality.[1] Indeed, a case against another so-called "heartbeat bill" that is to be heard in late 2021 from Mississippi may explicitly overrule the near fifty-year-old precedent in *Roe*.[2]

As a political scientist, these sorts of hugely impactful court rulings have always been of interest. Somewhat lacking in the literature, however, was an explanation of how such policy power developed for judges. Battles such as those in Texas are difficult to contextualise through a longer historical perspective, and with sensitivity to both legal reasoning and modern political science. I therefore set out to code a machine reading algorithm to read millions of words of law across decades and several countries. The aim was to create the longitudinal data needed to better comprehend contemporary case law, but to do so in such a way as not to

[1] *Whole Woman's Health v. Jackson* Docket no. 21A24.

[2] *Dobbs v. Jackson Women's Health Organization* Docket no. 19-1392.

denigrate complex legal documents to nothing more than "text as data". This book therefore offers a mixed-methods and comparative analysis of judicial politics from the Second World War to the present day, focussed primarily on five prominent democracies. The ambition is to help reconcile political science and legal scholarship, without falling between two stools. At any rate, the book aims to contextualise the fire and fury that emanates from the abortion debate in America, to understand how judges make and justify their decisions.

This book would have been simply impossible without the support, friendly criticism, kindness, and prodding I have received. Especially deep thanks are due to my doctoral supervisor—Professor David Robertson. We sadly lost David in 2017, but I will never forget his advice that I should think more like a playful toddler than a "serious academic". He is missed, but not forgotten.

I am also indebted to many others who have supported me, including Bill Child, Elias Dinas, Ruth Dixon, David Doyle, Peter Edge, Christopher Hood, Alex Lumbers, Paul Martin, Caroline Mawson, Karolina Milewicz, Nick Owen, Alan Renwick, Petra Schleiter, Noa Schonmann, Marc Stears, Zofia Stemplowska, James Tilley, Stuart White, Stephen Whitefield, and Radek Zubek. I should like, in particular, to acknowledge the research assistance from my wonderful former student Matthew Cook. And I am deeply grateful for the Jesus College Major Projects Research Grant that funded the project. In addition to which, the Political Studies Association, and its Parliaments Group, have been exceptionally kind in allowing me to present early draft chapters. Thanks to you Marc Geddes, Louise Thompson, and Alexandra Meakin, in particular. Also, many thanks are due and gladly given to Jemima Warren and Arun Kumar Anbalagan at Palgrave Macmillan for their patience and support from proposal to typescript.

Finally, I wish to thank my loving family. Claire, Teddy, and Jasper have helped me persevere with writing and push through the imposter syndrome. They also demonstrate how powerful language can be in creating a sum greater than its parts.

Oxford, UK — Matthew Williams
2021

A Note on Referencing

In this book, references made to laws will, where appropriate, describe their precise jurisdictional origins. For instance, disputes in UK public law most often proceed through the courts of England and Wales, rather than the separate jurisdictions of Scotland or Northern Ireland. As such, English law (more properly English and Welsh law) is in many instances also UK law. Similarly, US federal litigants may appeal to a Circuit Court whose geographic reach is lesser than its legal jurisdiction. The enormously powerful US Court of Appeals for the Ninth Circuit manages cases from the entire western seaboard, in addition to Hawaii and Alaska. It nonetheless has the capacity to pronounce on law for the entire federation, unless and until overruled in such by the US Supreme Court. When referencing court cases, the official court citation will be used, and, where appropriate, the law report from which the case was accessed.

As for legislation, there is nothing new in variable legislation between the states of the US, the Länder of Germany, and the Provinces/Territories of Canada. But, what is new are creeping discordances between laws of devolved Parliaments in the UK, and collectivités territoriales of France. Despite these, the book concentrates on national legislation, and references to legislation will be the essential details of a law's name and its year of promulgation.

Contents

List of Figures

List of Tables

PART I

Language in Contemporary Politics

CHAPTER 1

Introduction and State of the Art

For several decades, a global "judicialisation" of politics has been observed, entailing an "expansion of the province of courts or the judges at the expense of the politicians and of the administrators" (Tate and Vallinder 1995, 3; Sunkin 1994, 125; Ginsburg 2008). Why has this occurred? Governments have either lost directly as parties to litigation, or, they have lost indirectly, where court rulings curtailed present and future policy-making discretion. These consequences raise questions of justice and democratic theory (Waldron 2005). But this book aims to explain the history as to why and how judges' power expanded after the war. By focussing on power across seven decades, we will see that judges behaved with political consequence not necessarily when they wanted to, but when they had means, opportunity, and institutional incentives to. The global expansion of judicial power was not led by judges, therefore. Necessary changes in the matrix of judicial policy power—ideologies (Volcansek 1992; Jackson et al. 2010), incentives (Guarnieri and Pederzoli 2002), resources, litigants (Epp 1998), and legitimacy (Klarman 1996)—were, for the most part, exogenously rendered. Judges would simply have been too weak to have acted unilaterally.

As such, "the expansion of the province of courts" was preceded by an expansion in the scope, authority, and material capacity of states writ large. Whilst judicial policy rulings may indeed come "at the expense of the politicians and of the administrators", there has been a rising tide of

M. Williams, *Judges and the Language of Law*,
https://doi.org/10.1007/978-3-030-91495-0_1

state power that has lifted all institutional boats. Of interest, therefore, is the precise mechanism by which shifting ideologies of state power have connected with government-constraining litigation. There are a number of plausible hypotheses to test—including that governments simply break more laws. But the most viable explanation for a decades-long expansion of judicial power lies in changes to the primary resource of adjudication—the law itself. Changes to the conception and execution of statecraft can be observed as changes to the coordinative and communicative discourses used by states to manage policies (Schmidt 2008).

Put plainly, the language of legislation has changed. Laws have been, to an increasing extent, linguistically underdetermined. This indeterminate language of law represents the social ambivalence and loose policy bargains that preceded it. And, in turn, the indeterminacy of language enables post-promulgation discretion for policy implementation. This is a meso-level theory, where language connects macro-level social changes to individual court rulings at a micro-level. It is not simply that governments increasingly break laws, it is that the precise substance and correct procedural implementation of laws is less easily identifiable. The concept of lawfulness, meanwhile, has barely changed in centuries (Bennion 2008). In other words, the education and socialisation of judges, and the methods by which they determine the legality of executive decisions is broadly consistent through time. But the law itself (and in particular legislation) has changed rapidly with post-war reconstructions, welfare expansions, and other drivers of increased state capacities. Judges face demands from state and private litigants for laws to be clarified. Even when judges can be assumed to be pursuing their personal policy preferences, they are given cover to do so by a conspicuous discrepancy between the rule of law and individual pieces of legislation (see, for example, Ferejohn and Weingast 1991).

And, in resolving legislative indeterminacies, judicial rulings are more likely to be norm-conserving than norm-progressing (March and Olsen 1989). This is to ensure sustenance of the primary judicial resource—legitimate jurisdiction (Vanberg 2001). Where juris-*diction* etymologically describes an authority to speak of the law. In the rare, but prominent, instances where judges are a vanguard for progressive policy change, they will do so under the cover of supportive public or elite opinion (Klarman 1996), and they will defend their vanguardism according to extant principles of law. This is the optimal strategy for institutionally weak actors to maintain their perceived authority (Gibson et al. 1998; Helmke 2002).

Table 1.1 Dataset overview

Jurisdiction	*Time frame*	*Number of words of legislation*
Canada	2001–2020	7,266,607
France	1958–2019	12,336,391
Germany	1950–2018	8,466,537
UK	1948–2019	10,338,681
US	1948–2019	17,782,410
187 World constitutions	1789–2014	4,366,046
Total	7469 country years	60,556,672

An unlikely explanation for seven decades of expanded judicial power is that the judges simply wanted the power and took it (Roosevelt 2006). Such a proposition cannot be explained according to basic tenets of political science. Judges simply do not have the power, resources, or legitimacy to lead a self-serving expansion without extra-judicial support and stimulation (Hanretty 2013).

As Jeremy Bentham put it, "the power of the lawyer is in the uncertainty of the law" (D'Amato 1983). Needed, therefore, is a *langue durée* analysis of legal certainty (Hönnige 2011). This book offers both quantitative and process tracing histories of judicial power across the world, with focusses on five jurisdictions—Canada, France, Germany, the UK, and the US. Central to this endeavour is a natural language processing entity extraction algorithm. This is a computer program, written in Python script, that is capable of measuring relative meaninglessness in law from the semantic and syntactic variances across time. Natural language processing (or NLP) is used in search engines as an interface between human and computer languages. Law is broadly analogous to a computer program, with lines of encoded instructions capable of execution, save for the presence of syntactical bugs, pragmatic omissions, or semantic elisions. The NLP program has been used to great effect in past research on British legislation, and is now being applied to this global comparative history (Williams 2017a, b, 2018). Readers are welcome to test the program for themselves, and are welcome to access the entirely scrubbed plain text dataset of laws, that is described in Table 1.1.[1]

[1] Please visit matthewlippoldwilliams.com.

These data are complete, as far as availability allows, meaning that measures of confidence and statistical significance are unnecessary. These new data allow us to understand better the accretion of judicial power over decades. This was no overnight coup. Judges have faced demands for expanded political power since at least the 1960s (Stevens 2005). Understanding shock decisions—such as the UK Government's defeated case to prorogue Parliament in 2019[2]—becomes easier when adopting synoptic views through both time and space. Central to the causal mechanism is not simply an increased quantity of enacted law, although that is a primary indication of state expansion. For example, in criminal justice legislation, the UK Parliament's enactments of the 1950s amounted to just three-fifths of one per cent of the total output between 1950 and 2020. By contrast, 30% of all criminal justice legislation enacted in these seventy years came between 2000 and 2007, during the latter two-thirds of Britain's New Labour governments. More important to judicial power than this increased volume, however, is the increased indeterminacy of laws. Put plainly, judges face both institutional incentives and litigant demand to determine the indeterminate law. This is how they obtain political and policy influence.

Examples will help summarise this process of judicial power accretion. A 2021 case before Germany's Federal Constitutional Court (FCC) hinged on contested interpretations of "especially aggravated arson".[3] A Munich drug dealer was hiding from police in his grandparents' apartment. He barricaded the doors, took out a kitchen knife, and started a fire to stop anyone entering. The blaze forced his retreat to a balcony, where he was shot in both legs by police. Despite obviously committing a number of offences, his trial was delayed as police investigated whether this was an aggravated offence. The man was held in pretrial detention for 13 months. He issued a constitutional complaint to the FCC that his liberty was being deprived. The judges agreed and reprimanded the Bavarian authorities for their administrative inefficiencies. Prosecutors wanted evidence of aggravated arson, so as to secure a lengthier sentence. As such, it was necessary for them to establish a breach of section 306b Strafgesetzbuch (the Federal Criminal Code). To

[2] *R (Miller) v. The Prime Minister and Cherry v. Advocate General for Scotland [2019] UKSC 41.*

[3] BVerfG, Feb. 3, 2021, 2 BvR 2128/20.

demonstrate how the machine reading algorithm works, the following excerpt includes emphases on those words that are likely to contribute to indeterminacy:

> *Especially aggravated* arson. (1) Whoever, by committing arson within the meaning of section 306 or 306a, causes *serious* damage to *another* person's health *or* damage to a *large* number of people's health incurs a penalty of imprisonment... for a term of at *least* five years *if*... the offender... prevents the fire from being extinguished *or* makes extinguishing the fire *more difficult*.

Whether the defendant had caused "serious damage" and made "extinguishing the fire more difficult" had to be investigated. The FCC judges recognised how adjectives in the legislation were responsible for procedural delays:

> The prosecution has not insignificant legal difficulties. The problem is whether the complainant can also be accused of especially serious arson... the follow-up investigations into the scope of damage are of considerable importance, because this legal question does not arise if essential components of the building had burned.[4]

The FCC did not declare the law to be unconstitutional, as they are empowered to do. Indeed, they did not even construct away the indeterminacy, but left it open for prosecutorial discretion. They restricted the ruling to assertion of procedural proprieties in the face of fuzzy legalese. The stimulation for judicial intervention in policy was the language of law and a concomitant litigant claim for a determination.

In practically all cases, indeterminacies in law are not merely textual, but are also contextual, subtextual, or intertextual. For example, in the US, judges must reconcile state and federal legislation with constitutional rules of law, some of which are, despite their long-standing, highly indeterminate. In the 2015 US Supreme Court case of *Horne v. Department of Agriculture*,[5] no less an authority than Magna Carta was cited to determine the fate of many tonnes of state-expropriated raisins. Marvin Horne was ordered to hand over a little under half of his raisin crop to federal

[4] Ibid., para 25.

[5] 576 U.S. ___ (2015).

authorities under legislation designed to regulate supplies and prices of the crop. The court ruled that this federal legislation was unconstitutional given its lack of clarity and the strong constitutional protections for personal property. This was of course not a highly publicized case, but building a theory of judicial behaviour cannot rely solely on the most celebrated or maligned examples.

Indeed, whilst indeterminate law increases the potentiality and probability of judicial policy incursion, it does not guarantee it. Here we can resort to a famous example. In pursuit of *laïcité* (secularism), the French state enacted legislation to ban the wearing of all facial occlusions in public spaces. The ban included motorcycle helmets, but was widely understood to be a "Burqa Ban". In the case of *S.A.S. v. France*[6] a young woman took the French government to the European Court of Human Rights, having failed to convince domestic courts that the law was incompatible with her rights. The Strasbourg Court declared its misgivings, but upheld the ban's lawfulness. The court ruling included clear evidence of judicial uneasiness as to the case outcome. Evidence includes this cited "Viewpoint" from the Council of Europe's Commissioner for Human Rights:

> Prohibition of the burqa and the niqab will not liberate oppressed women, but might instead lead to their further exclusion and alienation in European societies. A general ban on such attire constitutes an ill-advised invasion of individual privacy and, depending on its terms, also raises serious questions about whether such legislation is compatible with the European Convention on Human Rights. (Hammarberg 2011)

Despite their substantive queasiness, the judges had no wiggle room to intervene against the French government. The contested legislation (Loi n° 2010–1192) whisked through the National Assembly with 335 votes in favour and just one solitary vote against. Besides this overwhelming democratic mandate, the legal language was tightly constructed:

> No one may, in public places, wear clothing that is designed to conceal the face.

[6] Application no. 43835/11.

This book therefore aims to situate judges in their historical and institutional contexts. It provides vast quantities of new evidence capable of testing long-standing hypotheses that legal certainty came under strain from state expansion. It thereby poses empirical challenges to the concept of judicialisation. The "judicial" prefix could be interpreted as focussing overly on the judges, as opposed to interrogating their exogenously imposed incentives. Secondly, the "isation" suffix could imply a continuous and secular trend towards judicial empowerment. The research presented here allows us to understand not only why judges have ruled against governments, but also why they often have not.

A principal motivation for this book is multi-disciplinarity. In these pages will be methods applied from political science, history, computer science, and literary scholarship that have been developed to test theory most commonly advanced in legal scholarship—that judges, generally speaking, react to their socio-legal environment rather than actively trying to manipulate that environment. The book will analyse the incentives for judges to manage textual indeterminacies in ways that either sustain or challenge government power. Key to this is understanding and carefully considering the legal raw materials of adjudication, and how judges seek to determine their meaning. In the words of the late, great, David Robertson (2010, 8): "far too little attention is paid to what judges actually say in judging, as opposed to simply the decisions they reach".

The book is therefore attempting to cross disciplinary barricades. It is a risky gambit that can encourage objections from all camps. Nevertheless, the origins and sustenance of judicial policy power is not a matter of concern solely to political scientists or law scholars, nor is it a matter that cannot be assisted with methods from history, computer science, and literary scholarship (Banakar and Travers 2005; Moretti and Pestre 2015). But, to avoid the book falling between disciplinary stools, it can be asserted that in essence it is a work of political science, in so far as it analyses power and the means of its faithful communication between and beyond state actors. And this is a timely study. Judicialisation is highly controversial. Judges are smeared as "activist", and resented for their presumed pursuit of their own anti-democratic agendas (Roosevelt 2006). The aim here is to acknowledge and revel in the complexity of judicialisation, and offer new theory and evidence of a historic motor for court "activism".

This introductory chapter proceeds by outlining a theory and its contribution to contemporary research. The chapter structure (as with the book's overall structure) describes a funnel—from macro-social origins, through meso-level linguistic changes, through to micro-level decision-making.

Theory

In a 2012 case, the UK Supreme Court ruled against the British government and delayed the deportations of seven Algerian nationals.[7] These men were suspected of a conspiracy to commit terrorist offences, but were spared deportation upon the presentation of evidence that they would likely be tortured on repatriation. This evidence depended on testimony from an anonymous witness. Anonymous testimony poses a challenge to principles of open justice,[8] but the court called for re-hearings so as to include the fateful testimony. This is an example of judicialisation. A court transferred a policy decision (when to deport threatening individuals) into a legal decision (what just limits to state power exist). More abstractly, judges transmogrified the issue from a focus on prospective and multipolar social goals, to the retrospective and bipolar interests of competing litigants. As we will see, the judges orchestrated this move so as to determine a rule of law in response to conspicuous uncertainty.

The stability of policy language is an emerging area of research for political science. The genre of law can be observed as generic patterns of intra-, inter-, and extra-institutional discourses (Gotti 2012). Degenerating rules of law—in the sense of lexico-grammatic deviations from genre expectations—create instabilities that will encourage litigation, and will open space for judicialisation (Williams 2017b). As Vivien Schmidt (2008, 314) has argued:

[7] *W (Algeria) and another v Secretary of State for the Home Department; PP (Algeria) v Same; Z (Algeria) and others v Same* [2012] UKSC 8.

[8] See, in particular, Lord Brown at paragraph 16 of the ruling. He described the potential consequences of an *ex partes* hearing, including, notably, a permanent injunction against the UK government referring to or using any intelligence that emerges in a closed hearing.

> institutional action can… be predicated on what I call foreground discursive abilities, through which agents may change (or maintain) their institutions. These discursive abilities represent the logic of communication, which enables agents to think, speak, and act outside their institutions even as they are inside them, to deliberate about institutional rules even as they use them, and to persuade one another to change those institutions or to maintain them.

Legislative genre changes indicate institutional changes (Gotti 2012). Genre in language is an observable implication of customary or normative behaviour. Institutions, being rules of the political game, are sustained by a shared and meaningful "logic of communication" (Hall and Taylor 1996; Pierson and Skocpol 2002). Modulations in the meaningfulness of this shared discourse affect the perceived clarity of policy goals (Chun and Rainey 2005), and affect the capacity of principals to delegate powers (Strøm et al. 2003). With indeterminate policy goals and delegation of authority, accountability is also implicated (Staton and Vanberg 2008). As such, legislative genre instability could be intentional or a form of institutional entropy. The point being that official languages gradually and almost imperceptibly change, thereby creating friction between normative expectations and linguistic reality. It is through massive datasets and efficient machine reading that we can observe these subtle entropic forces. The indeterminacy in legislation is caused by socio-political complexity, but it in turn triggers discontented litigation and judicial resolution. Legislative language is part effect and part cause, and situated at the meso-level.

Around the turn of the twentieth century, statute law operated as a precise "statutum". This was a command from the legislature to fix identified problems in common or civil laws. The contemporary model of statute law is not just of a command to fix but also an instrument to enable. Whilst governments seek policy manoeuvrability, state power is increasingly underdetermined and therefore lacking both mandate and accountability. By observing the tiny changes in legislative language across decades, we will see how spaces were gradually opened by legislators for executive, judicial, and bureaucratic discretion. This allows us to explain the micro-foundations of judicialisation without unverifiable assumptions of an individual judge's psychological state or policy preferences. Rather than assume judges wanted judicialisation, we can measure when they enjoyed discretion to pursue it, and when such discretion was denied by clear legal language.

We can also explain why judicialising court rulings tend towards liberality. The default legal power of democratic states over its citizen is either non-existent or highly constrained. When in doubt about the legitimacy of legislation, courts are incentivised to cut away state power. Added to which, we will discover that a major cause of indeterminacy in law is ambivalence regarding the rectitude and application of state powers. Modern democracies have become more tolerant of civic autonomy and diversity. There are resulting instabilities in law making, as principle, ideology, and other social foundations are either partially conceived or absent. The consequence is that legal discourse relies less on a cohering theory of statecraft. This has advantages for individual autonomy. But, at extreme levels of indeterminacy, the law will be incapable of managing "wicked" ecological problems (Rittel and Webber 1973; Chapman 2015). These being problems that affect not just individuals, but groups and communities. For instance, resolving the externalities of globalisation, ensuring social order, and mitigating the effects of climate change, all call for clear logics of communication in legislation. In the absence of such clarity, discretion will fall to the executive and judiciary to impose a logic.

An example, discussed further in Chapter 7, is the 1962 case of *Brody, Dansky, Rubin v. The Queen* that came before the Supreme Court of Canada.[9] Litigation turned on a single adjective: "undue". Specifically, the court was tasked with determining whether D.H. Lawrence's *Lady Chatterley's Lover* was obscene according to a legislative definition of exerting "undue exploitation" with sex. The novel was declared obscene both at trial and on appeal. By consequence, a bookseller was charged with an offence. But, he was exonerated on second appeal to the Supreme Court, when five of the four Justices determined the meaning of "undue", and, in doing so, defaulted to a constrained state:

> The phrase 'undue exploitation' is aimed at excessive emphasis on the theme of sex for a base purpose. Measured by the internal necessities of the novel, there was no such undue exploitation. There was no more emphasis on the theme of sex than was required in the treatment of such a serious work of fiction. No matter whether 'undue exploitation' is to be measured by the internal necessities of the novel itself or by offence against community standards, this novel does not offend.[10]

[9] *Brody, Dansky, Rubin v. The Queen, 1962 CanLII 80 (SCC), [1962] SCR 681.*

[10] Ibid., at p. 682.

That judges even had to determine "offence against community standards" was a consequence of indeterminate legislation. In a much better known judicial dictum, Justice Potter Stewart of the US Supreme Court ruled that indeterminate state obscenity laws could not apply to a cinema owner:

> It is possible to read the Court's opinion [on obscenity in past cases] in a variety of ways. In saying this, I imply no criticism of the Court, which, in those cases, was faced with the task of trying to define what may be indefinable. I have reached the conclusion... that, under the First and Fourteenth Amendments, criminal laws in this area are constitutionally limited to hard core pornography. I shall not today attempt further to define the kinds of material I understand to be embraced within that shorthand description, and perhaps I could never succeed in intelligibly doing so. But I know it when I see it, and the motion picture involved in this case is not that.[11]

Justice Stewart was consciously and openly using his own discretion to determine the law. It was a discretion he does not seem to have desired, but was thrust upon him by the effects of indeterminate legislation. The key point being that legislative genre shifts are an observable indication of barely perceptible, but nonetheless impactful institutional change that empowers judges. Existing research on institutional dynamics focusses on the stability of states (Bates et al. 1998); of veto players (Tsebelis 2002); of cabinets and coalitions (Martínez-Gallardo 2014); of party systems (Powell and Tucker 2014); and of policy substance (Rosenthal 2013). This book contributes by analysing institutional discourses under normal conditions, and in response to shocks (Thelen 1999). This yields new data to assess the capacity of legislatures to represent reality through shared language. Data will reveal and test different patterns of language use in "transformative" and "reactive" legislatures (Polsby 1990; Cox and Morgenstern 2001), and will describe the higher discursive stability obtained in consensual as opposed to majoritarian political systems (Lijphart 2012).

The theory also nuances judicial histories that (quite reasonably) describe deliberate reforms to judicial powers. For example, judges in the UK were pulled further into policy determinations by the introduction

[11] *Jacobellis v. Ohio*, 378 U.S. 184 (1964), p. 378.

of legal aid in 1949; membership of the European Economic Community; Order 53 of the 1978 Rules of the Supreme Court (application for judicial review); the *Supreme Court Act 1981*; the incorporation of the European Convention on Human Rights by the *Human Rights Act 1998*, the *Constitutional Reform Act 2005* and creation of a fully independent Supreme Court; and modernisation of the tribunals system with the *Tribunals, Courts and Enforcement Act 2007*. We will also see how the French Conseil constitutionnel was substantially empowered in 2008, when amendments to Article 61 of the Constitution allowed citizens to pursue a posteriori (concrete) constitutional review for the first time. This procedure, known as a *question prioritaire de constitutionalité* (QPC) was first used in 2010 and has led to judicialisation of varied policies, including a ban on the construction of cockfighting Gallodromes.[12] Such deliberate gifts of power have of course driven judicialisation. But, these reforms have only changed the judicial toolkit, they did not create the disputes that relied on these tools.

In describing judicial behaviour as triggered by exogenous linguistic instabilities, this book aligns with historical institutionalism in political science (Hall and Taylor 1996), and orthodox legal theories (Levi 1948; Dahl 1957; Merryman 1981; Edwards 1984; McGuire and Stimson 2004). These positions are at odds with legal realist theories (Robertson 1998). Whilst orthodox theories focus on law as the primary driver of jurisprudential change, realist theories nuance its importance and look in addition to the preferences of judges. Orthodox theories are institutionalist and structuralist, stressing the bounded rationality of judges (Gillman and Clayton 1999). Realists favour more of a mixture of structural and agency variables. They followed the nineteenth-century American pragmatists in this, as well as the Supreme Court Justice, Oliver Wendell Holmes Jr. (1920). Realists have hypothesised, for example, that a judge's behaviour depends about as much on what they eat for breakfast as it does on the law (Robertson 1998). In political science, realism is represented as attitudinalism—wherein the judges' preferences are complete, transitive, and lead their decision-making (Schubert 1965; Gibson 1983; Sisk et al. 1998; Segal and Spaeth 2002). Also from political science are strategic

[12] ECLI: FR: CC: 2015: 2015.477.QPC.

models that assume judges are preference maximising rationalists, but who are locked in a competitive policy game with other players. Strategic theories therefore determine Nash equilibrating decisions by which courts push their advantage when possible, and retreat when necessary (North and Weingast 1989; Eskridge Jr and Ferejohn 1992; Epstein and Knight 1998; Garrett et al. 1998; Carrubba et al. 2008). What links the attitudinalist and strategic positions is their focus on judicial preferences. What separates attitudinalism and strategic theories is the institutional constraints acknowledged by the latter.

Other theories argue that demand for change to judicial power came primarily from politicians, rather than judges or private litigants. Specifically, political elites deliberated orchestrated judicialisation of "high" or "mega" policy issues to depoliticise them. This allows elites to preserve their hegemony, whilst judges carry the burden of managing irreconcilable policy fights (Hirschl 2004). Examples of this "judicialise to depoliticise" action might include abortion in France, Germany, and the US.[13] Failures to grasp this policy nettle effectively forced courts to step in and settle on-going disputes. Other theories describe forces coming from the bottom up rather than from the top down. Notably, following a post-war "rights revolution" came heightened demands for individual autonomy from state power (Epp 1998). And, beyond self-regarding rights consciousness, was a growing other-regarding clamour for social justice. Public opinion demonstrably shifted in favour of empowering the previously disempowered. Examples include widespread support for desegregating US public schools that lead rather than followed the *Brown v. Board* Supreme Court ruling (Klarman 1996).

Other theories speak to cultural and historical relativism. Some contributions describe a universalising approach to justice. The global expansion of judicial power was therefore driven in part by economic ties and cross-border leverage with, for example, the European Union (Levitsky and Way 2006). Others stress enduring points of difference in administrations of justice across borders. Culturally and historically rooted theories stress diverging views on justice (Couso et al. 2010)—including revolutionary ideologies (Moustafa 2006), transitional practices (Herron and Randazzo 2003), and critical assessments of justice and fairness (Hutchinson 2017). On the latter point are theories on race, gender, and sexuality (Keck

[13] As will be analysed in later chapters.

2009; Cichowski 2013); analyses of justice in the Global South (Rios Figueroa 2007; Ugochukwu 2011); as well as publications in non-English languages and non-Western journals (Niwayama 2012).

As with many research questions, there is this tension between aspiring to generalise, whilst recognising contextual specificities. Theories of judicialisation have reached for generalised models with some successes (Stone Sweet 2000; Dyevre 2010). But convincing theories have nonetheless acknowledged contextual constraints on judges (Hönnige 2011; Hanretty 2013). This book places its primary empirical focus on five well-established Western democracies, but not before also tracking global patterns in constitutional loquacity. What becomes clear through these pages is that judicial models count for less than political constraints and opportunities on judges. In other words, whether the jurisdiction is common law or civil law matters less than whether separations of political power, policy complexity, and legislative indeterminacy create interpretative spaces for creative adjudication (Lester and Piore 2004, 264). The principal aim of this book is to theorise and observe the connection between macro-social complexity, through meso-level legal indeterminacies, to micro-level judicialisation. In short, the aim is to track input to outputs through the under observed black box in the middle (Easton 1965).

Previous research has convincingly tracked changes on the demand side of politics. Martin Shapiro, most notably, described "political jurisprudence" as led by litigant demands. Both private civilians, and state actors such as political parties, have the power and perceived right to challenge deleterious side effects of state expansion (Shapiro 1983). Shapiro specifically contended that a centralising and policy-steering state leads to: (i) diminished independence for judges, as they must react to dynamic political events (Hillbink 2012); (ii) rising demands for protection from government overreach; and, ultimately (iii) use of the judiciary as an alternative avenue for resolving policy disputes (Shapiro 1964). Alec Stone Sweet more abstractly argued that judges fulfil a basic political function—that of a third-party dispute resolver, intervening between disputants (Stone Sweet 2000, 12–20). He therefore argues, in a Weberian vein, that "triadic dispute resolution (TDR)" by judges will crowd out preexisting normative structures of dispute resolution. As society has become more tightly coordinated by an expanded bureaucracy, there is both policy agonism, and, ironically, a demand for yet more bureaucracy to resolve it. As Henry Maine put it a century and a half before Stone Sweet, there an irresistible move "from status to contract" in human affairs (Maine 1861).

This book contributes by identifying specific triggers of judicialisation. It is not just litigant demand that drives judicialisation, but the supplies of law (Clayton 2002). Legislation, in particular, is a promulgated political bargain. Where the bargain is incomplete, underdetermined, or complex, then the "contract" is open to post-promulgation bargaining (see, for example, Dotan and Menachem 2005). It can also mean that agents deviate from the intent of principals (Strøm et al. 2003). As such, judicialisation is a mechanism of clarifying what was or ought to have been agreed in legislation or executive regulation. By inverting Henry Maine's dictum, we can assume that an incomplete contract opens space for status to re-emerge, with the potential to further degrade a rules-based order and enable populism. The courts are incentivised to close a space that might otherwise be filled by charismatic politicians, or under-constrained bureaucrats. Epstein and O'Halloran used a transaction cost analysis to explain why legislators delegated power to the executive branch via incomplete legislation (Epstein and O'Halloran 1999). Huber and Shipan similarly explained why lawmakers sometimes draft detailed legislation to micro-manage policy implementation, and why they sometimes draft "vague" legislation to enable bureaucratic discretion (Huber and Shipan 2002; Staton and Vanberg 2008). They argue that discretion is in most cases deliberately gifted so as to achieve long-term policy objectives. What is most likely not intended when drafting vague legislation is that judges will intervene in deciding policy outcomes. This is because judges will likely follow institutional norms and curtail executive discretion.

Of course, any theory will simplify reality, but it is essential to identify and manage any possible weaknesses. A first-order problem with orthodox legal theories is thought to be their internal logic. David Robertson summarised the syllogism as he saw it, before himself converting to an orthodox position (Robertson 2010):

> (1) Discretion [for judges] does exist, because statutes are sometimes vague, or precedents missing or conflicting. (2) Most judges most of the time will try very hard to stick within the clear meaning of the statute or the guidance of precedent. Some will from time to time try to develop the law to fit modern needs, but this 'public policy horse' is dangerous, to be ridden seldom and cautiously. (3) Where 'difficult cases' do crop up, some judges will act from personal idiosyncrasy, but these are mainly

> self-cancelling unsystematic quirks, not representing an intrusion of class ideology, and too limited to fit the realist model of permanent intuition. (Robertson 1982, 2)

The problem with this logic for Robertson was that steps two and three did not follow from the first predicate, and thus there are different "observation languages" at work. The first predicate is institutional (discretion exists), but steps two and three rely on unrelated behavioural factors, namely caution and idiosyncrasy. To tidy up this syllogism, it is necessary to employ predicates that interconnect, such as:

> (1) Judicial discretion exists when rules of law are indeterminate. (2) It is institutionally normal for judges to resolve disputes by removing indeterminacies. (3) An optimal resolution to legal indeterminacy will be widely recognisable as evincing legal and institutional norms (Hart 1961). It will thus be "appropriate" not merely intuitive (March and Olsen 1989).

None of which means to say that the judicial rulings will be morally optimal according to this logic. Recognisable or appropriate decisions are inherently conservative. Even if judges actively recognise new law, they will be doing so in reaction to public opinion, policy ambivalence, and legal indeterminacy. In the very rare instances when judges fail to anchor their rulings in existing norms of law, their rulings will be at high risk of being disregarded, overturned, and their legitimacy disdained. Judges are in an acutely vulnerable institutional position. Without powers of sword or purse, judges cannot easily lead the state or society where it would not otherwise go (Vanberg 2001). Even a devil-may-care judge on the cusp of retirement simply lacks the capacity to steer justice on their own without encountering institutional breaks, including multi-judge panels and multi-level appeals. Policy impactful court rulings will most likely be norm-conserving and can thereby often be expected to include iniquities, discrimination, and even, ironically, prejudice. As ever, it is not possible to abstract an ought statement from an is statement. This book will not apologise for nor commemorate judicial rulings. The aim is to understand why judges are more actively involved in policy. There are moral implications that will be considered, but these are secondary to the book's empirical focus.

A second-order, but nonetheless crucial challenge, is falsifiability. Orthodox theories can be accused of assuming judges act in "good faith", by assuming that judges react to appropriate external triggers. But almost any court ruling could be described as reactive (Braman 2006). However, much the same criticism can be made against realist or attitudinalist studies that identify "activist" or "supremacist" behaviour (Dickson 2007; Rozenburg 1997). To ensure falsifiability, concepts must be parsimonious and empirical. Segal and Spaeth for instance, developed an attitudinalist theory to analyse the transformative *Bush v. Gore* ruling of the US Supreme Court (Segal and Spaeth 2002). Their book utilised the value-neutral concept of "judicial policy-making". By machine analysing the relative presence or absence of "interpretive spaces for judges" this book avoids the falsification problem. It is possible to observe when legislative norms are sustained or degenerated. We can therefore observe the counterfactual of when judges refuse to intervene in policy when legal language is plain. We can also observe and acknowledge disconfirmatory evidence, where judges intervene in policy despite there being no conspicuous indeterminacies of law. This approach is more robust than the typologies of behaviour, such as "activist" and "restrained", or "liberal" and "conservative" (Roosevelt 2006).

Another possible falsification problem lies with indeterminacy. Brian Flanagan, for one, argues persuasively that there cannot be a literal meaning to any law, and thus all legal language must to some extent be indeterminate (Flanagan 2010). If all legal language is indeterminate then it would be impossible to measure determinate law, and the existence of indeterminacy could not be falsified. But, whilst there may be no objectively determinable law, there will be changes to lexico-grammatical "genre" that can be measured through time. It is also possible to describe language that is more or less meaningless, in so far as it relies to a greater or lesser extent on subtext, context, or inter-textual reference to be comprehended. This position is underpinned by the theory of post-positivism analysed further in Chapter 2. As a brief prelude, Neil MacCormick (2005) argued that the language of law is not demonstrative, but persuasive. As such, pure positivism, in the sense of objective meaning, is impossible, but more or less inter-subjective clarity is possible. An example is the *Representation of the People Act 1983*, in which section 1(1)(c) states: "A person entitled to vote… is of voting age (that is, 18 years or over) on the date of the poll". Whilst a Martian may quibble with what 18 years means, anyone socialised within the UK will take no time at all to understand this language. Hence, the extent of indeterminacy will be relative to the interpreter rather than text. For instance, adjectives such as "reasonable" have more specific meanings to lawyers than to laypeople (Mayo 2003). Nevertheless, there are some elements of legal language that will be universally unknowable and requiring of construction (Bennion 2008, 2009). Even "reasonable" only attained meaning to lawyers through decades of judicial construction.

And, what about non-legislative judicialisation? Judges in Canada, the UK, and US make important policy-impacting rulings in common law. The case of *Miller v. Prime Minister*, that denied Boris Johnson a long prorogation in 2019, was settled in common law. This was an unusual case in which the Prime Minister was testing the extent of his own prerogatives. But that he broke the law was not the anticipated ruling, and, by so declaring, judges curtailed executive privileges in their ruling. Relatedly, courts can affect public powers in private law. The US case of *New York Times Co. v. Sullivan*,[14] for example, was a defamation lawsuit in which it was ruled that freedoms of speech are more generously protected with regard to public officials than private citizens. Public policy will be made in common law, and, as such, the book cannot explain all cases of judicialisation. However, discretion for judges in common law derives from the same stimulus to resolve indeterminacies in law. For instance judges may seek to establish what the law is on a subject that legislatures have, for whatever reason, failed to legislate. This is the ultimate legislative indeterminacy, and is a key factor in explaining common law developments in contributory negligence, and misfeasance in public office (Robertson 1998). Criminal law is perhaps the most policy sensitive area of common law creativity. In 1992, the UK House of Lords (then final court of appeal) effectively invented a crime of rape in marriage. This deviation from precedent was justified on the basis that the law on rape was unjust, and needed to be aligned with contemporary mores. This case underscores the point that indeterminacy is not inherent in any text, but is relative to shared sources of meaningfulness. But, as argued above, textual indeterminacies do provide a pretext to legitimate judicialisation. Whether indeterminacies pertain to constitutional law, or rapidly increased quantities of statute law, they offer the most secure basis for judicialisation. Abstracting a general pattern from a unique case like *Miller* will achieve very little.

[14] 376 U.S. 254 (1964).

Referring back to the case of seven Algerian nationals, it captures the theory's primary elements. On the macro-level, the case entailed policy ambivalence between managing borders, whilst not conspiring in torture or other human rights abuses. It was a balancing of security and liberty that is nothing new to law, but is being played out in newly globalised contexts. The litigation centred on section 5 of the *Special Immigration Appeals Commission Act 1997* (SIAC), which contained a power to admit secret witness testimony. Also in contention was section 3(5)(a) of the *Immigration Act 1971,* which contains the deportation power:

> 3(5) A person who is not a British citizen is liable to deportation from the United Kingdom if– (a) the Secretary of State deems his deportation to be conducive to the public good.

The Secretary of State (Home Secretary in this instance) may deport a foreign national if it is in the interests of public policy to do so. But there are questions begging as to the substance of this law, as well as to the process of its implementation. These questions are not answered by a legislative text, but must be interpreted from context, subtext, and intertextual reference to other laws. As regards process, how must the Secretary of State "deem" their decision? Can they reach a decision on a whim, or only after deliberation? In UK administrative law, it is illegal for a minister to reach snap judgements.[15] Instead, judges will expect publicly accessible reasons for a decision. Secondly, how will the "public good" be identified, and what is "conducive" to goodness? In UK immigration law, rules and regulations are commonly used to determine these matters. However, any delegated legislation can be changed by the government with relative ease, and it must cohere with the primary legislation, or else judges will rule to reimpose Parliament's primary version. Thirdly, and most pertinent to this case, how does the Home Secretary's deportation power cohere with powers for the Special Immigration Appeals Commission (also contained in primary legislation) to manage security-sensitive proceedings? SIAC wanted a method for hearing the secret evidence, without it being disclosed. The Home Secretary (Theresa May at the time) did not want to face a permanent injunction against disclosing that evidence. Such evidence could have hypothetically predicted a terrorist

[15] *Secretary of State for Education and Science v Tameside Metropolitan Council* [1977] AC 1014, HL.

attack overseas, and would thereby create a diplomatic incident if the British Government knew of the threat, but did not warn any other implicated governments.

In regard to legal substance, therefore, were related questions. Could the men be deported without admitting secret testimony of their risks to torture? When assessing the public good, what rational method for balancing security and human rights was to be adopted? On these points, the Supreme Court (and SIAC) were required to consider Parliament's commitment to border security against her commitment to the *European Convention on Human Rights*, enshrined in the *Human Rights Act 1998*. Article 3 ECHR was at issue in this case, as it enforces an unqualified prohibition on torture. The UK Parliament may, if it wishes, rely on the lack of a higher law constitution to override such human rights commitments in the name of public policy. To do so they need only use precise legislative language. However, in this instance, as is typical of the judicialisation of immigration policy, the decision conserved individual rights, at the cost of enabling wide government discretion. As Lord Dyson explained in his ruling:

> ... two conflicting considerations are in play here. On the one hand, the appellants say that, unless the order that they seek is made, they will be unable to place material before SIAC which may be crucial to their case that, if returned to Algeria, they face a real risk of ill-treatment... contrary to article 3 of the Convention. If they are able to persuade SIAC of this risk, their appeals will succeed. Thus, the appellants say that it is essential to their case that they are able to place this evidence before SIAC: the stakes could hardly be higher for them (short of a risk to life itself). They also rely on rule 4(3) of the SIAC Rules which provides that subject to paragraphs (1) and (2), SIAC 'must satisfy itself that the material available to it enables it properly to determine proceedings'. In other words, it has a duty to ascertain all relevant facts.[16]

The crucial words here are "properly to determine proceedings". It is inevitable in higher courts of appeal that the determination of fact and law will be highly complex. However, the default, norm-conserving ruling demonstrated in this case was to obtain as much actionable evidence as is reasonable to ensure justice is done. The ruling had the subsidiary

[16] Lord Dyson at para 30.

consequence of denying that Parliament had, in it is indeterminate law, intended for the government to avoid international embarrassment at the expense of individual liberties. This theme will recur through the book: when precisifying laws, courts narrow discretion for governments and thereby widen it for civilians.

Hypotheses and Chapters Summary

Hypotheses have been extracted from this theory and will be tested through the following eight chapters. They test for macro-, meso-, and micro-level drivers of judicialisation. Most of these hypotheses are historical, as testing for changes through time. The first two parts of the book rely on quantitative methods, and the book's third part relies on qualitative process tracing. All hypotheses link to changes in language at the meso-level, either exploring how that language changed, or assessing its effects on judicialisation. Measures look to stability (genre), change (degenrification), and textual clarity. The tests draw on six levels of linguistic variability:

1. Textual changes to the relative meaninglessness of language.
2. Subtextual changes to restore meaningfulness.
3. Contextual changes.
4. Intertextual reconciliation of legislation with international laws, or domestic constitutional and regulatory laws.
5. Transtextuality, where a text is transcended, taking it beyond intertextual interpretation by synthesis of law and norms.
6. Metatextual changes, where one text is used to critically analyse another text. Typically in law this leads to subordination of one law by another. This differs from intertextuality in so far as one law is used against another, as opposed to in concert with it.

Also of interest are paratextual changes, but these are not systematically analysed. Paratextual changes would include any elements technically extraneous to the text, but capable of elucidating meaning. For example, these may include explanatory notes, preambles, or any other supplementary materials (Ginsburg et al. 2014).

Chapter 2 focusses primarily on the text, interrogating why legislative language is more indeterminate and how indeterminacies are managed.

To explain indeterminacy, the psychological concept of ambivalence has been co-opted. First described by Swiss psychologist Eugen Bleuler, ambivalence is the condition of simultaneously holding both positive and negatively-valenced views on the same matter (Segal and Perl 2019). In policy terms, this might describe a desire to simultaneously reduce immigration, whilst also wanting to protect the rights of immigrants. The term is applied here metaphorically, and therefore does not adhere to its technical applications. Nonetheless, it captures a sense of social dissensus on policy issues that is communicated in incomplete or underdetermined legislative language. Of course, on many policy matters, there will be no ambivalence at all, but these are unlikely to call for language whose meaning can be debated. The Burqa banning legislation described above is an example. There was overwhelming consensus in favour of restriction, and the tightly constructed legislation captured this. But, there is evidence of a generalised trend to increased indeterminacy in legislation, and it begs the question why this might be so.

We could pithily summarise the linguistic patterns as "Campaigning in prose, but governing in poetry". The inversion of an old adage suggests that contemporary electioneering promises are clear, repetitive, and open to little interpretative flair (Weldon 1953). Policy, however, must reconcile the promissory with the practical. Policy and law making is far messier than the stump speeches suggest, and the resulting language is hence wide open to interpretation (Poole 2007; Thompson 2016). As Theodore Lowi argued in *The End of Liberalism*, vague legislation was symptomatic of political compromise (Lowi 1979). Ultimately, this is likely the consequence of power dispersal, and institutions incapable of reconciling pluralism. In other words, voters have more power, more autonomy, and more discrete demands. Consensus institutions that seek a pre-promulgation deal on policy will be better adapted to managing a logic of communication, than will adversarial or majoritarian institutions (Lijphart 2012). Pulling on this thread, we must consider why there is more power for a wider diversity of citizens. Partly it has come from wider distribution of material resources post-war (Boix 2003; Acemoglu and Robinson 2006), and partly it has come from ideological recognition of value in diversity (Epp 1998). Kenneth Arrow (1950) predicted that with a diverse range of preferences it becomes impossible to make a social choice without arbitration. Arbitration increasingly comes from judges, working out what was intended from a mess of underdetermined policy choices.

In addition to this, before the war states were not expected to provide a suite of public services "from cradle to grave" (Lloyd 1985). The changing role of democratic states—from guarantor to guardian—was underpinned by a newly demanding mindset from citizens. This in turn triggered competition between politicians in a marketplace of policy ideas, where over-promising was rewarded. Key variables for explaining legislative indeterminacy include, therefore, topic complexity, goal ambiguity, ideological fluidity, variable time horizons, resource scarcity, and international competition. These and other forces yield two different outcomes—slow and difficult policy change, or change achieved with incomplete bargains (Tsebelis 2002). Both scenarios have spurred judicialisation. A lack of policy change to manage pressing social problems encourages litigation. And, conversely, enactment of indeterminate legislation will also empower judges to tidy up any interpretative difficulties.

Besides voters simply having more power to make demands of their governments, the aftermath of war saw strengthened commitments to liberty, autonomy, and rights. Whilst lip service was paid to these ideas pre-war, there were conspicuous exceptions made for the rights of, *inter alia*, women, people of colour, and indigenous peoples. The late twentieth century saw a slow rejection of incoherent applications of liberty, albeit there is still much ambivalence centred on questions of equality and justice. Other guiding state philosophies have also atrophied. For example, explicit or hidden commitments to religiosity have been superseded by secularism. As David Robertson argued (2010, 7), in secularising societies there is no higher textual authority than liberal constitutionalism. This has inevitably elevated judges as keepers of exegetical order.

To explain judicial responses to legislative indeterminacy, Bryan Jones's work on bureaucratic complexity and bounded rationality provides anchoring (Jones 1999, 2001). In France and Germany, judges are bureaucrats, and trained as such. In common law jurisdictions, judges have more autonomy, but they nonetheless will react to policy complexity in a similar manner to their bureaucratic colleagues. A specific expectation of Jones's work is to leptokurtosis in patterns of bureaucratic behaviour. The thin tall peaks and fat tails of a leptokurtic distribution signify that the vast majority of bureaucratic decisions conform tightly to norms, and therefore cluster at the centre. But, in response to sustained policy complexity, there are a small number of extremely outlying decisions that pull the distribution wider than would be expected from a normal bell-shaped distribution. It is predictable behaviour, punctuated by infrequent but extreme deviations from normality. Jones uses tectonics as a natural science metaphor for this process. There is stability, until there is an earthquake. In a similar vein, courts are bounded, until forces exogenous to the judiciary compel an extreme response. The infrequent extreme breaches in normal behaviour are difficult to predict *ex ante*, but will entail a confluence of wicked problems, ideological solutions, and cover for the courts from accountability.

Having explained this theory of political language, Chapter 3 hunts for evidence, beginning at the grandest possible scale. The chapter tests hypotheses of linguistic change in all of the world's available constitutions. Figures 1.1 and 1.2 tease some findings from the machine reading of

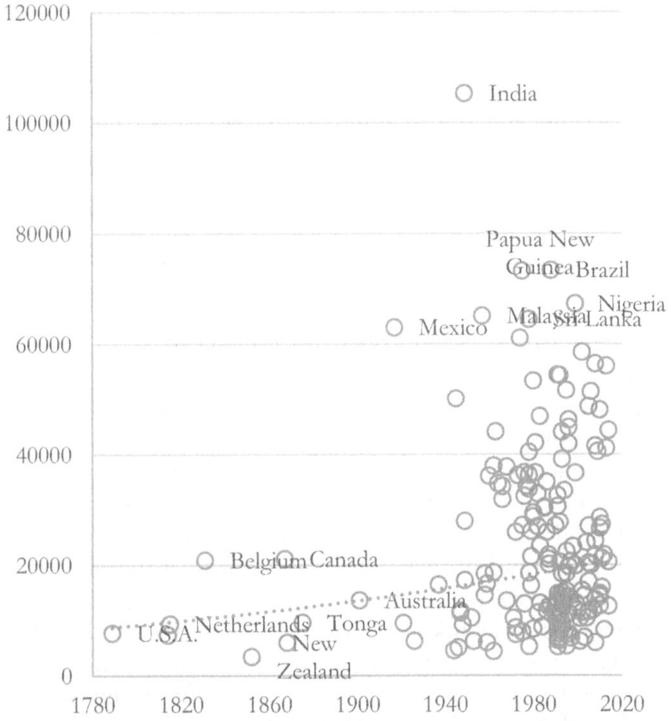

Fig. 1.1 Time vs word length, 1789–2020 (*Source* Author's creation using data from The Comparative Constitutions Project)

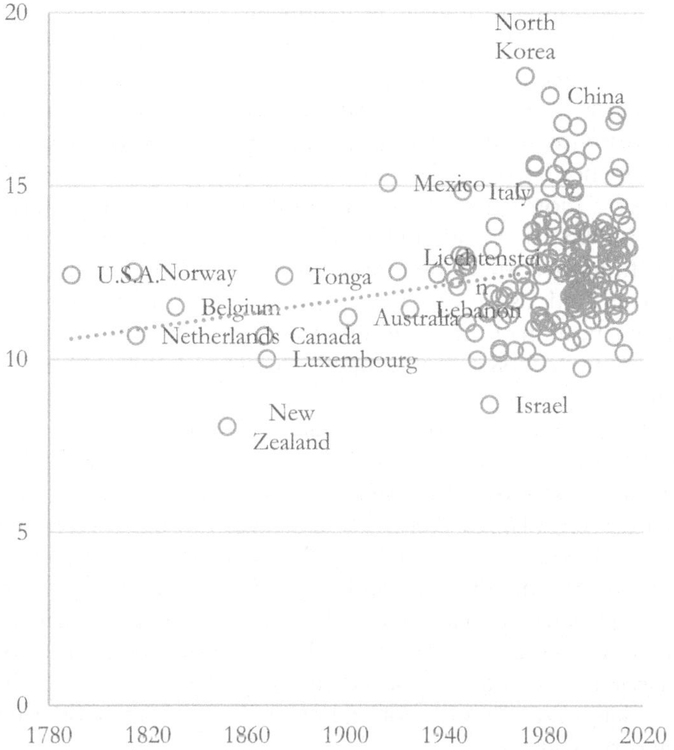

Fig. 1.2 Time vs indeterminacy (% words that are noun or verb qualifying) (*Source* Author's creation using data from The Comparative Constitutions Project)

4,366,046 words in 187 constitutions. Figure 1.1 describes a loose positive correlation between the age of the constitution and its word length. Figure 1.2 then describes a similarly wide but nonetheless positive correlation between the age of constitutions and their percentage of noun or verb qualifying parts of speech. Those constitutions promulgated more recently, have a higher percentage of these relatively indeterminate semantics. Of course, such a wide-angled analysis obviates specific instances where adjectives or conjunctions may be highly meaningful within their context. But of interest initially is identifying a general trend, later chapters of the book will be able to dive into the minutiae of how specific word choices affected litigation strategies and judicialisation.

Importantly, there is no correlation between word length and relative proportion of noun verb qualifying parts of speech. As such, word length does not predict relative indeterminacy. The basic linear model seeking correlation between the two variables yields a slope formula of $y = -0.000006x + 12.69$, and an R^2 of just 0.0002. For example, the US Constitution is short by international standards, but not especially determinate. And, as we will go on to observe in Chapter 6, entire legal careers have been made on a few adjectives and conjunctions in that great text, including “necessary and proper”, “cruel and unusual”, and “equal protection”.

But, before focussing on individual countries, Chapter 4 sustains the comparative endeavour with a method of difference analysis of five democracies. The chapter assesses how Canada, France, Germany, the UK, and the US adapted their legal languages to regular election cycles, and to the 2008 global financial crisis. We will observe, in line with expectations of Bryan Jones’s work on complexity, that patterns of language are more leptokurtic in majoritarian democracies, and more platykurtic in consensus democracies. In other words, consensus democracies demonstrate a relative advantage in sustaining inter-electoral genre stability in legislative language. They do not, to borrow Jones’s metaphor, experience as many earthquakes.

For instance, German institutions encourage consensual agreement on policy, thereby favouring legal clarity over underdetermined legislation (Lijphart 2012). This care in securing policy bargains derives in part from a historic mistrust of unaccountable authority. It is also tethered to pre-National Socialist norms of law, including the idea of *Rechtsstaat*, as well as the jurisprudence of Hans Kelsen captured in the constitutional *Grundgesetz* (Basic Law). Added to which are inter-regional lines of negotiation, including the *Beamtenstatus*, which encourages institutional discourses between central and local governments (Schröter 2007). Conversely, in France, the Fifth Republican constitution is significantly more centralised, executive dominated, and majoritarian than its German counterpart. Pierre Mazeaud, the former President of the Conseil constitutionnel, recognised a likely effect of this concentration of power in law. He denounced the use of indeterminate legislation with no clear enumeration of powers and duties. He claimed, specifically, that such laws were unintelligible and inaccessible to citizens (Mazeaud 2005). And, in the UK, a similarly executive-dominated polity was identified at the dawning of mass democracy. Lord Hewart described in 1929 that too much legislation sought "to subordinate Parliament, to evade the Courts, and to render the will, or the caprice, of the Executive unfettered and supreme" (Hewart 1929). My work to date demonstrates an extraordinary increase in legislative indeterminacy in the UK since Hewart's attack (Williams 2016, 2017a, b, 2018). There are few cultural, historical, and institutional fetters to British politicians crafting indeterminate powers, or non-specific duties.

But, despite the institutional differences, there is still evidence of rising legislative indeterminacy amongst all five of the democracies studied. Chapters 5–9 consider each country in turn, assessing results from machine reading all available criminal legislation, and then process tracing specific effects of language on judicial behaviour.

Tables 1.2 and 1.3 tease findings from these chapters. Table 1.2 describes the increased quantity of criminal legislation enacted in France, Germany, and the UK. The US and Canada have been omitted from this comparison, as it is not possible to find complete year-on-year criminal law enactments, but rather amendments to their respective criminal codes. This does not, however, preclude analysis of the changes to legislative language in those two jurisdictions. Data from France was included only after the inauguration of their Fifth Republic in 1958. Despite these

Table 1.2 Number of words of criminal justice legislation enacted in five jurisdictions

	France	*Germany*	*UK*
1950s		14,018	17,085
1960s	40,667	16,646	74,179
1970s	97,163	19,502	153,223
1980s	414,732	19,513	587,211
1990s	298,477	21,371	408,980
2000s	1,070,775	23,396	751,788
2010s	2,091,198	25,381	549,932
Minimum	40,667	14,018	17,085
Mean	668,835	19,975	363,200
Maximum	2,091,198	25,381	751,788
Standard deviation	719,700	3583	263,375

data deficiencies, Table 1.2 describes enormously increased quantities of criminal law enacted in both France and the UK, especially as compared to Germany. Regardless, all three countries saw the greatest quantities of law enacted after the millennium.

Table 1.3 describes changes in legislative indeterminacy through time. In the case of Canada, data are only available after 2000. In this table, the more accurate measure of per section or per article indeterminacy is used as opposed to percentages (Staton and Vanberg 2008). Percentages were used for the global comparisons because there is no consistency in the definition of "section" or "article" amongst the 187 countries. The problem with using percentages is that the numerator is affected by the denominator, as the number of words increases, the percentage of noun or verb qualifying words will decrease. Table 1.3 allows us to gauge how the language of legislation has changed in these five jurisdictions.

Despite the paucity of data from Canada, even there were nearly five more indeterminate parts of speech per section of criminal code in the 2010s as compared to the 2000s. In the US, the increase has been even more dramatic, from just over sixteen parts of speech per section in the 1960s, up to over eighty in the 2010s. The US constitution has many checks on majoritarian power, but these institutional limitations do not so often bite when it comes to criminal justice. As we will see in Chapter 6 (Table 1.3).

Table 1.3 Indeterminate parts of speech per section of legislation in five jurisdictions

	Canada	*France*	*Germany*	*UK*	*US*
1950			8.54	16.09	27.87
1960		8.42	10.16	15.97	16.30
1970		9.27	12.04	27.30	19.66
1980		10.93	12.23	25.40	26.10
1990		9.94	11.41	21.32	39.80
2000	33.86	19.46	14.34	22.20	48.33
2010	38.26	22.16	15.40	29.91	81.52
Minimum	33.86	8.42	8.54	15.97	16.30
Mean	36.06	13.36	12.02	22.60	37.08
Maximum	38.26	22.16	15.40	29.91	81.52
Standard deviation	2.20	5.37	2.17	4.95	20.87

Criminal justice legislation was chosen for analysis as these laws are central to any state's stateness. In other words, the capacity to secure or liberate citizens is a primary component of state authority. How this authority is managed, is therefore a central question to the development of modern states. These chapters offer narratives for each of the five countries on their post-war developments in criminal justice, including counterterrorism. Special attention will be paid to those laws presenting wide variances in the determinacy of language. The basic hypothesis of these chapters is that indeterminate exposition of policy is the primary cause of increased judicial discretion. It is therefore not simply the case that judges have taken power for themselves. This hypothesis will be tested in each state, allowing for consideration of the counterfactual, as in many cases judges refuse to rule against their governments, despite the substantive controversies of a case.

Chapters 5–9 therefore proceed with case selection on the independent variable. Those laws that display unusually high or unusually low indeterminacies per section for their time were analysed for their effects on judicial behaviour. To understand the judicial behaviour, the judges' own case reports were analysed within their broader socio-political contexts. The aim is to trace the judicial decision from macro political friction, through meso legislative language, to specific judicial determination. Of course, such process tracing is open to multiple interpretations, and proving beyond doubt there is a connection between judicial behaviour, legislative language, and socio-political context will be impossible. The best we can hope for is a persuasive circumstantial case. Hence, there is unlikely to be a smoking gun, but the threads of a case will start to become overwhelming that judges' behaviour is policy-oriented when there is a linguistic opportunity for them to engage. It is worth stressing that no studies of judicialisation have been able to provide systematic smoking gun evidence for models of behaviour, and we must work either with abstract formal modelling or indirect evidence (Vanberg 2001; Hanretty 2011). Having analysed over 60 million words of law, the concluding chapter considers some of the ethical implications, in particular as regards "judicial activism".

The Global Expansion of Judicial Power

The world's democracies have experienced an "expansion of the province of courts or the judges at the expense of the politicians and of the administrators" (Tate and Vallinder 1995, 13). This book aims to explain why, by adopting a long-range historical perspective, utilising machine reading techniques and vast data sets. A picture emerges of substantial changes to the primary raw material of adjudication—the law itself. A proliferation of plainly stated rules could be explained as a function of newly empowered and differentiated veto players, and the disempowerment of vested interests. Plain rules are efficient operational protocols, agreed through deliberate bargaining. In most contexts, however, we will observe the proliferation of indeterminate rules of law. These can be explained by rising policy complexity, mediated through poorly or un-differentiated veto players (with interests connected by party or institutional concentrations of power). Indeterminate rules will therefore be more pronounced in majoritarian polities where post-promulgation bargaining or bureaucratic discretion are valued. Alternatively, in consensus and majoritarian systems, we can expect indeterminacies in law when policy-makers are united in response to highly complex exogenous shocks, such as the 2008 financial crisis.

The primary driver of policy power for judges are litigant demands for clarification, supported by an ecosystem of public law lawyers seeking to profit from linguistic arbitrage. Judicialisation can become self-reinforcing, when judges become increasingly used to policy interventions. But, with weak institutional power and resources, judges need a pretext to be "active" policy-makers. The pretext will most safely be the text of law, its context, any relevant subtext, and a proliferation of intertextual sources of human rights law. There has therefore been a multi-decade, and barely perceptible shift in law's conceptual status from determinable code to individuated learning algorithm that is capable of refinement and reconfiguration. Interestingly, it is as if legislation is progressing from binary to analogue. Where laws were more likely in the past to describe that "x *will mean* y" they now demand more analogic reasoning "x *may, if necessary and reasonable, lead to* y" (Musolff 2004). This underdetermined language can yield discretion to state agents or citizens, but will ultimately be resolved by judges where disputes arise. Examples come from the UK's *Prison Act 1952*, section 8. In the original enactment, the section included, *inter alia*, the following language:

> Every prison officer while acting as such shall have all the powers, authority, protection and privileges of a constable.

This is an intertextual reference to enactments that empower constables, but it establishes a clear binary—every prison officer has the powers of a constable. A new section 8A was inserted by the *Criminal Justice and Public Order Act 1994*, and contains significant indeterminacies (emphases added):

> (1) An authorised person at a prison shall have the power to search *any* prisoner for the purpose of ascertaining whether he has *any* unauthorised property on his person.
> (2) An authorised person searching a prisoner by virtue of this section—
>
> (a) shall not be entitled to require a prisoner to remove *any* of his clothing other than an *outer* coat, jacket, headgear, gloves *and* footwear;
> (b) may use reasonable force where necessary; and
> (c) *may* seize *and* detain *any* unauthorised property found on the prisoner in the course of the search.
>
> (3) In this section "authorised person" means a person working at the prison, of a description for the time being authorised by the governor to exercise the powers conferred by this section.
> (4) The governor of a prison shall take *such* steps as he considers *appropriate* to notify to prisoners the descriptions of persons who are for the time being authorised to exercise the powers conferred by this section.
> (5) In this section "unauthorised property", in relation to a prisoner, means property which the prisoner is not authorised by prison rules or by the governor to have in his possession *or*, as the case *may* be, in his possession in a *particular* part of the prison.

The reliability of such side-by-side comparisons is undermined by obvious selection biases. This is why analysing all criminal justice laws since 1950 and all laws of any description since 2000 yields a firmer basis for concluding that legislative language has changed. For example, UK criminal legislation increased in quantity from 91 sections enacted in the 1950s, to 1444 sections in the 2010s. And, indeterminacies have increased from 16 parts of speech per section in the 1950s, to 30 in the 2010s. It was possible from these data to select laws with relatively high levels of indeterminacy, so as to assess their effects on judicialisation. And, the counterfactual will be observed, where laws of little to no indeterminacy, when such are litigated, yield no discretion for the courts.

State expansion necessitated new forms of legislative authorisation for civic and governmental action. Essentially, greater discretion is required to implement complex social policies without the strictures of legal precision. Legislatures have therefore been the biggest losers, by having to delegate significant discretionary power to agents, including the citizenry, central executive, local government, NGOs, tribunals, and, ultimately, the judiciary. Friedrich von Hayek and Harry Jones both anticipated that a state committed to civic welfare would empower judges. Hayek's "red light" position holds that collectivist welfare and individual liberties are exclusive goals, and cannot be reconciled. Jones's "green light" position held that an accommodation between liberty and collective welfare was possible, but difficult to administer (Harlow and Rawlings 2006). Legislation is insufficient to manage policy complexity and ambivalence. Other actors, including judges, are needed to complete the task of obtaining a legitimate "logic of communication".

Recent scholarship on democratic participation notes that legislation is an old solution that is ill-suited to contemporary problems. Decentralisation and citizen assemblies may, for example, be better at managing complexity with legitimacy (Dowding et al. 2003). But rapidly rising demands led to the adaptation of legislative tools already at hand to jobs they are not necessarily best suited to. Situations where policy solutions precede problems have been described with the "garbage-can model" by Cohen, March, and Olsen (1972). Added to this reversal of expectations, policies can (due to their underdetermined language) lead changes in politics, rather than politics always preceding policy (Lowi 1972, 299). In short, legislation does not consummate policy battles in complex, multipolar, and ideologically dissonant domains. Modern legislation still bears hallmarks of its medieval origins. A command or "statutum" (the derivation of statute) would be delivered by sovereign monarchs to courts and other agents (Goldsworthy 2004). Such commands were typically short and precise, employing imperative rather than indicative language. Lord Thring, the UK's first ever head draftsman, described the essence of legislation:

> Clearness is the main object to be aimed at in drawing Acts of Parliament. Clearness depends, first, on the proper selection of words; secondly, on the arrangement and construction of the sentences. An enactment in its simplest form is a declaration of the legislature, directing or empowering the doing or abstention from doing of a particular act or thing. (Thring 1902, 61)

No doubt legislation has never attained perfect "clearness", and, indeed, clarity can lead to unworkable arbitrariness (Endicott 2011). For instance, the earliest retained draftsmen in nineteenth-century Britain had been conveyancing lawyers. Judges often complained that their Acts were excessively detailed, in a vain attempt to anticipate all eventualities. An example includes one of the earliest pieces of criminal justice legislation, the *Criminal Jurisdiction Act 1802*, section one:

> From and after the passing of this Act, if any person who now is, or heretofore has been, or shall hereafter be employed by or in the service of his Majesty, his heirs or successors, in any civil or military station, office, or capacity out of Great Britain, or shall heretofore have had, held, or exercised, or now has, holds, or exercises, or shall hereafter have, hold, or exercise any publick station, office, capacity, or employment, out of Great Britain, shall have committed, or shall commit, or shall have heretofore been, or is, or shall hereafter be guilty of any crime, misdemeanor, or offence, in the execution, or under colour, or in the exercise of any such station, office, capacity, or employment as aforesaid, every such crime, offence, or misdemeanor may be prosecuted or enquired of, and heard and determined... here in England.

If legislation increasingly describes an incomplete policy bargain, and judges have recognised tools for managing its completion, we should not be surprised at their rising global power. As Martin Shapiro argued, a strong rule of law is rather like having a ferocious junkyard dog. Most of the time, the dog defends, but occasionally it will bite its owner (Shapiro and Stone Sweet 2002, 163). We will therefore uncover little evidence that judges have behaved unconstitutionally or anti-democratically, as they are fulfilling a role defined for them amidst rapidly changing rules of law. Conversely, we will find evidence that politicians have not only defended judicial independence and autonomy, but have in many instances enhanced the judicial toolkit by subscribing to new international rules of human rights law. Added to which, we will come across cases where politicians were explicitly (or no doubt secretly) grateful that judges took a political hot potato off their plates (Hirschl 2004). And, of course, we will come across instances where politicians have succeeded in controlling who becomes judges in the first place. Hence, another important source of policy influence for judges that is exogenous to the judiciary, comes from their politicisation. What we will not find, despite good faith attempts, is evidence that judges were "activist" in pursuit of their own policy agendas without any external push.

References

Acemoglu, Daron, and James A. Robinson. 2006. *Economic Origins of Dictatorship and Democracy*. Cambridge: Cambridge University Press.

Arrow, Kenneth. 1950. A Difficulty in the Concept of Social Welfare. *Journal of Political Economy* 58 (4): 328–346.

Banakar, Reza, and Max Travers. 2005. *Theory and Method in Socio-legal Research*. Oxford: Hart Publishing.

Bates, Robert H., et al. 1998. *Analytic Narratives*. Princeton, NJ: Princeton University Press.

Bennion, Francis A.R. 2008. *On Statutory Interpretation: A Code*, 5th ed. London: LexisNexis.

Bennion, Francis A.R. 2009. *Understanding Common Law Legislation: Drafting and Interpretation*. Oxford: Oxford University Press.

Boix, Carles. 2003. *Democracy and Redistribution*. Cambridge: Cambridge University Press.

Braman, Eileen. 2006. Reasoning on the Threshold: Testing the Separability of Preferences in Legal Decision-Making. *Journal of Politics* 68 (2): 308–321.

Carrubba, Clifford J., Matthew Gabel, and Charles Hankla. 2008. Judicial Behavior Under Political Constraints: Evidence from the European Court of Justice. *American Political Science Review* 102 (4): 435–452.

Chapman, Kelly. 2015. *Complexity and Creative Capacity: Rethinking Knowledge Transfer, Adaptive Management and Wicked Environmental Problems*. London: Routledge.

Chun, Young Han, and Hal G. Rainey. 2005. Goal Ambiguity in U.S. Federal Agencies. *Journal of Public Administration Research and Theory* 15 (1): 1–30.

Cichowski, Rachel. 2013. Judicial Politics and the Courts. In *The Oxford Handbook of Gender and Politics*, ed. Georgina Waylen, Karen Celis, Johanna Kantola, and S. Laurel Weldon. Oxford: Oxford University Press.

Clayton, Cornell W. 2002. The Supply and Demand Sides of Judicial Policy-Making (Or, Why Be so Positive about the Judicialization of Politics). *Law and Contemporary Problems* 65 (3): 69–88.

Cohen, Michael D., James G. March, and Johan P. Olsen. 1972. A Garbage Can Model of Organizational Choice. *Administrative Science Quarterly* 17 (1): 1–25.

Couso, Javier A., Alexandra Huneeus, and Rachel Sieder. 2010. *Cultures of Legality: Judicialization and Political Activism in Latin America*. Cambridge: Cambridge University Press.

Cox, Gary, and Scott Morgenstern. 2001. Latin America's Reactive Assemblies and Proactive Presidents. *Comparative Politics* 33 (2): 171–189.

D'Amato, Anthony. 1983. Legal Uncertainty. *California Law Review* 71 (1): 1–55.

Dahl, Robert A. 1957. Decision-Making in a Democracy: The Supreme Court as a National Policy-Maker. *Journal of Public Law* 6: 279–295.

Dickson, Brian. 2007. *Judicial Activism in Common Law Supreme Courts*. Oxford: Oxford University Press.

Dotan, Yoav, and Hofnung Menachem. 2005. Legal Defeats—Political Wins: Why Do Elected Representatives Go To Court? *Comparative Political Studies* 38 (1): 75–103.

Dowding, Keith, Jurgen De Wispelaere, and Stuart White, eds. 2003. *The Ethics of Stakeholding*. Basingstoke: Palgrave Macmillan.

Dyevre, Arthur. 2010. Unifying the Field of Comparative Judicial Politics: Towards a General Theory of Judicial Behaviour. *European Political Science Review* 2 (2): 297–327.

Easton, David. 1965. *A Framework for Political Analysis*. New Jersey: Prentice-Hall.

Edwards, Harry T. 1984. Public Misperceptions Concerning the Politics of Judging: Dispelling Some Myths About the DC Circuit. *University of Colorado Law Review* 4 (2): 619–646.

Endicott, Timothy. 2011. The Value of Vagueness. In *Philosophical Foundations of Language in the Law*, ed. Andrei Marmor and Scott Soames. Oxford: Oxford University Press.

Epp, Charles. 1998. *The Rights Revolution: Lawyers, Activists and Supreme Courts in Comparative Perspective*. Chicago: University of Chicago Press.

Epstein, David, and Sharyn O'Halloran. 1999. *Delegating Powers: A Transaction Cost Politics Approach to Policy-Making Under Separate Powers*. Cambridge: Cambridge University Press.

Epstein, Lee, and Jack Knight. 1998. *The Choices Justices Make*. Washington, DC: CQ Press.

Eskridge Jr, William N., and John Ferejohn. 1992. Making the Deal Stick: Enforcing the Original Constitutional Structure of Law-Making in the Modern Regulatory State. *Journal of Law, Economics and Development* 8 (1): 165–189.

Ferejohn, John, and Barry Weingast. 1991. *Limitation of Statutes: Strategic Statutory Interpretation*. New York: Columbia Center for Law and Economic Studies.
Flanagan, Brian. 2010. Revisiting the Contribution of Literal Meaning to Legal Meaning. *Oxford Journal of Legal Studies* 30 (2): 255–271.
Garrett, Geoffrey R., Daniel Kelemen, and Heiner Schulz. 1998. The European Court of Justice, National Governments, and Legal Integration in the European Union. *International Organization* 52 (1): 149–176.
Gibson, James L. 1983. From Simplisticity to Complexity: The Development of Theory in the Study of Judicial Behavior. *Political Behavior* 5 (1): 7–49.
Gibson, James L., Gregory A. Caldeira, and Vanessa A. Baird. 1998. On the Legitimacy of National High Courts. *American Political Science Review* 92 (2): 343–358.
Gillman, Howard, and Cornell Clayton. 1999. *Supreme Court Decision-Making: New Institutionalist Approaches*. Chicago: The University of Chicago Press.
Ginsburg, Tom. 2008. The Global Spread of Constitutional Review. In *The Oxford Handbook of Law and Politics*, ed. Gregory A. Caldeira, R. Daniel Kelemen, and Keith E. Whittington. Oxford: Oxford University Press.
Ginsburg, Tom, Nicholas Foti, and Daniel Rockmore. 2014. We the Peoples: The Global Origins of Constitutional Preambles. *George Washington International Law Review* 46 (1): 305–341.
Goldsworthy, Jeffrey. 2004. *The Sovereignty of Parliament*. Oxford: Oxford University Press.
Gotti, Maurizio. 2012. Text and Genre. In *The Oxford Handbook of Language and Law*, ed. Lawrence M. Solan and Peter M. Tiersma. Oxford: Oxford University Press.
Guarnieri, Carlo, and Patricia Pederzoli. 2002. *The Power of Judges: A Comparative Study of Courts and Democracy*. Oxford: Oxford University Press.
Hall, Peter A., and Rosemary C. Taylor. 1996. Political Science and the Three New Institutionalisms. *Political Studies* 44 (5): 936–957.
Hammarberg, Thomas. 2011. *Council of Europe Commissioner for Human Rights*, 39–43. Strasbourg: Council of Europe Publishing.
Hanretty, Christopher. 2013. The Decisions and Ideal Points of British Law Lords. *British Journal of Political Science* 43 (3): 703–716.
Harlow, Carol, and Richard Rawlings. 2006. *Law and Administration*. Cambridge: Cambridge University Press.
Hart, H.L.A. 1961. *The Concept of the Law*. Oxford: Clarendon.
Helmke, Gretchen. 2002. The Logic of Strategic Defection: Judicial Decision-Making in Argentina under Dictatorship and Democracy. *American Political Science Review* 96 (2): 291–303.

Herron, Erik, and Kirk Randazzo. 2003. The Relationship Between Independence and Judicial Review In post-Communist Courts. *Journal of Politics* 65 (2): 422–438.

Hewart, Gordon. 1929. *The New Despotism*. London: Ernest Benn.

Hillbink, Lisa. 2012. The Origins of Positive Judicial Independence. *World Politics* 64 (4): 587–621.

Hirschl, Ran. 2004. *Towards Juristocracy: The Origins and Consequences of the New Constitutionalism*. Cambridge, MA: Harvard University Press.

Hönnige, Christoph. 2011. Beyond Judicialization: Why We Need More Comparative Research about Constitutional Courts. *European Political Science* 10: 346–358.

Huber, John D., and Charles R. Shipan. 2002. *Deliberate discretion? The Institutional Foundations of Bureaucratic Autonomy*. Cambridge: Cambridge University Press.

Hutchinson, Allan. 2017. The Politics of Constitutional Law: A Critical Approach. In *The Oxford Handbook of the Canadian Constitution*, ed. Peter Oliver, Patrick Macklem, and Nathalie Des Rosiers. Oxford: Oxford University Press.

Jackson, Donald W., Michael C. Tolley, and Mary L. Volcansek. 2010. *Globalizing Justice: Critical Perspectives on Transnational Law and the Cross-Border Migration of Legal Norms*. Albany, NY: State University of New York Press.

Jones, Bryan D. 1999. Bounded Rationality. *Annual Review of Political Science* 2: 297–321.

Jones, Bryan D. 2001. *Politics and the Architecture of Choice: Bounded Rationality and Governance*. Chicago: University of Chicago Press.

Keck, Thomas. 2009. Beyond Backlash: Assessing the Impact of Judicial Decisions on LGBT Rights. *Law & Society Review* 43 (1): 151–186.

Klarman, Michael. 1996. Rethinking the Civil Rights and Civil Liberties Revolutions. *Virginia Law Review* 82 (1): 1–67.

Lester, Richard, and Michael Piore. 2004. *Innovation: The Missing Dimension*. Cambridge, MA: Harvard University Press.

Levi, Edward H. 1948. An Introduction to Legal Reasoning. *The University of Chicago Law Review* 15 (3): 501–574.

Levitsky, Steven, and Lucan A. Way. 2006. Linkage Versus Leverage. Rethinking the International Dimension of Regime Change. *Comparative Politics* 38 (4): 379–400.

Lijphart, Arend. 2012. *Patterns of Democracy: Government Forms and Performance in Thirty-Six Countries*. New Haven: Yale University Press.

Lloyd, Trevor O. 1985. *Empire to Welfare State: English History 1906–1985*. Oxford: Oxford University Press.

Lowi, Theodore J. 1972. Four Systems of Policy, Politics, and Choice. *Public Administration Review* 32 (4): 298–310.

Lowi, Theodore. 1979. *The End of Liberalism: The Second Republic of the United States*. London: Norton.
MacCormick, Neil. 2005. *Rhetoric and the Rule of Law: A Theory of Legal Reasoning*. Oxford: Oxford University Press.
Maine, H.S. 1861. *Ancient Law: Its Connection with the Early History of Society and Its Relation to Modern Ideas*. London: John Murray.
March, James, and Johan Olsen. 1989. *Rediscovering Institutions: The Organisational Basis of Politics*. New York: The Free Press.
Martínez-Gallardo, Cecilia. 2014. Designing Cabinets: Presidential Politics and Ministerial Instability. *Journal of Politics in Latin America* 6 (2): 3–38.
Mayo, Moran. 2003. *Rethinking the Reasonable Person: An Egalitarian Reconstruction of the Objective Standard*. Oxford: Oxford University Press.
Mazeaud, Pierre. 2005, January 3. Echange de voeux à l'Elysée le 3 janvier 2005. Retrieved January 16, 2013, from Counseil Constitutionnel: http://www.conseil-constitutionnel.fr/conseil-constitutionnel/francais/documentationpublications/le-conseil-au-jour-le-jour/le-conseil-en-2004/voeux-a-l-elysee.5147.html.
McGuire, Kevin T., and James A. Stimson. 2004. The Least Dangerous Branch Revisited: New Evidence on Supreme Court Responsiveness to Public Preferences. *The Journal of Politics* 66 (4): 1018–1035.
Merryman, John H. 1981. On the Convergence (and Divergence) of the Civil Law and the Common Law. *Stanford Journal of International Law* 17 (2): 357–388.
Moretti, Franco, and Dominique Pestre. 2015. Bankspeak: The Language of World Bank Report. *New Left Review* 92: 75–99.
Moustafa, Tamir. 2006. Law Versus the State: The Judicialization of Politics in Egypt. *Law and Social Inquiry* 28 (4): 883–930.
Musolff, Andreas. 2004. *Metaphor and Political Discourse: Analogical Reasoning in Debates about Europe*. Basingstoke: Palgrave Macmillan.
Niwayama, Hideo. 2012. Political Science of Courts. *Bulletin of the Senshu University Law Institute* 44: 1–8.
North, Douglas, and Barry Weingast. 1989. Constitutions and Commitment: The Evolution of Institutions Governing Public Choice in Seventeenth-Century England. *Journal of Economic History* 49 (4): 803–832.
Pierson, Paul, and Theda Skocpol. 2002. Historical Institutionalism in Contemporary Political Science. In *Political Science: State of the Discipline*, ed. Ira Katznelson and Helen V. Milner. New York: W. W. Norton.
Polsby, Nelson. 1990. Legislatures. In *Legislatures*, ed. Philip Norton, 129–148. Oxford: Oxford University Press.
Poole, Steven. 2007. *Unspeak: Words Are Weapons*. New York: Grove Press.

Powell, Eleanor N., and Joshua Tucker. 2014. Revisiting Electoral Volatility in Post-Communist Countries: New Data, New Results and New Approaches. *British Journal of Political Science* 44 (1): 123–147.

Rios Figueroa, Julio. 2007. Fragmentation of Power and the Emergence of an Effective Judiciary in Mexico, 1994–2002. *Latin American Politics & Society* 49 (1): 31–57.

Rittel, Horst W.J., and Melvin M. Webber. 1973. Dilemmas in a General Theory of Planning. *Policy Sciences* 4 (2): 155–169.

Robertson, David. 1982. Judicial Ideology in the House of Lords: A Jurimetric Analysis. *British Journal of Political Science* 12: 1–25.

Robertson, David. 1998. *Judicial Discretion in the House of Lords*. Oxford: Clarendon Press.

Robertson, David. 2010. *The Judge as Political Theorist: Contemporary Constitutional Review*. Princeton, NJ: Princeton University Press.

Roosevelt, Kermit. 2006. *The Myth of Judicial Activism: Making Sense of Supreme Court Decisions*. New Haven CT: Yale University Press.

Rosenthal, Maoz. 2013. Policy Instability in a Comparative Perspective: The Context of Heresthetic. *Political Studies* 62 (1): 172–196.

Rozenburg, Joshua. 1997. *Trial of Strength: The Battle Between Ministers and Judges Over Who Makes the Law*. London: Richard Cohen Books.

Schmidt, Vivien. 2008. Discursive Institutionalism: The Explanatory Power of Ideas and Discourse. *Annual Review of Political Science* 11: 303–326.

Schröter, Eckhard. 2007. Reforming the Machinery of Government: The Case of the German Federal Bureaucracy. In *Public Governance and Leadership*, ed. Rainer Koch and John Dixon. Frankfurt: DUV.

Schubert, Glendon. 1965. *The Judicial Mind*. Evanston IL: Northwestern University Press.

Segal, Hanna, and Jeffrey Perl. 2019. The Achievement of Ambivalence. *Common Knowledge* 25 (1): 51–62.

Segal, Jeffrey A., and Harold Spaeth. 2002. *The Supreme Court and the Attitudinal Model Revisited*. Cambridge: Cambridge University Press.

Shapiro, Martin. 1964. *Law and Politics in the Supreme Court: New Approaches to Political Jurisprudence*. New York: Free Press of Glencoe.

Shapiro, Martin. 1983. Recent Developments in Political Jurisprudence. *Political Research Quarterly* 36 (4): 541–548.

Shapiro, Martin, and Alec Stone Sweet. 2002. *On Law, Politics and Judicialization*. Oxford: Oxford University Press.

Sisk, Gregory. C., Heise, Michael., and Morriss, Andrew. P. 1998. Charting the Influences on the Judicial Mind: An Empirical Study of Judicial Reasoning. *New York University Law Review* 73: 1377–1500.

Staton, Jeffrey K., and Georg Vanberg. 2008. The Value of Vagueness: Delegation, Defiance and Judicial Opinions. *American Journal of Political Science* 52 (3): 504–519.
Stevens, Robert. 2005. *The English Judges: Their Role in the Changing Constitution*. Oxford: Hart Publishing.
Stone Sweet, Alec. 2000. *Governing with Judges: Constitutional Politics in Europe*. Oxford: Oxford University Press.
Strøm, Kaare, Wolfgang C. Müller, and Torbjörn Bergman. 2003. *Delegation and Accountability in Parliamentary Democracies*. Oxford: Oxford University Press.
Sunkin, Maurice. 1994. Judialization of Politics in the United Kingdom. *International Political Science Review* 15 (2): 125–133.
Tate, C. Neal., and Torbjorn Vallinder. 1995. *The Global Expansion of Judicial Power*. New York: New York University Press.
Thelen, Kathleen. 1999. Historical Institutionalism in Comparative Politics. *Annual Review of Political Science* 2: 369–404.
Thompson, Mark. 2016. *Enough Said: What's Gone Wrong with the Language of Politics?* London: Penguin.
Thring, Henry. 1902. *Practical Legislation: The Composition of Acts of Parliament and Business Documents*. London: John Murray.
Tsebelis, George. 2002. *Veto Players: How Political Institutions Work*. Princeton NJ: Princeton University Press.
Ugochukwu, Basil. 2011. The Pathology of Judicialization: Politics, Corruption and the Courts in Nigeria. *The Law and Development Review* 4 (3): 59–87.
Vanberg, Georg. 2001. Legislative-Judicial Relations: A Game-Theoretic Approach to Constitutional Review. *American Journal of Political Science* 45 (2): 346–361.
Volcansek, Mary L. 1992. *Judicial Politics and Policy-Making in Western Europe*. London: Cass.
Waldron, Jeremy. 2005. The Core of the Case Against Judicial Review. *Yale Law Journal* 115: 1346–1407.
Weldon, Thomas D. 1953. *The Vocabulary of Politics*. London: Penguin Books.
Wendell Holmes Jr, Oliver. 1920. *Collected Legal Papers*. London: Constable.
Williams, Matthew. 2016. Indeterminate Sovereignty and the Rule of Law. *British Politics* 11 (1): 26–48.
Williams, Matthew. 2017a. The Grammar of Politics: A Brief History of Legislative Language in Britain. *Political Quarterly* 88 (2): 248–257.
Williams, Matthew. 2017b. Legislative Language and Judicial Politics: The Effects of Changing Parliamentary Language on UK Immigration Disputes. *British Journal of Politics and IR* 19 (3): 592–608.
Williams, Matthew. 2018. *How Language Works in Politics: The Impact of Indeterminate Legislation on Policy*. Bristol: Bristol University Press.

CHAPTER 2

Modern Political Language

With universal suffrage, the function, quantity, and qualities of legislation all changed. Determining optimal legislative language became, for the most part, a numbers game. If policy content and delivery were likely to please enough voters in important districts, then legislation was pursued. Governments enforcing those laws also underwent fundamental changes in response to democratic pressures. Adjudication, by contrast, is the only method of governance still used in democracies that has not much changed. Maintaining peace by resolving disputes with justice is as old as law itself. Being considered a good judge remains more a matter of peer review, than democratic accountability. And yet, the global expansion of judicial power happened in step with this transition to mass democracy. Judicial power may have changed, but there is little reason or evidence to suggest that the judicial method changed. To be sure, there have been significant changes to the tools used in pursuit of justice, such as with the Universal Declaration of Human Rights in 1948, Germany's Basic Law promulgated the following year, the preamble to the French Fourth Republican Constitution becoming justiciable in 1971, the Canadian Charter of Rights and Freedoms of 1982, and the UK's *Human Rights Act 1998*. And yet, despite these changes, much of what it means to be judicious has survived the transition to mass democracy and the recovery from war.

M. Williams, *Judges and the Language of Law*,
https://doi.org/10.1007/978-3-030-91495-0_2

So, why has judicial power increased? State expansion was transacted using new forms of political discourse, the most impactful of which is legislation. Legislative language is hence a precise locus where the effects of policy demand can be observed. In pre-democratic legislatures, societal pressures were exerted by a propertied elite. Legislation responded either to their demands, or was designed to resolve specific pathologies in customary, code, or common laws. With mass democracy, legislation had to respond to a far wider array of constituencies, and needed to do so with time and resource efficiencies. Legislation thereby became more than a communication between state institutions, and is now in some instances a direct line of communication from state to citizens. Legislators will now enact laws—sometimes with accessible titles and easily gobbeted content[1]—in part to respond to demands, and in part to show they are doing something. Legislation thus has mixed substantive and theatrical functionalities. The very concept of law has therefore changed, slowly and barely perceptibly, with the age of democracy. Indeed, even autocracies (as will be seen in the following chapter) have adopted new forms of constitutional language to allow for maximal adaptability to mercurial elites and variable circumstances. Laws are less capable of ruling by textual determination alone. The rule of modern law is flexible, anticipatory, and participatory. The text of contemporary law does not structure reality but is structured by reality. Legislation adapts to context, is sensitive to subtextual interpretations, and is intended to be read intertextually within a growing corpus of higher law. As Lester and Piore (2004, 264) have argued:

> ... language evolves from clarity to ambiguity – in precisely the opposite direction of evolution that one finds in analytical problem-solving. Language development evolves, in other words, toward the creation of interpretative space.

If legislative texts are insufficient to determine policy outcomes, then the text needs to be supplemented or augmented. Such transtextual or metatextual impositions are performed by authoritative judges. Interpretative spaces in laws, and judges closing down those spaces, are nothing new, but the frequency with which judges are called on, and have opportunities, to

[1] For example the *Uniting And Strengthening America By Providing Appropriate Tools Required To Intercept And Obstruct Terrorism (USA Patriot Act) Act 2001.*

delimit interpretative spaces have increased. Institutions, being the rules of the political game, are increasingly utilising indeterminate rules. This is indicative of a form of institutional entropy, that can only be arrested by the imposition of meaningfulness. This links to Vivian Schmidt's (2008) ground-breaking theory of "discursive institutionalism". She argued that a "logic of communication" exists between and beyond political institutions of power. This logic can be said to exist when specific policies can be inferred from broader principles. Rules of law become indeterminate when disequilibria in the law-making environment unbuckle principles, ideologies, and other social foundations from the text of law itself. Rules of law thereby become words with only partially determined meanings, rather than being meaningful ideas committed to words (Crowley 1989). This in turn means that legal discourse relies less on a cohering theory and more on individual whim to be executed. This has advantages for removing constraints on individual wisdom, and thereby links to the observed "presidentialization" of global politics (Poguntke and Webb 2005). But, at extreme levels of indeterminacy, the law will be less capable of managing "wicked" problems (Chapman 2015). For instance, resolving the externalities of globalisation, ensuring social order, and mitigating the effects of climate change, all rely on policy goals and managed delegation of tasks. In short, complex governance calls for logics of communication in legislation to coordinate the state apparatus and its resources.

Indeterminacy or Ambiguity?

Core concepts for this study are legislative indeterminacy (Bix 1993) and genre (Gotti 2012). Legislative genre describes the extent of stability or change in indeterminacies through time. Legislation here refers to public and primary laws enacted by a legislature. These can be contrasted with private or hybrid enactments, which are also passed by legislatures but are specific legislative requests from non-state organisations. Legislation in the UK will cover only enactments of the UK Parliament, not the devolved legislatures, nor Measures of the Church of England's General Synod. The book will focus on primary legislation, but will make references where necessary to subordinated secondary legislation, regulations, or rules.

Indeterminacies in legislative language refers to language where more than one interpretation would be possible without misreading (Dyevre 2010; MacCormick 2005; Poscher 2012; Solan 2012). This is similar to ambiguity of language (Empson 1953), but where ambiguity typically concentrates on semantic and syntactic elements of language, indeterminacy broadens the area of study to include pragmatics, the third element of semiotics (Morris 1946). In other words, ambiguity denotes uncertainty intrinsic to text, where indeterminacy refers additionally to extrinsic causes of interpretative confusion. As such, legislation may be unambiguous on its face, and yet still be difficult to implement. Examples of semantic and syntactic indeterminacy stretch back multiple centuries, and include *Heydon's Case*[2] of 1584 where the Baron of Exchequer created the so-called Mischief Rule as a way to make sense of Parliament's legislative intent. A more recent thought experiment was H.L.A. Hart's (1958) law banning vehicles from a park. The sentence "no vehicles are allowed in the park" has little semantic nor syntactic ambiguity, and yet it is still capable of indeterminacy as a change in context can affect the pragmatics. A simple byelaw banning vehicles seems clear on its face, but would create an indeterminate problem where, in Hart's example, a jeep was intended for use as a war memorial. There may also be questions raised as to whether pushchairs, roller-skates, or even walking frames are sufficiently vehicular to be banned.

Indeterminate laws include textual ambiguities, but also include interpretative spaces for agents to make new rules. Interpreting law is a form of speech act, wherein the utterance of an empowered agent is making law, not simply declaring it (Austin 1962). This is how indeterminate language enables politicians, bureaucrats, and judges to make law whilst implementing it. Roughly we may say that an ambiguous law is one where the focus is on the correct interpretation of a text, where indeterminate law has a broader concern for the correct allocation of power. An example of litigating ambiguities comes from a case decided by the UK House of Lords in the 1990s. The case was *Knowles v Liverpool City Council.*[3] A workmen's compensation statute held an employer liable for injuries caused by defective "equipment".[4] The Act's underlying principle was in

[2] (1584) 76 ER 637.

[3] In full: Knowles v Liverpool City Council [1993] 4 All ER 321.

[4] *Employer's Liability (Defective Equipment) Act 1969*, section 1(1).

keeping with a long line of workers' protection legislation, dating from 1897. In this particular case, a labourer hurt his hand when a paving stone he was unloading shattered and cut him. The court had to decide whether the employer, Liverpool City Council, was liable for the injury. Equipment typically brings to mind a tool or appliance, rather than a material. But, the Lords found for the worker, likening the paving stone to anything that *equips* the doing of work. They could do so because the term equipment is ambiguous on its face, and a good argument could have been made for the opposite decision. Preceding case law had, through a process of lexical inflation, extended the meaning of equipment to include an entire ship in one instance. Ambiguities and indeterminacies describe an incomplete set of items or phenomena, and are thereby liable to this sort of expansive interpretation. Unless, that is, the expansion of meaning facilitates the diminution of rights by a powerful litigant. For example, in the case of *Hotak v London Borough of Southwark*, the adjective "vulnerable" was given a narrow construction by the UK Supreme Court. This was to stop local authorities denying housing assistance by expanding the definition of vulnerable to an extent that excluded most claimants, including the disabled litigant in this case.[5]

"Indeterminacy" is therefore used here to describe and measure three semiotic elements—semantics, syntactics, and pragmatics. As such, the book builds on previous studies of legislative language that have focussed more on semantic and syntactic elements of language, including "ambiguity" (Edelman 1992), "indefiniteness" (Freund 1921), "irrelevant considerations" (Taylor 1976), and "vagueness" (Post 1994). As Marmor and Soames (2011, 6–7) have contended:

> …successful communication is determined by contextual and normative aspects… over and above the strictly semantic properties of the words used. As a consequence, the study of these factors – 'pragmatics' broadly conceived – has taken on a larger role in theories of linguistic communication.

The book also contributes to works in legal scholarship that have observed growth in *casus omissus*. H.L.A. Hart (1961) noted that legislation had, in his lifetime, become more prone to having these "gaps" which allowed

[5] [2015] UKSC 30.

judges to decide how to fill them. Even in situations where the indeterminacy in law is a gap in the legislation, this is still a positive source of confusion despite being literally nothing (Auchie 2004). This is because legal sovereignty cannot be delegated into a vacuum.

The most common development in pragmatic indeterminacy has been to enable executive and regulatory discretion through delegated powers. Here the law is drafted with indeterminate language so that an agent can with discretion flesh out its meaning and adapt it to differing contexts. Despite the significant increase in the volume of legislation, this is not theorised to be a direct cause of political power for judges. If there was a considerable volume of determinable law, the judiciary would not be called upon so often to clarify its meaning. Simply increasing the volume of legislation cannot on its own change the qualitative behaviour of judges. It is the qualification of nouns and verbs (through use of adjectives, adverbs, conjunctions, and modal verbs) as well as the delegation of authority (through enabling verbs) that empowers judges to interpret away confusions. It must be stressed that expansively indeterminate language is nothing new. Rather its incidence has increased such that the genre—or generic patterns of legislative language—have been affected. In the early twentieth century, delegated powers were used sparingly and in response to critical emergencies. But we will see that such language is increasingly generic, rather than extraordinary.

In pre-war Britain, for example, there was the *Official Secrets Act 1911*, the *Public Order Act 1936*, and the *Emergency Powers (Defence) Act 1939* which all delegated powers to the government in response to emergencies. But the *Income and Corporation Taxes Act 1988* was, on its own, nearly 400,000 words (excluding schedules), making it more than twice as voluminous than the entire legislative output for the year 1911, when the infamously liberty-inhibiting *Official Secrets Act* was enacted. That 1911 Act in fact contained no enabling verbs (such as "make" or "amend") that are often used to delegate powers. It also had somewhat fewer adjectives than the average 1911 statute, but moderately more conjunctions. The 1988 Act had more adjectives and conjunctions than the average 1988 statute, but fewer enabling verbs. But even the average 1988 statute had, compared to the 1911 average, twice as many adjectives per section, as well as many more conjunctions, indeterminate modal verbs ("may", "might"), and enabling verbs. The genre of legislation had changed substantially, and seemingly unusual laws, such as the 1911 and 1988 Acts were in fact broadly in keeping with genericisms of legislation for their respective years. Clearly such legislation is not new, and this thesis is not arguing that there was a single identifiable point in time that marks a "critical juncture" (Collier and Collier 2002), but rather there has been an increase in state size and responsibilities which was achieved with increased indeterminacy of legislative language.

The effects of such language on judicial power includes, most broadly, the continuity of policy bargaining outside the legislature. Also the distillation of multipolar policy disputes into bipolar questions of justice gives judges the capacity to reframe complex policy issues. There has also grown an industry of law firms in major democracies that profit from arbitrage in indeterminate legalese. Firms, interests groups, and even social movements will find and train litigants to press policy claims in court, where they can obtain more leverage than they would in a legislature. A clear example of this was an alliance of law firms and interest groups that overturned California's constitutional ban on same-sex marriages (Proposition 8) in *Hollingsworth v. Perry*.[6] The more technical legal effects of indeterminate language were set out by Justice Charles Gonthier on behalf of the Canadian Supreme Court in *R. v. Nova Scotia Pharmaceutical Society*.[7] As he noted, the problem caused by language is beyond a simple matter of semantic dispute:

> A vague provision does not provide an adequate basis for legal debate, that is for reaching a conclusion as to its meaning by reasoned analysis applying legal criteria. It does not sufficiently delineate any area of risk, and thus can provide neither fair notice to the citizen nor a limitation of enforcement discretion. Such a provision is not intelligible, to use the terminology of previous decisions of this Court, and therefore it falls to give sufficient indications that could fuel a legal debate. It offers no grasp to the judiciary. This is an exacting standard, going beyond semantics.

Ambivalence and Cybernetics

Legislators are less able to describe and encode desirable futures in legislation. These inadequacies of expression are caused by uncertainties from plural public demands, from global economics, and the decline of guiding ideologies in Western politics (Robertson 2010). There is uncertainty as to what principles do or should underlie political action. And yet there is

[6] 570 U.S. 693.

[7] 1992 CanLII 72 (SCC), [1992] 2 SCR 606.

overloading demand for continuous activity (Flinders 2008; Foster 2005; King 1975). The result is a preponderance of pragmatic solutions to complex problems, where individual discretion, and circumstantial adaptability, are prioritised over clear enunciations of value. Indeed, the very need to describe and control an unknown future is relatively new to legislation. Historically, legislation was a corrective instrument to repair other sources of law. Or, if legislation was future-oriented—such as in tax-raising finance laws—it would more likely define the future rather than be defined by it.

The broadest cause of this communicative inefficiency is increased distribution of power within and between states. Old power elites are increasingly forced to share power (Boix 2003), and thereby inclusive language that is capable of efficient adaptation is increasingly favoured (Acemoglu and Robinson 2006). Indeterminacies in shared discourse would therefore be predicted by Kenneth Arrow's Impossibility Theorem (Arrow 1950). As choices for citizens proliferate, it becomes impossible to obtain a mutually acceptable collective choice. Impossible, that is, unless some form of dictatorship is established to remove agenda items. This holder of authority will include government ministers, bureaucrats, and judges that can delimit the range of choices available. The externalities of which include "goal ambiguity" (Chun and Rainey 2005), "bureaucratic drift" (McCubbins et al. 1987), accountability gaps (Whitefield 2006), and, of course, judicialisation.

Bryan Jones has described the instability of bureaucracy as consequent on rising social complexity. Bureaucrats conform to patterns of bounded rationality, where their choices are curtailed by norms until overwhelming external pressure readjusts those norms suddenly and fundamentally—a process that Jones's likens to an earthquake (Jones 2001). Complex systems are intended to contain and manage social pressures, but occasionally reach a dramatic breaking point. Judges are akin to bureaucrats—or even classified as such in civil law jurisdictions—so will similarly behave under conditions of bounded rationality until social pressures become overwhelming. Several authors—from Marx, to Weber, to Alvin Gouldner—have written of a further layer of tension in bureaucracy, between rational efficiency in systems and individual subjectivity (Adler 1993). The objective and the subjective clash in a manner akin to "ambivalence". First coined by Eugen Bleuler, ambivalence is a state of simultaneous and contradictory affect (Segal and Perl 2019). In other words, an individual will feel positive and negative valences towards the same thing, simultaneously. This forces bureaucrats (and judges) to face a stark choice between their bounded rationality in maintaining systemic norms, whilst also recognising their personal preferences. And, these personal preferences will themselves be informed by feelings such as sympathy towards individuals affected by policy. Indeed, these individual feelings of conflict are indicative of social ambivalence as to what the optimal policy will be.

For example, where immigration is on the one hand favoured as a solution to the problems of an ageing population with skills shortages, on the other hand immigration control is popular to protect public services from being overloaded, and is desired to manage social relations. Added to which are individual cases of acute injustice for individual immigrants subject to efforts at managing their immigration via these complex and competing goals. Also, simply processing failed asylum and immigration claims raises dilemmas. An efficient system for deporting undeserving claimants is ideal. But hasty decisions can be unjust due to anything from procedural unfairness, all the way to deporting an individual back to their underserved death or torture. Democracies face on-going battles between public reason and emotion therefore. Publicly accessible reason is expensive. Political authority backed by reason requires on-going investment in time, commitment, and publicity. As Zygmunt Bauman (1991) argued, sovereignty is the "power to define and to make definitions stick – everything that self-defines or eludes the power assisted definition is subversive". Without definite language, political power is, like everything else, prone to degrade in the face of complexity. This can be seen from the temptation we all face from time to time to act on gut instinct rather than reason and evidence. Disorganised power may be able to solve specific problems quickly, but in the long term it is crude, arbitrary, incomprehensible, and unreasonable. All of which means that disorganised power is likely to be perceived as unjust. Whether disorganised power *is* unjust is beyond this book's bailiwick.

Modern governance is therefore complex as regards shared choices, and the individual effects of those choices. But, even more complexity is created by attempted adherence to international norms. There are hence at least three levels of control—individual, state, and global—that need to be reconciled in legislative language. Ernst Haas (1958), in his early neofunctionalist theory, argued that nation states would decline in the face of regional and international dissemination of principles, policies, and laws. He specifically contended that a process of "technocratic automaticity" would foster closer and closer integration in Europe (see also

Rhodes 1996). Observed in the European Union, however, is a pattern closer to Jones's prediction of norm-confirming behaviour punctuated by occasional but severe crises—including Black Wednesday, the Greek sovereign debt crisis, and Brexit. Even at the international level there is a pressure exerted for order amidst complexity. But the pressure again creates ambivalence between the desire for rational optimisation and individual subjectivity.

In linguistic terms, there is either insufficient lexical complexity to manage social complexity, or there are contradictions between generalist policies and individual human rights protections. Requisite complexity in communication is a defining attribute of cybernetics (Wiener 1948). Legislation, like any command language, defines variables (such as new offences) and flow control (the concatenation of decisions to administer those offences). Requisite complexity allows a command language (such as a computer program) to execute without patches and updates. It is language that can almost literally self-execute, and any "crashing" of the system will require a reboot to an essential operating kernel. In law, a reboot may be to a constitutional norm that is capable of guiding appropriate decision-making. This analogy of legislation to a computer program is ill-fitting. Indeed, cybernetic theories have for some time been unfashionable in studies of bureaucracy (Deutsch 1963; Easton 1965; Lippucci 1998). Nonetheless, the reference to cybernetics is not entirely misplaced, as encoding social organisation does entail similar design requirements to the coding of software. And, extending the metaphor, much modern software is designed to learn from environmental data and adapt, just as legislation uses open language to adapt to changes in social complexity.

State efficacy is, as Napoleon realised, encoding rules. It is the conceptualising and administration of reality into forms that can be manipulated and utilised in linguistic space. The failure of a code is hence a failure of the state to be understood and to project power. Of course, Napoleon was not concerned that the state code be democratic or pluralistic. As such, this difficulty for modern states in managing complexity is something to be celebrated. It is a consequence of a simple loss of control by elites over the *lingua franca* of state authority. This is not a straightforward linear trend, as there have been relatively determinable laws enacted depending on a variety of forces analysed further in Chapter Four. Nonetheless, we will see the ambivalence of modern statecraft throughout contemporary constitutional laws and legislation. Exemplary is this following balancing act of free movement and public safety in the German Basic Law, Article 10:

(1) All Germans shall have the right to move freely throughout the federal territory. (2) This right may be restricted only by or pursuant to a law, and only in cases in which the absence of adequate means of support would result in a particular burden for the community, or in which such restriction is necessary to avert an imminent danger to the existence or the free democratic basic order of the Federation or of a Länd, to combat the danger of an epidemic, to respond to a grave accident or natural disaster, to protect young persons from serious neglect or to prevent crime.

Measuring Indeterminacy—Methodology

So how can we measure the potential of a legislative text to adapt to context, changing subtexts, or be read intertextually with other laws? The solution is to measure relative meaninglessness, rather than meaningfulness. Determining how meaningful a text is cannot be achieved with machine reading technologies, because it depends on so many variables, including the subjective assessment of an interpreter. What can be measured are the interpretative spaces created in a text by specific parts of speech (Lester and Piore 2004). This approach builds on research by Epstein and O'Halloran (1999), and Huber and Shipan (2002). Huber and Shipan compared American and European attempts to regulate social and labour policies through legislative language. Their book analysed changes to legislative word lengths. They contended that longer laws were more controlling and shorter laws more enabling of bureaucratic discretion. Theirs was a work contributing to the delegation literature, assessing how principals manage agents (Strøm et al. 2003; Schleiter and Morgan-Jones 2009). Other notable political science research on word length looks to the "substantive restrictions" of longer constitutions (Tsebelis and Nardi 2016), and the wider policy effects of relative "garrulity" (Voigt 2009; Bjørnskov and Voigt 2014).

Word length intuitively matters with regard to relative meaningfulness. The basic assumption being that longer laws lay down more detailed instructions and are therefore more capable of exerting control over policy implementation. However, a begging question remains. Are all words equal in their capacity to transmit meaningfulness, such that increasing word count increases meaningfulness? If we imagine trying to play an unfamiliar board game with a small list of clear instructions, including the ultimate game objectives, this is likely to be an easier game to play than an alternative with a very long list of instructions, some of which are highly specific, others of which are broad and deliberately open up play to discretionary improvisation. Technological advances in natural language processing (NLP) used in search engines, allows us to measure not only variable legislative lengths, but also their semantics and syntax. By these methods we can (and this book does) test hypotheses as to the origins and effects of these differing linguistic patterns.

Ultimately, the methods used here assess readability. A well-known method to achieving this task is called the Gunning Fog Index (GFI) (Gunning 1952). This index utilises an algorithm to measure the "fog", or relative complexity, of a text. The algorithm takes average sentence length, with the percentage of complex words (three or more syllables), and multiplies it by 0.4. The preceding paragraph to this (beginning "Word length intuitively…") has a GFI of 17.9. This score suggests that the paragraph can be understood by a person who left full-time education after the age of 18. The GFI has been used in studies of bureaucracy to measure "Mission Comprehension Ambiguity" (Chun and Rainey 2005). When analysing legal texts, however, reading age is of lesser importance, because all lawyers and judges have at less an undergraduate education. This book therefore develops hand-coding methods used by legal scholars for decades and has automated it.

Constructing the Discourse Analysis Codebook

Discourse analysis is a method of close textual reading that is not often used in political science. It can, nonetheless, be used to great effect in analysing structured languages, such as legislation. Typically, discourse analysis measures language structure and its situated meaning—being the meaning of language in context. Discourse analysis also measures the wider cultural understandings of language (Gee 2005). As such discourse analysis is more often used in social anthropology, cultural studies, and literature. Content analysis is a more familiar text-as-data method in political science (see, for example, Evans et al. 2007). However content analysis is more appropriate for assessing the subject matter of communications, such as speeches, social media posts, newspaper articles, and election manifestoes (Krippendorff 1980). Discourse analysis focusses on the structure of communication, rather than its content. As such discourse analysis has, since the 1960s, been the preferred method to measure the language of law (Trosborg 1995).

Discourse analysis uses a codebook of measures to observe theoretically important parts of language. Most previous research has concentrated on the semantic and syntactic features of language, rather than its pragmatic features. For instance, regarding semantics, Brenda Danet performed a lexical study to show how legal language is "frozen" by employing more archaic terms than day-to-day speech (Danet 1985). She also recognised the use of common terms with uncommon meanings, the use of tautological doublets such as "null and void", the use of unusual prepositional phrases, and a frequent use of the determiner "any".

Yet more discourse analyses of legal language have focussed on syntactics. For instance, Danet assessed "whiz" deletion, where a sentence omits the wh-words—such as in "agreement [*which is*] herein obtained or applied" (Danet 1980). Marita Gustafsson (1975) showed that in a sample of legal documents there were far more clauses per sentence than in other highly structured languages. This supports the decision not to use the Gunning Fog Index, which would yield high scores for such long sentences. In a similar vein, Butt and Castle launched a campaign for more "plain language" in legal documents (Butt and Castle 2001). They also pointed out the potential confusion caused by use of the vague modal verb "may", which, unlike "shall", does not determine behaviour. Other parts of speech studied include the high incidence of prepositional phrases (Charrow and Charrow 1979), and the use of complex conditional phrases relying on conjunctions such as "if", "when", and "or" (Crystal and Davy 1969).

This project is concerned with pragmatics, as well as semantics and syntactics. Pragmatics evaluates language in terms of its probable effect in context and in accordance with normal usage. There have been relatively few analyses of legal pragmatics, but an important contribution by Dennis Kurzon focussed on "speech acts" in legal discourse (Kurzon 1997). This drew on J.L. Austin's (1962) linguistic philosophies in *How to Do Things with Words*. A speech act is where the speaking is part of the doing. In other words, a speaker creates reality through speech, and does not merely represent reality. In law, an indeterminacy can be used to create a new socio-legal reality if there is sufficient interpretative space to do so. The language of law is insufficient to represent reality, but affects reality in its usage. This is difficult to measure automatically. But, we can pinpoint, in simple terms, those parts of speech that deliberately enable a language user to make the law clearer. These include the modal verbs "may" or "might" already discussed. Also of importance are enabling verbs, including "make" and "amend", that specifically empower agents of a legislature to change the law. Measuring these parts of speech in legal language has a long heritage, but is now possible on a much larger scale, without the need for statistical sampling (Trosborg 1995; Kurzon 1997; Hiltunen 2012). Indeed, it is now possible to analyse every word of available law, in different languages, across space and through time.

All available constitutions from 187 countries and legislation from five countries were analysed using parts of speech tagging (POST) with the Natural Language Toolkit (NLTK), run on Python script. An excerpt of the program is below, and the full program can be trialled online.[8] The software can even discriminate between homonyms, and accurately tag the parts of speech. For example, "free" can be a noun, an adjective, or a verb, and the software is capable of determining which it is from its sentence position (as in "We the free, being free, have a duty to free."). Furthermore, the software can, with the "Snowball plug-in", identify and tag parts of speech in different languages. Although, following tests, it was clear that first translating the texts into English and then tagging them was more accurate. All data, which have been meticulously scrubbed and prepared for analysis, are freely available on request.

```
while True:
    print('Enter the number of sections, if known. If not, simply enter "1" to finc
        the totals rather than the averages.')
    sec = int(input())
    class SampleApp(tk.Tk):
        def __init__(self):
            tk.Tk.__init__(self)
            self.title("Discourse Analysis")
            self.entry = tk.Entry(self)
            self.button = tk.Button(self, text="Analyse", command=self.on_button)
            self.button.pack()
            self.entry.pack()
        def on_button(self):
            raw = self.entry.get()
            tokenizer = RegexpTokenizer(r'\w+')
            tokens = tokenizer.tokenize(raw)
            sents = sent_tokenize(raw)
            print('Length: ' + str(len(tokens)) + ' words.')
            print('Length: ' + str(len(sents)) + ' sentences.')
            print('The average section is ' + str(len(tokens)/sec) + ' words long.
                ')
            tagged = nltk.pos_tag(tokens)
            allAdj = [word for word,pos in tagged if pos in ['JJ']]
            allAdv = [word for word,pos in tagged if pos in ['RB']]
```

[8] www.matthewlippoldwilliams.com/test.

As an example of how parts of speech tagging works, the following excerpt from the UK's *Data Retention and Investigatory Powers Act 2014* (DRIPA) includes highlights where the program tags relevant elements:

> The Secretary of State *may* [indeterminate modal verb] by notice (a "retention notice") *require* [enabling verb] a *public* [adjective] telecommunications operator to retain *relevant* communications data *if* [conjunction] the Secretary of State considers that the requirement is *necessary and proportionate* for one *or more* [determiner] of the purposes falling within paragraphs (a) to (h) of section 22(2) of the Regulation of Investigatory Powers Act 2000 (purposes for which communications data *may* be obtained).
>
> (2) A retention notice *may*—
>
> (a) relate to a *particular* operator *or any* [determiner] description of operators,
>
> (b) *require* the retention of *all* data *or any* description of data,
>
> (c) *specify* the period *or* periods for which data is to be retained,
>
> (d) contain other requirements, *or* restrictions, in relation to the retention of data,
>
> (e) *make different* provision for *different* purposes,
>
> (f) relate to data whether *or* not in existence at the time of the giving, *or* coming into force, of the notice.

The essential observations are that this kind of linguistic indeterminacy has increased across the world; it has grown more rapidly and haphazardly in majoritarian political systems; and it has demonstrably created interpretative discretion for judges. The DRIPA legislation was controversial when enacted. It allowed then Home Secretary Theresa May to intercept digital communications so as "to safeguard national security and economic well-being". This law was not unusual in its linguistic construction when compared to other laws enacted by the Westminster Parliament in 2014. But, it did out-lie the UK legislative language enacted in 2013 and 2015. DRIPA was indeterminate on its face, and inconsistent with generic patterns of language use. The policy of loosely restrained mass surveillance was declared unlawful by the Court of Appeal for England and Wales.[9] The Court relied on European Union law to reach this verdict, and they could do so because the law was indeterminate on at

[9] *Secretary of State for the Home Department v. Watson and Others* [2018] EWCA Civ 70.

least three counts: it was incomplete, it contradicted other rules of law, and it provided scant guidance as to its practical implementation.

Hence, the measure of indeterminacy includes noun or verb qualifiers (adjective, adverbs, conjunctions, and determiners) as well as discretionary modal (may/might) and enabling (make/amend) verbs. The sum of these parts of speech per section describe indeterminacy, and allow for comparisons to assess changes in patterns of language use. These parts of speech, as recognised in the preceding research cited above, tend to affect relative meaninglessness (Trosborg 1995). Where meaning is very difficult to quantify across time and different languages, meaninglessness does depend on certain basic assumptions that are universal to grammars across the world. We will still encounter a great quantity of relatively clear legal language, such as the *National Horse of Canada Act 2002*:

> The horse known as the Canadian horse is hereby recognized and declared to be the national horse of Canada.

Of course, "national" is an adjective, but is not included in the measurements because it poses no interpretative problems. Other adjectives such as "Canadian" were also identified and omitted to avoid over-estimates of indeterminacy. Choices as to which adjectives (such as "national") to omit were taken from qualitative assessment of statutory interpretation manuals, interpretative guidance in legislation, and judicial opinions. In the end, it is safest to omit a measurement than to commit to one falsely. Omitting certain adjectives yields a greater risk of type two errors, which is preferable in hypothesis testing to admitting false positives. Nonetheless, measurement error is unavoidable when utilising such vast data sets. There are robustness safeguards in place and cross validations to attenuate these errors. Cross validation of quantitative findings to qualitative coding has been performed in intricate detail on randomly selected laws, so as to assess that the parts of speech tagger is accurate, and maintains its accuracy in translations (Williams 2016).

Canada provided the testing ground for ensuring the data processing was seamless in translated languages. This is because all Canadian federal legislation is published in French and English. Indeed, Canada is not only a bilingual, but also bijural (civil and common law) jurisdiction. An example, pertinent to criminal justice, is section 43(2.1) of the Canadian *Human Rights Act*. It describes the power for officials to forcefully enter property. Indeterminacies identified by the computer program in

English, were also tagged in the French version, and the French-to-English translated version. Different languages can therefore be coded, but care is needed to address discrepancies (indeterminacies highlighted in the English version):

> Subject to *such* limitations as the Governor in Council *may* prescribe in the interests of *national* defence *or* security, an investigator with a warrant issued under subsection (2.2) *may*, at any *reasonable* time, enter *and* search *any* premises in order to carry out *such* inquiries as are *reasonably necessary* for the investigation of a complaint.

> Pouvoir de visite (2.1) Sous réserve des restrictions que le gouverneur en conseil peut imposer dans l'intérêt de la défense nationale ou de la sécurité, l'enquêteur muni du mandat visé au paragraphe (2.2) peut, à toute heure convenable, pénétrer dans tous locaux et y perquisitionner, pour y procéder aux investigations justifiées par l'enquête.

The phrase "reasonably necessary" in English translates to "justifiées par l'enquête" in French. Both versions enable a wide range of discretion to interpreters. Of note, there are remarkably few cases where discrepancies between French and English versions of Canadian law yielded a specific cause of action.[10] Overall, the advantage to machine reading is that there is no need for inter-coder reliability tests, nor do we need to rely on confidence intervals for the outputs. The entire universe of available data has been utilised, yielding non-parametric and complete statistics.

Determining Indeterminacies

How do judges resolve indeterminacies in law? And why might their interpretations differ from those of other state agents, including members of the elected government? The most straightforward answer is that judges rule against governments when they have the means, motive and opportunity to do so. Such an answer is positivist, in so far as judges constrain governments when a balance of power favours and enables them (Maravall and Przeworski 2003). According to a positivist argument, norms and values are of lesser importance than capacity. If judges feel they can rule against government, without risk of being overruled themselves, they are

[10] A notable exception is *Canadian Pacific Ry. Co. v. Robinson* (1887) 14 SCR 105.

much more likely to act. This positivist argument is not how judges would likely describe their own behaviour, but is seemingly obvious to the point of trite—judges make politically sensitive rulings when they are able to. The theory needs embellishments to more accurately capture the specific means, motives, and opportunities.

Firstly, ascertaining when the balance of power favours courts requires us to identify the principal power of judges—their authority to determine the meaning of laws. To make those determinations stick, judges must not advocate a preposterous interpretation of language. A constrained construction that went against normal usage, precedent, and public mood would likely be disapplied on appeal, or overturned by future legislation. Judges are at serious risk of losing their legitimacy, both within and beyond the judiciary. Even a whiff of inappropriate "activism" could see a judge disrespected by their peers, ignored by other state institutions, and, at worst, removed from office (Vanberg 2001). Judges do not have unrestrained decision-making power. Their rulings must deal with a disputed interpretation of law, and not a fabricated trifle. And their interpretations must be persuasive to others with power. Because judges are conspicuously powerless. Without a direct democratic mandate (in most cases) judges rely on vicarious legitimation. This can either come from other state institutions (such as when one branch of government does not agree with another), or can come when public opinion generally favours the judicial interpretation against the government's. An example of both scenarios is *Obergefell v Hodges*, when the US Supreme Court legalised same-sex marriage throughout the country.[11] Not only did the Obama Administration support the court ruling, against the wishes of various state governments, but public opinion across the country was also willing to accept the change.

A more nuanced description of judicial interpretation is therefore post-positivist, rather than simply positive. Power does not lie in the hands of judges, but is wielded by them according to vicarious consent from others with power. This is the crucial contribution of Neil MacCormick (2005). The institutional role of the judges is a form of practical reasoning, where a source of law purporting to provide a positive source of validity cannot be recognised due to indeterminacy, and interpretation resolves this problem. Language is the cause of the problem, and a synthesis of

[11] 576 U.S. 644 (2015).

language and norms are the solution. Thus post-positivism goes beyond the deconstructionism of Derrida and the post-modernists who claim there is "nothing outside the text" (Derrida 1997). It also goes beyond the legal realists who ascribe everything to the whim of individual judges.

The precise method of legal interpretation adopted is less important than the aim of being persuasive to a powerful audience. Hence it is a form of rule utilitarianism, where what matters is maximising perceived certainty in the rule of law, and the optimal means of achieving this is a rule-bound normative approach called the "logic of appropriateness" where the resolution of indeterminacy will be most persuasive (March and Olsen 1989). This normative institutionalism combines institutions and norms to explain the behaviour of judges. In other words, institutionalism cannot be separated from interpretivism, and difficulties in interpretation arising in a new legal problem are based on an institutional problem of recognising valid law. As MacCormick put it: "Law is institutional normative order". And indeterminate law threatens this order with collapse into uncertainty. As MacCormick goes on to contend (2005, 2):

> Respecting the rule of law is of profound political value in states... To have properly published and prospective laws, equality of citizens before them, and limitation of official power with respect to them, are foundations for democratic liberty and essentials for a stable economy. This would not be possible if laws and arguments about them gave only a sham of intelligibility. In that case, once it came to applying them, anything would go, on account of the radical indeterminacy of legal texts and absence of any reasonable grounds for preferring one construction of them to another.

The political behaviour of judges can be traced back to this "radical indeterminacy". It has undermined normative legal order, and has required judicial interventions to restore certainty. MacCormick's post-positivism therefore synthesises positivism with interpretivism. H.L.A. Hart (1961) had previously argued that the meaning of law entirely depends on its textual content, and was therefore positivist. Ronald Dworkin, contrarily, argued that law is far more than a simple disagreement over the meaning of words. He accused Hart of falling into a "semantic sting", where the complexity of legal discourse is denigrated to a battle over dictionary definitions. For Dworkin (1986, 239–240), interpreting the meaning of law is a hugely complex socio-cultural task, requiring the ability to ensure justice is achieved in accordance with accepted principles. In a similar vein, MacCormick suggested that to resolve incoherence in law requires the tethering of individual judgements to judicial and political reasoning that can be accepted.

Therefore to understand why judges display more political behaviour, we must analyse how positive law has changed and created spaces for interpretation. As Guido Calabresi (1982) has argued in relation to American law, judges created a "Common Law for the Age of Statutes". Rapid changes in legislation spurred judges to assimilate these new laws with extant legal principles. Hence, where a literal interpretation of legislation is impossible, judges utilise the language of the legislation as far as they can; they interrogate the legislators' intent; they assess the general scheme of legislation; and they decide on a means of ensuring justice for litigants (Cross et al. 1995). Having done all of this, judges will also be expected to synthesise domestic legislation with principles of customary law, international law (such as European Union law and the European Convention on Human Rights), and even academic analyses (Volcansek 1997).

Nonetheless, distinguishing adjudication from legislation is not easy, and is not uncontroversial (Shapiro and Stone Sweet 2002). In determining away indeterminacies judges will make law. Specifically, judges offer transtextual and metatextual interpolations and interpretations (Genette 1992). Where transtextuality is the cohering of one text with others, and metatextuality is the critiquing of one text by reference to others. As conceptual markers, therefore, legislation and adjudication are "fuzzy" with a "family resemblance" to each other (Goertz 2006). Fundamentally the difference is that judges are at least nominally independent and under-resourced. They are under-resourced in the sense that they lack the bureaucracy, treasure, and mandate to make good on their judgements. As mentioned, therefore, judges' power is derivative and vicarious. They are therefore strongly incentivised to determine law in line with recognised and generally approved sources of meaning (Klarman 1996). An optimal case resolution offers "integrity" to the legal system, where past principle and current problem are synthesised (Dworkin 1986, 225). An appropriate resolution to a case is more than fitting the case to conventional reasoning, it is also the reification of that conventional reasoning in new and unforeseen circumstances. As Dworkin suggests (1986, 228), adjudication is like writing a chapter in a novel with multiple authors—case law builds on principles established in earlier cases and propels the story forwards. Joseph Raz similarly argued that a rule of law is a means to (quoted in Kavanagh 2009, 349):

> …facilitate the integration of particular pieces of legislation with the underlying doctrines of the legal system.

This does not mean there is a Nash equilibrating resolution to each case that can be identified objectively. This is why judges, especially of the senior appellate levels, must cajole and persuade their audiences. Even in civil law jurisdictions, where there is less of a tradition of lengthy opinion writing, judges, as we will see in the coming chapters on France and Germany, clearly feel a need to explain how their ruling is a viable instantiation of legal principles to the facts of a case. Of course, there will be occasions where judges are thought to have made a mistake. And this is why the democracies studied for this book have multiple layers of appeal, and panels of judges deciding the most complex cases. No single judge can steer this oil tanker on their own.

But, clearly the most controversial aspect is when judges are perceived to be activist. This term is sometimes ranged against progressive or liberating rulings that empower weaker litigants against the strong. So why would indeterminacies in law ever favour a weaker litigant? Why, specifically, do judges not simply respect interpretations of law offered by the government? First, and most obviously, there is no "the government" to speak of. Instead there are vertically and horizontally disaggregated instruments of governance that attempt to coordinate using legislation. We will therefore encounter plenty of examples of federal and state governments on opposing sides of litigation, or situations where one government minister is claiming to represent the intent of an entire legislature, despite stark disapproval from legislators. Second, indeterminacies in law are not just state empowering. Previous research found evidence that whilst conjunctions expand powers, adjectives and adverbs will often impose fuzzy limits on those powers (Williams 2018). Think of a scenario when you are asked to select "the *red* ball" as opposed to when someone offers you a choice between "bat *and* ball". The latter is clearly more expansive. And, of course, legislation does not merely create powers, but also imposes duties, and establishes licencing criteria. So legislative intent will often be best served by supporting weaker litigants. Thirdly, where there is a doubt, natural justice will tend to suggest that any benefit of said doubt be offered to litigants with the most to lose.

Ultimately, "activism" is post-positive. In that, we will see plenty of cases where judges follow what they perceived to be draconian judgements, where the law was determinate. And, when judges do rule for weaker litigants, they will do so cautiously and in a manner that minimises any risk of their ruling being disrespected or overruled (Williams 2017). Even some of the most celebrated cases of judicial power, like *Brown v Board*, or the German *Census Ruling*, demonstrate far more political savvy and caution than critics of judicial power are likely to concede. The *Census Ruling* (*Volkszählungsurteil*) of 1983, is not widely known outside of Germany, but was a major check by the Federal Constitutional Court on powers to collect data.[12] The court developed a jurisprudence of informational self-determination, which was at least in part metatextual, in so far as the German Basic Law was used to critically assess the census legislation. But, the court ruling was careful not to over-extend the privacy rights. Several sections of the legislation complained of by litigants were ruled to be compatible with the Basic Law. The court nonetheless ordered that extra safety regulations be employed to prevent data collection from violating constitutional rights. It was only a part of one section (section 9) on the use and sharing of data that was ruled to be unconstitutionally void. In an earlier draft of this section, considered by the court, the legislature proposed a modest range of data that could only be shared with municipalities, and subject to tight conditions. In the final legislative text, these conditions were watered down and instead there were broad powers to share almost all data.[13] The court went so far as to analyse inter-party voting patterns on section 9 as it passed through the Bundestag, so as to be absolutely clear what power lay behind which constructions of language.[14] This behaviour from judges is undoubtedly of political significance. But the aim is to understand and explain why the judges intervened in this way. The evidence from their ruling suggests a desire to reconcile legislative and constitutional languages. Both sets of texts were indeterminate to a degree that new textual ligatures needed to be fashioned. It may have been that the judges were motivated by their own policy goals, but that is an untestable psychological hypothesis. What

[12] BVerfG, Dec. 15, 1983, 1 BvR 209, 269, 362, 420, 440, 484/83.

[13] Ibid. at paras. 82–83.

[14] Ibid. at para. 85.

is observable is the fact that there was an opportunity for a judicial intervention in policy that was created by a lack of legal positivism. Put plainly, there was no discernible law, especially in this context of social and technological change. The concomitant absence of a logic of communication enabled the judges' decision. Their motivations to decide are of lesser importance than their opportunities to decide.

Conclusion

Modern legislation can trace its origins to what was in effect a deed of property. Needing a tax base for war, the earliest European Parliaments developed in peripheral, multi-ethnic feuding states, many of which were isolated from the continent by sea or mountains—Iceland, the Isle of Man, Leon, and England being the earliest examples. The original parliamentary model was of a forum for the rich and powerful to *parley.* From this discourse would emerge a settled communiqué that could be recognised as an authoritative reallocation of funds. But, of course disputes would arise and the system worked with strong judges in tow. A strong central monarchy constrained by parliament and courts was an efficient mechanism for managing pluralism and growth whilst limiting blood feuds.

Legislatures must today manage increased state responsibilities, leading to complex and sometimes incompatible policy goals. The state must at once be powerful enough to manage social demands, but must also be constrained and prevented from abusing its position. Reconciling these varied forces of public and private power in a settled "logic of communication" is simply more difficult and can explain the rise in post-legislative disputation. As the linguistic turn in philosophy would have us expect, the most prominent debates in public policy can be derived from debates about what words mean and how they are to be used. When critics of powerful judges complain that "political correctness has gone mad" they are actually complaining of an externality in traded language. Lawyers trade in linguistic arbitrage, and have incentives to open markets to new disputants. Judges must reconcile the competing linguistic claims in a manner that can be accepted by those with power, or which is at least unlikely to be overturned.

If law is more difficult to determine, judges attain greater policy-making power. It is not a power that judges have strived for, more likely they have had it thrust into their hands by legislators who are understandably incapable of reconciling ambivalent demands into a coherent text. Judges are better placed at making a determination because they face no pressure from direct accountability, and can take unpopular decisions. But, given the relative powerlessness of judges, they repair legislative indeterminacies according to a logic of appropriateness. In short, their rulings must be persuasive if they are to stand.

References

Acemoglu, Daron, and James A. Robinson. 2006. *Economic Origins of Dictatorship and Democracy*. Cambridge: Cambridge University Press.

Adler, Paul. S. 1993. The Sociological Ambivalence of Bureaucracy: From Weber via Gouldner to Marx. *Organizational Science* 23 (1): 244–266.

Arrow, Kenneth. 1950. A Difficulty in the Concept of Social Welfare. *Journal of Political Economy* 58 (4): 328–346.

Auchie, Derek. 2004. The Undignified Death of the Casus Omissus Rule. *Statute Law Review* 25 (1): 40–67.

Austin, John L. 1962. *How to Do Things with Words*. Oxford: Clarendon Press.

Bauman, Zygmunt. 1991. *Modernity and Ambivalence*. Cambridge: Polity Press.

Bix, Brian. 1993. *Law, Language, and Legal Determinacy*. Oxford: Clarendon.

Bjørnskov, Christian, and Stefan Voigt. 2014. Constitutional Verbosity and Social Trust. *Public Choice* 161 (1): 91–112.

Boix, Carles. 2003. *Democracy and Redistribution*. Cambridge: Cambridge University Press.

Butt, Peter, and Richard Castle. 2001. *Modern Legal Drafting: A Guide to Using Clearer Language*. Cambridge: Cambridge University Press.

Calabresi, Guido. 1982. *A Common Law for the Age of Statutes*. Cambridge, MA: Harvard University Press.

Chapman, Kelly. 2015. *Complexity and Creative Capacity: Rethinking Knowledge Transfer, Adaptive Management and Wicked Environmental Problems*. London: Routledge.

Charrow, Robert P., and Veda R. Charrow. 1979. Making Legal Language Understandable: A Psycholinguistic Study of Jury Instructions. *Columbia Law Review* 79 (7): 1306–1374.

Chun, Young Han, and Hal G. Rainey. 2005. Goal Ambiguity in U.S. Federal Agencies. *Journal of Public Administration Research and Theory* 15 (1): 1–30.

Collier, Ruth Berins, and David Collier. 2002. *Shaping the Political Arena: Critical Junctures, the Labor Movement, and Regime Dynamics in Latin America*. Princeton, NJ: Princeton University Press.

Cross, Rupert, John Bell, and George Engle. 1995. *Cross: Statutory Interpretation*. London: LexisNexis Butterworths.

Crowley, Thomas. 1989. *The Politics of Discourse: The Standard Language Question in British Cultural Debates*. Basingstoke: Macmillan Education.

Crystal, David, and Derek Davy. 1969. *Investigating English Style*. Harlow: Longmans.

Danet, Brenda. 1980. Language in the Legal Process. *Law and Society Review* 14 (3): 445–564.

Danet, Brenda. 1985. Legal Discourse. In *Handbook of Discourse Analysis: Volume One*, ed. Teun van Dijk. London: Academic.

Derrida, Jacques. 1997. *Of Grammatology*. Baltimore: John Hopkins University Press.

Deutsch, Karl. 1963. *The Nerves of Government*. New York: New York Free Press.

Dworkin, Ronald. 1986. *Law's Empire*. London: Fontana.

Dyevre, Arthur. 2010. Unifying the Field of Comparative Judicial Politics: Towards a General Theory of Judicial Behaviour. *European Political Science Review* 2 (2): 297–327.

Easton, David. 1965. *A Framework for Political Analysis*. New Jersey: Prentice-Hall.

Edelman, Lauren B. 1992. Legal Ambiguity and Symbolic Structures: Organizational Mediation of Civil Rights Law. *The American Journal of Sociology* 97 (6): 1531–1576.

Empson, William. 1953. *Seven Types of Ambiguity*. London: Chatto and Windus.

Epstein, David, and Sharyn O'Halloran. 1999. *Delegating Powers: A Transaction Cost Politics Approach to Policy-Making Under Separate Powers*. Cambridge: Cambridge University Press.

Evans, Michael, Wayne Mcintosh, Jimmy Lin, and Cynthia Cates. 2007. Recounting the Courts? Applying Automated Content Analysis to Enhance Empirical Legal Research. *Journal of Empirical Legal Studies* 4 (4): 1007–1039.

Flinders, Matthew V. 2008. *Delegated Governance and the British State: Walking Without Order*. Oxford: Oxford University Press.

Foster, Christopher D. 2005. *British Government in Crisis, or, the Third English Revolution*. Oxford: Hart Publishing.

Freund, Ernst. 1921. Use of Indefinite Terms in Statutes. *Yale Law Review* 30 (5): 437–455.

Gee, James P. 2005. *An Introduction to Discourse Analysis: Theory and Method*, 2nd ed. London: Routledge.

Genette, Gérard. 1992. *The Architext: An Introduction*. Berkeley: University of California Press.
Goertz, Gary. 2006. *Social Science Concepts: A User's Guide*. Oxford: Princeton University Press.
Gotti, Maurizio. 2012. Text and Genre. In *The Oxford Handbook of Language and Law*, ed. Lawrence M. Solan and Peter M. Tiersma. Oxford: Oxford University Press.
Gunning, Robert. 1952. *The Technique of Clear Writing*. New York: McGraw-Hill.
Gustafsson, Marita. 1975. *Some Syntactic Properties of English Law Language*. Turku, Finland: University of Turku.
Haas, Ernst B. 1958. *The Uniting of Europe: Political, Social, and Economic Forces 1950–1957*. Stanford: Stanford University Press.
Hart, H.L.A. 1958. Positivism and the Separation of Law and Morals. *Harvard Law Review* 71: 593–629.
Hart, H.L.A. 1961. *The Concept of the Law*. Oxford: Clarendon.
Hiltunen, Risto. 2012. The Grammar and Structure of Legal Texts. In *The Oxford Handbook of Language and Law*, ed. Lawrence M. Solan and Peter M. Tiersma. Oxford: Oxford University Press.
Huber, John D., and Charles R. Shipan. 2002. *Deliberate Discretion? The Institutional Foundations of Bureaucratic Autonomy*. Cambridge: Cambridge University Press.
Jones, Bryan D. 2001. *Politics and the Architecture of Choice: Bounded Rationality and Governance*. Chicago: University of Chicago Press.
Kavanagh, Alison. 2009. *Constitutional Review Under the UK Human Rights Act*. Cambridge: Cambridge University Press.
King, Anthony. 1975. Overload: Problems of Governing in the 1970s. *Political Studies* 23 (2–3): 284–296.
Klarman, Michael. 1996. Rethinking the Civil Rights and Civil Liberties Revolutions. *Virginia Law Review* 82 (1): 1–67.
Krippendorff, Klaus. 1980. *Content Analysis: An Introduction to Its Methodology*. London: Sage.
Kurzon, Dennis. 1997. 'Legal Language': Varieties, Genres, Registers, Discourses. *International Journal of Applied Linguistics* 7 (2): 119–139.
Lester, Richard, and Michael Piore. 2004. *Innovation: The Missing Dimension*. Cambridge, MA: Harvard University Press.
Lippucci, Alessandra. 1998. Cybernetic Legal Analysis and Human Agency. *Res Publica* 4 (1): 77–116.
MacCormick, Neil. 2005. *Rhetoric and the Rule of Law: A Theory of Legal Reasoning*. Oxford: Oxford University Press.
Maravall, José M., and Adam Przeworski. 2003. *Democracy and the Rule of Law*. Cambridge: Cambridge University Press.

March, James, and Johan Olsen. 1989. *Rediscovering Institutions: The Organisational Basis of Politics*. New York: The Free Press.
Marmor, Andrei, and Scott Soames (eds.). 2011. *Philosophical Foundations of Language in the Law*. Oxford: Oxford University Press.
McCubbins, Mathew, Roger Noll, and Barry Weingast. 1987. Administrative Procedures as Instruments of Political Control. *Journal of Law, Economics, and Organization* 3 (2): 243–277.
Morris, Charles W. 1946. *Signs, Language, and Behaviour*. New York: G. Braziller.
Poguntke, Thomas, and Paul Webb. 2005. *The Presidentialization of Politics: A Comparative Study of Modern Democracies*. Oxford: Oxford University Press.
Poscher, Ralf. 2012. Ambiguity and Vagueness in Legal Interpretation. In *The Oxford Handbook of Language and Law*, ed. Lawrence M. Solan and Peter M. Tiersma. Oxford: Oxford University Press.
Post, Robert C. 1994. Reconceptualizing Vagueness: Legal Rules and Social Orders. *California Law Review* 82: 491–508.
Rhodes, Rod A.W. 1996. The New Governance: Governing Without Government. *Political Studies* 44 (4): 652–667.
Robertson, David. 2010. *The Judge as Political Theorist: Contemporary Constitutional Review*. Princeton, NJ: Princeton University Press.
Schleiter, Petra, and Edward Morgan-Jones. 2009. Citizens, Presidents and Assemblies: The Study of Semi-Presidentialism Beyond Duverger and Linz. *British Journal of Political Science* 39 (4): 871–892.
Schmidt, Vivien. 2008. Discursive Institutionalism: The Explanatory Power of Ideas and Discourse. *Annual Review of Political Science* 11: 303–326.
Segal, Hanna, and Jeffrey Perl. 2019. The Achievement of Ambivalence. *Common Knowledge* 25 (1): 51–62.
Shapiro, Martin, and Alec Stone Sweet. 2002. *On Law, Politics and Judicialization*. Oxford: Oxford University Press.
Solan, Lawrence M. 2012. Linguistic Issues in Statutory Interpretation. In *The Oxford Handbook of Language and Law*, ed. Lawrence M. Solan and Peter M. Tiersma. Oxford: Oxford University Press.
Strøm, Kaare, Wolfgang C. Müller, and Torbjörn Bergman. 2003. *Delegation and Accountability in Parliamentary Democracies*. Oxford: Oxford University Press.
Taylor, G.D.S. 1976. Judicial Review of Improper Purposes and Irrelevant Considerations. *The Cambridge Law Journal* 35 (2): 272–291.
Trosborg, Anna. 1995. Laying Down the Law—Discourse Analysis of Legal Institutions. *Special Issue of Journal of Pragmatics* 23 (1): 1–5.
Tsebelis, George, and Dominic Nardi. 2016. A Long Constitution Is a (Positively) Bad Constitution: Evidence from OECD Countries. *British Journal of Political Science* 46 (2): 457–478.

Vanberg, Georg. 2001. Legislative-Judicial Relations: A Game-Theoretic Approach to Constitutional Review. *American Journal of Political Science* 45 (2): 346–361.

Voigt, Stefan. 2009. Explaining Constitutional Garrulity. *International Review of Law and Economics* 29 (4): 290–303.

Volcansek, Mary L. 1997. *Law Above Nations: Supranational Courts and the Legalization of Politics*. Gainesville, FL: University Press of Florida.

Whitefield, Stephen. 2006. Mind the Representation Gap: Explaining Differences in Public Views of Representation in Postcommunist Democracies. *Comparative Political Studies* 39 (6): 733–758.

Wiener, Norbert. 1948. *Cybernetics: Or Control and Communication in the Animal and the Machine*. Cambridge, MA: MIT Press.

Williams, Matthew. 2016. Indeterminate Sovereignty and the Rule of Law. *British Politics* 11 (1): 26–48.

Williams, Matthew. 2017. The Grammar of Politics: A Brief History of Legislative Language in Britain. *Political Quarterly* 88 (2): 248–257.

Williams, Matthew. 2018. *How Language Works in Politics: The Impact of Indeterminate Legislation on Policy*. Bristol: Bristol University Press.

PART II

Quantitative History

Quantitative history can only respond to broad "When?" and "How far?" questions. "Why?" questions are best dealt with by process tracing analyses, provided in Part III. Nonetheless, a synoptic view gives us a sense of which "Why?" questions are worth asking, and which parts of the world are best compared. The two chapters in this part present results from machine reading languages of law. The first chapter (Chapter 3) looks to all of the world's available constitutions (187 in all), and the second chapter (Chapter 4) assesses all legislation enacted in five countries of interest since 2000. The five countries were selected because of their institutional and historic variances, and their similarities as advanced liberal democratic economies—the UK, the US, Canada, France, and Germany. The book is structured as a funnel, from widest to narrowest points of analysis. Such funnelling allows us to understand the causal mechanism, from language creation and dissemination, through to individual court rulings.

CHAPTER 3

The "New Constitutionalism" in 187 Countries

Constitutions are both a cause of, and solution to, indeterminacies in public discourse. They are central to our understanding of state power, civic freedom, and, hence, policy influence for judges. This chapter finds evidence of a "new constitutionalism" that has been theorised (Stone Sweet 2000; Gill and Cutler 2014). We will be searching through the contents and language in all available constitutions to uncover what, in fact, is "new", and what might be considered to have been "older" approaches to constituting a polity. To solve these empirical tasks, a novel method for classifying constitutions is offered that pays close attention to the language used. Classifying constitutions is most commonly a matter of describing their cultural and intellectual origins, or their distributions of executive power (presidential/parliamentary). Whilst these typologies tell us a great deal about a constitution's origins, they often rely on qualitative judgements as to which constitutions fit where. The taxonomy proposed here can be automated, and encourages some lesser considered comparisons. A three-part, continuous measure of relative constitutional indeterminacy is thereby offered. Using machine reading technology, 4,366,046 words in 178,663 sentences of 187 constitutions have been analysed. Findings demonstrate increased indeterminacies in constitutional language since 1989. There is also evidence that higher "indeterminacy volume" in a constitutional text is correlated with limited political freedoms, with institutional rigidities, and with lower GDP

M. Williams, *Judges and the Language of Law*,
https://doi.org/10.1007/978-3-030-91495-0_3

per capita. These correlations pertain, even when controlling for other variables.

The extent to which constitutions are designed has long been debated (Lijphart 1977; Horowitz 2002). It is a debate that raises important questions for comparative analysis of constitutions (Ferejohn et al. 2007). Specifically, how can we best classify constitutions, identify their potential to change, and anticipate their likely effects? Classifying constitutions is often led by considerations of their cultural and intellectual origins, such as whether they were influenced by British imperialism, American-style separations of power, the Napoleonic Code, or the Austro-Germanic *Grundnorm* (Rockmore et al. 2017). This "family tree" approach has much to commend it as a foundation for analysis, but it tells us more about how a constitution is perceived, and can be problematic when perceptions and realities diverge.

Alternative approaches to classification rely on form and function. These include executive structures (Linz 1990), federalism (Riker 1964; Stepan 2001), electoral rules (Renwick 2010), principal-agent delegation (Strøm et al. 2003), or judicial power (Stone 1992). These institutional typologies are parsimonious by necessity—where a regime is classified, for example, as being either presidential or parliamentary.[1] It can also be difficult to measure the intersection of different institutional rules, such as executive and electoral rules.[2] Constitutionalism depends on the capacity of governors and governed to follow rules. As rules are constructed from language, they must be comprehensible in multiple contexts if they are to work. And yet, wide interpretative spaces are opening in modern constitutional language (Lester and Piore 2004, 264). This means that constitutional language does not structure policy outcomes, and is more likely itself to be restructured by changes to context.

Constitutionalism is, in theory, the encoding of a nation's principles, with instructions for their realisation. Citizens in contemporary polities are, however, less capable of declaring or declaiming their preferred encodings of political reality (Elster 1995). Philosophies to underpin social or economic ambitions have become in many cases complex hybrids, and therefore lack coherence. As discussed previously, power

[1] Of course, non-binary classifications of executive type also exist. See, in particular, Siaroff (2003).

[2] A notable exception being Lijphart (2012).

is less concentrated amongst nation-state elites, and is distributed vertically amongst international actors, and horizontally amongst domestic elites and citizens. Even where elites can be ideologically and materially dominant—as in autocracies and hybrid regimes—the ability to define sovereign power is subject, most notably, to the uncertainties of international political economy. This has encouraged in most cases the encoding of constitutional texts that enable adaptation to context, can sustain multiple subtexts, and can dovetail intertextually with a corpus of global rules and norms. There are, specifically, three core elements of constitutional language that affect comprehensibility: word length (Tsebelis and Nardi 2016); lexico-grammatical indeterminacy (Schmidt 2008; Williams 2018); and age (Horowitz 2002). These three elements describe an "indeterminacy volume", being an observable implication of "interpretative space".

Comparing Constitutions

This three-part measure of constitutional meaningfulness is derived from three seminal pieces of research. On the length of constitutions, Tsebelis and Nardi (2016) described the "positively bad" consequences of long constitutions. Their study of OECD constitutions demonstrated that "substantive restrictions" were the consequence of relative garrulity (Voigt 2009). These restrictions inhibited comprehensibility, as was measured from researchers' interpretations of texts (Melton et al. 2013). The authors also demonstrated consequences for governance, including corruption and poor economic performance. Their models are reused in this chapter, with an assessment of which particular parts of speech pose the greatest threat to institutional efficacy. Substantive restrictions may be positively bad, but so too are under-substantiated restrictions. Those are restrictions (or licences) that have little prima facie meaning that can be reimagined by those with power in relation to context. Such provisions are, by their lack of definition, unlikely to have been created through extensive inter-group bargaining, and will not so readily be subject to accountability. Indeterminate provisions therefore violate a central tenet of any social contract—that the text of agreement must dominate and structure responses to context, rather than have context capable of significantly reshaping the text.

There will be no "logic of communication" if, rather than text structuring our interpretation of context, context reformulates the text.[3] As an important, albeit controversial example, consider how "equal protection" in the US Constitution's Fourteenth Amendment has had its meaning adapted through interpretation—from post-slavery reconstruction, to the decriminalisation of abortion, and to the recognition of same-sex marriages. The point here is not moral, in the sense of disapproving the adaptability of text to changing social norms and contexts. The point is empirical, that indeterminate constitutional language allows powers to be expanded or shrunk, duties to be embellished or shirked, and rights to be denied or aggrandised. The most likely course through these will, as ever in politics, be led by the distribution of power in a society. Where power is concentrated in a small elite, textual indeterminacy will most likely lead to power expansion, duty shirking, and denial of rights. All of which will be in accordance with the rule of law, but only because the law is not sufficiently fixed in meaning to rule (Bix 1993).

In addition to length and linguistics, the third element is history. Specifically, research by Donald Horowitz moves our focus from text, past context, to intertextuality. He considered how newer constitutions were not obviously the products of design, but were complex "idiosyncratic hybrids" (Horowitz 2002, 16). Nineteenth-century constitutions forged during the "first-wave" of democratisation saw cross-pollinations of design (Huntington 1993), but nonetheless retained distinct revolutionary principles. The American founding fathers, for instance, took design ideas from antiquity and British parliamentarism, and added in some of their own problematic compromises. Despite this complexity, the text transcended mere hybridity. It was considered a bold innovation in government, for which there were no obvious peers. Modern constitutions of the "third-wave", by contrast, were in some cases imposed, and in other cases assembled from extant examples. For Horowitz (2002, 16), modern constitutions simply cannot be said to have been designed:

> In spite of all this cross-boundary involvement and in some ways because of it, constitutions that have been designed, as opposed to merely constructed, are difficult to find... Suffice it to say here that the results

[3] See theoretical work on post-structuralism and discourse analysis in, for example, Lyotard et al. (2006).

since 1989 do not suggest the triumph of constitutional design or even of comparative learning, however great the, efforts have been.

This lack of design intent again inhibits a "logic of communication" because there is no kernel of meaning, no basic undergirding philosophy. Instead there is a muddle of institutional forms put together. This means that we increasingly see constitutions without constitutionalism (Prempeh 2007). That is, texts without internal clarity and coherence. All of which further discourages an approach to classifying constitutions on the basis of typology, rather than taxonomy. Because, in typologies, constitutions are classed by their supposed association to archetypes, rather than their actual, often messy, inexactitude.

Let us take a pairwise comparison.[4] The US and Ecuadorean constitutions enjoy a degree of "family resemblance" (Stern 2004). Notably, Ecuador took on America's model of presidential executive, but its unicameral legislature and mixed-methods electoral system are striking differences. Classifying the relativity of these constitutions is therefore difficult if led by heritage, or first-order institutional principles (such as executive power). Arguably more instructive is how far each constitution fails to specify the distributions of power and rights. The US Constitution has a much smaller indeterminacy volume of 0.34, defined as the product of its word length in log words, its proportion of adjectives, adverbs and conjunctions, and its age since the dawn of constitutionalism (measured in years of operation since 1789). Indeed, the US could have a volume of 0 given its constitution was formally adopted in 1789, and was promulgated 0 years after the dawning of constitutionalism. To avoid mathematical problems such as this, the start date of US constitutional law is taken to be from ratification of the Bill of Rights in 1791. Still, the text was a relatively coherent design, only partially influenced by other existing constitutions of the time. In addition to which, the complete text is only 7764 words long (including the 27 amendments), just 6.22% of these words are adjectives or adverbs, and 6.21% are conjunctions. Ecuador has the world's most expansive indeterminacy volume of 4.32, derived

[4] Data for these comparisons was obtained from the Comparative Constitutions Project and Constitute Project from https://comparativeconstitutionsproject.org/ccp-rankings/, accessed from September 2018 to September 2021. See also Elkins et al. (2014).

from its 56,428-word constitution, 10.5% of these words being adjectives or adverbs, and 6.37% of them being conjunctions. All of which is contained in a constitution that was promulgated 219 years after 1789 (in 2008), meaning that it is likely, as per the argument of Horowitz, to be a confusing hybrid of multiple constitutional "designs" from which little time has passed to crystallise its meaning.

The relative meaningfulness in each constitution can be seen from the following comparisons of their freedom of expression provisions:

> Congress shall make no law respecting an establishment of religion, or prohibiting the free exercise thereof; or abridging the freedom of speech, or of the press; or the right of the people peaceably to assemble, and to petition the Government for a redress of grievances.
>
> US Constitution, First Amendment.

This is a short and plainly worded rule. There are few adjectives or adverbs that qualify the interpretation of nouns and verbs—*free* exercise, and *peaceably* assemble are notable counterexamples. There are five conjunctions (four *ors* and one *and*). These conjunctions string together conditions on the freedom of expression. The manner and form of these conditions can lead to several plausible but exclusive interpretations of the law. In Ecuador, the freedom of expression provision is worded as follows. The text has been edited down from its original 123 words:

> The State shall recognize young people as strategic players in the country's development... The State shall foster their incorporation into the labor force in fair and decent conditions, with emphasis on training, guarantee of access to first employment, and promotion of their entrepreneurial skills... The State shall guarantee their freedom of expression and association, the free functioning of student councils and types of associations.
>
> Ecuadorean constitution, Title II, Chapter 3, Section 2, Article 39.

This provision is long, and qualified by adjectives, adverbs, and conjunctions. A government lawyer of even moderate talent would be able to defend against a perceived failure to "recognize young people as strategic players" or to furnish "fair and decent [labor] conditions". An even starker contrast lies with Poland's concise provisions:

> The freedom to express opinions, to acquire and to disseminate information shall be ensured to everyone.
>
> Polish Constitution, Article 54, Section 1.

Note, the comprehensibility of the Polish law is a function not only of its diminutive length, but its relative lack of adjectives and adverbs. Regrettably, the Polish government has sought to circumvent these restrictions by firing judges. So textual clarity is insufficient for good governance. Nonetheless, the Polish use of verbs is also plain, with, notably, the modal auxiliary verb "shall" used rather than "may". The reason for operationalising indeterminacy without verbs is for the sake of parsimony. Where in previous and succeeding chapters we will include analysis of modal and enabling verbs, this and the following chapter look specifically to the qualification of linguistic variables and flow control (that is noun or verb qualifying adjectives, adverbs, and conjunctions). In the qualitative chapters we will also assess the capacity to generate new variables and flow control through verbs.

Combining the product of word length, linguistics, and youthfulness as a volume is perhaps geometrically dubious. This is especially given that word length and lexical variables are measurements of the same text. Perhaps it would be clearer to describe the factor variable as an "indeterminacy area", being the proportion of indeterminate words, multiplied by their youthfulness. But volume is analytically clearer than area. Because, a key point is that both word length and lexical indeterminacy are important separately and collectively. What matters is not just the number of words, but the types of words used. By taking the log number of words multiplied by the proportion of adjectives, adverbs, and conjunctions we obtain relative indeterminacy, which is then multiplied by age in log years. For example, there are short constitutions, that contain significant indeterminacies of language, and, by their youthfulness, are more likely to have been influenced by a confusing mixture of design ideas. For instance, Guinea-Bissau's 8844-word constitution is a little longer than this chapter, and is the thirty-second shortest of the 187 constitutions surveyed. But, it was promulgated in 1984, some 200 years after the dawning of modern constitutionalism, and it is in the world's top ten constitutions for proportion of adjectives and adverbs. Its short word length might otherwise hide the capacity of the text to carry multiple subtexts, and be expanded in context. As per Article 58 below:

> In accordance with national development, the State will progressively create the conditions required for the full accomplishment of the economic and social rights established by this Part.
>
> Constitution of Guinea-Bissau, Article 58.

Despite this article being short, it is capable of multiple reimaginings. And hence, a short constitution may be the tip of an extra-textual iceberg. Thus the volumetric taxonomy tells us about both relativity, and individuality of each subject—as does the phylogenetic taxonomy used in zoology. The resulting indeterminacy volumes are for the most part intuitive, and reinforce existing research on constitutions. But some results are more surprising, and therefore useful. Tonga and Lebanon, for instance, have close similarities to Canada in their constitutional languages. Grouping countries by jurisprudential traditions does make sense, but it is a typology imbued in cultural history. It could even be predicated on classification of core civilisations, and overly focussed on totemic western contributions to rules of law (Said 1978). By considering the potential interplay of text and context, this approach considers information processing, retrieval, and bargaining. These are the fundamental components of institutional theory, and indeterminacies in constitutional cybernetics affect them all.

Constitutions that establish indeterminate rules of law pose broader implications. The enlightenment notion of a social contract is challenged. Whilst the first consequences of indeterminacy are incomprehensibility, also consequent, but subject to other variables, will be suboptimal governance. Space is available for charisma to have a substantial effect, through discretionary decision-making. Where constitutions constrain the public sphere, especially via indeterminate rules, the consequences will likely be centralised policy-making and delivery. This may have advantages for flexibility, but disadvantages of haste, unpredictability, and under-scrutinised policy change (Strøm et al. 2003). Possible counter-arguments would stress that an incomplete constitutional text can spare excessive pre-promulgation bargaining. This can avoid the sometimes "evil" consequences of sealing moral problems indefinitely into the constitution (Graber 2006; Chapman 2015). The Connecticut Compromise, by which America's Constitution was rendered acceptable to its founders, led significantly to the US Civil War, because slavery and discrimination were written into the national rulebook. Furthermore, countries with significant ethnic, religious, or national cleavages could better develop their public spheres through incremental adaptation of institutions, which, like a learning algorithm, are more flexible and inclusive (Lerner 2010). Take Iraq's constitution as an example:

> Acknowledging God's right over us, and in fulfilment of the call of our homeland [we] marched for the first time in our history towards the ballot boxes by the millions… invoking the pains of sectarian oppression inflicted by the autocratic clique and inspired by the tragedies of Iraq's martyrs, Shiite and Sunni, Arabs and Kurds and Turkmen and from all other components of the people.
>
> Iraqi Constitution, Preamble.

It is unrealistic to expect a nation such as Iraq to have developed a plainly worded, short, or philosophically coherent constitution (McGarry and O'Leary 2007). In such cases, constitutions tend towards being mere "parchment barriers", as James Madison put it (Hamilton et al. 2009, No. 48). Superficially clear constitutions that are ignored will not determine policy outcomes, as mentioned with regard to certain freedoms in Poland. A constitutional text cannot hope to structure the means by which communities gather and manage information. Politicking is largely extra-textual. But Iraq is not an established democracy with a rule of law. Drawing inferences from its constitutional text will be difficult as a result. It is in free countries, as defined by the Freedom House Index, where the policy effects of indeterminate constitutions are most significant. Brazil has the highest indeterminacy volume of any free nation (3.85). This textual indeterminacy is a reflection of Brazil being a large, and highly diverse polity. Nonetheless, there will most likely be significant effects of constitutional indeterminacy that are independent of these sociodemographic factors. The textual indeterminacy obviates a "logic of communication" between and beyond Brazilian institutions. This can in turn delimit the capacity of individuals and social movements to press claims via official mechanisms. Indeterminate language therefore contributes to Brazil's institutional weaknesses.

This linguistic fixation is, as mentioned, narrowly focussed on the meso-level of a highly complex causal mechanism. Countries such as the US (0.34) and New Zealand (1.18), with small indeterminacy volumes, will of course experience moments of institutional failure. Just as those free nations such as Portugal (3.71) and Timor (3.10) with higher volumes will not always suffer "positively bad" consequences from lacking a logic of communication. The point is that where institutional powers, duties, and rights are more plainly promulgated it will better empower citizens relative to elites (Levitsky and Ziblatt 2018).

Hypotheses and Data

There are five hypotheses derived from the taxonomy. Two concern the causes of indeterminacy, and three consider its consequences. The five hypotheses tell a story of why indeterminacy is more common, and why it produces observable policy effects. As regards causes, all 187 constitutions were tested. As regards consequences, the 84 free countries are tested with some omitted in tests due to incomplete data. Hypotheses concern time, democratic freedoms, textual comprehensibility, and governance:

H1 Newer constitutions contain more indeterminacies of language (adjectives, adverbs and conjunctions) than older constitutions.

A linear association of time and indeterminacy is expected. The aim is to test whether newer constitutions, influenced by globalisation of legal norms, are more linguistically complex than older constitutions. Adjectives and adverbs add qualifications, and will therefore tend to limit powers, duties, and rights (Williams 2017a). This may constrain state power, but only indeterminately. Conjunctions can be used to expand or restrict powers and duties, by conjoining a string of competencies or conditions (Williams 2017b).

H2 Constitutional indeterminacy correlates with a country's Freedom score.

A linear association is expected, where freer countries have less indeterminate constitutions than unfree countries. This uses Freedom House's Freedom in the World scores. A correlation cannot support a causal proposition here. Indeterminate constitutional language does not so much cause countries to deviate from free politics. Indeterminacy in constitutional language is both consequence of and contributor to a country's lack of freedom. What is interesting is the correlation.

H3a Indeterminate constitutions are more rigid (less likely to be amended).

This utilises Elkins et al.'s (2009) amend_rate metric. As Tsebelis and Nardi (2016) demonstrated, longer constitutions impose more substantive restrictions and are more rigid. Even more rigid are those constitutions that impose both substantive and indeterminate restrictions. Such constitutions tend to empower elites and enfeeble civil society. Elites become invested in informal interpretations and less willing to consent to formal amendments. This rigidity can reinforce elite dominance of constitutionalism.

H3b Constitutions with high levels of adjectives and adverbs are more difficult to interpret.

This utilises Melton et al.'s (2013) inter-coder readability scores. Researchers were asked to read and interpret the world's constitutions. Using content analysis, the similarity of their interpretations were measured. Where multiple interpretations of the same text are possible, those with superior material, social, and cultural power will be better placed to determine their preferred interpretations. Might will often be right, including in liberal democracies where indeterminacies are resolved by potentially expensive litigation (Williams 2018). This subsidiary hypothesis looks to those parts of speech most important for creating textual indeterminacy, namely adjectives and adverbs. Conjunctions are more important for creating contextual indeterminacy, where deciding whether the text applies to this "or" that "and" the other, "but" not this, demonstrates potentially complex Boolean decision trees (Williams 2017a).

H4 Constitutional indeterminacy is correlated with low GDP per capita.

The dependent variable here is gross domestic product purchasing power parity (GDPPPP) averaged from 2008 to 2016.[5] The data frame here matches that used by Tsebelis and Nardi (2016, 471–476). Again, the direction of causation can be debated here—do indeterminate constitutions frustrate growth, or do poorer countries struggle to determinate rules of law? The models could indeed be partly endogenous (where cause and effect are dependent on omitted variables). But, it is theoretically most plausible that institutional performance affects development, not that underdevelopment creates indeterminate institutions. Put plainly,

[5] Data from the World Bank.

poorer countries should not be any more inclined to write unclear constitutional rules, whereas unclear constitutional rules can inhibit growth and redistribution. There will be other variables relevant to this story, such as cultural, regional, and historical variables. But herein lies the crux of any institutional theory—the rules of the political game are expected to have significant effects, which are partly independent of the forces that created those rules. Economic performance is expected to be affected by the indeterminate distribution of institutional powers and duties.

Method

Constitutional texts were taken from the Comparative Constitutions "Constitute Project" (Elkins et al. 2014). This website provides English translations of the world's constitutions. There are some potential limitations to analysing these. Firstly, and most importantly, English translations of constitutions may lead to perceived linguistic indeterminacies that do not exist in the original text, or are not considered as indeterminate. For instance, certain adjectives may seem vague in English, but have a settled meaning in the original language. Even in English, certain adjectives like "executive" are not indeterminate in meaning. As ever, the aim is to draw probabilistic inferences. Those constitutions with proportionately more adjectives, adverbs, and conjunctions are more likely to affect inter- and extra-institutional communication.

A second risk associated with the dataset is identifying the official constitution. There are cases where countries have amended their constitutions, sometimes to include largely inoperative addenda. New Zealand is a good example. Their original constitution was promulgated by the UK Parliament in 1852. It is short and plainly worded. But an amended version from 2014 is available on the Constitute website. It includes the Treaty of Waitangi as one of its schedules, alongside several other very long schedules. To avoid distorting the data, scheduled material have not been included for any nation, although amendments have been included. It is just the primary operative elements of each constitution that have been coded.

With regard to operationalisation, it is important to ask how and why indeterminacy is measured. Firstly, the language measured is prone to indeterminacies, but will not be completely incomprehensible. Even in autocracies with little or no public discourse, there is still a perceived need to draft some at least partially meaningful sentences on founding principles. North Korea's constitution contains significant indeterminacies, but is of course not entirely incomprehensible (parts of speech tagged by the program are italicised):

> The DPRK is a *revolutionary* state which has inherited *brilliant* traditions formed during the *glorious revolutionary* struggle against the *imperialist* aggressors, in the struggle to achieve the liberation of the homeland and the freedom and *well-being* of the people.
>
> North Korean Constitution, Article 2.

This exegetical passage has meaning and utility. But in a country with a rule of law, citizens might wish to litigate if the state pursued policies that deviated from the "glorious struggle" or inhibited "freedom and well-being".

The three-part indeterminacy measure is justified on the basis that word length, proportion of adjectives, adverbs, and conjunctions, and years since 1789 all interact. It would not be appropriate to use an additive measure, because of this interaction. The interaction is not strong, as demonstrated by factor analyses. Cronbach's α coefficient for internal consistency amongst variables has a p-value of 0.28. McDonald's ω coefficient has a p-value of 0.59. There is little statistical evidence to reject the null in favour of a common factor. Nonetheless, as *H1* will test, there is inter-correlation between the three variables, and there are substantive theoretical justifications for subsuming them into a single metric.

To make the three-part variable mathematically appropriate, the natural logarithm of word length has been used (following the example of Tsebelis and Nardi). If just the total number of words were used, then India, with its 105,346-word constitution, would be wildly outlying. In addition to which the proportion of words that are adjectives, adverbs, or conjunctions, and the log to base 10 of years since 1789 are applied. The reason for using the natural log for word length and a log to base 10 for age is because age is less significant than word length, and ought to be weighted less. Take Angola for example. Its constitution was promulgated in 2010, being 221 years after the dawning of modern constitutionalism. It is 26,697 words long, of which 10% are adjectives and adverbs, and another 6% are conjunctions. Taking the product of its log length, textual indeterminacies, and log age gives a relatively high indeterminacy volume of 3.71. But this score is not unduly skewed by youthfulness alone.

$$Ind.volume = \log_e(length) \times \left(\frac{adjectives, adverbs, andconjunctions}{wordlength}\right) \times \log_{10}(age)$$

$$Ind.volume_{Angola} = \log_e(26,697) \times \left(\frac{4150}{26,697}\right) \times \log_{10}(2010 - 1789)$$

$$Ind.volume_{Angola} = 10.19 \times 0.1554 \times 2.34 = 3.71$$

For multivariate regression analyses, all variables have been normalised 0–1 to make for comparable coefficients. Descriptive statistics (without normalisation) are displayed in Table 3.1.

Data Diagnostics

Diagnostics were run to test the core assumptions of regression analysis. Importantly, there needed to be independence between all explanatory variables, between the explanatory and the response variables, and the response variable had to be immune from auto-correlation with time. As regards the explanatory variables, variance inflation factors are recorded where there may be any doubt as to the multicollinearity of variables. These variance inflation factors do not provide evidence to reject the null of independence of all variables. This gives some confidence that errors are homoscedastic, and therefore do not deviate from the normality assumptions of Ordinary Least Square regression analysis. In multivariate analyses, model specification was led by theory, and past research (especially Tsebelis and Nardi 2016).

The response variables in all regressions do not offer evidence against the null hypothesis of time series stationarity. That is, they do not auto-correlate, which would distort the theorised impact of the explanatory variables. Priestly-Subba Rao tests for stationarity were used. When indeterminacy in adjectives, adverbs, and conjunctions was the response variable, and time was the explanatory variable, there was no evidence that indeterminacies begat more indeterminacies as time progressed. The p-value of 0.1034 is low, but not sufficiently low to reject the null of stationarity. Whilst indeterminacies have increased with time, there have been sufficient variations at all time periods to suggest that the changes in

Table 3.1 Descriptive statistics

Frame	*Variable*	*Description*	*Min*	*Mean*	*Median*	*Max*	*SD*
Constitution	YEAR	Year of enactment (years since 1789)	2	173.85	189	225	45.74
	REL	Interpretability (inter-coder reliability % from Elkins et al.)	60.46	76.54	77.05	92.13	6.37
	LOGLEN	Constitution length (in log words)	8.16	9.82	9.83	11.57	0.71
	LEVELS	Binary measure of devolved sub-national government (Elkins et al.)	0	0.82	1	1	0.39
	LAWCOM	Binary measure of common law origin (Elkins et al.)	0	0.31	0	1	0.47
	EXE	Executive powers (0–7 additive index from Elkins et al.)	0	4.37	4	7	1.71
	LEG	Legislature power (mean of 32 binary measures from Elkins et al.)	0	0.29	0.33	0.62	0.11
	JID	Judicial independence (0–6 additive index from Elkins et al.)	0	2.59	2	6	1.48
	SCO	Scope (% of 92 topics from Elkins et al.)	0.21	0.58	0.6	0.81	0.11

(continued)

Table 3.1 (continued)

Frame	*Variable*	*Description*	*Min*	*Mean*	*Median*	*Max*	*SD*
Text	LOGADJ	Presence of adjectives and adverbs (in log words)	4.93	7.24	7.35	8.89	0.72
	LOGCON	Presence of conditional conjunction (in log words)	2.15	2.92	2.91	3.70	0.34
	INDVOL	Indeterminacy = Log length x (Adj % + Con%) x Log age	0.34	2.66	2.68	3.85	0.54
Context	GDPPPP	GDP per capita PPP, averaged 2008–2016 (World Bank)	2.90	4.09	4.13	5.16	0.54
	EDUSEC	% of labour force with a secondary education in 2016 (World Bank)	42.50	59.41	58.25	79.50	7.62
	NATRES	Natural resources rent as % of GDP in 2016 (World Bank)	0.00	2.36	0.47	23.01	4.76
	TRADE	Trade as % of GDP in 2016 (World Bank)	24.61	99.32	89.99	407.43	57.62
	FDI	Foreign direct investment as % of GDP in 2016 (World Bank)	−37.17	4.27	2.71	54.61	10.22
	SAVE	Gross savings as % of GDP in 2016 (World Bank)	4.89	22.52	21.58	62.86	9.34

(continued)

Table 3.1 (continued)

Frame	*Variable*	*Description*	*Min*	*Mean*	*Median*	*Max*	*SD*
	CORRINV	Transparency Intl Corruption Perceptions Index inverted 2016–2017	11	42.27	43	67	15.97

language are not simply the result of changes in time. An important final point to note is that data are universal, rather than based on samples. All available constitutions and data on countries have been used. There is no need therefore for calculations of confidence intervals.

Results

Results begin with descriptive tests for H1–H2, and are followed by causal tests for H3a–H4.

H1 Newer constitutions contain more indeterminacies of language (adjectives, adverbs and conjunctions) than older constitutions.

Constitution length in log words is positively correlated with years since 1789. Newer constitutions are, on average, longer than older constitutions (assuming a linear trend, $y = 9.1 + 0.004x$, $R2 = 0.04$, $p = 0.008^{***}$). Word length alone only gives us one dimension, the presence of adjectives, adverbs, and conjunctions tells us in addition how constitutional language is qualified, and how policy information will likely be processed by institutions operating under the constitution. Figure 3.1 displays the sum of log adjectives, adverbs, and conjunctions regressed on time in years since 1789.

The slope in Fig. 3.1 (0.007x) is steeper than was that for total length in log words (0.0004x). Inevitably, the slope starts from a lower starting point, but being steeper suggests that of all the parts of speech, adjectives, adverbs, and conjunctions have increased in greater proportion. A slope for constitutions enacted after 1989 is flat, implying that indeterminacy peaked at the "third wave" constitution-forming moments of the post-Soviet era. There is of course wide variance in these findings. Nonetheless, there is a statistically significant correlation of time, constitution length,

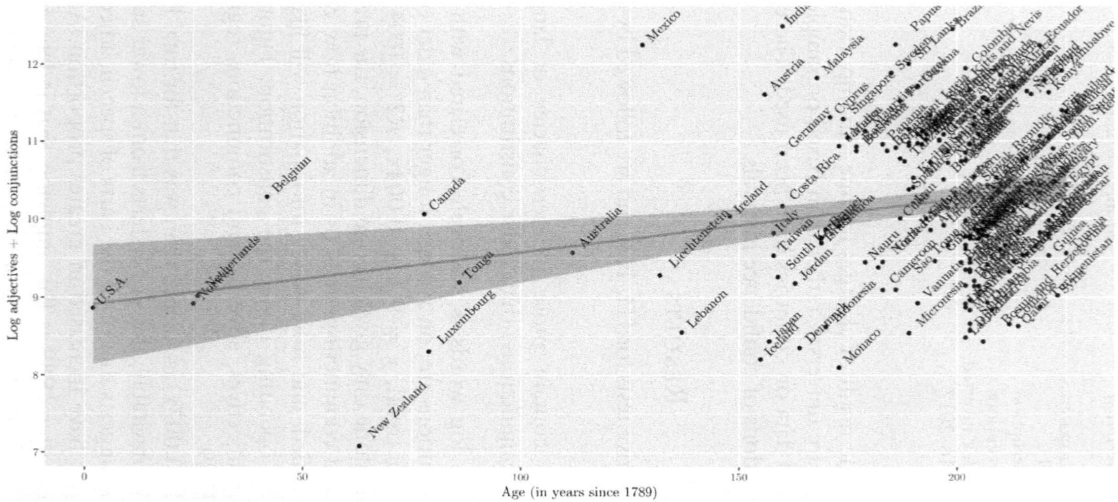

y = 8.9 + 0.007x, R^2 = 0.04, p = 0.0009***

Fig. 3.1 Indeterminacies in constitutional language regressed on age in years since 1789 (*Source* Author's creation using data from The Comparative Constitutions Project)

and constitutional indeterminacy. And, wide variances are to be expected from a large and diverse dataset. These findings support the creation of a three-part indeterminacy volume measure to compare constitutions. There is evidence that the language of modern constitutions is both more garrulous and more prone to indeterminacies (Fig. 3.2).

And what are the implications of this? Does classifying constitutions by their relative indeterminacies dovetail with other important political science indicators?

H2 Constitutional indeterminacy correlates with a country's Freedom score.

There is evidence to reject the null in favour of H2 that indeterminacy volume is correlated with a country's Freedom score. The 1–7 Freedom in the World score is a composite measure of political rights and civil liberties, where higher scores denote lesser freedoms.

H3a Indeterminate constitutions are more rigid (less likely to be amended).

Indeterminate constitutions are more rigid in the sense of being less likely to be amended. Formal amendment procedures are, typically, a more inclusive method of fixing problems with the national code. If a constitution contains significant indeterminacies, it can more easily be amended informally. There will be vested interests concerned to sustain the informal interpretation of constitutional language and opposed to a formal re-wording, thus making the text subject to subtextual and intertextual fixity. Elkins et al. (2014) created the amend_rate metric, which is the predicted probability of a constitutional amendment being promulgated. It is a compound of institutional, historical and cultural variables. Figure 3.3 shows its relation to indeterminacy volume.

There is a statistically significant cubic, rather than linear, relationship. The slope nonetheless demonstrates a positive relationship, where an indeterminacy volume of 1.5> has an equal 0.5 probability of amendment. All higher indeterminacy volumes are more likely than not to remain unamended.

H3b Constitutions with high levels of adjectives are more difficult to interpret.

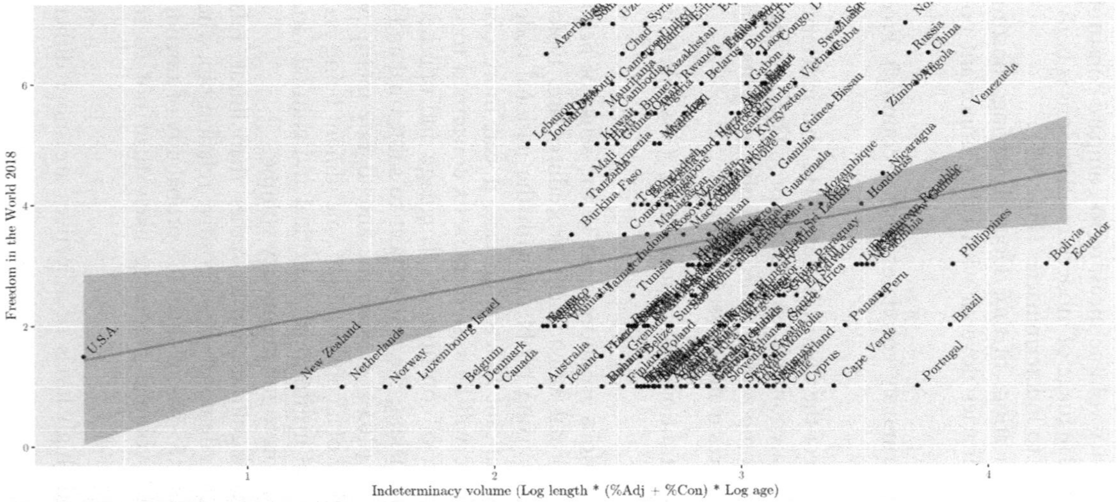

y = 1.19 + 0.77x, $R^2 = 0.04$, p = 0.007***

Fig. 3.2 Freedom in the World score regressed on indeterminacy volume (*Source* Author's creation using data from The Comparative Constitutions Project)

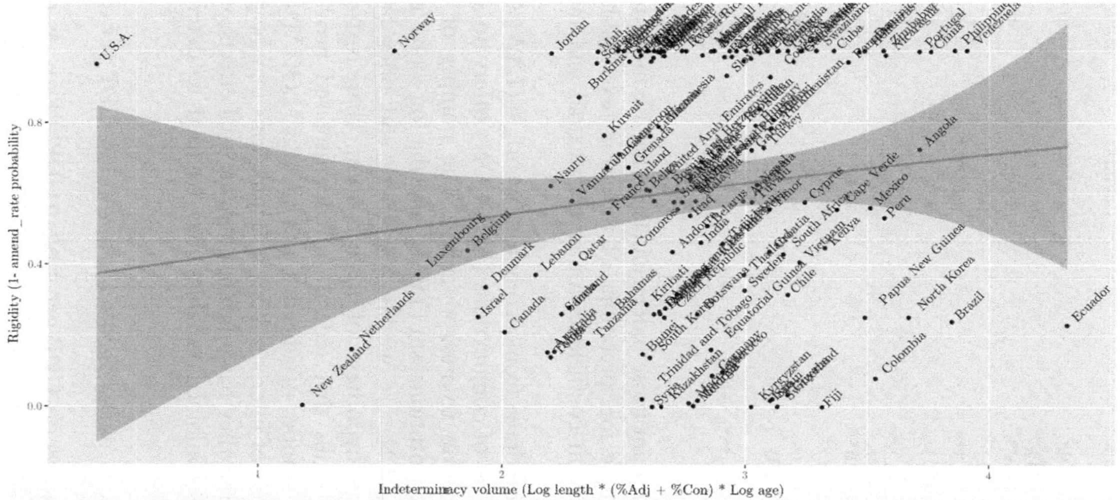

y = 0.61 – 0.81x³, R² = 0.05, p = 0.03**

Fig. 3.3 Constitutional rigidity regressed on indeterminacy volume (*Source* Author's creation using data from The Comparative Constitutions Project)

Table 3.2 Interpretability regressed on textual and other variables

Variable	*Binary*	*Constant*	*Multiple* R^2
YEAR	−0.19*	0.65***	0.04
	(0.11)	(0.08)	
LOGLEN	−0.19*	0.60***	0.04
	(0.11)	(0.05)	
LEVELS	−0.13**	0.61***	0.05
	(0.06)	(0.05)	
LAWCOM	0.06	0.49***	0.02
	(0.05)	(0.03)	
LOGADJ	−0.26**	0.66***	0.06
	(0.12)	(0.07)	
LOGCON	−0.16	0.58***	0.03
	(0.10)	(0.05)	

Note Standard errors in parentheses. $^{***}p < 0.01$. $^{**}p < 0.05$. $^{*}p < 0.1$. $N = 84$

It is interesting to pinpoint those indeterminacies that are most important to sustaining multiple interpretations of the same text. Table 3.2 displays bivariate regression coefficients for several textual and institutional variables.

Whether a constitution draws from a common law origin (LAWCOM), or contains high numbers of conjunctions (LOGCON) offers no statistical significance in relation to interpretability. The number of years after the dawning of constitutionalism (YEAR) and the log word length of constitutions (LOGLEN) are weakly correlated, and offer limited evidence to reject the null hypotheses of no correlation. There is stronger evidence to reject the nulls that federal and decentralised provisions (LEVELS) and a high number of adjective and adverbs (LOGADJ) are correlated with low levels of interpretability. Conjunctions may be prima facie easy to interpret, but they have significant contextual effects, where various conditions and conjoined variables may be used to determine multiple outcomes.

H4 Constitutional indeterminacy is correlated with low GDP per capita.

Modelling the influences on GDP per capita (GDPPPP) is, as noted by Tsebelis and Nardi (2016, 469), difficult and controversial. As such, a range of important explanatory variables have been included in bivariate and multivariate regressions, so as to avoid egregious omitted variable

Table 3.3 GDP per capita (PPP) regressed on textual and other variables

Frame	*Variable*	*Bivariate*	*(1)*	*(2)*	*(3)*	*(4)*
Textual	INDVOL	−0.53***	−0.4***	−0.41***	−0.05	−0.26**
		(0.13)	(0.1)	(0.1)	(0.08)	(0.11)
	YEAR	−0.48***				
		(0.09)				
	LOGLEN	−0.37***				
		(0.1)				
Legal	LEVELS	0.07				
		(0.06)				
	LAWCOM	−0.07				
		(0.05)				
	EXE	0.01				
		(0.12)				
	LEG	0.12				
		(0.1)				
	JID	−0.18*				
		(0.11)				
	SCO	−0.12				
		(0.13)				
Contextual: Economy	EDUSEC	0.1				
		(0.13)				
	NATRES	−0.18**	−0.12	−0.2		
		(0.08)	(0.09)	(0.1)		
	TRADE	0.31**	0.28**	0.19*	0.19***	0.21***
		(0.12)	(0.13)	(0.11)	(0.07)	(0.07)
	FDI	0.27*	−0.06			
		(0.15)	(0.18)			
	SAVE	0.23*		0.2*		
		(0.13)		(0.11)		
Contextual: Corruption	CORRINV	−0.45***			−0.42***	−0.87***
		(0.04)			(0.05)	(0.17)
	INDVOL*CORRINV					0.64***
						(0.23)
	CONSTANT		0.41***	0.37***	0.39***	0.52***
			(0.1)	(0.08)	(0.05)	(0.07)
	Multiple R^2		0.32	0.42	0.72	0.75
	Adjusted R^2		0.28	0.37	0.7	0.74
	N		69	58	63	63

Note Standard errors in parentheses. ***$p < 0.01$. **$p < 0.05$. *$p < 0.1$

biases. Table 3.3 presents results from bivariate analysis, and four multivariate models.

From the bivariate regressions there is evidence to reject the null hypotheses with regard to a negative correlation between GDP per capita and indeterminacy volume (INDVOL); years since 1789 (YEAR); and length in log words (LOGLEN). Given that INDVOL contains YEAR and LOGLEN, they cannot be used together in the same multivariate models. And the relative strength of INDVOL suggests it is the more powerful predictor to use. Other variables such as the decentralisation of power (LEVELS) and the extent of executive powers (EXE) do not demonstrate strong nor statistically significant bases for rejecting their null hypotheses. This is interesting, in that the range of executive powers enumerated is not as important as the indeterminacy of language used to frame those powers. Rents from natural resources (NATRES), trade openness (TRADE), and corruption (CORRINV) also offer statistically significant grounds to reject their respective null hypotheses, and suggest a negative correlation with GDP. Corruption is measured, as per Tsebelis and Nardi (2016, 473), with Transparency International's Corruption Perceptions Index, which is inverted such that high scores denote greater perceived corruption.

Models 1 and 2 were built from the bivariate results and from theory. Savings (SAVE) and investment (FDI) were not included in the same regressions, as per Tsebelis and Nardi (2016, 462). The most interesting models are 3 and 4. Model 3 suggests a suppression effect when corruption is included with indeterminacy volume, as the latter coefficient loses its strength and statistical significance. Variance inflation factors for model 3 suggest no significant multicollinearity (INDVOL = 1.23, CORRINV = 1.24, TRADE = 1.01). The square root of the inflation factors should be over 2 for evidence to reject the null and in favour of multicollinearity. Nonetheless it is justifiable from a theoretical perspective to create an interaction term INDVOL*CORRINV as is used in model 4. Model 4 presents strong and statistically significant coefficients. There is evidence to reject the null, giving some evidence that GDP per capita (PPP) is correlated with trade openness, and negatively correlated with corruption and constitutional indeterminacy. Corrupt regimes are both more likely to produce indeterminate rules of law, and will more likely take advantage of indeterminacies to rule in the interests of sectoral elites. Model 4 provides evidence for textual, contextual, and subtextual interactions with effects on GDP per capita.

Conclusions

Constitutions are typically understood as a *modus vivendi*—a mechanism for inter-communal coordination. To the extent that constitutions are deliberately designed, the intent is typically to enable resolution of unknown and indeterminate collective action problems. Clearly, without knowing the future, the language must to an extent be capable of adaptation to unforeseen events. But, if there are no clear guiding philosophies, principles, and policies, then there is no logic of communication. This dramatically unbalances the relationship between senders and receivers of communication. The senders—typically elites—can determine ad hoc what language means for them, rather than what it means in itself or for the community. What matters is not just the length of a constitution, but the comprehensibility of its encodings. At the other extreme, constitutional minimalism (i.e. short constitutions) are also associated with elite dominance and limited socioeconomic progression. The theory being that there is a lack of coordinative infrastructure, and hence limited participation and redistribution. The US Lochner Era, and its minimalist constraints on a growing federal bureaucracy would be an example. The lack of any codified constitution in the UK could be another. In these instances, there is little textual foundation for non-libertarians to build an expansive state on.

It seems, therefore, that constitutions enable civic coordination when they have the requisite detail to manage coordination problems, but without laying down long and indeterminate restrictions. In other words, a short constitution may be just as indeterminate, depending on its language, as a long and baggy constitution. The American constitution, as we will see in Chapter Six, creates a wide range of philosophical disputes and coordination problems. It is simply difficult to gauge in many instances what the correct substance and process of US constitutional law is. The constitutional text is the tip of a vast subtextual and intertextual iceberg. To have a handle on US constitutional law, it may be necessary to read vast quantities of case law, academic publications, and so on. The extent to which an average American citizen "knows" the constitution is therefore debatable (Kammen 1986). Of course, much the same can easily be said of the UK, or indeed any modern democracy. But we do have some basis for concluding that certain constitutions carve out greater or lesser interpretative spaces that can be dominated by powerful actors, including judges.

The aim here was to offer an alternative classification method for constitutions, based not on what they purport to say, but on what they fail to say plainly. The three-part indeterminacy volume is a taxonomy rather than a typology, in that it avoids association by archetypes and family trees. This approach is intended to support extant typologies, rather than supplant them. Findings suggest significant overlap between the new taxonomy and existing typologies. And, importantly, the taxonomy has here been used to support research into democratic freedom and economic performance. The taxonomy therefore offers both intrinsic and functional utilities.

The theory as to why newer constitutions are increasingly indeterminate offers a new insight to institutionalist theory, by digging to its very roots. If institutionalised politics depends on the predictable application of rules, then the language of those rules is an important variable in institutional operation. Disruption in the processing of socially relevant information is a cybernetic failure, with institutional consequences. The empirical implications are the wider applicability of indeterminacy volume in future research. This could include using learning algorithms, with naïve Bayes or support vector machines, to classify laws (not just constitutions) as liable to promote or retard various socially desirable goods. The parsimonious and replicable methodology used here has broad applicability in studies of social sciences and law. And more philosophically, it enables us to consider how far text dominates or is dominated by context.

More proximately, the taxonomy allows for case selection. For the following chapters, we will interrogate five countries in close detail. The aim is to understand why, in these countries, judges have become more politically powerful. It would be unscientific to select countries where judges have been shown to be "activist", and work backwards to find the cause. Rather, we need countries that differ substantially in their institutions, such that we would expect them to produce different logics of communication in legislation, and therefore different levels of political behaviour in judges. This is case selection on the independent variable (institutional variance), rather than on the dependent variable (judicial policy power). The following chapter digs deeper into these institutional differences between the five countries, but we can see from Table 3.4 that they differ significantly even in their constitutions' indeterminacy volumes. Omitted from this table is the UK, for which there is no single codified constitutional text. The UK, nonetheless, offers a good comparator, because it differs significantly in institutional form to the

Table 3.4 Constitutional characteristics of four democracies

	Word length	*Adjectives, adverbs, and conjunctions*	*Noun or verb qualifiers as % of word length*	*Years of promulgation since 1789*	*Indeterminacy volume*
Canada	21,118	2253	10.7	151	2.01
France	14,562	1660	11.4	60	2.43
Germany	27,991	3553	12.7	69	2.86
United States	7764	965	12.4	229	0.34

others, and from this we can expect (and will see in the following chapter) significant effects on its legislative logic of communication.

References

Bix, Brian. 1993. *Law, Language, and Legal Determinacy*. Oxford: Clarendon.

Chapman, Kelly. 2015. *Complexity and Creative Capacity: Rethinking Knowledge Transfer, Adaptive Management and Wicked Environmental Problems*. London: Routledge.

Elkins, Zachary, Tom Ginsburg, and James Melton. 2009. *The Endurance of National Constitutions*. Cambridge: Cambridge University Press.

Elkins, Zachary, Tom Ginsburg, James Melton, Robert Shaffer, Juan F. Sequeda, and Daniel P. Miranker. 2014. Constitute: The World's Constitutions to Read, Search, and Compare. *Journal of Web Semantics* 27: 10–18.

Elster, Jon. 1995. Forces and Mechanisms in the Constitution-Making Process. *Duke Law Journal* 45 (2): 364–396.

Ferejohn, John, Frances Rosenbluth, and Charles Shipan. 2007. Comparative Judicial Politics. In *The Oxford Handbook of Comparative Politics*, ed. Carles Boix and Susan Stokes. Oxford: Oxford University Press.

Gill, Stephen, and A. Claire Cutler. 2014. *New Constitutionalism and World Order*. Cambridge: Cambridge University Press.

Graber, Mark A. 2006. *Dred Scott and the Problem of Constitutional Evil*. Cambridge: Cambridge University Press.

Hamilton, Alexander, James Madison, and John Jay. 2009. *The Federalist Papers*. New York: Palgrave Macmillan.

Horowitz, Donald L. 2002. Constitutional Design: Proposals versus Processes. In *The Architecture of Democracy: Constitutional Design, Conflict Management, and Democracy*, ed. Andrew Reynolds. Oxford: Oxford University Press.

Huntington, Samuel P. 1993. *The Third Wave: Democratization in the Late Twentieth Century*. London: University of Oklahoma Press.
Kammen, Michael G. 1986. *A Machine That Would Go of Itself: The Constitution in American Culture*. New York: Knopf.
Lerner, Hanna. 2010. Constitution-Writing in Deeply Divided Societies: The Incrementalist Approach. *Nations and Nationalism* 16 (1): 68–88.
Lester, Richard, and Michael Piore. 2004. *Innovation: The Missing Dimension*. Cambridge, MA: Harvard University Press.
Levitsky, Steven, and Daniel Ziblatt. 2018. *How Democracies Die: What History Tells Us About Our Future*. London: Viking.
Lijphart, Arend. 1977. *Democracy in Plural Societies: A Comparative Exploration*. New Haven, CT: Yale University Press.
Lijphart, Arend. 2012. *Patterns of Democracy: Government Forms and Performance in Thirty-Six Countries*. New Haven: Yale University Press.
Linz, Juan. 1990. The Perils of Presidentialism. *Journal of Democracy* 1 (1): 51–69.
Lyotard, Jean-François, Keith Crome, and James Williams. 2006. *The Lyotard Reader and Guide*. Edinburgh: Edinburgh University Press.
McGarry, John, and Brendan O'Leary. 2007. Iraq's Constitution of 2005: Liberal Consociation as Political Prescription. *International Journal of Constitutional Law* 5 (4): 670–698.
Melton, James, Zachary Elkins, Tom Ginsburg, and Kalev Leetaru. 2013. On the Interpretability of Law: Lessons from the Decoding of National Constitutions. *British Journal of Political Science* 43 (2): 399–423.
Prempeh, H. Kwasi. 2007. Africa's 'Constitutionalism Revival': False Start or New Dawn? *Icon-International Journal of Constitutional Law* 5 (3): 469–506.
Renwick, Alan. 2010. *The Politics of Electoral Reform: Changing the Rules of Democracy*. Cambridge: Cambridge University Press.
Riker, William H. 1964. *Federalism: Origin, Operation, Significance*. Boston: Little Brown.
Rockmore, Daniel, Chen Fang, Nicholas Foti, Tom Ginsberg, and David Krakauer. 2017. The Cultural Evolution of National Constitutions. *Journal of the Association for Information Science and Technology* 69 (3): 483–494.
Said, E.W. 1978. *Orientalism*. London: Routledge and Kegan Paul.
Schmidt, Vivien. 2008. Discursive Institutionalism: The Explanatory Power of Ideas and Discourse. *Annual Review of Political Science* 11: 303–326.
Siaroff, Alan. 2003. Comparative Presidencies: The Inadequacy of the Presidential, Semi-Presidential and Parliamentary Distinction. *European Journal of Political Research* 42: 287–312.
Stepan, Alfred. 2001. Toward a New Comparative Politics of Federalism, (Multi)Nationalism, and Democracy: Beyond Rikerian Federalism. In *Arguing Comparative Politics*, ed. Stepan Alfred. Oxford: Oxford University Press.

Stern, David G. 2004. *Wittgenstein's Philosophical Investigations: An Introduction*. Cambridge: Cambridge University Press.
Stone, Alec. 1992. Where Judicial Politics Are Legislative Politics: The French Constitutional Council. *West European Politics* 15 (3): 29–49.
Stone Sweet, Alec. 2000. *Governing with Judges: Constitutional Politics in Europe*. Oxford: Oxford University Press.
Strøm, Kaare, Wolfgang C. Müller, and Torbjörn Bergman. 2003. *Delegation and Accountability in Parliamentary Democracies*. Oxford: Oxford University Press.
Tsebelis, George, and Dominic Nardi. 2016. A Long Constitution Is a (Positively) Bad Constitution: Evidence from OECD Countries. *British Journal of Political Science* 46 (2): 457–478.
Voigt, Stefan. 2009. Explaining Constitutional Garrulity. *International Review of Law and Economics* 29 (4): 290–303.
Williams, Matthew. 2017a. The Grammar of Politics: A Brief History of Legislative Language in Britain. *Political Quarterly* 88 (2): 248–257.
Williams, Matthew. 2017b. Legislative Language and Judicial Politics: The Effects of Changing Parliamentary Language on UK Immigration Disputes. *British Journal of Politics and IR* 19 (3): 592–608.
Williams, Matthew. 2018. *How Language Works in Politics: The Impact of Indeterminate Legislation on Policy*. Bristol: Bristol University Press.

CHAPTER 4

Regulating the Extent of the State in Five Democracies

This chapter interrogates how legal language—specifically legislation—changes through time. How do lexico-grammatical norms of legislation change within an election cycle? And does it matter if there are changes to a "logic of communication" (Schmidt 2008)? These questions contribute to our understanding of institutional stability amidst the buffeting of global events. Evidence in this chapter is taken from machine reading 47 million words of legislation in five countries. Findings suggest that policy executives reacted to the global financial crisis of 2008 with substantial changes to legal language (Gotti 2012). Unstable rules of law reflected instabilities of politics and policy unleashed by a crisis (Roitman 2013). However, in countries with fewer institutional and partisan veto players, the instabilities endured and are expected to have fed back into further political and policy instabilities (Tsebelis 2002). In other words, where institutions permit executives to dominate the law-making process, there will be lesser stability in the language of law. Germany is the only country of the five studied that measurably recovered linguistic stability in its rule of law after the global financial crisis. The lack of a stable genre for legal language is liable to increase judicial policy power, as judges will be called on to resolve disputes over discourse.

The five nations offer notable divergences in history, culture, and institutions that will add flesh to the bones of Chapter 3's synoptic time series analyses. The wholly new observations presented in this chapter became

M. Williams, *Judges and the Language of Law*,
https://doi.org/10.1007/978-3-030-91495-0_4

possible with the improved availability of digital legal sources, as well as the machine reading technologies described. All data were meticulously processed for machine reading, and are available for anyone to replicate these studies, or to use in pursuit of other research questions.

Theory and Hypotheses

We begin with a brief review of the theory presented in Chapter 2. Genre changes in legislation—being changes to generic linguistic forms—signify barely perceptible institutional changes. Institutions are rules of the political game, and are disseminated in a shared and meaningful language (Hall and Taylor 1996; Pierson and Skocpol 2002). Changes to the meaningfulness of that language, however, affect the delegation and accountability of power (Strøm et al. 2003), and affect the clarity of policy goals (Chun and Rainey 2005). Indeed, unstable discursive institutions will affect the balance of power between the senders and receivers of formal communications (Schmidt 2008). The degree of stability in state discourses also helps us measure a form of institutional resilience and crisis management (see, for example, Ostrom 2000). Institutions capable of sustaining patterns of language through changes in political and economic climate arguably present greater institutional resilience. Although, of course, adaptability in the face of crisis may be of short-term utility in managing the unexpected circumstances. It is the scale of change in discursive norms, and the extent of recovery to pre-crisis norms of language use, that are of particular theoretical interest here. Unstable patterns of language use will encourage those with capacity or resources to contest meaningfulness through litigation, or other less formal routes. Unstable legal language stimulates extra-legislative bargaining over meaningfulness. This therefore empowers judges to resolve such disputes. As will be demonstrated, where Germany recovered rule of law norms after the global financial crisis, the UK did not. We could conclude from this that the British Parliament is more flexible and adaptive, which may very well be in the public interest. But, the increased space opened for judicialisation in the UK is clear from the findings.

Specifically, quantitative text analyses allow us to measure the stability (and instability) of legal language within an election cycle, and between election cycles (Williams 2018; Zittel et al. 2019). This allows the testing of hypotheses against 85-country years' worth of panel data of primary legislation from 2001 to 2018 in Canada, France, Germany, the UK, and the US. Stability in legislative language will be assessed both cross-sectionally and temporally. Findings will be non-parametric statistics, utilising every available primary law in the five countries. Such are the advantages of modern machine reading, that statistical models and probability tests are not necessary as all data have been included in the analyses. These findings will give us some sense of how legal language normally operated in the five jurisdictions, and how it changed in response to events. Not only will this speak to studies of how legislatures respond to shocks, but it will also contribute to comparative analyses of legislatures under normal circumstances—be they more "transformative" or "arena" legislatures (Polsby 1990), "reactive" legislatures (Cox and Morgenstern 2001), or based in "consensus" as opposed to "majoritarian" systems (Lijphart 2012).

The dependent variable of interest here is noun or verb qualifiers per section of legislation (NVQPS). Specifically, the machine reading program picked out and enumerated all adjectives, adverbs, coordinating conjunctions, and conditional conjunctions. These parts of speech qualify the interpretation of core sentence components, making meaning more reliant on context and diminishing the capacity of a text to determine context. Some illustrative examples are offered of legislation from two of the five countries in the year they experienced above-average per section incidence of noun or verb qualifiers. A related example from the UK—the *Data Retention and Investigatory Powers Act 2014* (DRIPA)—has already been discussed in Chapter 2. The parts of speech coded by the computer program are italicised:

Canada's *Personal Information Protection and Electronic Documents Act 2000*, as amended in 2011:

> Section 4.8.1 'Individuals shall be able to acquire information about an organization's policies *and* practices without *unreasonable* effort. This information shall be made available in a form that is *generally understandable*.'

Germany's *Federal Constitution Protection Act 2009*:

> Section 3 'The task of the *constitutional* authorities of the Federal *and* State Governments is the collection *and* analysis of information, in *particular* of *appropriate and personal* information, news *and* documents... directed against the *free democratic basic* order.'

There are two vectors of interest—the frequency distribution of noun or verb qualifiers in five countries' laws, and their changes through time. These provide us with a sense of how the rules of law normally employ language, and how these norms were affected by events. The first hypothesis pertains to the distribution shapes of noun or verb qualifiers.

H1 In political systems with more institutional or partisan veto players, language use will more closely fit a normal distribution.

The idea here is that veto players increase the stability of policy (Tsebelis 2002), and also increase the stability of legal language use (Williams 2018). In political systems with proportionate electoral laws, and sustained checks on executive power, there will be more generic use of legislative language. A clear quantification of the fragmentation or concentration of powers in these five democracies comes from Arend Lijphart's *Patterns of Democracy* (2012). Table 4.1 provides his measurements for each of the five countries on the executive-parties and federal-unitary dimensions. Lower scores denote more majoritarian polities. Higher scores denote more consensus polities, which must enact policy change only with the consent of a number of disaggregated veto players:

France and the UK—as intuition would suggest—are the most majoritarian oriented of the five democracies. Canada and the US are majoritarian with regard to executive parties, but more consensus oriented with regard to the federal-unitary measure. Germany is the only all-round consensus democracy of the five. The alternative hypothesis to H1, therefore, is that in systems with fewer institutional or partisan veto players (such as in France and the UK) the distribution of legal language will be right-skewed and leptokurtic, rather than normal. This means that

Table 4.1 Comparison of five countries according to their executive-parties and federal-unitary scores, 1945–2010

	Executives-parties dimension	*Federal-unitary dimension*
Canada	−1	1.73
France	−0.86	−0.22
Germany	0.78	2.41
United Kingdom	−1.09	−1.06
United States	−0.67	2.25

outlying observations will more likely be seen on the high rather than low end of noun or verb qualifiers (right-skewed), and hence more indeterminate. And it also means that there are indeed more outlying observations than would be expected if the distribution was normal (leptokurtic describes a thin peaked and fat tailed distribution). Another expectation, derived from H1, is that in systems with sustained policy stability (such as created by gridlock in the US) will present platykurtic distributions—those with fewer outlying observations than a normal distribution. A platykurtic distribution has a wide peak and thin tails when compared to a normal, bell-shaped, distribution.

Leptokurtosis in a distribution (a higher than normal propensity to out-lie) is associated with bounded rationality (Jones 1999). That is, a propensity within a community to process new information mostly through routinised thinking, rather than critical thinking. This leads to high and slender peaks, with a clustering of observations at the mean, because the mean represents routine. But, in unusual circumstances, actors have few institutional barriers to breaking with routine, and thereby processing information with creativity, with emotion, with fear, or with other potentially extreme reactions. This explains a high number of mean-deviant outliers. In short, the UK is expected to present a leptokurtic distribution, whilst Germany presents a platykurtic distribution. This does not mean that the German system is the more rational, but that it is less bounded to the rationality of a single agency (such as Her Majesty's Government).

The following longitudinal hypotheses consider word length, noun or verb qualification, and inter-electoral genre stability.

H2 In political systems with more institutional or partisan veto players, the output of legislation will have increased in response to crisis.

This hypothesis is derived from the works of Epstein and O'Halloran (1999), and Huber and Shipan (2002). In systems with few checks on executive power, such as France and the UK, word length will have reduced during the crisis as the executive is distracted away from pursuing more quotidian policy, and because fewer words impose fewer "substantive restrictions" on bureaucratic discretion (Tsebelis and Nardi 2016). In Germany, in particular, the veto players constraining executive discretion will have sought more, not less, legislative output.

Next, we turn to linguistic indeterminacy.

H3 In political systems with fewer institutional or partisan veto players, the output of legislation will have increased in indeterminacy.

Not only do systems with fewer veto players enact a lesser volume of laws, that which they do enact is expected to be more indeterminate in meaning and capable of multiple post-legislative interpretations.

H4a In all political systems, the lowest level of inter-electoral genre stability will have been observed in the election span covering the global financial crisis.

This hypothesis suggests that no systems were fully immune to the exogenous shock that was the global financial crisis of 2008. However:

H4b In political systems with more institutional or partisan veto players, the level of inter-electoral genre stability will have reverted to higher levels in the first succeeding electoral cycle.

Various other hypotheses were tested, out of interest, but cannot be utilised for methodological reasons and are not presented. Firstly, tests for correlation between stability in legal language and economic variables (such as tax take, and the gross domestic savings as a percentage of GDP) displayed strong correlations. However, given the primary dependent variable here (inter-electoral genre stability) varies with time, it is not appropriate to use correlation analyses, as there is no stationarity in time series. For the same reasons, tests as to correlation between the effective number of legislative parties and genre stability could not be presented (Laakso and Taagepera 1979). The aim of this chapter is to describe changes to legislative genre through time. It is an attempt at quantitative history, rather than correlation analysis.

Methods and Data

First a note on case selection. The five countries selected vary on the key predictors of interest—the number of institutional and partisan veto players. They were also highly exposed to global economic shocks, and, as advanced democracies, all value the rule of law and the procedures by which rules of law are manifest. These nations also have large and mostly complete datasets available. The US (2001–2011) did not provide full data for the entire period (up to 2018), but both offer sufficient data for purposes of comparison during and after the 2008 financial crisis.

Inter-electoral genre stability is measured as the inverted mean change in noun or verb qualifiers for each year of a legislature, from the year of election to the final full year before the next election. This needs unpacking. First, the per section frequency of noun or verb qualifiers per year was calculated using the computer program, and then normalised to be between 0 and 1. Normalisation allowed for reliable cross country comparisons. The normalisation formula is as follows (4.1).

$$\frac{x_i - x_{\min}}{x_{\max} - x_{\min}}. \tag{4.1}$$

Having calculated the noun or verb qualifiers per section per year and normalised the data, it was then necessary to assess year-on-year changes. These changes were then squared so that negative changes would become positive, and larger changes would be magnified. An average of these measures of year-on-year changes in legislative language was calculated for an election cycle. An average was needed rather than sum because election cycles vary in length, and a sum would exaggerate linguistic volatility. These averages were then inverted ($1/n$) to give a measure of legislative stability, where higher numbers signify greater genre stability between elections. The reason for inversion from volatility to stability is to fit in with extant theory and empirical work on policy stability (Tsebelis 2002). The formula for calculating inter-electoral genre stability is as follows (4.2).

$$IGS(x) = \frac{1}{\sum_{t=1}^{n}(q_t + 1 - q_t)^2 \ldots (q_n - q_{n-1})^2} = (\mu\Delta q^2)^{-1} \tag{4.2}$$

IGS	Inter-electoral genre stability.
x	A specific country's election cycle.
q	Noun or verb qualifiers.
t	Time in calendar years starting with the year of election.
n	The total number of years of an election cycle finishing with last full year of legislative business.

To illustrate how the calculations of inter-electoral genre stability work, Table 4.2 displays the calculations step-by-step for the UK between 2001 and 2018. Note that 2018 has a score as the last year of measurement in all cases, although 2019 was, coincidentally, an election year for the UK.

Table 4.2 Inter-electoral genre stability calculations UK, 2001–2018

Year	*Noun or verb qualifiers per section*	*NVQPS Normalised*	*Volatility* $(t + 1 - t)^2$	*Inter-electoral genre stability*
2001	18.25	0.02		
2002	19.05	0.08	0.004	
2003	19.68	0.13	0.002	
2004	20.95	0.22	0.009	204.59
2005	18.47	0.04	0.034	
2006	18.77	0.06	0.000	
2007	19.72	0.13	0.005	
2008	17.98	0.00	0.017	
2009	19.79	0.14	0.018	66.94
2010	19.90	0.14	0.000	
2011	20.46	0.19	0.002	
2012	26.75	0.65	0.219	
2013	22.41	0.33	0.104	
2014	29.46	0.86	0.276	8.32
2015	26.80	0.66	0.039	
2016	31.40	1.00	0.117	12.81
2017	25.42	0.55	0.198	
2018	21.44	0.26	0.088	6.98

Furthermore, in line with the theory of Huber and Shipan (2002), few legislatures are likely to curtail discretion during an exogenous shock. Hence, most change to legal language during and after the financial crisis will have been towards greater indeterminacy to enable discretion. This links to the classic "arena" and "transformative" typologies for legislatures (Polsby 1990). Where arena legislatures will likely follow the executive's lead in response to a crisis, transformative legislatures will more likely revert to a more consistent linguistic output after a crisis, so as to ensure the continued efficacy of their command language. Descriptive statistics for all countries are provided in Table 4.3.

A potential problem with this method is that instability in legal genre could mean a sharp decrease in legal indeterminacy within an election cycle. Because, unstable genre could mean two very different scenarios—rapidly increasing indeterminacy, or rapidly decreasing indeterminacy. There is little consistency between these scenarios, except that they are both dynamic. Actually, dynamism is the variable of interest. Even if dynamic legislative language could be changing in different directions, it

Table 4.3 Descriptive statistics (2001–2018)

Variable	*Country*	*Min*	*Mean*	*Median*	*Max*	*SD*
Word length	Canada	111,681	353,956	342,386	837,211	178,748
	France	273,754	462,390	448,879	723,140	128,429
	Germany	204,161	413,275	381,630	733,053	135,224
	UK	148,744	431,398	364,502	1,042,328	196,599
	US (2001–2011)	939,397	1,577,135	1,663,630	2,343,819	439,593
NVQPS	Canada	7.49	18.19	18.26	27.80	5.03
	France	15.54	19.51	19.10	26.77	3.26
	Germany	18.28	22.52	22.66	26.20	2.23
	UK	17.98	22.04	20.18	31.40	3.99
	US	17.41	21.11	21.07	25.95	2.70
IGS	Canada	2.70	15.26	10.22	30.48	10.96
	France	7.37	21.77	8.39	62.90	23.76
	Germany	3.68	13.03	12.33	23.79	7.18
	UK	6.98	59.93	12.81	204.59	75.71
	US	3.50	57.07	5.55	263.10	103.03

is the fact of change that matters. Change affects expectations from actors and encourages contestation in court. Such contestation will come from parties with vested interests in certain linguistic forms. For instance, a President might rail against tighter legal language. Or litigants and judges may contest and seek to clarify looser legal language. Furthermore, in line with the theory of Huber and Shipan (2002), few legislatures are likely to curtail executive discretion during a crisis. Hence, most change to legal language during and after the financial crisis will have been towards greater indeterminacy of meaning to enable discretion.

Results

The first results, displayed in Figs. 4.1, 4.2, 4.3, 4.4, and 4.5, describe the observed noun or verb qualifiers as compared to normal distributions.[1] These figures test H1—In political systems with more institutional or partisan veto players, language use will more closely fit a normal distribution. The figures describe the cumulative probability of a section of legislation having specified numbers of noun or verb qualifiers. Under a

[1] Source: Author's creation.

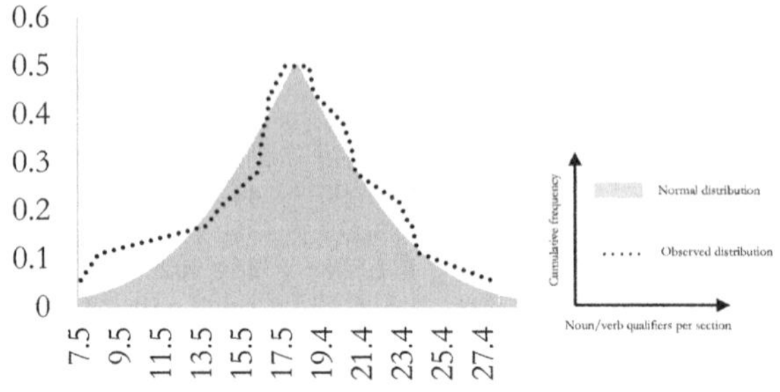

Fig. 4.1 Canada

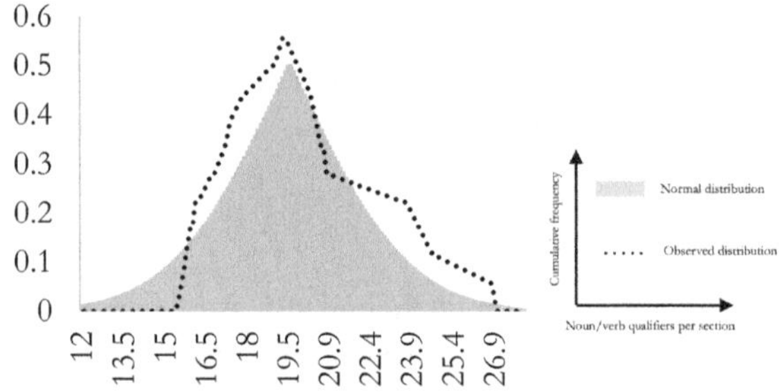

Fig. 4.2 France

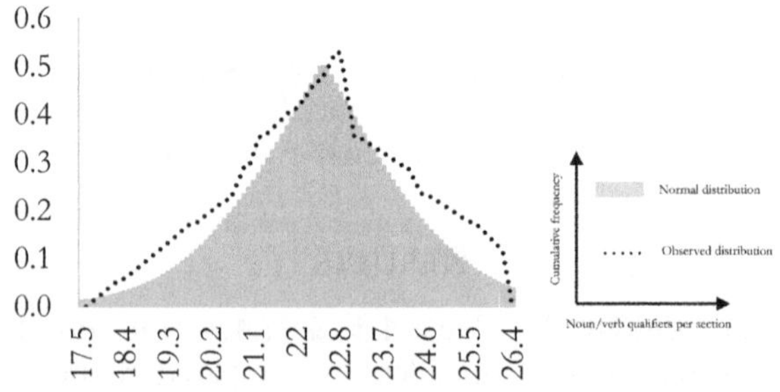

Fig. 4.3 Germany

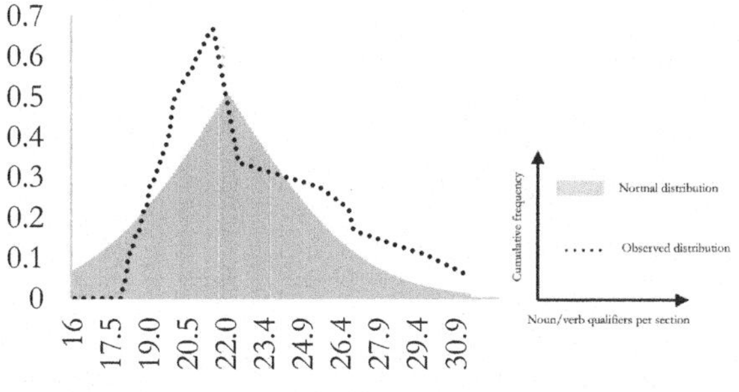

Fig. 4.4 UK

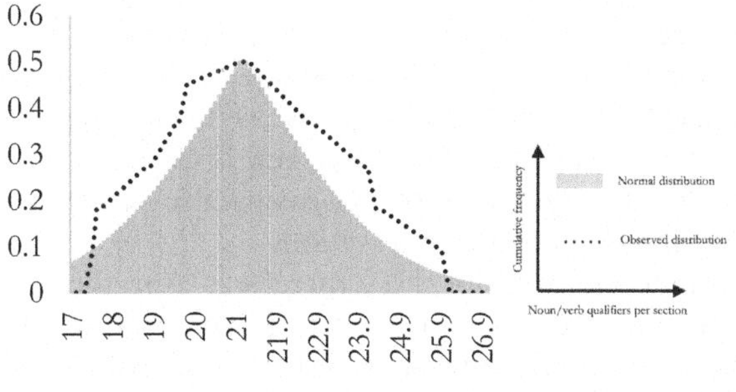

Fig. 4.5 US

normal distribution, half of all sections will be equal to or less than the mean, and half will be equal to or greater than the mean. The distributions will thus be symmetrical about the mean in a normal distribution, and the median will equal the mean. For instance, Canada's average noun or verb qualifiers per section across the period is 18.19. Assuming normality (which is akin to assuming there is genre to language) we would expect symmetry about the mean, with 68% of observations falling within one standard deviation.

Table 4.4 provides the statistics on kurtosis (a measure of outlying) and skew (a measure of distance between mean and median):

Canada and the UK, both Westminster systems, are moderately leptokurtic with positive scores obtained. All other countries present platykurtic distributions, but most notable of these is the US with −1.

Table 4.4 Kurtosis and Skew by Country, 2001–2018

Country	*Kurtosis*	*Skew*
Canada	0.36	−0.40
France	−0.37	0.73
Germany	−0.64	0.02
UK	0.15	1.14
US (2001–2011)	−1.00	0.33

This suggests that US legislative language very rarely deviates more than two standard deviations about the mean. Measures of skewness also help us consider deviations from a normal distribution. Here we see France and the UK as right-skewed, as one would expect given their few veto players and executive dominance. What this signifies is that the French and British cabinets are better able to propose legislation with high levels of indeterminacy. The US is also right-skewed, but less so than France and the UK. The country with the least skew is Germany, with mean and median very closely aligned (0.02). Germany also presents a platykurtic distribution with few outlying observations.

There is some support for H1, therefore, that the relatively high number of institutional and partisan veto players in Germany constrains legislative language within normative patterns. Canada's left-skew with kurtosis can be explained by relatively high party system volatility in that country, making for more partisan veto players. There was a high number of effective legislative parties of 3.27 in the 39th Parliament (2006–2008) to a low of 2.42 in the 41st Parliament (2011–2015). The UK not only had the lowest average number of effective legislative parties of the five nations, but as a Westminster system it lacks institutional veto players to stop a government (even the 2010–2015 coalition) from presenting legislation that favours executive discretion.

The following Figs. 4.6, 4.7, 4.8, 4.9, and 4.10 describe changes to the word lengths of legislation enacted each year in the five countries.[2] These test H2—In political systems with more institutional or partisan veto players, the output of legislation will have increased in response to crisis. The UK has seen a marked decline in legislative output, from an average of 600,000 words to around 250,000 words. Not only post-crisis political instability explains this, but so too do the policymaking distractions

[2] Source: Author's creation.

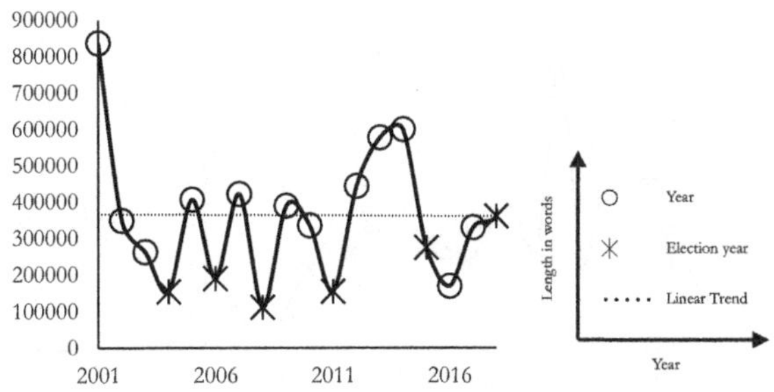

Fig. 4.6 Canada

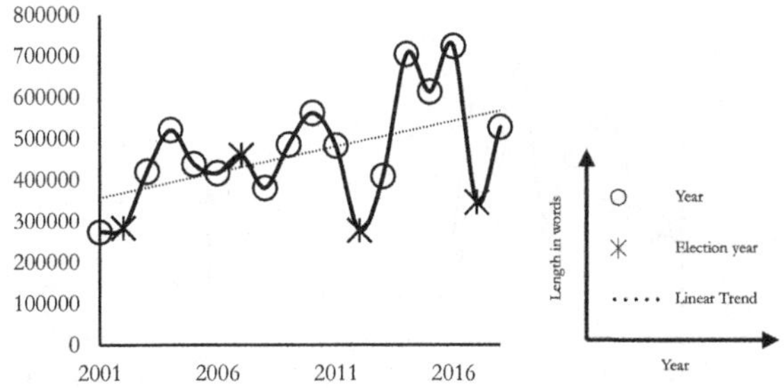

Fig. 4.7 France

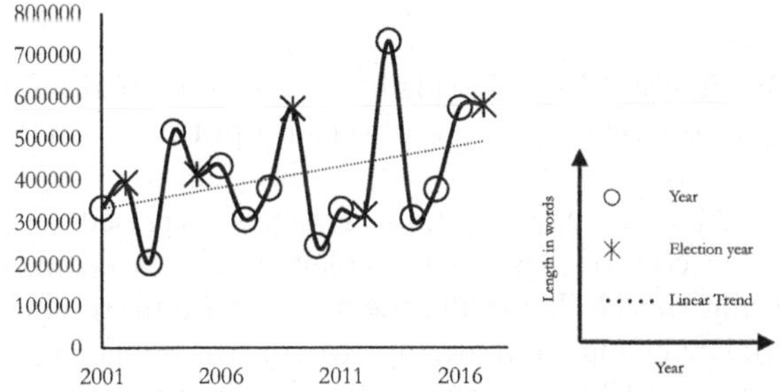

Fig. 4.8 Germany

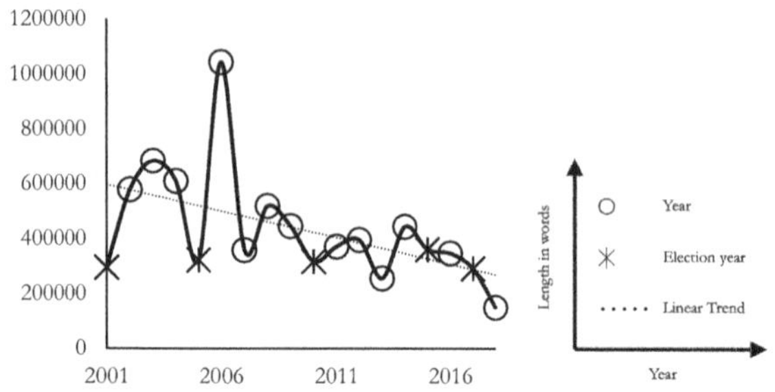

Fig. 4.9 UK

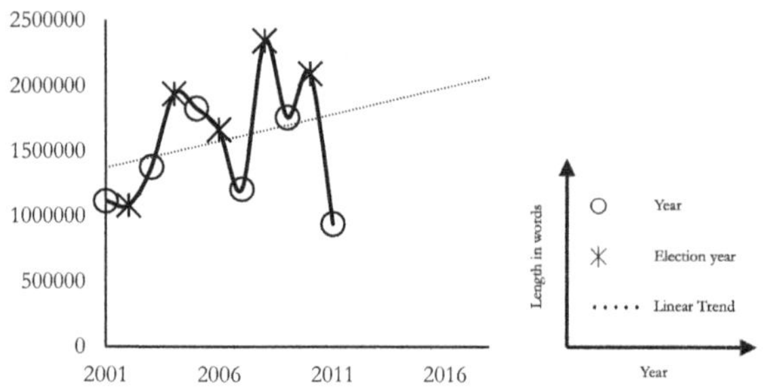

Fig. 4.10 US

created by Brexit after 2016. Canada has also seen reductions in legislative output, but this is based on an exceptional output of law in 2001. Otherwise Canada has seen fluctuating output throughout. France, Germany, and the US all saw increased output. France's increased output disconfirms H2 as that country has few veto players. The peaks in output were observed during the Hollande Presidency, and are more likely explained as dynamic policy change and attempt to control bureaucratic discretion in what was an unusual Socialist dominated administration. Germany and the UK most close support H2. Germany saw the greatest increase in legislative output, from an average of around 330,000 words to nearly 500,000. Of course, H2 simplifies the many possible explanations for increased legislative output across nations, but the findings do mostly conform to theories that imposing "substantive restrictions" through longer laws will more likely be observed in systems where veto players are able to dominate executive discretion (Tsebelis and Nardi 2016).

Figures 4.11, 4.12, 4.13, 4.14, and 4.15[3] test H3—In political systems with fewer institutional or partisan veto players, the output of legislation will have increased in indeterminacy. The greatest increases in noun or verb qualifiers per section can be observed in France and the UK. These countries have the fewest veto players of the five. The UK, in particular, saw a 50% increase in the average incidence of qualifiers, from 18 per section to 27. Indeterminacies in French law increased more haphazardly, with spikes in 2007 and 2014, corresponding to the reformist administrations of Nicolas Sarkozy and François Hollande. Canada and the US saw lesser rises in indeterminate parts of speech per section. Only Germany

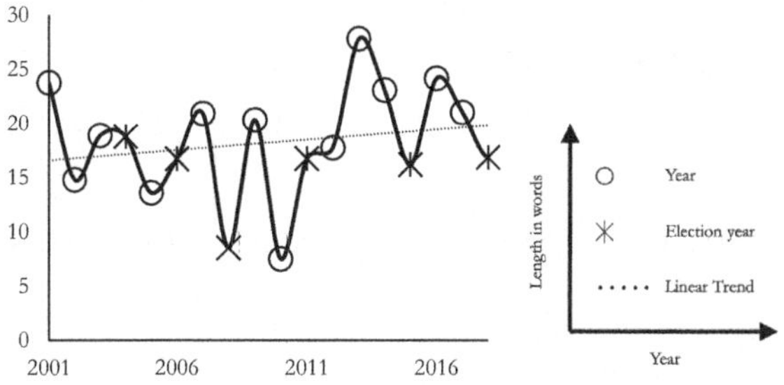

Fig. 4.11 Canada

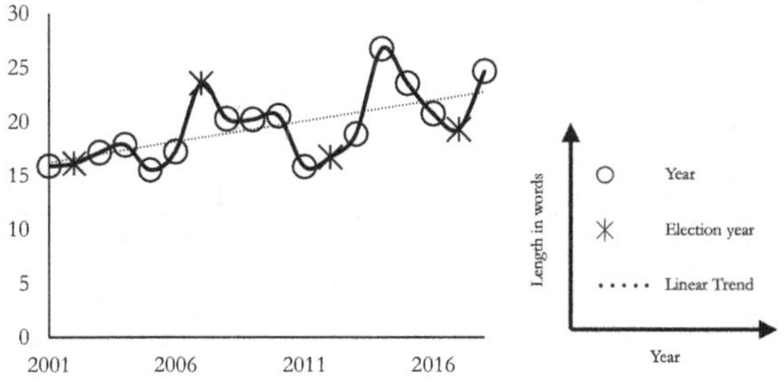

Fig. 4.12 France

[3] Source: Author's creation.

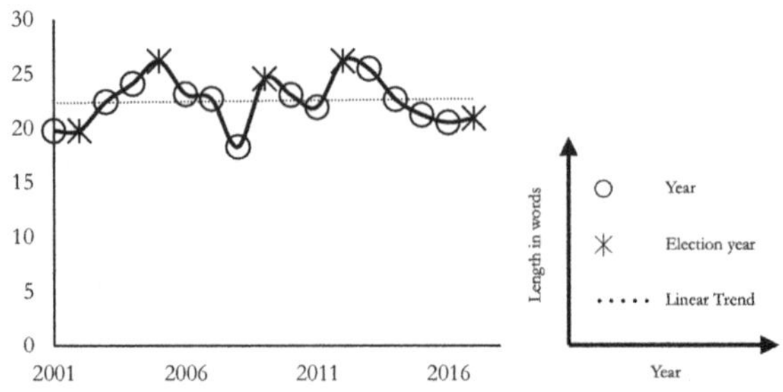

Fig. 4.13 Germany

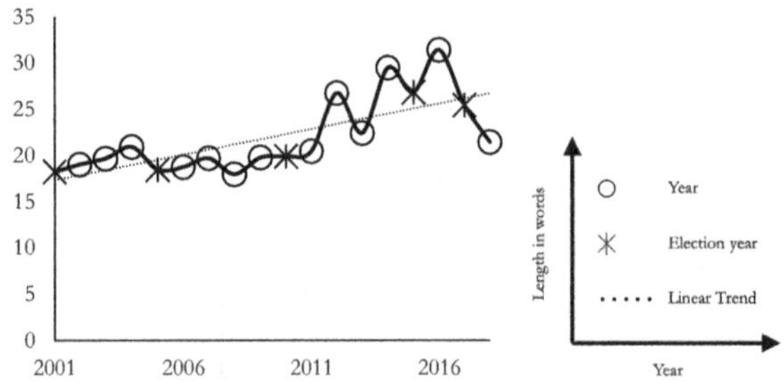

Fig. 4.14 UK

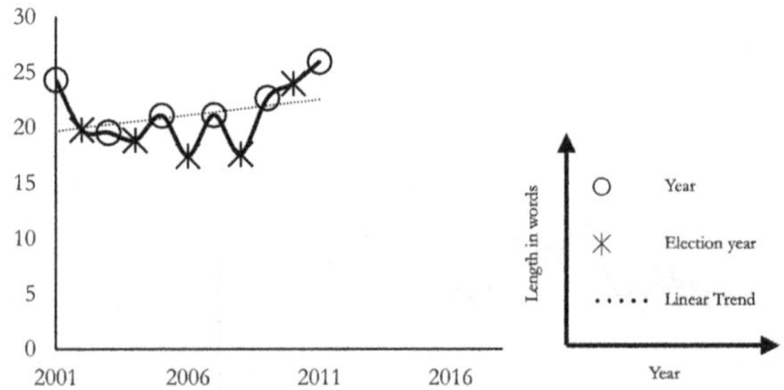

Fig. 4.15 US

saw no change in average indeterminacy, fitting the expectations of H3. Interestingly, both Germany and the US display cyclical patterns in indeterminacy output, peaking during election years. This is most likely where incoming legislatures seek policy change immediately after an election, when mandates are still considered fresh and viable. But, after a honeymoon period, the veto players start to bite and constrain indeterminacies in rules of law.

Figures 4.16, 4.17, 4.18, 4.19, and 4.20 test H4a and H4b—In all political systems, the lowest level of inter-electoral genre stability will have been observed in the election span covering the global financial crisis. But in political systems with more institutional or partisan veto players, the level of inter-electoral genre stability will have reverted to higher levels in the first succeeding electoral cycle. The figures support H4a as each of

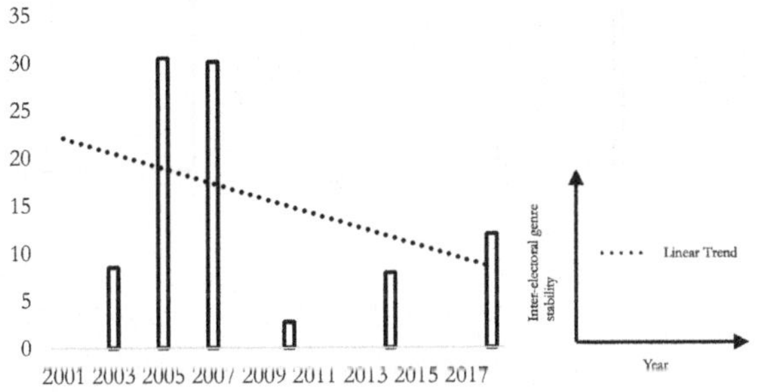

Fig. 4.16 Canada

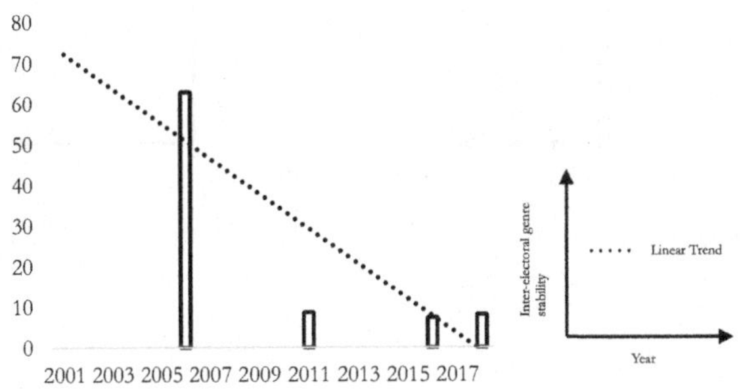

Fig. 4.17 France

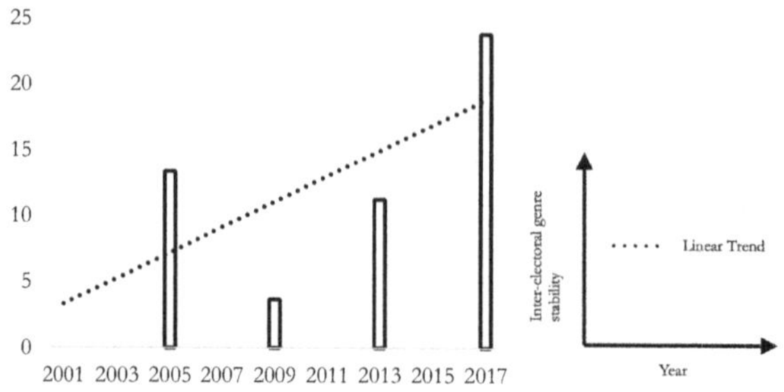

Fig. 4.18 Germany

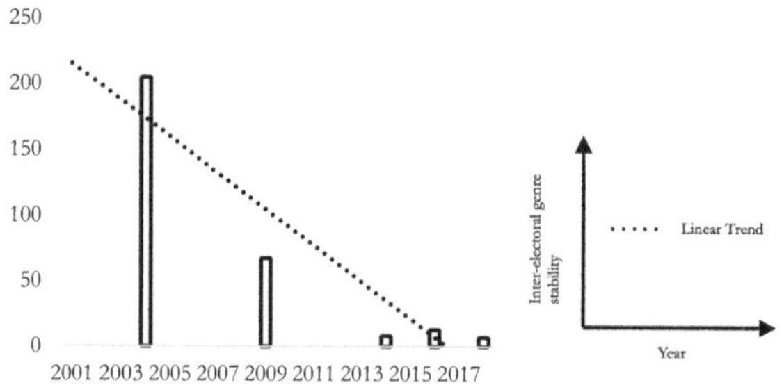

Fig. 4.19 UK

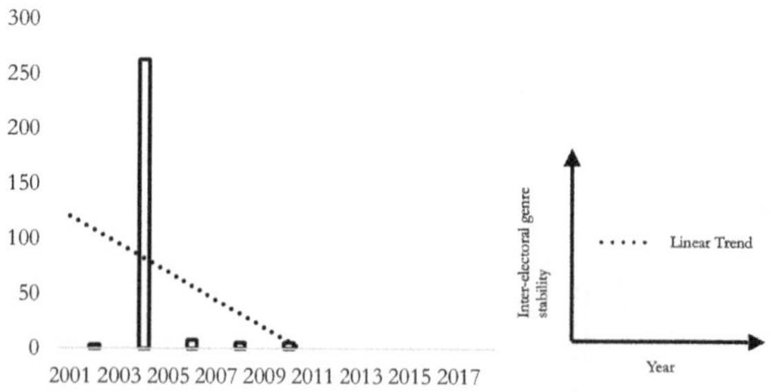

Fig. 4.20 US

the five systems reported the lowest levels of genre stability during the election span containing the 2008 crisis. The only exception is the UK where the post-Brexit Parliament after 2017 registered even lower levels of stability in legislative genre.

The US presents a particularly interesting case, as also having low genre stability in the election period containing the September 11th terrorist attacks, followed by very high consistency in language used. Canada similarly saw lower genre stability in that period, which may in part be explained by legislative responses to national security threats, such as the Canadian "Security Budget" of 2001. Otherwise the five countries all experienced sharp falls in legislative genre stability after the financial crisis. Germany, it must be noted, had consistently lower stability levels than the other four nations. The stability index is comparable as being derived from normalised statistics. The UK and US, by contrast, have levels of genre stability peaking at 200> , where Germany never exceeds 25. So Germany has a lower average genre stability.

That Germany has relatively low but more consistent genre stability can be explained by the transformative potential of the Bundestag, and its comparative immunity from US-style gridlock. Also, its instability in language use represents a third possibility to the two outlined above. It was noted that two possibilities could explain high inter-electoral instability—rapid increases or rapid decreases in indeterminacy. The third possibility, and that which is much less likely to create friction points and judicialisation, is fluctuating high/low indeterminacy. Germany presents this form of wave-pattern in language use, with peaks in election years and troughs in the years preceding an election. It also presents the greatest multi-election consistency in legislative genre. Where the US moved from a genre stability score of greater than 250 to less than 10 in one election cycle, Germany only saw maximum changes of 10 points between election cycles. It would be wrong to conclude, therefore, that the German Bundestag is incapable of maintaining a logic of communication. Furthermore, as outlined above, where discursive institutions fail and meaning is contested, the German state has a reliable kernel of meaning to fall back on in its Basic Law. Such undergirding constitutionalism is not available in the UK.

Furthermore, Figs. 4.16, 4.17, 4.18, 4.19, and 4.20,[4] offer evidence in support of H4b. All systems with fewer veto players (notably France and the UK) present little recovery from the post-crisis slump in genre stability. Meanwhile Canada and Germany recovered within the succeeding election cycle. It is worth noting that Canada has few institutional veto players at the Federal level, but with Provinces, Territories, and recent experiences of minority government, it has more veto players than the executive-dominated British and French systems.

For the US there is insufficient evidence to reject H4b. It did not see a recovery in stability after the 2008 crash, but that could be explained as a brief period of unified government under the Obama administration that stripped away partisan veto players. More evidence of longer term trends are needed, and will be possible when Congress assents to publishing more recent statutes at large. The expectation is, that after 2011, higher levels of genre stability returned to the US as Congress sought to constrain a Presidency with which it has had sustained policy disagreements.

More generally, any historical relationship between the global financial crisis and inter-electoral genre stability needs further investigation. Nonetheless we have evidence that legislative logics of communication can be measured across time and space by considering relative meaninglessness in rules of law. These measurements also backup a contention that legislative language will be more volatile in executive-dominated systems, and more stable in consensus-oriented systems.

Conclusion

How does legal language change? This was the principal question for this chapter. Presented was a theory of how lexico-grammatical norms of legislation change within an election cycle in different political systems. Findings from machine reading 47 million words of legislation in five countries suggest that policy executives reacted to exogenous shock with substantial changes to legal genre. But, that these changes were not sustained in those countries with more institutional and partisan veto players. In such systems, veto players were capable of thwarting the bounded rationality of executive policymakers.

[4] Source: Author's creation.

More specifically, Germany with the most institutional and partisan veto players reverted to a stable use of legislative language after the 2008 financial crisis. It also saw no substantial change in reliance on noun or verb qualifying parts of speech across nearly two decades. This is exceptional consistency in the use of language, making its political command language theoretically less liable to produce post-promulgation contestation in court. France and the UK have, conversely, both substantially changed their logics of communication since the millennium turned. These executive-dominated systems both produced less law, with more linguistic indeterminacy. And neither substantially recovered legislative norms after the 2008 crisis passed. The lack of institutionalised consensus in France and the UK has allowed each office-winning coalition the opportunity to shift legislative language to suit its proximate interests. This will likely disturb actors with a vested interest in conserving legislative norms. This may be no bad thing if the government wishes to break powerful interests and has a mandate to do so. The problem is that where meaning in the rule of law is highly contestable, those with political connections and substantial resources will be able to have their preferred interpretations dominate. The essential rationale for having a representative Parliament lies in its capacity to *parley* on behalf of its constituents through carefully regulated law-making processes. Indeterminacies and instabilities in the language of law subvert the principle of contesting legal meaning within Parliament. Instead, rules of law are fought over outside Parliament.

References

Chun, Young Han, and Hal G. Rainey. 2005. Goal Ambiguity in U.S. Federal Agencies. *Journal of Public Administration Research and Theory* 15 (1): 1–30.

Cox, Gary, and Scott Morgenstern. 2001. Latin America's Reactive Assemblies and Proactive Presidents. *Comparative Politics* 33 (2): 171–189.

Epstein, David, and Sharyn O'Halloran. 1999. *Delegating Powers: A Transaction Cost Politics Approach to Policy Making Under Separate Powers*. Cambridge: Cambridge University Press.

Gotti, Maurizio. 2012. Text and Genre. In *The Oxford Handbook of Language and Law*, ed. Lawrence M. Solan and Peter M. Tiersma. Oxford: Oxford University Press.

Hall, Peter A., and Rosemary C. Taylor. 1996. Political Science and the Three New Institutionalisms. *Political Studies* 44 (5): 936–957.

Huber, John D., and Charles R. Shipan. 2002. *Deliberate Discretion? The Institutional Foundations of Bureaucratic Autonomy*. Cambridge: Cambridge University Press.

Jones, Bryan D. 1999. Bounded Rationality. *Annual Review of Political Science* 2: 297–321.

Laakso, Markku, and Rein Taagepera. 1979. Effective Number of Parties: A Measure with Application to West Europe. *Comparative Political Studies* 12 (1): 3–27.

Lijphart, Arend. 2012. *Patterns of Democracy: Government Forms and Performance in Thirty-Six Countries*. New Haven: Yale University Press.

Ostrom, Elinor. 2000. Collective Action and the Evolution of Social Norms. *Journal of Economic Perspectives* 14 (3): 137–158.

Pierson, Paul, and Theda Skocpol. 2002. Historical Institutionalism in Contemporary Political Science. In *Political Science: State of the Discipline*, ed. Ira Katznelson and Helen V. Milner. New York: W. W. Norton.

Polsby, Nelson. 1990. Legislatures. In *Legislatures*, ed. Philip Norton, 129–148. Oxford: Oxford University Press.

Roitman, Janet. 2013. *Anti-Crisis*. Durham: Duke University Press.

Schmidt, Vivien. 2008. Discursive Institutionalism: The Explanatory Power of Ideas and Discourse. *Annual Review of Political Science* 11: 303–326.

Strøm, Kaare, Wolfgang C. Müller, and Torbjörn Bergman. 2003. *Delegation and accountability in parliamentary democracies*. Oxford: Oxford University Press.

Tsebelis, George. 2002. *Veto Players: How Political Institutions Work*. Princeton NJ: Princeton University Press.

Tsebelis, George, and Dominic Nardi. 2016. A Long Constitution Is a (Positively) Bad Constitution: Evidence from OECD Countries. *British Journal of Political Science* 46 (2): 457–478.

Williams, Matthew. 2018. *How Language Works in Politics: The Impact of Indeterminate Legislation on Policy*. Bristol: Bristol University Press.

Zittel, Thomas, Dominic Nyhuis, and Markus Baumann. 2019. Geographic Representation in Party-Dominated Legislatures: A Quantitative Text Analysis of Parliamentary Questions in the German Bundestag. *Legislative Studies Quarterly* 44 (4): 681–711.

PART III

Qualitative History

Parts I and II considered the macro-level social origins of legal language, and the meso-level changes to that language. Part III brings us to the micro-level, where we can observe the effects of legal indeterminacies on judicialisation. To reiterate the book's central questions—When and how do judges decide to make policy and law? When do judges decide not to influence policy and defer to other state authorities? When, in other words, does the weaker party triumph against the state in court? The answer is where there is a textual doubt, the benefits of which can be given to weaker litigants without judges facing direct accountability (institutional overruling) or indirect accountability (protest, delegitimisation, and resource depletion). Judges will also tend to justify their ruling in accordance with existing norms of law. Even if their ruling departs from public policy practice, their ruling will emphasise the vindication of constitutional or linguistic authorities. Judges will seek to obtain a logic of communication, even in novel cases.

The following chapters describe a six-point typology, to explain patterns in five nations' criminal case laws. Post-war clashes of liberty and security will be scrutinised in Canada, France, Germany, the UK, and the US. Six typological categories are tested per chapter as to the significance of legislative language on judicial behaviour. Specifically, the connection between legislative genre volatility and the power of judges is traced through these five jurisdictions, and 250 country years. These qualitative chapters build on the theory of Part I and the quantitative evidence of Part II. Critical analyses of all published cases pertaining to criminal justice heard by senior courts have been performed. Illustrative examples are then provided of cases where indeterminacies in legislative text were the subject of a lawsuit.

We shall assess the descriptive typology, a causal theory, and interrogate the counterfactual. This can be achieved by considering the effects of, for instance, Germany's more consistently determinable legal language, as contrasted to France and the UK's more indeterminate and volatile legislative languages. As described in Part I, the narrative focusses on how macro-historical change in attitudes and culture affect judicial behaviour through the prism of command languages, and their determinability. A story will be told of how politicians managed post-war demands for enhanced state functionality using flexible legal instruments. The consequence of an enhanced public sphere was not only enlarged bureaucracies, but also an increased resort to "governing with judges" (Stone Sweet 2000).

An example from the US of policy-making in response to a "wicked problem" is instructive (Rittel and Webber 1973). The example comes from Title VII of the *Combat Methamphetamine Epidemic Act* (CMEA) of 2005 (21 USC 801), Section 771, 48(G). All parts of speech that were coded by the computer program have been italicised:

> A regulated seller *may* take *reasonable* measures to guard against employing individuals who *may* present a risk with respect to the theft *and* diversion of scheduled listed *chemical* products, which *may* include, notwithstanding State law, asking applicants for employment whether they have been convicted of *any* crime involving *or* related to *such* products *or* controlled substances.

The opioid crisis in America is such a complex problem that words almost fail policy-makers. More specifically, the structuring of policy goals in definitive verbiage would, if attempted, produce undesirable rigidities of form or execution (Endicott 2011). Instead, a scaffold has been erected to allow executive agencies and courts to determine what is "reasonable". Besides the computer-identified coding of adjectives, conjunctions, and indeterminate modal verbs, there are some very indeterminate noun-phrases in the above excerpt. The concept of "risk" is, for one, highly contestable. Such noun-forms are difficult to machine analyse consistently, because they do not qualify meaning. Assessing qualified meaning can be automated, where assessing meaning itself cannot fully be automated as it is subjective and must be contextualised.

Herein comes the value of qualitative analysis. Whilst Part II demonstrated the success in quantifying sources of relative meaninglessness, Part III will consider how judges moved from confusion to determination. How, in short, do judges decide cases under conditions of legal indeterminacy? How did judges move from a problem in identifying meaning to a solution that is unlikely to be overturned? It will be shown that despite the enhanced political discretion enjoyed by judges as a result of contemporary legalese, they showed reticence in exploiting these opportunities. Unless, that is, there was (a) a particularly compelling basis in contemporary theories of justice to compel policy change, and (b) there was sufficient political cover (from other state actors or public opinion) to avoid judges having their decisions overruled. In other words—and as described in Part I—political behaviour in judges conforms to a logic of appropriateness with a tripartite confluence of macro-level ideology, meso-level language, and micro-level cover from accountability. These forces must coincide to enable political decision-making from judges. At this confluence, judges create a new logic of communication from the threads of existing laws and norms.

Back to the example, opioid countermeasures were adapted from the CMEA in legislation throughout America's States. Newly criminalised activities encouraged a flurry of litigation in state and federal courts, as citizens called on judges to clarify the policy. But there was no tripartite confluence of macro, meso, and micro forces that could shield judges, and so, despite the indeterminacy in law, there were no major cases of courts overturning or changing the new legislation. Kansas' Supreme Court captured the litigating strategy of one defendant, who appealed on the basis of not knowing the law:

> It shall be unlawful for any person to knowingly or intentionally purchase at retail during a 30 day period more than 9 grams of ephedrine base, pseudoephedrine base, or phenylpropanolamine base in a scheduled listed chemical product ….
>
> The State's argument that [this law] K.S.A. 2007 Supp. 65-7006(d) is not unconstitutionally vague is persuasive. There is nothing in the language of the statute, which clearly prohibits the acquisition of more than 3.6 grams of pseudoephedrine base or ephedrine base in any one transaction or more than 9 grams in any 30-day period, that would leave persons of common intelligence guessing as to what is prohibited or that would be open to arbitrary and discriminatory enforcement. To the extent that there is any

> ambiguity because a person of common intelligence may not know how the weights are calculated, that ambiguity is external to [the law].[1]

As the judges put it, "There is nothing... that would leave persons of common intelligence guessing as to what is prohibited or that would be open to arbitrary and discriminatory enforcement". They refused to intervene in political decision-making, because the indeterminacy of the law was insufficient. By resorting to considering "persons of common intelligence" they have adopted an interpretative method redolent of the English law "man on the Clapham Omnibus".[2] Whilst some may doubt that judges keep such company, it demonstrates an attempt to apply common or practical reasoning, rather than reaching for a more abstract and idealised construction. Critics of judicial activism imply that judges can barely contain their desire to push forth a political agenda. But these critics struggle to explain the many instances in which judges appear to demure and acknowledge legal norms rather than subvert them.

A principal problem in these qualitative chapters will be in establishing causation. Given how complex and multifaceted judicial behaviour is, how can the effects of legislative language be isolated? This is the reason for analysing individual cases. In previous chapters, the primary evidence was descriptive statistics and correlation analyses. The difficulty with these methods is in describing causation. Also, as suggested above, committing political power into language is just one step, the language then creates its own communities of power. The causal mechanism is partly cyclical—or endogenous. This does not mean that correlation analyses cannot work (Williams 2017b), but that a mixed-methods research design offers the best possible insights as to how changing legal language affects judicial behaviour.

Also, the range of evidence is limited to five Western democracies. It is therefore best to describe this as a mid-range rather than a general, or universal analysis of judicialisation (Dyevre 2010; Geddes 2003). This is justifiable on account of data availability, and the salience of judicialisation in those five democracies. Also, importantly, with these focussed comparisons, we are able to obtain the advantages of depth with a degree of breadth. Existing studies of judicialisation tend to consider courts separately to the other accoutrements of state power. But as Christoph

[1] *State of Kansas, v. Kevin Teter.* May 11, 2012, Opinion Filed No. 105, 495.

[2] *McQuire v. Western Morning News* [1903] 2 K.B. 100 at 109.

Hönnige has argued, this misses the bigger picture of how courts interact with other branches of government, and how judges take resources and incentives to act from inactivity or indeterminacy elsewhere in the state (Hönnige 2011). We will be able to observe these forces at work in five of the world's most prominent legal jurisdictions.

These chapters borrow a great deal from theories of bureaucratic decision-making, as discussed in Parts I and II. Specifically, Bryan Jones's expectation of leptokurtosis in bureaucratic behaviour is expected of judges in the face of indeterminate law (Jones 1999, 2001). The thin peak and fat tails of a leptokurtic distribution suggests that the vast majority of judicial decisions confirm norms and are therefore "average", whilst a much lesser number extremely out-lie this central tendency. The pattern is of normative behaviour, punctuated by infrequent but extreme deviations. Normative judicial behaviour conserves extant powers and privileges. Deviating judicial behaviour recognises, but rarely creates, new power constellations (Hart 1961). The approach in these chapters is to show the varied ways in which judges confirm state powers, and explain the less frequent examples of judicialisation—where "expansion of the province of courts [comes] at the expense of the politicians and of the administrators".[3] The infrequent extreme breaches in normal behaviour are difficult to predict *ex ante*, save for the confluence of wicked problems, ideological solutions, legislative indeterminacy, and cover for judges from accountability. The prism through which these political resources come together is at the meso-level with underdetermined, or indeterminate legal language. When meaningfulness in state communication disappears it is likely to be asserted by judges. Judicial "activism" is explicable as post-structural and post-positive recognition of a new reality through clear language.

In methodological terms, the approach is to test six typological expectations. These will offer some descriptive evidence that judicial behaviour is derived from linguistic stimuli. Indefeasible predictions remain elusive, but we shall be in a better position to conceptualise and rationalise when and why judges behave politically. Key requirements are to provide evidence that (a) judges do not systematically impose themselves politically in favour of the weaker party, and (b) to provide evidence that when

[3] Tate and Vallinder, *The Global Expansion of Judicial Power*, p. 13. Also Sunkin (1994: 125). As the judicial role expands, it is said that "governing with judges also means governing like judges", where behavioural tropes from the legal profession are adopted by executive and legislative actors (Stone Sweet 2000: 204).

courts do change law and policy it is in most cases fed by political forces beyond their control, rather than the judges merely acting in their own self-interest.

Case selection has been led on the independent variable—legislative indeterminacy. Legislative language is not fully independent as a variable, but is dependent on context and its judicial reification. This is why qualitative analysis is applied here, because cause and effect feedback on each other and limit the applicability of frequentist analyses. The essential point is that cases have not been selected on the supposed dependent variable—political behaviour in judges. Starting with language—as opposed to tracing back from "hard cases"—has both theoretical and empirical advantages. The theoretical advantage is to explain both when judges do overrule governments, but also when they demur. Why, for instance, have British judges established a leadership role with regard to privacy law, but have shied away from euthanasia, or votes for prisoners? It is simply not the case that courts are actively engaged in policy across the gamut. The empirical advantages are, therefore, avoidance of selection bias and improved falsifiability. On that last point, counterfactuals will be tested—when judges overrule governments despite the law being crystal clear, or when judges do not overrule governments despite an indeterminacy in law. At root, the theory is simple and falsifiable, and preliminary findings suggest it has strong explanatory power across time and space.

These qualitative chapters utilise a "most different systems" research design, as the five countries differ substantially in their legal systems and levels of legislative genre volatility (Przeworski and Teune 1970). The historical method is applied to analyse primary documents (constitutions, legislation, and case reports) from these five jurisdictions. All legislation and all published cases brought to superior courts between 1950 and the present were analysed. Determining relevant "criminal laws" was done by searching and cross referencing government websites with secondary commentary. The research design is replicable. Another researcher could also analyse all available criminal cases from these five top courts, and identify compelling evidence for how courts use and create authoritative language. The ambition is not to present precise statistical estimates of how often courts behave according to certain prompts. Such accuracy is impossible given that each case heard by a superior court will be the tip of a jurisprudential iceberg. The aim instead is to show evidence that political behaviour in the courts is not the only (or indeed even preferred) method of case resolution, and that where the courts do create new legal meaning it is reactive to the state of law. Nor will I hide cases where there is politicking despite little evidence of legal indeterminacy.

So as to describe long-term trends, it is important not to select court cases that evince judicial power and try to work backwards to a theory. Famous (or indeed infamous) cases will often not be representative of judicial behaviour. Which is not to say that the theory of linguistic judicialisation cannot and will not speak to well-known cases. For instance, possibly the apogee of judicial power in America came under the Warren Court (1953–1969). Chief Justice Earl Warren had served as Governor of California and run for US Vice President in the 1948 election. It was perhaps safe to describe him, more so than most judges, as a "politician in robes". Less easy to explain, if we focus on an agent-centred theory, is how the Supreme Court Justices collectively enlarged the scope of civil rights in landmark cases under his stewardship, such as *Miranda v. Arizona*.[4] Warren's politics may be widely known (or at least presumed), but why would the other eight Associate Justices have enabled his ambitions? The landmark school desegregation case of *Brown v. Board of Education of Topeka*[5] is particularly in need of explanation in this regard.

This unanimous ruling came barely six months after Warren's Chief Justiceship was inaugurated. In it, the justices declared racial segregation of public schools to be unconstitutional. It is considered by some proponents and critics as a political, rather than legal, decision (Roosevelt 2006). But it is possible to identify a confluence of the three forces described by this book's theory—there was overwhelming public opposition to segregation, there was severe and protracted legislative indeterminacy that encouraged litigants, and there was sufficient political cover for the justices. In short, the use of indeterminate instruments of oppression in State laws was ripe for correction. In fact, there were reams of law on segregation, and not just constitutional and statutory, but also the common law rulings in cases such as *Plessy v. Ferguson*,[6] or later pre-Brown cases such as *Shelley v. Kraemer*.[7] By the time of *Brown v. Board*, the federal government had not legislated on segregation since the *Civil Rights Act* of 1866, but many states had so legislated (Klarman 1996).

[4] 384 U.S. 436 (1966).

[5] 347 U.S. 483.

[6] 163 US 537.

[7] 334 US 1.

The central interpretative problem for the courts was profound indeterminacy in the Fourteenth Amendment to the US Constitution relative to State laws:

> No State shall make or enforce any law which shall abridge the privileges or immunities of citizens of the United States; nor shall any State deprive any person of life, liberty, or property, without due process of law; nor deny to any person within its jurisdiction the equal protection of the laws.

Much of the fight came down to deriving meaning from a single adjective—equal. Separate, it was ruled in *Brown*, could not mean equal. The effects of this textual reification have, of course, rumbled on. Cases, such as 2007s *Parents Involved in Community Schools v. Seattle School District No. 1*[8] have kept the Supreme Court's segregation jurisprudence on the agenda well into the twenty-first century. These days the courts also have to contend with indeterminacies in the *Civil Rights Act 1964*, especially Title VII, section 703:

> (a) It shall be an unlawful employment practice for an employer—(1) to fail or refuse to hire or to discharge any individual, or otherwise to discriminate against any individual with respect to his compensation, terms, conditions, or privileges of employment, because of such individual's race, color, religion, sex, or national origin; or (2) to limit, segregate, or classify his employees in any way which would deprive or tend to deprive any individual of employment opportunities or otherwise adversely affect his status as an employee, because of such individual's race, color, religion, sex, or national origin.

The point is not to criticise Congressional drafters for sloppy writing. The point is not moral, but empirical. How else could the US be governed, given its continental scale, cultural diversity, institutional fragmentation, and with increasingly distributed social power? Phrases such as "tend to deprive any individual of employment opportunities" will of course encourage litigation, and therefore empower judges. But what else was to be done? Congress and the President created legislation that reflected US society: where power is increasingly indeterminate language will be indeterminate. Judicialisation was a consequence of these social and institutional changes wrought through understandably indeterminate rules of law.

[8] 551 U.S. 701.

The broader view is to see judicialisation of what had been the private sphere. Judges were merely dragged along on the coattails of an expanded post-war state expansion. The very idea that the US Federal Government could regulate the make-up of school classrooms would have seemed perversely intrusive to that country's founding fathers. Hence, it is counter-intuitively possible to argue that modern judges are much less powerful than their nineteenth-century forebears. Adjudication, certainly in common law jurisdictions, used to be isolated from the state bureaucracy and expected to create new rules of law to settle private disputes. In the twentieth and twenty-first centuries, common law judges have come to look a lot more like civil law judges (Calabresi 1982). In that, judges are accountable public servants, and they are expected to limit their creative impulses to ensuring that laws work as intended, not that new laws are made.

Clearly this diminished role for individual authority figures coincides with the age of mass democracy. Revelatory of a diminished status in the democratic age is this statement from the preeminent British judge, Lord Bingham[9]:

> ... [T]here now exists no power in the courts to create new criminal offences, as decided by a unanimous House in *Knuller v. Director of Public Prosecutions* [1973] A.C. 435... Statute is now the sole source of new criminal offences.

The Law Lords clipped their own wings, in other words. This is hardly the work of an agenda-pursuing political force. Bingham went on to hammer home their self-imposed enfeeblement:

> And Mr Crow [counsel] submits that s.1 of the 1946 [United Nations] Act gives express power to provide for the trial and punishment of persons offending against any Order. But the principle of maximum certainty requires that a citizen must be able to have an adequate indication of the legal rules applicable.[10]

Section 1 of the *United Nations Act 1946* granted near eye-watering executive power to the British Government in wartime:

[9] *R v. Jones* [2007] 1 A.C. 136 at 28.

[10] Ibid at 45.

> If… the Security Council of the United Nations call upon His Majesty's Government in the United Kingdom to apply any measures to give effect to any decision of that Council, His Majesty may by Order in Council make such provision as appears to Him necessary or expedient for enabling those measures to be effectively applied, including (without prejudice to the generality of the preceding words) provision for the apprehension, trial and punishment of persons offending against the Order.

British judges are technically members of the executive branch. This is why their courts are festooned with the royal Lion and Unicorn emblem, and not the Portcullis of Parliament. And yet, Bingham ruled in this case that executive discretion militated against the "principle of maximum certainty", so he ruled that new criminal offences must come from Acts of Parliament. Such a self-negating declamation does not fit a theory that judges will expand their powers at every opportunity.

Logics of Appropriateness and Communication

What are observable implications of the theory? When does judicial behaviour have political consequences? In a sense this is a trite question. At certain levels of the judiciary, all of their decisions will have political consequences. But we are most interested in those decisions that expand the province of courts at the expense of executives and bureaucrats. These would be cases where judges overrule a government interpretation of their powers or duties. Judges behave in this way when managing textual indeterminacies, or when determining the relation between text and its subtext, context, or intertextuality. Under some circumstances the meaning of legislation is so open as to require transtextual or metatextual interpretation. Transtextual interpretations are those which transcend the text, and utilise a range of alternative sources to determine meaning. Metatextual interpretations are those which critique the text as suboptimal, and thereby improve the meaning from alternative sources. Metatextual interpretations are the most overtly policy influencing, but will still be shown to be institution-conserving for the most part, not activist. These six elements—text, subtext, intertext, context, transtext, and metatext—have been adapted here to cohere with a seminal analysis of political behaviour in the USSupreme Court by Richard Hodder-Williams (1997). The first four categories describe instances where judges do not substantially alter the text. The latter two categories will describe when judges "read in" or "read down" language to make sense of legislation.[11]

1. Empirical (Textual)—Litigants bring cases concerning public policy to court as an alternative means of settling their political grievances. The selection of cases by docket control will prioritise those with the most important legal questions to be resolved. Therefore "Empirical" here refers to the source of disputes. Whilst in all jurisdictions surveyed here, the apex courts can manage their own docket, such management is corporate, rather than individualistic. As such, no individual judge can steer case selection in their own interests, and the path of least resistance is to select those cases raising the most difficult interpretations of law. The specific expectation is that there are increased incentives for judicialisation as a consequence of changes to the language of legislation through time.

2. Definitional (Subtextual)—Judges are expected to clarify rules of law. This will often be achieved through subtextual references to existing interpretations of the same or similar language. Judges look back to past decisions to define away new indeterminacies. To define is to constrain. And, where definition is anchored to past decisions it conserves the constellation of power that has built up around that use of language. Hence definition will in most cases be to the advantage of the institutional litigant, not the weaker appellant seeking to reimagine state powers. A state authority would not typically appeal a case they expected to lose. If precedent was squarely against their position, they would not expend time nor treasure in a doomed fight.

3. Systemic (Intertextual)—Apex courts oversee complex legal systems. The top court in a system has a responsibility to the integrity and order of that system. That will require the court to instruct, and sometimes to constrain the rule-expanding ambitions of lower courts. It is expected that in cases dealing with indeterminate legislation, the apex courts will seek to maximise coherence in legal and quasi-legal institutions by the imposition of regularities and safeguards. This will entail not only the conservation of subtextual interpretations (as above), but also intertextual interpretation as a means to resolve indeterminacy. In other words, to settle a case, apex courts will interpret new laws in conjunction with

[11] These interpretative methods are described in UK law in the cases of *R v A (No. 2)* [2001] UKHL 25, and *R v Lambert* [2001] UKHL 37.

existing laws, and especially existing procedural laws (such as constitutional or administrative law) so as to maintain regular separations of power and democratic accountability. Top courts will use a hierarchy of domestic and international laws to rein in lower court colleagues.

4. Prudential (Contextual)—Apex courts have many strengths, but factual analysis, including vast-scale data processing and management, is not one of them. Appellate courts work best in the abstract realm of law and principle, and typically leave the verification of facts to more junior tribunals. Whilst appeal courts will apprise themselves of case facts, they will also acknowledge their vastly inferior capacity to determine complex social facts, as compared to, in particular, the executive and legislative branches. This will include cases such as whether euthanasia should be decriminalised. The courts simply do not have the mandate to judge whether the public support such a step. Judges may be conscious of an injustice for a litigant, but nonetheless rule in accordance with the state. In such cases, judges defer to another agent with greater capacity, competence, or collective legitimacy (Strøm et al. 2003). This deference comes in the form of ruling in favour of the stronger litigant.

Courts will judicialize policy under the following two circumstances:

5. Influence-seeking (Transtextuality)—Gérard Genette (1992) described transtextuality as an all-encompassing analysis of a text. Beyond just intertext, the meaning of a text is here developed from open and even secret sources of meaningfulness. This is admittedly, and ironically, a stretched interpretation of transtextuality. The way it is being used here is perhaps more clearly described using Hodder-Williams's framework. Judges do not seek influence, *per se*, but will often obtain policy influence when a text is so indeterminate, or so obviously in conflict with other rules of law. Under these circumstances, judges must transcend the text to determine its meaning from whatever sources may be available.

In concrete terms, influence-seeking refers to cases where judges constrain other state actors, but do not make new powers for themselves. It is a negative, rather than positive application of power. An example would be where judges explicitly constrain the scope of their decision to the immediate case facts and deny its wider applicability. This gives the courts influence in the immediate case, but no wider or on-going policy impact. A notable illustration is *Bush v. Gore*, where a USSupreme Court majority declared that their decision had no implications wider than the immediate case facts. Their ruling also stopped the application of Floridian law, but did not create new rules of law. Of course, in that case, the implications of ruling for George W. Bush were enormous, but the judges were explicitly not making policy on manual ballot recounts for future elections.

6. Policy-orientated (Metatextual)—This is an interpretation that also transcends a text, but also tacitly or explicitly denies the legitimacy of that text (Genette 1992). It is a critique of one text by another. Such interpretations do tend to have on-going policy significance. The most obvious instances of this would include declarations of unconstitutionality. Under the circumstances, constitutional law is used to distinguish or even obliterate a piece of ordinary legislation.

Influence-seeking and policy-oriented decisions are triggered by extreme degenrification of legal language. Courts have to transcend a text when there is no reliable subtext to tether their decision. The precise point at which degenrification enables judicialisation is impossible to pinpoint ex ante. This is why the method here is descriptive and historical, rather than providing causal inferences. The aim, in other words, is to explain and understand judicialisation, but we are not yet in a position to predict it. Nonetheless, we will be able to explore some causal propositions. The likelihood of a court ruling being overturned can help explain whether it is a constraining or enabling intervention. Where a court ruling conforms to public opinion, it will be difficult for politicians to reverse it without adverse electoral consequences. This can support a policy-oriented response to extreme indeterminacy. A more circumspect influence-seeking judgement may not enjoy obvious public support—either because of divisions or indifference on the matter—but there will be sufficient elite-level dissensus to minimise the likelihood of a counter-decision.

An example of a policy-oriented decision was when the UK House of Lords criminalised rape in marriage by using principles of natural justice.[12] An example of more circumspect influence-seeking came when that same court ruled the Director of Public Prosecutions had to give detailed guidance on whether an individual would be charged with assisted suicide if he helped his chronically ill wife travel to be euthanised.[13] The latter case did not adjust law *tout court*, it had tight

[12] *R v. R* [1991] UKHL 12.

[13] *R (Purdy) v. DPP* [2009] UKHL 45.

limitations. Specifically, the court ordered a public authority other than itself to declare new policy. But then how do courts know what public opinion is, given that it has been argued they lack the mandate to claim to know such facts? Public opinion is ascertained by courts more through institutional rather than social data. In other words, courts will observe a concerted effort by, say, state legislatures to mitigate the effects of federal laws. In *Brown v. Board*, not only did the Warren Court make use of Brandeis Briefs containing social data, they could also see that a majority of US States had legislated to overturn Jim Crow segregationist laws. These institutional facts would have offered cover for them to challenge at a federal level any state law that went against this trend—as was the case in 1950s Kansas.

An implication of the theory is that judges may refuse to react to severe legal indeterminacy with transtextual or metatextual repairs. This in itself could be a politically significant act. Such "restraint" is, as argued, likely to be institutionally inappropriate, as rejecting the separation of powers. For instance, *Liversidge v. Anderson*[14] is a much lamented example of excessive deference paid by courts to the UK Government. The government's wartime internment order was not challenged nor even clarified in court, despite its indeterminate and genre-deviant language:

> If the Secretary of State has reasonable cause to believe any person to be of hostile origin or associations and that by reason thereof it is necessary to exercise control over him, he may make an order against that person directing that he be detained.

In deciding this case, judges kicked legal uncertainty further down the road, and hence the decision was institutionally inappropriate. In his dissentient remarks, Lord Atkin complained in the following now celebrated defence of English liberties:

> ...the minister has been given complete discretion whether he should detain a subject or not. It is an absolute power which, so far as I know, has never been given before to the executive, and I shall not apologise for taking some time to demonstrate that no such power is in fact given to the minister by the words in question...
>
> In this country, amid the clash of arms, the laws are not silent. They may be changed, but they speak the same language in war as in peace. It has

[14] [1941] UKHL 1.

> always been one of the pillars of freedom, one of the principles of liberty for which on recent authority we are now fighting, that the judges are no respecters of persons and stand between the subject and any attempted encroachments on his liberty by the executive, alert to see that any coercive action is justified in law. [15]

As a general philological point, language is fundamentally meaningless. It is just a set of symbols that facilitates communication according to socially determined interpretations. It is nonetheless possible to identify relative patterns in how communities use language. It is through norms of usage that at least a recognition of meaningfulness emerges. Outlying deviations from these normal usages will stimulate either a closing down of their scope, or a recalibration of meaning to a new normal. Judges facilitate this conservation or adaptation of norms.

We will, of course, see instances where judges miscalculated their opportunity to judicialise. This will be clear where a transtextual or metatextual interpretation of law is slapped down on appeal or in a constitutional amendment. As the theory would have us expect, judges will not be able to sustain a stretched interpretation of law where that law is insufficiently indeterminate; does not represent a deviation from genre; and where the stretched interpretation does not cohere with public or elite interests. An example is *Re S (A Care Plan)*, where the England and Wales Court of Appeal was overruled by the House of Lords for excessively intervening in the making of local authority child care orders. There will be other such examples, which will hopefully make clear that the aim here is not to defend judicialisation in a moral sense, but explain it in historical and empirical senses. The following chapters start with scene setting, before proceeding conceptually, following Hodder-Williams's typology.

References

Calabresi, Guido. 1982. *A Common Law for the Age of Statutes*. Cambridge, MA: Harvard University Press.

Dyevre, Arthur. 2010. Unifying the Field of Comparative Judicial Politics: Towards a General Theory of Judicial Behaviour. *European Political Science Review* 2 (2): 297–327.

[15] Ibid at p. 284.

Endicott, Timothy. 2011. The Value of Vagueness. In *Philosophical Foundations of Language in the Law*, ed. Andrei Marmor and Scott Soames. Oxford: Oxford University Press.

Geddes, Barbara. 2003. *Paradigms and Sand Castles: Theory Building and Research Design in Comparative Politics*. Ann Arbor, MI: University of Michigan Press.

Genette, Gérard. 1992. *The architext: An introduction*. Berkeley: University of California Press.

Hart, H.L.A. 1961. *The Concept of the Law*. Oxford: Clarendon.

Hodder-Williams, Richard. 1997. Six Notions of 'Political' and the United States Supreme Court. *British Journal of Political Science* 22 (1): 1–20.

Hönnige, Christoph. 2011. Beyond Judicialization: Why We Need More Comparative Research About Constitutional Courts. *European Political Science* 10: 346–358.

Jones, Bryan D. 1999. Bounded Rationality. *Annual Review of Political Science* 2: 297–321.

Jones, Bryan D. 2001. *Politics and the Architecture of Choice: Bounded Rationality and Governance*. Chicago: University of Chicago Press.

Klarman, Michael. 1996. Rethinking the civil rights and civil liberties revolutions. *Virginia Law Review* 82: 1–67.

Przeworski, Adam, and Henry Teune. 1970. *The Logic of Comparative Social Inquiry*. Chapel Hill, NC: Oxford University Press.

Rittel, Horst W.J., and Melvin M. Webber. 1973. Dilemmas in a General Theory of Planning. *Policy Sciences* 4 (2): 155–169.

Roosevelt, Kermit. 2006. *The Myth of Judicial Activism: Making Sense of Supreme Court Decisions*. New Haven CT: Yale University Press.

Sunkin, Maurice. 1994. Judialization of Politics in the United Kingdom, *International Political Science Review* 15: 125–133.

Stone Sweet, Alec. 2000. *Governing with Judges: Constitutional Politics in Europe*. Oxford: Oxford University Press.

Strøm, Kaare, Wolfgang C. Müller, and Torbjörn Bergman. 2003. *Delegation and Accountability in Parliamentary Democracies*. Oxford: Oxford University Press.

Williams, Matthew. 2017. Legislative Language and Judicial Politics: The Effects of Changing Parliamentary Language on UK Immigration Disputes. *British Journal of Politics and IR* 19 (3): 592–608.

CHAPTER 5

Rule of Law Without a Constitution in the UK

"End the human rights farce!" So went a 2011 headline in the UK's *Daily Telegraph* newspaper. The sentiment has echoed through British newspapers since the turn of the millennium.[1] More provocative still was *The Daily Mail's* channelling of Robespierre in 2016, denouncing three judges as "Enemies of the People".[2] This was that newspaper's assessment of a legal challenge successfully brought by Gina Miller, an anti-Brexit activist, by which a vote was forced in the House of Commons on when to trigger Britain's formal departure from the European Union.[3] The UK Supreme Court came even more prominently into public consciousness with the second successful case brought by Miller. In it, the Government's attempted prorogation of Parliament in 2019 was declared unlawful by a unanimous decision of all twelve Justices. The case name was *R (Miller) v. The Prime Minister*[4] The UK Prime Minister had been defeated by the unquestionably weaker litigant.

[1] https://www.telegraph.co.uk/news/uknews/crime/8485717/End-the-Human-Rights-farce-Amy-died.-He-got-a-slapped-wrist.html, accessed 11 March 2020.

[2] https://www.dailymail.co.uk/news/article-3903436/Enemies-people-Fury-touch-judges-defied-17-4m-Brexit-voters-trigger-constitutional-crisis.html, accessed 11 March 2020.

[3] *R (Miller) v. Secretary of State for Exiting the European Union* [2017] UKSC 5.

[4] *R (Miller) v. The Prime Minister and Cherry v. Advocate General for Scotland* [2019] UKSC 41.

M. Williams, *Judges and the Language of Law*,
https://doi.org/10.1007/978-3-030-91495-0_5

An important starting point for this chapter, therefore, is to acknowledge just how controversial the power of British judges has become, and to assess public criticisms of "activist" judges. Critics have highlighted, in particular, violations of supposed common sense under the *Human Rights Act 1998* (HRA). This Act of Parliament empowered British judges to apply almost all of the *European Convention on Human Rights* (ECHR) to domestic litigation.[5] A notable example came when the detention of nine suspected terrorists was declared unlawful, on the grounds of discrimination. In another case, it was decided that men who had immigrated to the UK in a plane that they had hijacked should have their deportations delayed, because of fear for their rights if repatriated. A case personally criticised by Theresa May, when Home Secretary, was that an immigrant had supposedly been spared deportation because of his family life in the UK. Part of the evidence in support of which was his owning a cat.

These were cases at home. Meanwhile, the European Court of Human Rights receives around 1700 petitions each year against the British government.[6] Although the UK was described as "top of the class" in the 47-member Council of Europe, the court nevertheless ruled that some British prisoners ought to vote in elections.[7] The court was also able to temporarily block the deportation of the radical cleric Abu Qatada to Jordan.[8] These rulings from domestic and international courts were ferociously criticised. Judges stepped in the way of UK public policy, and in some of these cases they did so by adapting law in support of sometimes dangerously anti-democratic characters. The cases appear to be evidence that judges, especially since the HRA, get to answer some of the most hotly contested "who gets what, when and how" questions of British politics (Lasswell 1936). And, besides these attention-grabbing cases has been a general ratcheting up of human rights jurisprudence. This implies that with every defeat, the British Government becomes more likely to be constrained and defeated in future litigation under human rights law. This "neo-functionalist" (Haas 1958) accretion of power in courts was

[5] The HRA omitted from domestic integration Article 13 ECHR, on the right to an effective remedy,.

[6] https://www.echr.coe.int/Documents/Facts_Figures_2020_ENG.pdf, accessed 11 March 2021.

[7] *Hirst v United Kingdom (No 2)* (2005) ECHR 681.

[8] *Othman (Abu Qatada) v. United Kingdom.*

observed from the inside by no less an observer than former Supreme Court Justice Lord Sumption in his Reith Lectures 2019.[9]

A specific example of how human rights law supposedly grew beyond its original scope is in regards to privacy. The state intervening to protect its citizens' privacy is perhaps at face value an absurd notion. The law of privacy was nonetheless changed by judges in the early 2000s, again enabled by the HRA. Footballers and celebrity chefs were among the first to take solace from a new device: judge-made super-injunctions. These were injunctions against publishing a news story where the existence of the injunction was itself the subject of an injunction. Besides "super-injunction", "meta-injunction" could describe the device which was intended to avoid even a rumour of guilt. With these super-injunctions the court used the *Human Rights Act*, even though that law was intended to protect individuals from the state rather than from other citizens—such as newspaper proprietors. Whilst the expansion of judicial power has not only benefitted ne'er do-wells, foreigners, and philandering celebrities, the results have shifted a modicum of power from the strong to the weak (Williams 2017). And whilst judge-made law is nothing new in Britain, it has been on the rise since the 1960s, and particularly since the HRA came into force in October 2000 (Stevens 2005). Powerful judges pose challenging questions for those concerned as to the present and future state of British democracy. In particular, how is it ever right for unelected elites to support a weak litigant, assuming that the stronger litigant has a larger constituency of support?

Has there in fact been "a human rights farce" in twenty-first-century Britain? Are human rights just another sense in which political correctness has gone mad? The characters may seem outlandish, the circumstances unusual, but the court decisions can all be explained according to existing rules of law, adapted in the face of exceptional legislative indeterminacy. First consider the above mentioned case of foreign terrorist suspects whose detention was ruled to be illegal as discriminatory. This was the *Belmarsh Prisoners'* case. It is cited as a notorious example of the *Human Rights Act* being used to protect the interests of terrorist suspects, and thereby frustrating the government's national security strategy.

[9] https://www.bbc.co.uk/programmes/m00057m9, accessed 24 November 2020.

The dispute concerned policy in the aftermath of the September 11th attacks. Nine men, all non-citizens, brought legal action against the government who had ordered they be indefinitely detained in London's Belmarsh prison, pending their deportations. They were detained under the *Anti-terrorism, Crime and Security Act 2001*. The Act was indeterminate on three counts. It lacked meaning by being incomplete, it contradicted other rules of law, and it made little sense as a practical measure. It was these last two reasons in particular that spurred judges to rule in favour of the incarcerated men. Although, this was unquestionably not a case where public opinion offered support to the judges' ruling. On the first source of indeterminacy, the Act delegated broad discretion to the government to deal with security threats. Section 21 allowed the Home Secretary to certify an individual as being an international terrorist if the Minister:

> reasonably– believes that the person's presence in the United Kingdom is a risk to national security, and suspects that the person is a terrorist.

This language has no literal meaning until translated by the Home Secretary. An individual certified as an international terrorist on the grounds that the Home Secretary believes and suspects them of being a terrorist could challenge that certification, and the courts would need to define what a reasonable belief or suspicion might be. "Reasonable" has an interpretation in English law, but only because its meaning has been elaborated by judges settling past cases. In the *Belmarsh* case, the government was ruled to have behaved reasonably in their certifications, so there was no court interference on that point. The case was lost by the government on a separate matter, arising from section 23 of the Act. This section was declared to be incompatible with the *European Convention of Human Rights* (ECHR). It states:

> (1) A suspected international terrorist may be detained under a provision specified in subsection (2) despite the fact that his removal or departure from the United Kingdom is prevented (whether temporarily or indefinitely) by–
> a. a point of law which wholly or partly relates to an international agreement, or
> b. a practical consideration.

This language may be described as both ambiguous and indeterminate. It is ambiguous in that the words used have contested meanings, and it is also indeterminate because some key information is entirely omitted. With regard to ambiguity, the noun modifying adverb "partly" and the adjective "practical" are examples. Meanwhile, pragmatic indeterminacy comes from "suspected international terrorist". The use of the passive form of the verb "to suspect" begs the questions: suspected by whom and suspected how? These three words mean nothing until the Home Secretary has made known her suspicions under section 21. As mentioned, this portion of the law was settled by the government to the judges' satisfaction in the *Belmarsh* case. What the judges could not accept was how the law affected other laws and did so without being able to achieve its aims of managing national security. It is a well-established principle that law should not apply differently to different people unless Parliament explicitly requests this. Tax law, for instance, discriminates wildly between individuals. A progressive tax regime could not operate otherwise. The problem in this particular case is that the policy went against Parliament's self-imposed commitment not to discriminate without justification. This commitment lies in Article 14 of the European Convention. It is a worthy discipline. Laws that discriminate without justification create arbitrary distinctions that cannot be understood by citizens.

Parliament was calling for foreign-born suspects to be detained without trial. Foreign terrorist suspects were a small minority of all terrorist suspects. Detaining them alone would be as effective as detaining only left-handed terrorist suspects. A minority of terrorists would be detained because of a shared characteristic that has no direct bearing on the likelihood of their committing a terrorist offence. There is little justification in watering down a commitment not to discriminate if it is in pursuit of a symbolic gesture. Although Parliament had said in the 2001 Act that detention should not be prevented by a point of law "which wholly or partly relates to an international agreement", Article 14 of the European Convention is not an international agreement, it is enshrined in domestic law via the *Human Rights Act*. On the one hand Parliament called for unrestricted detention of suspected international terrorists (in the 2001 Act) whilst on the other it called for judges to prevent unjustified discrimination (under the HRA). Such policy conflict can best be resolved by reference to basic principles of justice. In this case it was clear that the intent of the legislation was to counter a terrorist threat, but the language used could not achieve that aim.

One could argue the symbolism of detaining a small minority of dangerous individuals is of benefit in deterring terrorism. Also, if Parliament had changed its mind on Article 14, it was not for the courts to go back to an earlier understanding of that law. No Parliament of the past, it is said, may bind its successors. Apart from anything, the courts have nothing close to the government's knowledge on terrorist threats. These are all valid points, but the primary reason the 2001 Act does not work is because it creates power without limits. Limited power is a democratic essential. Citizens must be able to determine what their government can, and, crucially, cannot do. If Parliament is to keep track of what the government does, then it cannot do so with language like that in sections 21 and 23. It was not establishing a rule of law, but a rule by individual.

The Home Secretary could decide whether and to what extent foreign-born residents could be detained without it being clear when that power had gone too far. One could describe Parliament's use of language here as so vague it establishes an unfalsifiable statement of power. In other words, it is impossible to say "if the Home Secretary does *x* she will be breaking the law". Provided the Home Secretary believes and suspects an individual is a terrorist, their detention is lawful. This psychological condition would be very difficult to prove or disprove, and all sorts of abuses would be possible if an unscrupulous Home Secretary were in charge. The only way the Home Secretary could unambiguously break this law would be to detain, without trial, a British citizen believed and suspected to be a terrorist. Without this ability to know when a law is broken there is no determined law at all.

Furthermore, the court ruling in *Belmarsh* did not lead to the prisoners' release. When judges use the *Human Rights Act* they may at most declare an incompatibility under section 4 of that Act. Nothing actually changes in the impugned law when a declaration is made of an incompatibility with the ECHR. Instead the problem is merely flagged, allowing Parliament to fix it, if it wishes to. Unlike in nations with co-equal branches of government, British courts are crown servants, and the crown is subordinate to Parliament. It just so happens that Parliament has never failed to react to judicial declarations under the HRA. This in itself suggests the judges must have been right on each occasion, otherwise we would expect the politicians to have ignored their rulings.

The HRA is not a power for judges to use proactively, it is a reparatory tool. This court ruling initiated a debate in Parliament that in turn led to new counter-terrorism legislation. This was somewhat more effective as a rule of law. Parliament created control orders for all terrorist suspects (foreign and domestic) under the *Prevention of Terrorism Act 2005* (PTA). In the *Belmarsh* case, the government, Parliament and the media were understandably perturbed by the unusual incursion of judges into national security policy. However, it is inaccurate to argue that such intervention from the bench is unconstitutional or illegitimate. Parliament depends on the courts to ensure its laws work. As we will go on to observe, there has been a glut in the supply of law, much of which lacks sufficient determinacy to rule.

Judicial Review in the UK

Without a codified constitution, there is no constitutional review in the UK. Hence, to all intents and purposes, there is no way for Acts of the sovereign Parliament to be declared null by a court. Nonetheless, there has been judicial review of executive decisions stretching beyond noted cases, such as *Dr. Bonham's Case* in the reign of James I. Despite this long heritage, judicial review fell moribund after the Glorious Revolution, until a flowering with administrative rulings after the Second World War. There came enhanced substantive and procedural requirements for new executive actions. Common law was strained by judges beyond the traditional *ultra vires* doctrine. *Ultra vires* is a legality test adapted from commercial privity in the nineteenth century. The principle of which was to classify when individuals had gone beyond the power granted to them in legislation.

Some have argued that *ultra vires* is the foundation stone of all judicial review in English law (Forsyth 1996). The role of the judge in this conception was to make a declaration of the law by determining the *vires*, or limits. Recent scholarship however has argued that *ultra vires* could not have been the basis for the considerable developments in judicial review since the 1960s (Craig 1998; Oliver 2000). These authors contend that statutory interpretation requires more than simply identifying the *vires*, and that it occasionally entails establishing *vires* by adapting existing principles of law to new social or legal contexts. By laying down substantive and procedural limits, it could be argued that courts were drafting a constitution of higher laws that bind all other subordinating laws, including Acts of Parliament.

Not all accept this to be true (Forsyth 2000), and it is important to note that it is only in relatively unusual "hard cases" that the legality conditions are set out by judges to resolve a dispute. Whilst these cases have a disproportionate impact on the rule of law, it would be wrong to say that *ultra vires* has been abandoned as a foundation for judicial intervention in public policy (Elliott 2000). Nevertheless it is argued here that a modern state acting within the rule of law cannot have its actions evaluated simply according to enumerated powers when those powers are indeterminately communicated. In such a situation, judges will make new *vires* from older rules of law so as to resolve the uncertainty at dispute.

Legal scholarship and political science have aimed to solve the mystery of why judicial power developed at pace after 1960. The bench-mark year of 1960 is of course arbitrary, but it is a useful line in the sand to consider variation over the twentieth and twenty-first centuries. One much noted cause of change were the *dramatis personae*, such as the partnership of Lords Reid and Wilberforce in the House of Lords, the impact of Lord Denning as Master of the Rolls, or the emergence, following 1954, of less reactionary Lords Chancellor in succession to Viscount Simonds (Blom-Cooper et al. 2009). These individuals oversaw turning-point cases of the 1960s, with long-term repercussions for the political role of judges (Feldman 2004; Loveland 2006). Notable cases included *Ridge v. Baldwin*,[10] *R v. Minister of Agriculture ex p Padfield*,[11] and *Anisminic v. Foreign Compensation Commission*.[12] They were helped in this by expanded access for citizens to legal services with the *Legal Aid Act 1949*.

Besides individual judges, it is of course important to associate challenges to government as coincident with an end to consensus and deference in 1960s British politics. The "sick man of Europe", then struggling to find a role without an Empire, was not universally trusted nor respected by its citizens. There were also self-imposed international limits to what Parliament or the government could achieve. We have mentioned already the ECHR, a foundational document of the Council of Europe. Added to which were memberships of the European Common Market (now EU), the United Nations, and, more recently, the Asian Infrastructure Investment Bank. All of these imposed limits on what laws and

[10] [1964] AC 40.

[11] [1968] AC 997.

[12] [1969] 2 AC 147, [1969] 2 WLR 163.

policies could be made in the UK. In theory, any of these standards can be ignored by Britain withdrawing from global society. Whether this is the right course of action is not the concern of this book. What can be argued here is how power is arranged in Britain. The UK Parliament consented to limits on her sovereignty, because these were accepted as being in the interests of the country. These then created opportunities for judicialisation when taken with increasingly indeterminate rules of law.

An implication is that unchecked sovereignty for the UK Parliament is a fantasy. Walter Bagehot concluded as much when he listed the various "efficient" constraints within England's (sic) Constitution that made the "formal" rules palatable. The formal rule is that Parliament is an unconstrained sovereign. The reality is that could not and has never operated, and has only ever been asserted rhetorically. As social policies expand, the tension between formal and efficient resolves in favour of the latter. Parliament is simply not an efficient mechanism for orchestrating a complex bureaucracy. It therefore has to delegate policymaking and implementation functions to state agents. Communicating discretion requires indeterminate language. It is impossible to predetermine the substance and implementation of a law, and simultaneously yield discretion. The solution, as A.V. Dicey noted, is to abet Parliament's sovereignty with the rule of law (Dicey 1915).Parliament sets out its will, but its commands may be misunderstood or ignored. In the ensuing dispute over what Parliament really wanted to say, courts will help realise its sovereignty by clarifying what was intended. The sheer complexity of modern public law has meant that the parochial and personal essences of common law are being adapted to a catholicity and abstraction that would be more often associated with civil law jurisdictions (Calabresi 1982).

This chapter will demonstrate that whilst *dramatis personae* and notable cases are important, they in turn depended on the extent of indeterminate legislation and are therefore of secondary, not primary, importance. Ultimately, the story is dominated not by actors, but by institutions and their adaptation to events. The aim of this chapter is not to dispel previous contributions to the debate, but to offer an account that is capable of addressing the begging questions—why then, and why those judges? The key variable was the hugely expanded executive power of the post-war state, and the indeterminacy of legislation needed to scaffold this change. It is often said that "hard cases make bad law", this chapter simply points out that "indeterminate legislation makes hard cases".

Empirical—Textual Changes

Noticing and commenting on the increased volume of enacted UK legislation is far from original (Seaward and Silk 2003). It escaped nobody's notice that the *Income and Corporation Taxes Act 1988* was extremely long. The 1988 Act was, on its own, at nearly 400,000 words, twenty-five times longer than the entire legislative output for the year 1905 (Williams 2018). Nor has the widened scope of policy occupied by state regulation gone unnoticed (Ewing 2010). Nor, indeed, is it novel to link the policy power of judges to this rising tide lifting all state boats (Lee 1994). What is novel here are the uses of quantitative analysis of linguistics and political science to explain why, on a case-by-case basis judges determined aspects of policy.

The first step to take is in testing the claim that law did in fact become increasingly indeterminate. These textual changes affect the genericisms of legal language, and thereby encourage extra-legislative dispute over meaning. An overview of these data pertaining to all public laws was presented in Part Two, but here we can disaggregate the findings further, and in specific relation to criminal justice legislation. And, here again we see the universal data set. There was no sampling required with the machine reading technology, and the emergent patterns are not subject to intervals of confidence. Beginning with some descriptive statistics, Table 5.1 summarises the increased output of criminal legislation from 1950 to 2020.

In terms of word length, the legislative output of the 1950s was 3/5ths of 1% of the total output from 1950 to 2020. By contrast 30% of all surveyed legislation was enacted during the 2000s under the New Labour governments (Ormerod and Laird 2015). But linguistic variance in this output is the crucial variable for this book and is described by Table 5.2.

The most indeterminate law surveyed was the *Criminal Finances Act 2017* with 68.7 indeterminate parts of speech per section. This can in part be explained because the law contained very long sections that amended other laws (notably the *Proceeds of Crime Act 2002*). But this does not diminish the likelihood of this law being difficult to interpret. As an example, take section 2, that sets out the use of "Unexplained wealth orders" and empowers courts in the following terms:

Table 5.1 Increased legislative output

Decade	*Sum of sections*	*Sum of word length*
1950s	91	17,085
1960s	294	74,179
1970s	513	153,223
1980s	2106	587,211
1990s	1308	408,980
2000s	2753	751,788
2010s	1444	549,932
Average statute	73	21,730
Standard deviation	91	26,492
Minimum	2 (*Restriction Of Offensive Weapons Act 1959, Sexual Offences Act 1993*)	94 (*Sexual Offences Act 1993*)
Maximum	462 (*Proceeds Of Crime Act 2002*)	120,190 (*Highways Act 1980*)
Total	8509	2,542,398

> Application for interim freezing order (1) This section applies where the High Court makes an unexplained wealth order in respect of any property. (2) The court may make an interim freezing order in respect of the property if the court considers it necessary to do so for the purposes of avoiding the risk of any recovery order that might subsequently be obtained being frustrated.

This legislation empowers courts to act with discretion "in respect of any property... [when] the court considers it necessary to do so". This in fact is an example of deliberate judicialisation, orchestrated by politicians. Most UK legislation, when enabling law and policymaking, does so for the benefit of the government and quasi-governmental entities. Figs. 5.1 and 5.2 describe quantitative findings from machine reading all post-war criminal justice legislation.

Figure 5.1 describes a sharp increase in indeterminate parts of speech per section in the 1970s, followed by a quadrupling in the quantity of law enacted in the 1980s. Figure 5.2 shows that the total number of indeterminate parts of speech enacted (adjectives, adverbs, conjunctions, indeterminate modal verbs, and enabling verbs) shot up from 14,004 in the 1970s to 53,500 in the 1980s. There was a decrease in the 1990s, followed by a further spike post-millennium to 61,105 indeterminate

Table 5.2 Increased legislative indeterminacy

Decade	*Average of adjectives/section*	*Average of conjunctions/section*	*Average of indeterminate modal verbs/section*	*Average of enabling verbs/section*	*Average of compound indeterminacies/section*
1950s	4.05	10.83	1.38	0.29	16.56
1960s	7.17	9.33	1.36	0.25	18.11
1970s	9.74	14.69	1.72	0.40	26.56
1980s	8.42	12.30	1.76	0.34	22.81
1990s	8.26	11.47	1.80	0.45	21.98
2000s	8.95	10.85	1.74	0.60	22.14
2010s	13.32	14.13	2.31	0.80	30.56
Averages statute	9.05	12.05	1.79	0.49	23.38
Standard deviation	4.32	4.86	0.95	0.39	9.61
Min	0.00	1.50	0.23	0.00	3.75 (*Tattooing of Minors Act 1969*)
Max	30.71	29.61	6.44	1.93	68.69 (*Criminal Finances Act 2017*)

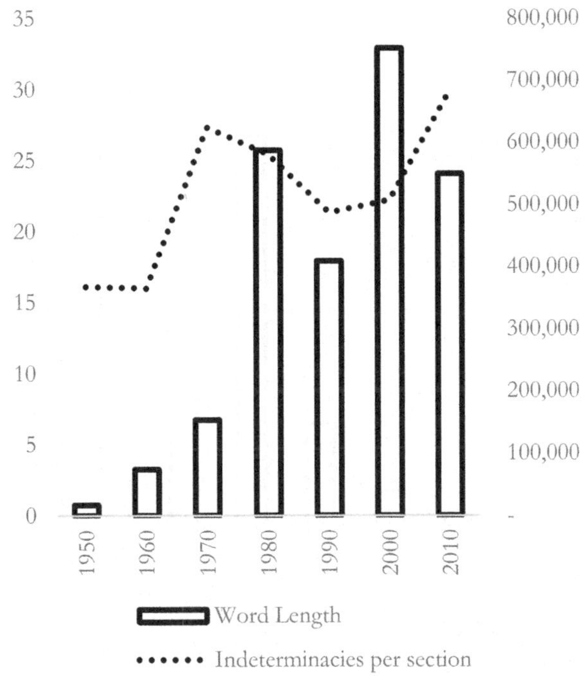

Fig. 5.1 Comparison of changes in indeterminacy (primary *y*-axis) and word length (secondary *y*-axis) in all criminal justice legislation 1950 2020 (*Source* Author's creation)

parts of speech. There was another decrease in the 2010s, but with 43,194 indeterminate parts of speech across all criminal justice law, that decade saw thirty times the number of indeterminate words as compared with the 1950s (1464 parts of speech).

In all, 2.5 million words of criminal justice legislation were machine read. That is equivalent to more than three copies of the King James Bible. With the increased indeterminacies of language, we would expect wider interpretative spaces for judges. As a former Supreme Court Justice, Lord Toulson, testified (Ormerod and Laird 2015, 19):

> To a worryingly large extent, statutory law is not practically accessible today, even to the courts whose constitutional duty it is to interpret and enforce it.

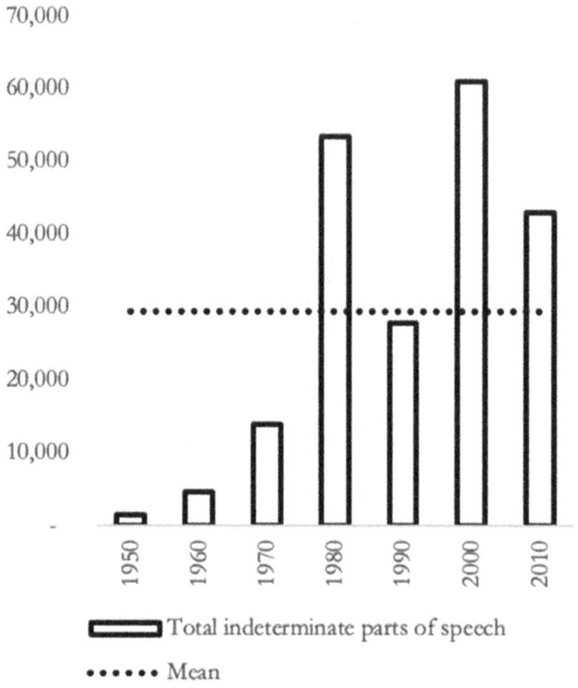

Fig. 5.2 Total indeterminacies (number of coded parts of speech) in all criminal justice legislation 1950–2020 (*Source* Author's creation)

In some cases, modern legislation was enacted to make targeted improvements to judge-made common law. For example, under common law, the survivor of a suicide pact was convicted of murder. The last person to be so charged was hanged in 1944.[13] The *Homicide Act 1957* softened the position, stating that if a defendant had a settled intent of dying as a pact, but failed to, then they were guilty of manslaughter. In this case, legislation introduced texture to otherwise arbitrary law.[14] Nonetheless, the sophistication of this statutory scheme still enables judges and juries to determine intent.

[13] *R v. Croft* [1944] 1KB 295.

[14] See, for example, *(Nicklinson) v. Ministry of Justice (CNK Alliance Ltd intervening) (R (AM) v. Director of Public Prosecutions (CNK Alliance Ltd intervening), Nicklinson v. Ministry of Justice)* 12 Mar 2012 [2012] EWHC 304 (QB).

Ironically, judges themselves used common law to rule that statute law would be the sole source of newly defined criminal offences. This is ironic in so far as judges used common law to rule that common law is subservient to statute law. The case, referenced above, was *Knuller v. Director of Public Prosecutions* in 1973.[15] As a precedent, it was then applied to settle a 2007 case concerning anti-Iraq War protests, and how the term "offence" was to be interpreted in s.68(2) of the *Criminal Justice and Public Order Act 1994*.[16] One of the judges hearing that case, Lord Hoffmann, made plain the balance of powers as regards criminal law:

> New domestic offences should in my opinion be debated in Parliament, defined in a statute and come into force on a prescribed date. They should not creep into existence as a result of an international consensus to which only the executive of this country is a party.[17]

And this was not just Lord Hoffman's opinion, but that of the entire court. As such, courts have themselves made plain that Parliament is solely responsible for developing new criminal offences, and it has been very busy in so doing since the war. The consequent role of judges is to settle disputes as to what Parliament intended. A further irony, therefore, is that although statute law has supplanted common law in creating offences, this does not mean that judges have lost policy power in determining the scope of laws. The sheer quantity of statute law has increased interpretative demands on the bench. These demands, at their most basic, constitute definitional questions as to what the law means and how individual concepts fit into a wider scheme.

Definitional—Subtextual Changes

Text adapts to changes in subtext, and vice versa. Subtextual shifts are occasioned by changes to (at least) technology, power balances, and time horizons. Terms such as "equal", for example, are understood very differently in the twenty-first century, because technology makes inequalities more easily observable, because material power is more equally

[15] [1973] A.C. 435.

[16] *R v. Jones* [2007] 1 A.C. 136.

[17] Ibid., para 62.

distributed, and because expectations are that progress to equality will proceed more quickly. Especially rapid changes to meaning are associated with social and culture ructions, brought on by wars, economic crises, climate crises, and, more recently, pandemics. Words such as "assisted",[18] "recklessly",[19] "riotously",[20] and "terrorism" were reinterpreted by courts as appellants claimed their meaning had shifted since the laws containing these words were promulgated. Nonetheless, the expectation is that judges will interpret new laws by drawing on existing law and precedent, and this will mostly favour the stronger litigant. In other words, judicialisation of subtext is unusual, as judges defer to those with an electoral mandate as being better placed to interpret contemporary usage of words.

In this section, we will see that, even in cases where a loss will be devastating for the weaker litigant, courts often defer to interpretations from legislators and policy executives. Courts even accepted that a man could trick his wife into an unwanted miscarriage, and did so by relying on a narrow reading of law. The point being, that despite shifting subtextual sands, appeal courts will defer to legislators by narrowly defining language, unless the indeterminacy in law encourages a rethink. We will start by describing cases of strict construction, and end this section looking at when (and why) more expansive interpretations are admitted in court.

There is near constant pressure on courts to adapt the meaning of old laws to new scenarios. This pressure comes most often from non-state actors. The British Government is relatively unconstrained by constitutional limits, and can bring in new legislation with few veto players able to intervene. This means that the state will rarely seek new interpretations of language in court, as they can obtain as much in Parliament with greater efficiency and efficacy. And, as such, when semantics are the subject of contestation, it will most often be the weaker litigant who seeks to expand a concept, adapt its scope, adapt its demographic applicability, or adapt its

[18] *R (Conway) v. Secretary of State for Justice (Humanists UK intervening)* 5 Oct 2017 [2017] EWHC 2447 (Admin).

[19] *O (A Child) v. Rhodes (Rhodes v. OPO)* 20 May 2015 [2015] UKSC 32.

[20] *Mitsui Sumitomo Insurance Co (Europe) Ltd v. Mayor's Office for Policing and Crime (Royal & Sun Alliance Insurance plc v. Mayor's Office for Policing and Crime, Lace International Ltd v. Mayor's Office for Policing and Crime)* 12 Sep 2013 [2013] EWHC 2734 (Comm).

connectivity to other rules of law. When courts deny expansive interpretations, like these, they are therefore, most often, ruling in favour of the state. And this happens even in cases where an injustice is consequent on a narrow use of language.

Sometimes the weaker litigant is weak in the sense not only of relative material disadvantage, but also by lacking public or political support. Suspected terrorists, for example, are usually despised by all but their acolytes, and could only realistically be protected by democratically unaccountable courts. But even courts have very infrequently gone against the state's counter-terrorism measures, even when those measures were couched in indeterminate language. For instance, is supporting an insurgency an act of terrorism? When a British man uploaded videos to the internet of insurgent attacks on coalition forces in Iraq and Afghanistan, he claimed he was not inciting terrorist violence, but national self-defence.[21] By his perception, terrorists (as defined by the *Terrorism Act 2006*) could not include freedom fighters resisting international invasion. At the Court of Appeal, his conviction for terrorism offences was affirmed, because it was ruled that there was no basis in international or domestic law justifying his argument. It was nonetheless conceded that changes to *opinio juris* may in future describe insurgency violence as a legitimate act of self-defence, but that day had not yet come. The court therefore explicitly noted the interplay of subtext and textual interpretation. As circumstances change, so too do the meanings of words. But, established meaning is not lightly discarded by courts.

In a related case brought to the Supreme Court, two appellants claimed that encouraging violent overthrow of the International Security Assistance Force (ISAF) in Afghanistan was not unlawful.[22] Again, the court took advantage of their independence from politics to reach a nuanced judgement, that nonetheless vindicated the UK government's strict interpretation. The court remitted both cases for rehearing, thereby giving the litigants another bite at the cherry, but they guided lower courts to adopt a narrow and domestic definition of terrorism, in recognition of the fact that the term enjoys no global consensus as to its meaning. The court also determined the appropriate balance of proof needed. In

[21] R v. Gul (Mohammed) [2012] 1 WLR 3432, CA.

[22] DD (Afghanistan) v. Secretary of State for the Home Department [2012] UKSC 54; [2013] 1 AC 745; [2012] 3 WLR 1263; Case details, SC(E).

English criminal law, the defendant must be guilty "beyond a reasonable doubt". But the offence here was in relation to article 1F of the *Refugees' Convention*, which states that there must be "serious reasons for considering" a breach. The court ruled that "serious reasons" was stronger than "reasonable grounds", but that there was no requirement for satisfaction "beyond a reasonable doubt". The court therefore used a variety of subtextual sources to determine a burden of proof that suited the government and was to the disadvantage of the defendants.

Nuance in these judgements was a consequence of indeterminacies in the concept of "terrorism". In other cases, however, the language of statute law is plain, and, despite pressure to stretch a meaning in line with principles of justice, the courts refuse. When, for example, do 24 weeks of pregnancy elapse? In a 2019 High Court case, judges were encouraged by appellants to acknowledge that the twenty-fourth week meant 24 weeks + 0 days, not 23 weeks + 6 days as understood by the government.[23] The dispute came down to language in section 1 of the *Abortion Act 1967*, as amended:

> (1) ... a person shall not be guilty of an offence under the law relating to abortion when... the pregnancy has not exceeded its twenty-fourth week.

The Secretary of State sought to clarify when, precisely, the time for a legal abortion elapsed, and wrote a letter to practitioners of the effect that after midnight at 23 weeks and 6 days the pregnancy had "exceeded" the allowable window. A mathematician might take issue with a proof that $24 + 0 = 24 >$, but, when considered as fractions of a day, it makes more sense to conclude, as the court did, that 24 days plus some minutes is indeed in excess of 24 days. Similarly constrained was the Court of Appeal's decision in the 2010 case of *R v. Ahmed*.[24] The defendant had taken his three months pregnant wife for an abortion she did not want. Unable to speak English, she had no idea what procedure was to be administered, until a nurse was able to explain the situation to her in Urdu. The husband was charged under section 59 of the *Offences against the Person Act 1861* with "procuring a miscarriage". He was so convicted

[23] *R (British Pregnancy Advisory Service) v. Secretary of State for Health and Social Care* 5 Jun 2019 [2019] EWHC 1397 (Admin).

[24] 29 Jul 2010 [2010] EWCA Crim 1949.

but appealed, successfully, against his conviction. His appeal focussed on the interpretation of "thing" in the 1861 Act:

> Whosoever shall unlawfully supply or procure any poison or other noxious thing, or any instrument or thing whatsoever, knowing that the same is intended to be unlawfully used or employed with intent to procure the miscarriage of any woman... shall be liable... to be kept in penal servitude.

The defendant made his case that, whilst he had instigated an unwanted abortion, he had not procured the items (things) needed to administer the termination. Quite how distressing it must have been for a mother to be misled into an abortion, and for that to be legal, is an ethical question beyond these pages. What is pertinent here is how restrained the courts were in applying a strict construction of "thing", even though its understanding in 2010 differed from 150 years earlier. A further pair of examples where interpretation was not stretched in court concerned the adverb "substantially". This word has interesting connotations of scale and importance that are volatile in response to changes in technology and social norms. Specifically at issue was section 2(1)(b) of the *Homicide Act 1957* as amended by section 52 of the *Coroners and Justice Act 2009:*

> A person ("D") who kills or is a party to the killing of another is not to be convicted of murder if D was suffering from an abnormality of mental functioning which—(b) substantially impaired D's ability to do one or more of the things mentioned in subsection (1A).

Substantially could be interpreted in any combination of the following three ways—(i) substantially is anything more than minimally, (ii) substantially means maximally impaired, and (iii) substantially is a spectrum to be determined according to the case facts. In the 2014 Court of Appeal case, *R v. Golds*, at issue was whether the trial judge had erred in not defining "substantially" for the jury's benefit.[25] Instead the judge had allowed the jury to interpret as they would every day. This, it was ruled on appeal, was an acceptable direction, given that numerous precedents had rendered the adverb as closest to (ii) in the options listed above—substantially means maximally, as would commonly be understood. Rather than take control

[25] 02 May 2014 [2014] EWCA Crim 748. This decision was later affirmed by the UK Supreme Court in [2016] UKSC 61.

of the dictionary, the courts deferred to the popular participation mechanism of jury consideration. In a 2016 case at the High Court—*Henderson v. Dorset Healthcare University NHS Foundation Trust*—a spectral understanding of substantially (as in (iii) above) was rejected.[26] Again the maximal understanding of substantially was taken as the correct interpretation. In this case, the defendant had been convicted of manslaughter when she stabbed her mother to death. The defendant claimed she was substantially impaired by a severe psychiatric disorder. The dispute came down to whether she could claim damages from a negligent health trust. But, to do so would require the quantum of negligence to be calculated as a function of how substantially impaired she had been. The court instead ruled that only a monist or unitary—non-spectral—rendering of the adverb was law.

There are cases where a stretched meaning is desired by the state, despite the relative ease with which new legislation can be enacted in the UK. Let us start with laughing gas. Nitrous oxide has become a popular recreational drug, yet not one who's popularity was not anticipated by statutes on psychoactive substances. Central to two cases was section 7 of the *Psychoactive Substances Act 2016:*

> 7 (1) A person commits an offence if– (a) the person is in possession of a psychoactive substance,

The 2016 Act had been deliberately drafted as a catch-all, to regulate the possession and supply of so-called "designer" narcotics. But, in the case of *R v. Rochester*, it was contended by the defence that nitrous oxide was not, in fact, psychoactive, and that possession of 165 canisters was inconsequential.[27] This claim was dismissed by the Court of Appeal, who ruled that even an indirect psychoactive effect was within the remit envisaged by Parliament. In another case, claimants sought to define nitrous oxide as a medicinal product and therefore perfectly legal to possess and supply.[28] But, given that the defendants had no therapeutic aspiration for

[26] 19 Dec 2016 [2016] EWHC 3275 (QB).

[27] 17 Aug 2018 [2018] EWCA Crim 1936.

[28] *R v. Chapman (Sonny) (R v. Tesfay (Abel), R v. Chroussis (Nicholas), R v. Bryce (Armande))* 1 Nov 2017 [2017] EWCA Crim 1743.

their holdings, their interpretation was judged to be about as far-fetched as claiming that street heroine was in fact medical-grade diamorphine.

These are examples where new narcotic fads adapted the definition of "psychoactive" in law. In many cases, text and subtext are reconciled by developing ligatures between rules of law, thereby enhancing the law's integrity (Dworkin 1986). This involves counsel digging into historical laws and cases to find patterns in language use. And, increasingly, resort is made to the proceedings of Parliament (published in Hansard) and the Explanatory Notes of Bills as means to assess how legislators interpreted the words used. Assiduous detective work runs counter to a claim that judges wontly stretch meanings, unless, that is, we are to believe that they are desperately trying to cover their tracks. It seems more likely that judges are deliberately trying to understand how text reconciles with subtext, and are not engaging in an elaborate conspiracy to control language for their own benefit. Two cases are exemplary—one concerning assisted suicide, the other turned on the meaning of "cheating". In a 2012 High Court case, it was necessary to ascertain if encouraging suicide over the internet was an offence.[29] Section 2 of the *Suicide Act 1961* made it an offence to assist in another's self-annihilation, but had not anticipated the internet as the medium of encouragement. This section was then amended by section 59 of the *Coroners and Justice Act 2009*, in order to update the language. Barristers made reference to Hansard in order to explain what Parliament had—through the voice of the Bill's ministerial sponsor—likely intended[30]:

> Both the Law Commission and an independent review identified confusion about the scope of the law on assisted suicide ... [Section 59] does not substantively change the law, but it does simplify and modernise the language of section 2 of the Suicide Act 1961 to increase public understanding and to reassure people that the provision applies as much to actions on the Internet as to actions off-line.[31]

[29] *R (Nicklinson) v. Ministry of Justice (CNK Alliance Ltd intervening) (R (AM) v. Director of Public Prosecutions (CNK Alliance Ltd intervening), Nicklinson v. Ministry of Justice)* 12 Mar 2012 [2012] EWHC 304 (QB).

[30] Reference in *ratio decidendi* to Hansard was first made in the case of *Pepper v. Hart* [1992] 3 WLR 103. Whilst the courts are tasked with ascertaining the mischief Parliament had intended to manage through its legislation, it was customary to infer intent from the final Act, not the utterances of individual members.

[31] Hansard (HC Debates), 26 January 2009, col 35.

In a 2017 case,[32] the Supreme Court was tasked with defining what cheating meant, and whether the accused's state of mind ought to be determinative. A professional gambler had won £7.7m playing cards in a London casino. He had used a technique of observing minute disfigurations on cards, by which he could tell their face values as the deck cycled. The man claimed he did not intend to cheat and was therefore liable to his winnings. The casino called on the Supreme Court to narrow an existing subjective understanding of cheating (where intent matters),[33] to a more objective test as to whether a neutral observer would cry foul. The highest court obliged the casino and denied the winnings. In doing so, they narrowed the definition of cheating and relied on Explanatory Notes to a parliamentary Bill prepared by the sponsoring Department (DCMS):

> [t]he word 'cheating' is not defined [in subsection 42(1) of the *Gambling Act 2005*] but has its normal everyday meaning.[34]

Again, when asked to define words, the courts here sought integrity in rules of law, and deferred to Parliament. But this very concept of "normal everyday meaning" begs questions as to who controls the shared interpretation, and how it can be identified. Courts have been clear on this point as well—where interpretation is indeterminate, with no means of resolution according to rules of law, it is up to Parliament to settle the meaning through the democratic process. This is the case, even when judges feel an injustice has been done. Legal texts are often described as "living instruments" and it is up to legislators to prune away any dead matter. An often-quoted dictum of Lord Bingham describes the constitutional position of judges in these terms[35]:

> There is, I think, no inconsistency between the rule that statutory language retains the meaning it had when Parliament used it and the rule that a statute is always speaking. If Parliament, however long ago, passed an Act applicable to dogs, it could not properly be interpreted to apply to cats;

[32] *Ivey v. Genting Casinos (UK) Ltd (trading as Crockfords Club)* [2017] UKSC 67.

[33] *R v. Ghosh* [1982] EWCA Crim 2.

[34] https://www.legislation.gov.uk/ukpga/2005/19/notes/division/5/3/7/1/7, accessed on 28 February 2021.

[35] *R (Quintavalle) v. Secretary of State for Health* [2003] UKHL 13, [2003] 2 AC 687 at 9.

> but it could properly be held to apply to animals which were not regarded as dogs when the Act was passed but are so regarded now. The meaning of 'cruel and unusual punishments' has not changed over the years since 1689, but many punishments which were not then thought to fall within that category would now be held to do so.

In this vein, a much-contested adverb is "reasonably", which is interpreted very differently depending on whose reason is taken as a yardstick. Mrs Owens went all the way to the UK Supreme Court to seek a divorce from her octogenarian husband, on the basis of language in subsection 1(2)(b) of the *Matrimonial Causes Act 1971*:

> [Mr Owens] has behaved in such a way that [Mrs Owens] cannot reasonably be expected to live with [him]

A so-called "no fault divorce" was not historically available. Mr Owens had not acted in any particular manner that could objectively be described as unreasonable, but the totality of his actions had subjectively led Mrs Owens to want out of the marriage. As Lady hale put it:

> I have found this a very troubling case. It is not for us to change the law laid down by Parliament—our role is only to interpret and apply the law that Parliament has given us.[36]

Lord Wilson similarly encouraged legislators to step up:

> Parliament may wish to consider whether to replace a law which denies to Mrs Owens any present entitlement to a divorce in the above circumstances.[37]

This dialogue between court and Parliament led to a legislative amendment in the *Divorce, Dissolution and Separation Act 2020*, which created no fault divorces for the first time in English law. There are more formal mechanisms by which language can be updated by Parliament upon the directions of a senior court. Section 4 of the *Human Rights Act 1998* (HRA) empowers courts to declare an incompatibility between primary

[36] *Owens v. Owens* [2018] UKSC 41 at 46.

[37] Ibid at 45.

legislation and the European Convention on Human Rights (ECHR). Subsection 4(6) of the Act nonetheless makes plain that:

> A declaration under this section ('a declaration of incompatibility')—(a) does not affect the validity, continuing operation or enforcement of the provision in respect of which it is given; and (b) is not binding on the parties to the proceedings in which it is made.

The section 4 power is literally declaratory, and not substantive. "So far as it is possible to do so", courts may use section 3 of the 1998 Act to ensure that "primary legislation and subordinate legislation [is] read and given effect [to] in a way which is compatible with the Convention rights". Uses of sections 3 and 4 HRA have been analysed in greater detail elsewhere.[38] The important point to note here is that use of section 3 must not alter any "fundamental feature" of the legislation.[39] It is not, therefore, an unfettered legislative power, and its use is reviewable by Parliament. For example, in a 2016 Supreme Court case, a lady being evicted for rent arrears sought to rely on her rights to a private and family life (Article 8 ECHR), and encouraged the court to "read down" mandatory repossession language in section 21(4) of the *Housing Act 1988*.[40] Her case, in essence, was that as a lifelong sufferer of psychiatric and behavioural difficulties, it would not be proportionate to evict her, as it would risk her becoming homeless. The justices acknowledged that using section 3 HRA could ensure a more balanced use of the 1988 Act's repossession power. But they also ruled that this was not possible in a case such as this where the landlord was a private entity. The *Human Rights Act* does not, bar exceptional circumstances,[41] apply "horizontally" between private litigants. It only applies "vertically" between state and citizenry.[42]

[38] For a detailed analysis of the *Human Rights Act*, see Williams 2018.

[39] *Re W (children: care plan) Re S (children: care plan)* [2002] UKHL 10 All ER (D) 212 (Mar) at 40.

[40] *McDonald (by her litigation friend Duncan J McDonald) (Appellant) v. McDonald and others (Respondents)* [2016] UKSC 28.

[41] Under Sect. 6 HRA, the court itself is a public authority bound by the ECHR and can apply convention rights between disputing private parties.

[42] Ibid at para 62.

Article 8 ECHR is a *bête noire* of those who see human rights (in particular rights administered by a continental court) as anti-democratic. The right to a private and family life is invoked most frequently in immigration and asylum claims, which, until recent reforms, made up over 75% of all judicial review cases (Williams 2017). The perception, held even by past and serving Home Secretaries, is that Article 8 has become something of a trump card, used to prevent or delay immigration proceedings on flimsy grounds. There is substantial evidence against these specific criticisms. And, more generally, the HRA is not the law-making tool its critics claim it to be. There are substantive and procedural limitations against judges developing new legal language using the HRA. In substantive terms, the rights are old-fashioned, negative, and derivative of common law, from whence they largely emerged in 1950. The Convention Rights did not, therefore, make substantial changes to rules of law that were already long in the tooth by 1998. They did, however, make for more user-friendly procedures. Where, since 1966, British litigants could appeal against their state to the Strasbourg-based European Court of Human Rights, from 2000 Convention Rights could also be litigated at home. But there are significant limitations to their applicability. Only a "victim" may bring a claim,[43] and must do so within a year of the transgression occurring.[44] Nor does the HRA entitle litigants to substantial financial damages,[45] and it is therefore not an attractive option for litigant or counsel when compared to civil litigation strategies. And, ultimately, judicial powers in the HRA are utterly in subservience to Parliament, giving courts no co-equal status as is enjoyed by, for example, the US Supreme Court.

It is difficult to find cases where the HRA substantially frustrated government delivery of public goods. Even in counter-terrorism cases, there is simply no evidence that government policy was frustrated to an extent of rendering the country unsafe (Volcansek and Stack 2011). The complaints of Home Secretaries and others betray either a selection bias with regards to the cases considered, or a deliberate attempt to blame courts for problems in their own policies. An example of the courts deferring to state authority concerns the hugely controversial stop and search

[43] HRA s 7(1).

[44] HRA s 7(5)(a).

[45] HRA s 8.

powers available to police officers under section 60 of the *Criminal Justice and Public Order Act 1994*.[46] A young black woman was stopped and had her bag searched whilst riding a bus. The search had allegedly been undertaken because there was heightened gang activity in London at that specific time, and 17 hours of enhanced searching powers were authorised for police. In addition to which, the young lady appeared nervous when confronted by the officers. It is perhaps unsurprising that the claimant appeared nervous, but she had no offensive weapons in her possession and made a judicial review claim that her Article 8 right to privacy had been breached. The Metropolitan Police contended instead that no laws had been broken. They specifically submitted that their powers to search were "necessary in a democratic society for the prevention of disorder or crime" and these powers had, in this case, been administered proportionately. The Supreme Court (affirming the Divisional Court and Court of Appeal) duly dismissed the young lady's claim.

In another case regarding stop and search, the European Court felt it had to clarify its preferred interpretation of Article 8, in reaction to a UK court's seeming acquiescence to state power. In the British hearing of *R (Gillan) v. Commissioner of Police of the Metropolis*, two individuals were stopped and searched under the *Terrorism Act 2000* for "Articles concerned in terrorism" after they attended an arms fair with intent to protest.[47] Lord Bingham spoke for his fellow Law Lords (then the highest appeal court) in downplaying any deprivation of liberty or intrusion:

> the [stop and search] procedure will ordinarily be relatively brief. The person stopped will not be arrested, handcuffed, confined or removed to any different place. I do not think, in the absence of special circumstances, such a person should be regarded as being detained in the sense of confined or kept in custody, but more properly of being detained in the sense of kept from proceeding or kept waiting. There is no deprivation of liberty.[48]

The case made it to the Strasbourg court, where the judges could not entirely endorse Bingham's assessment:

[46] *R (Roberts) v. Comr of Police of the Metropolis* [2015] UKSC 79.

[47] [2006] UKHL 12.

[48] Ibid at para 25.

> The court observes that although the length of time during which each applicant was stopped and searched did not in either case exceed 30 minutes, during this period the applicants were entirely deprived of any freedom of movement. They were obliged to remain where they were and submit to the search and if they had refused they would have been liable to arrest, detention at a police station and criminal charges. This element of coercion is indicative of a deprivation of liberty within the meaning of article 5.1. In the event, however, the court is not required finally to determine this question in the light of its findings below in connection with article 8 of the Convention.[49]

As is typical of British cases at the Strasbourg court, nothing substantially happened. Even the much maligned Strasbourg ruling on the voting rights of prisoners led to no changes in UK law.[50] There is, therefore, a conspicuous gap between the perceived and real political power of UK and European judges. Perhaps the most confounding fact against any charge of judges being politicians in robes, is how accountable each court is within a highly rule-bound institutional system.

Systemic–Intertextual Changes

Figure 5.3 offers a schematic description of UK domestic courts and their interrelationships. This figure omits international courts to which the UK is answerable via treaties (such as the European Court of Human Rights, or the International Criminal Court). It also omits the supranational Court of Justice of the European Union (CJEU), which could enforce rulings above UK courts up to the conclusion of British withdrawal from the EU in January 2020. Even this simplified schematic nonetheless shows there is institutional complexity that diminishes the agency of individual judges. Justice, in short, is a team sport. There are, specifically, multiple lines of delegation and accountability, making for a web of veto players. Crowning this schematic could have been Parliament, to whom the courts bear ultimate responsibility. Hence, individual judges making decisions based on their own preferences is implausibly unlikely to succeed, unless their amendments to the *status quo* are acceptable to a complex and disaggregated ecosystem of power.

[49] *Gillan and Quinton v. United Kingdom* (2010) 50 EHRR at 57.

[50] *Hirst v. United Kingdom (No 2)* (2005) ECHR 681.

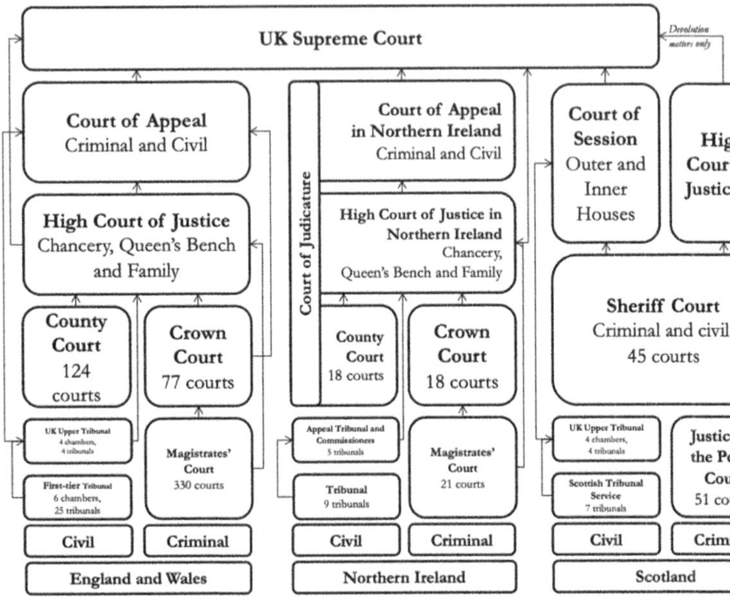

Fig. 5.3 UK courts schematic (*Source* Author's creation)

Cases where judges rule against the state are not only statistically improbable, therefore, but depend on a there being a cause that unites a web of actors with unaligned preferences. And there are no formal mechanisms to aggregate preferences. There are informal means of preference accommodation—such as socialisation into professional patterns of thought (Griffith 1977)—but the legal profession is ultimately subservient to Parliament in all matters. Drawing back to the central interest in textuality, we are here interrogating how inter-textual divergences (between interpretations of different courts, or between courts and Parliament) are reconciled to a single authoritative interpretation. This section will move up the legal hierarchy—starting with courts, then to devolved legislatures, and finally to international institutions.

An essential and precursor point to make is that judges are accountable for their decisions. Whilst there are many cases decided by individuals acting alone, there is always the possibility of an appeal, engaging the mechanisms of oversight described in Fig. 5.3. Even cases that are superficially easy to resolve can progress by stages up the judicial hierarchy to the very apex. A case concerning when a prisoner could be released is a clear example of this. In *R (Noone) v. Governor of Drake Hall Prison*,[51] Lord Phillips opened his judgement in the following arresting terms:

> The road to hell is paved with good intentions. In this case the good intentions were to introduce mandatory rehabilitation for very short term prisoners by coupling time spent in custody with a release period under licence. This was known as 'custody plus'. Hell is a fair description of the problem of statutory interpretation caused by transitional provisions introduced when custody plus had to be put on hold because the resources needed to implement the scheme did not exist.[52]

In this case, a woman had been convicted of multiple offences of theft with sentences set to run both consecutively and concurrently, to a total of 27 months. Early release on license was available for sentences of less than 12 months under the *Criminal Justice Act 1991*. For sentences of less than 12 months imposed with concurrent or consecutive sentences of more than 12 months, the *Criminal Justice Act 2003* was intended to determine early release under so-called "Custody Plus". But the resources for this were not made available, and the critical sections were not brought into effect, leaving the prison governor unsure as to how to calculate the early release of Rebecca Noone. The judge at first instance ruled against the governor and Secretary of State and ordered a recalculation. The Court of Appeal then reversed that decision, and the Supreme Court then reversed that decision and reaffirmed the first ruling. This back and forth led to a defeat for the government, but on an issue where there was considerable indeterminacy in the law, and where the system constrained the autonomy of individual judges. In basic numerical terms, the case drew in a larger number of judges at each level of the hierarchy, culminating with five Justices of the Supreme Court.

In the case of *Hague v. Deputy Governor of Parkhurst Prison and others*, three courts (Divisional Court, Court of Appeal, and Supreme Court) were asked whether prisoners could be falsely imprisoned and thereby sue for damages.[53] It may seem an odd consideration, but in an

[51] [2010] UKSC 30.

[52] Ibid at para 1.

[53] *Hague v. Deputy Governor of Parkhurst Prison and others; Weldon v. Home Office* [1991] 3 All ER 733.

entirely separate case, Lord Justice Ackner raised the following thought experiment[54]:

> ...it must be possible to conceive of hypothetical cases in which the conditions of detention are so intolerable as to render the detention unlawful and thereby provide a remedy to the prisoner in damages for false imprisonment. A person lawfully detained in a prison cell would, in our judgment, cease to be so lawfully detained if the conditions in that cell were such as to be seriously prejudicial to his health if he continued to occupy it, eg because it became and remained seriously flooded, or contained a fractured gas pipe allowing gas to escape into the cell. We do not therefore accept as an absolute proposition that, if detention is initially lawful, it can never become unlawful by reason of changes in the conditions of imprisonment.

This dictum was disapproved by the Supreme Court in *Hague*, effectively voiding its validity to decide future cases. The Supreme Court ruled that isolating a prisoner could be unlawful, but this did not raise any possibility of damages from a private lawsuit, it was a breach of public law. The Court of Appeal had already ruled that the isolation of Hague was unlawful, but refused to grant a writ of certiorari to strike down the orders used for the isolation. Again, judges are part of a decision-making network. It is very difficult to act unilaterally, without running the risk of being disapproved and overturned.

Courts therefore communicate amongst themselves, but also must consider the systemic web of law-making authorities. How, for instance, should a court in England deal with a complainant from Northern Ireland who felt her access to an abortion had been denied, simply because of where in the UK she was from?[55] The Northern Ireland Assembly had at that stage not made provision in their devolved health care for abortions, on moral and religious grounds. It was possible for citizens of Northern Ireland to have an abortion in Great Britain, but at their own expense, and not through the NHS. The complainant felt this was not only a statutory breach of the *Abortion Act 1967*, but also breached rights to equality and privacy in the ECHR. The Supreme Court backed up rulings from two lower tribunals that the claimant and her mother had not made their

[54] *Middleweek v. Chief Constable of the Merseyside Police* [1990] 3 All ER 662 at 668.

[55] *R (on the application of A and B) (Appellants) v. Secretary of State for Health (Respondent)* [2017] UKSC 41.

case. There was dissent in the Court from Lady Hale and Lord Kerr (one of the Northern Irish Justices on the Supreme Court). Nonetheless, it was ruled that the Secretary of State for Health had:

> ...to afford respect to the democratic decision of the people of Northern Ireland; was entitled to have in mind the undeniable ability of Northern Irish women lawfully to travel to England and to purchase private abortion services there; and was entitled to decide not further to alter the consequences of the democratic decision by making such services available to them free of charge under the public scheme in England for which he was responsible.[56]

An extraordinary example of courts intervening in devolved matters is *Cadder v. HM Advocate* at the Supreme Court.[57] Since the formation of the Union in 1707, Scottish criminal law had never had a means of appeal outside of Scotland, until the *Human Rights Act 1998*. This finally made the apex court "supreme" in name and in reality. But, review of Scots criminal law in London is extremely rare. Nonetheless, in this case, Peter Cadder convinced the UK Supreme Court that his conviction in Scotland was unsafe, because he had been interviewed by police without a solicitor. The ruling against Scots criminal procedure threw into doubt any other convictions obtained on the basis of an unsupported police interview, of which there were estimated to be thousands.

A key role for the courts is therefore to act as a medium for communication between institutions. This makes sense if we assume the courts are applying rules of law equally across the entire system, rather than assuming judges are independent-minded and act on their own preferences. This communicative function is demonstrated not just intranationally, but also inter-nationally. For example, a case arose where two people contested the state's right to hold their biometric data indefinitely.[58] Both had been suspected of major crimes, but were later acquitted. Their DNA and fingerprints were nonetheless stored under provisions in the *Police and Criminal Evidence Act 1984*, as amended. The Divisional Court held in accordance with precedent and dismissed

[56] Lord Wilson at para 20.

[57] [2010] UKSC 43.

[58] *R (on the application of GC) v. The Commissioner of Police of the Metropolis* [2011] UKSC 21.

the appeal. They were acting according to their authority. But, they recognised that there was a near identical case decided on the opposite grounds at the European Court of Human Rights. Because of the clashing jurisdictions, the Divisional Court granted a "leap frog" certificate for the claimants to appeal straight to the Supreme Court, bypassing the Court of Appeal. On this appeal, the Justices were told that the Government intended to enact a Bill to rectify breaches of Article 8 ECHR in the retention of personal data. Given that, the Court was comfortable in overturning precedent and ruling that indefinite retention of data was in breach of human rights. Here we therefore see intersecting communication between Parliament and the European Court, mediated by the UK Supreme Court. It is to identifying such jurisdictional intersections that we now turn.

Prudential—Contextual Changes

A substantial constraint on any judge's behaviour, are their real and perceived inadequacies in assessing context. Where text, subtext, and inter-textual interpretations of law are their proverbial bread and butter, ascertaining the context within which these textual elements should operate is not a judge's strength. There are two prominent reasons for this: capacity and legitimacy. Courts are simply not well placed to aggregate social data. And, even when reliable briefs are provided to make up for this informational shortfall, courts typically lack legitimacy to determine an acceptable reading of context. As such, courts are often prudent in their jurisprudence. Meaning that they defer to actors with greater decision-making capacity, competence, or legitimacy (Strøm et al. 2003). The etymology of "jurisdiction" is the capacity to speak about the law—hence juris-*diction*. Courts limit themselves to this legal abstraction, and are less comfortable with ascertaining social facts. Which is perhaps most clearly evident from the reliance on juries to determine facts, with judges advising on the law. The implications of which are that courts will typically defer to others for interpreting context, where there is a doubt, and if that contextual data is essential to resolving a case. Let us start at the level of individual competence and expand up to the broadest institutional competences.

At an individual level, there are some state officials who can simply be expected to know best the context in which policy and law are enforced. Police officers are a prominent example. The abstract law concerning policing needs to be squared with the complex reality of day-to-day police work, and courts are poorly placed to speak to the latter. A tragic example involved the killing of a young black man in East London called Mark Duggan. He was shot dead by a police officer on the grounds that there was an "imminent threat" if he was not so violently engaged. His death sparked riots in London and elsewhere in England during the hot August of 2011. But an inquest and subsequent judicial review returned verdicts of "lawful killing".[59] Duggan's mother sought a judicial review of this verdict, claiming that a police officer's mistaken calculation of an "imminent threat" could not justify a conclusion of lawful killing. In its judgement, the High Court raised the epistemological difficulty of ascertaining a true belief[60]:

> In the result, for the purposes of the criminal law the necessity to respond to an imminent attack must be judged on the assumption that the facts were as the defendant believed them to be, whether or not mistaken, and if mistaken, whether or not the mistake was objectively reasonable.

In short, the defendant police officer was mistaken about the existence of a threat, but nonetheless entitled in law to believe it. And, beyond individuals, judges defer to institutions with greater competence in aggregating social facts and popular legitimacy. The constitutional subservience of judges to Parliament is set out perfectly in this dictum from Lord Bingham with regard to the ban on fox hunting:

> There are of course many... who do not consider that there is a pressing (or any) social need for the ban imposed by the [Hunting] Act [2004]. But after an intense debate a majority of the country's democratically-elected representatives decided otherwise. It is of course true that the existence of duly enacted legislation does not conclude the issue ... Here we are dealing with a law which is very recent and must ... be taken to reflect the conscience of a majority of the nation. The degree of respect to be shown to the considered judgment of a democratic assembly will vary according to the subject matter and the circumstances. But the present case seems to me pre-eminently one in which respect should be shown to what the House of Commons decided. The democratic process is liable to be subverted if, on

[59] *R (Duggan) v. North London Assistant Deputy Coroner* 14 Oct 2014 [2014] EWHC 3343 (Admin).

[60] Ibid at para 36.

> a question of moral and political judgment, opponents of the Act achieve through the courts what they could not achieve in Parliament.[61]

Bingham is careful not to rule out judicial oversight of enacted legislation *tout court*, but there is no enumerated power for British courts to nullify an Act of Parliament, even if an Act nullifies the courts. Ouster clauses, on that point, are a rarely used constitutional instrument whereby Parliament denies the courts a role in arbitrating disputes arising from policy. Barristers can find creative work-arounds when confronted with ouster clauses,[62] but not when the ousting language is plainly stated. One such example is section 67(8) of the *Regulation of Investigatory Powers Act 2000*:

> determinations, awards, orders and other decisions of the Tribunal (including decisions as to whether they have jurisdiction) shall not be subject to appeal or be liable to be questioned in any court.

This judicial ouster was softened by the subsequent enactment of the *Investigatory Powers Act 2016*, but this did not help Privacy International in their 2017 lawsuit. The group brought suit claiming that the Home Secretary had unrestrained power to allow for electronic surveillance by the Government Communications Headquarters (GCHQ). The court deferred to the institutional prerogative of ousting their jurisdiction. It would have been difficult to interpret the clear language of section 67(8) in any other way. A similar case regarding bulk surveillance was raised by the National Council for Civil Liberties in 2019.[63] In that case, reliance was placed on EU law and the ECHR, to, in effect, go over the heads of domestic authorities. This is therefore a case pertaining to all levels of authority to which judges may defer—the Home Secretary, Parliament, and international laws. To whom should the courts defer when different authorities are in contest? The answer for the courts was that (a) the authorities were not in fact contesting the interpretation, and that at any rate (b) the position of Parliament was to be followed:

[61] *R (Countryside Alliance) v. Attorney General* [2008] AC 719, para 45.

[62] *Anisminic Ltd v Foreign Compensation Commission* [1969] 2 AC 147.

[63] *R (National Council for Civil Liberties) v. Secretary of State for the Home Department (National Union of Journalists intervening)* 29 July 2019 [2019] EWHC 2057 (Admin).

> We can readily understand that the Claimant... and others in society have concerns about the existence of 'bulk' powers to obtain large amounts of data, much of which will be of no interest to the intelligence and security agencies. Similar concerns have been expressed both within and outside Parliament. Having had regard to those concerns, Parliament decided to enact the Investigatory Powers Act 2016 in the form which it did... The primary focus of the arguments before this Court has been on the ground that the 2016 Act does not contain sufficient safeguards against the risk of abuse of power and that, accordingly, it is inconsistent with the requirement that interference with human rights must be 'in accordance with the law'. For the reasons we have given above we do not accept those arguments.[64]

In some cases, the courts speak directly to their loss of voice. In cases of human trafficking, for example, it is no longer up to judges to determine whether an individual is being exploited, as per section 45(4)(b) *Modern Slavery Act 2015*. That fact-determining task is for a jury.

> Formerly, there was a lacuna in that regard, which the courts sought to fill by expanding somewhat the notion of abuse of process, which required the Judge to make relevant decisions of fact. That is no longer necessary, and cases to which the 2015 Act applies should proceed on the basis that they will be stayed if, but only if, an abuse of process as conventionally defined is found.[65]

The *Modern Slavery Act 2015* had, through clear and determinable language, denuded judicial discretion and patriated jurisdiction from the Convention on Actions Against Trafficking (Council of Europe) as well as the EU Directive on Preventing and Combating Trafficking in Human Beings. The point being that where politicians can aggregate their policy preferences around determinable language, there is no clear scope for judicial discretion.

[64] Ibid at para 394.

[65] *R v. DS* 28 Feb 2020 [2020] EWCA Crim 285 at para 40.

Influence-seeking—Transtextual Changes

Judges will engage creatively in interpreting legal texts under two conditions—where either the process of implementation or the substance of law is indeterminate. As demonstrated above, the language of criminal justice legislation has become increasingly indeterminate, thereby enabling judicialisation. When matters of procedure arise, and courts overrule other law-makers, it may be described as influence-seeking in line with Hodder-Williams's (1997) conceptualisation. But, in reality, the courts are not so much seeking influence as obtaining it. They do so by providing transtextual means of resolving textual indeterminacies. This means that other texts of an authoritative nature are used to flesh out the meaning of an uninterpreted text. Given there is no codified constitution in the UK, transtextual interpretation can be highly controversial, depending on which sources of law are considered authoritative. Ultimately, however, the courts are intervening to change how law is used, rather than what it says. This interdiction ranges from the most basic level of claiming a role for the courts, to intervening in how laws are implemented by bureaucracies. The effect of transtextual interpretation is usually to constrain the government rather than enable the judiciary. It is, therefore, a negative power.

Starting from where the courts assert their voice, we have already seen a case where ouster clauses were accepted in regards to secret intelligence surveillance. Typically, such clauses do not inhibit judicial oversight because, (a) they are insufficiently determinate in language to achieve such an outcome, and (b) they pertain to matters of lesser consequence than state security, meaning that the courts are less likely to be overruled if they decide against the government. The UK Supreme Court, for example, made a declaration under the *Human Rights Act 1998* that section 82(1) and Schedule 3 of the *Sexual Offences Act 2003* were incompatible with Article 8 of the ECHR.[66] A child of 11 committed a sexual crime of such seriousness that he was to be placed on the sex offenders' register for life, with no mechanism of review by a court. It was this lack of any review by a court or tribunal that was declared disproportionate to the otherwise legitimate aim of reducing sexual crimes. In this case, the transtext used was the common law and European Convention on Human Rights. Lord

[66] *F and Another, Regina (on The Application of) v. Secretary of State for The Home Department* [2010] UKSC 17.

Justice Dyson in the Court of Appeal, failed to find any domestic authorities that could provide justification for denying any review. Therefore, the courts sought authoritative texts that were able to provide meaning where legislation was indeterminate.

The government will find creative ways to oust the jurisdiction of courts when it suits their purposes. But, even in matters pertaining to security, the courts will not simply turn their face. A prominent example came with regard to UK involvement in a practice known as extraordinary rendition, whereby suspected terrorists were abducted to US facilities for interrogation. In a 2017 case, the British government sought immunity from judicial oversight of their involvement in rendering suspects to US detention facilities, where they were subsequently tortured.[67] The Supreme Court held that there was no basis in common law, statute law, or international treaty to claim immunity, given that the UK was the defendant in a British lawsuit. State immunity only applies when a foreign power is in such a circumstance. It might be a strange jurisdictional development should the British government be able to claim immunity from the machinations of its own justice system.

But the most sacrosanct questions of jurisdiction concern the relationship between Parliament and the courts. According to the *Bill of Rights 1688* there is no recourse to the courts for anything done in parliamentary business. This privilege has meant that Members of Parliament are immune from prosecution or lawsuit for anything done as part of their legislative business. It would be impossible, for example, for an MP to be sued for anything said on the floor of the House of Commons. Does it, however, apply to anything done within the environs of the Palace of Westminster? In the aftermath of the 2009 expenses scandal, three MPs claimed that their fraudulent use of parliamentary expenses could not be prosecuted under the *Theft Act 1968*, on account of their privilege as parliamentarians.[68] The Supreme Court dismissed this casuistry and remitted all cases back to the Crown Court for trial, whereupon the men were all sent to prison. Lord Phillips, then president of the Supreme Court, dismissed their arguments in the following terms:

[67] *Belhaj and another (Respondents) v. Straw and others (Appellants); Rahmatullah (No 1) (Respondent) v. Ministry of Defence and another (Appellants)* [2017] UKSC 3.

[68] *R v. Chaytor and others* [2010] UKSC 52.

> The Theft Act extends to England and Wales. In other words, it forms part of the law of England and Wales. The Houses of Parliament and their dépendances are in England and so the criminal law of England applies to what is done there. The most famous illustration of this elementary point is, perhaps, the murder of the Prime Minister, Mr Spencer Percival, in the lobby of the House of Commons in 1812. John Bellingham was arrested, prosecuted, tried for murder at the Old Bailey, convicted and executed—all according to the common law of England. If the assassin had been a fellow MP, then by the law of England he too would have committed murder. The same would have applied if the MP had assassinated the Prime Minister in the chamber of the House of Commons. Less dramatically, if a Member of Parliament were to steal money from a fellow member's wallet in a room in the House of Commons or from the till in the Members' Dining Room, he would commit theft under section 1 of the Theft Act 1968.[69]

In short, parliamentary privilege does not enable members to become petty thieves. Even more controversial than the courts claiming a right to speak, are cases where the courts tell the government what to do. Such cases are rare, but when they arise can elicit a degree of indignation from elected officials who have the legitimacy and accountability to make decisions on public policy. To cover themselves from charges of impropriety, courts engage a textual indeterminacy and ensure their decision is such that they are unlikely to be overruled. For example, in a 2016 case it was disputed as to whether or not more should have been done by the Home Office to protect a boy brought to the UK from Vietnam by human traffickers. The Home Office contended that he was a man, rather than a boy, but the Refugee Council ascertained that he was in fact 15. The Home Office released him from detention but put in place no safeguards against him being re-trafficked.[70] At the Court of Queen's Bench, it was ruled that this decision went against the "the credible suspicion threshold" set out by the European Court of Human Rights in their jurisprudence an Article 4. The concept of a "credible suspicion" is highly indeterminate, and there was little in either domestic or international authority to resolve it. The court therefore relied on analogous cases from the European Court, whilst considering the boy's vulnerabilities. The case outcome was

[69] Ibid at para 99.

[70] *R (TDT (Vietnam)) v. Secretary of State for the Home Department (Equality and Human Rights Commission intervening)* [2016] EWHC 1912 (Admin), QBD.

that a declaration was made of a breach in the Home Secretary's Article 4 duty. As far as the government was concerned, this made no substantive difference, but was an embarrassing climb down.

Even when courts intervene in the implementation of duties and powers, the intervention rarely makes a difference, and is typically limited to declaring a past mistake, or encouraging a modest rethink. Encouraging the government to rethink its implementation of laws is particularly unusual. Nonetheless, a difficult case came in 2009 with *R (Purdy) v. Director of Public Prosecutions*.[71] The claimant was dying of primary progressive multiple sclerosis, and she sought guidance from the Director of Public Prosecutions (DPP) as to whether her partner might be prosecuted if he assisted in her travelling to Switzerland, where she could commit suicide in a specialist facility. Less than a decade earlier, the courts had shied away from intervening in a very similar case concerning euthanasia.[72] But this time the court ruled that under Article 8 ECHR, the DPP would have to provide guidance as to his policy for cases of assisting the suicide of someone incapable of committing the act themselves. What this case did not lead to was the courts determining the content of policy, instead, in line with Hodder-Williams (1997), it is an example of the courts maintaining or asserting their influence. What was achieved was a court order that policy be made, not that the courts must make it. In the judgement of Lord Hope:

> Decisions in this area of the law are, of course, highly sensitive to the facts of each case. They are also likely to be controversial. But I would not regard these as reasons for excusing the Director from the obligation to clarify what his position is as to the factors that he regards as relevant for and against prosecution in this very special and carefully defined class of case. How he goes about this task must be a matter for him, as also must be the ultimate decision as to whether or not to prosecute. But, as the definition which I have given may show, it ought to be possible to confine the class that requires special treatment to a very narrow band of cases.[73]

[71] [2009] EWCA Civ 92; [2009] 1 Cr App R 455, CA; 30 Jul 2009 [2009] UKHL 45.

[72] *R(Pretty) v. Director of Public Prosecutions* [2001] UKHL 61.

[73] *R (Purdy) v. Director of Public Prosecutions* [2009] UKHL 45 at para 55.

Policy-Oriented—Metatextual changes

This final section looks at when court rulings affect the substance of law. Again, the conceptual label of "policy-oriented" is not entirely apposite. Hodder-Williams (1997) was using the term in regards to the US Supreme Court, where, as co-equal to Congress, it is not a stretch to describe their constitutional jurisdiction as being led by policy orientations. To describe British judges as oriented towards policy is not accurate, however, for reasons of consistency, the label is applied nonetheless. What it specifically means here is that courts apply metatextual analysis to alleviate textual indeterminacies by critical reference to other texts. In other words, the courts go beyond the words available in an indeterminate text in order to establish new understandings of law. Courts will only make innovative legal interpretations of significance when there is significant legislative indeterminacy, and a low likelihood of the case being overturned.

The *Miller v Prime Minister* case discussed above is not strictly an example of this. In that case, it was not statute law, but indeterminate royal prerogatives that were being interpreted. The prerogative to prorogue Parliament was at issue. This prerogative is not simply couched as a textual indeterminacy, as there is no single text that contains the power. Rather there is a web of loosely connected sources outlining the power, including common law and academic publications. As a constitutional convention, it is already in transcendence of textual sources of law. The UK Supreme Court surprised many in ruling against the Prime Minister's judgement that a five-week prorogation was lawful. They could do so because of the power's exceptional indeterminacy, coupled with the low probability of their being overruled. It would have required an Act of Parliament to have voided the ruling, which was very unlikely given the government's then small majority. In addition to which, elite and public backlashes were unlikely, given opposition to the unusual use of the prorogation power. It had even been pointed out that Boris Johnson may have lied to the Queen as regards his use of her prorogation powers. A possibility which strengthened the judicial hand against the government. In the end, a unanimous and unusually large panel of twelve Justices ruled against the Prime Minister.

The *Miller* case is interesting, but far too unusual to be capable of explaining judicialisation. The process by which courts have expanded their powers relative to governments and bureaucrats has happened over decades, and is predominantly focused on interpretations of statute law, rather than unwritten constitutional conventions. There are simply insufficient opportunities for the courts to have accrued any influence in ruling over these seldom used and even less often challenged powers of the state. And, as regards the data selection for this book, the *Miller* case does not pertain to criminal justice. The power of courts under the *Human Rights Act* is perhaps a better source of evidence for judicialisation. However, as discussed above, and in a preceding publication, the HRA does not often yield policy power (Williams 2018). The courts are highly constrained as to what, how, and even when the HRA may be used. As is typical of the common law, the courts cannot use it as part of their *ratio decidendi* unless it has been submitted by counsel. And, because of the derisory financial rewards that can be awarded under the legislation, barristers are not infrequently keen to avoid using it, even when it may be relevant. Added to which, are the dialogic mechanisms within the legislation. Under the HRA, courts cannot simply resolve a new line of policy in common law, they have to make a declaration to Parliament of an incompatibility, and then it is up to legislators to act. It just so happens that Parliament has always responded to these declarations of incompatibility, but they were absolutely not compelled to. And, having so responded, Parliament effectively cauterised the problem and forestalled any further developments in common law.[74] Judges can utilise section 3 of the Act to "read in" or "read down" statutory language, but may only do so under very tight constraints that the judges set for themselves.[75]

A far better source of evidence of expanded judicial power at the expense of government is proportionality review. The legality principle states that government decisions must be in accordance with law. Proportionality review takes this a step further by interrogating whether or not a government power is in proportion to human rights. This sort of analysis is utilised under the HRA, but actually predates it, and is used beyond that legislation's limitations. In other words, a government decision may be taken within established interpretations of law, and yet be declared unlawful for being out of proportion. This review of proportions appears, *prima facie*, to be an entirely subjective means of resolving legal

[74] A noted counter example to this would be the string of court cases consequent on the *Belmarsh* decision, wherein parliament legislated multiple times to declarations of incompatibility brought about the detention of terrorists without trial.

[75] *R v A (No 2)* [2001] UKHL 25, and *R v Lambert* [2001] UKHL 37.

disputes. It is also seen as a foreign imposition on English law. The Court of Justice of the European Union (CJEU) and the European Court of Human Rights (ECtHR) applied tests of proportionality that were more stringent than the common law's more limited reasonableness formula (Voeten 2008). As Britain became enmeshed in continental jurisprudence over post-war decades, the British (more properly English) approach of assessing reasonableness slowly merged with proportionality review. At the CJEU and ECtHR, proportionality review turns on whether a government objective can justifiably infringe rights, even when it is otherwise lawful. Such a balancing of policy against rights would be difficult to incorporate into the English tradition, where there is no law higher than that enacted by Parliament. Therefore, the most appropriate judicial mode of action was not to fully adopt proportionality on the same lines as the ECtHR, but to "take it into account" and assimilate it as an extension of the "*Wednesbury*" reasonableness test that adds rights to the calculus on top of reason. Specifically, there was developed a "heightened *Wednesbury*" test of reasonableness, as set out in *R v. Ministry of Defence ex p Smith*.[76] As per Lord Steyn in *R v. Secretary of State For The Home Department, Ex Parte Daly*[77]:

> There is a material difference between the Wednesbury and Smith grounds of review and the approach of proportionality applicable in respect of review where convention [ECHR] rights are at stake... The starting point is that there is an overlap between the traditional grounds of review and the approach of proportionality. Most cases would be decided in the same way whichever approach is adopted. But the intensity of review is somewhat greater under the proportionality approach... the doctrine of proportionality may require the reviewing court to assess the balance which the decision maker has struck, not merely whether it is within the range of rational or reasonable decisions.

The assimilation of proportionality review was accelerated by an extraordinary expansion of state power, coupled with increased concern for and protection of rights. All of which comes together in judicialisation via indeterminate legislation. A pre-HRA example of courts denying the state power to excessively interfere in rights was *R v. Secretary of State for*

[76] [1996] 1 All ER 256; [1996] QB 517.

[77] [2001] UKHL 26 at 26–27.

the Home Department ex p Simms.[78] In this case, Law Lords ruled that the Home Secretary's blanket ban on interviews between prisoners and journalists breached a claimant's right to investigating the soundness of his conviction. The claimant sought judicial review of the Home Secretary's decision, and relied on indeterminacy in the Prison Rules, under the authority of which his rights had been curtailed. The Rules were made by secondary legislation under the *Prison Act 1952*. The 1952 Act did not specifically deny prisoners access to journalists, and the judges had to assume that, without explicit authorisation, Parliament could not have intended this outcome. As per Lord Hoffmann:

> Parliamentary sovereignty means that Parliament can, if it chooses, legislate contrary to fundamental principles of human rights... But the principle of legality means that Parliament must squarely confront what it is doing and accept the political cost. Fundamental rights cannot be overridden by general or ambiguous words... In the absence of express language or necessary implication to the contrary, the courts therefore presume that even the most general words were intended to be subject to the basic rights of the individual.[79]

This is evidence of judges utilising metatextual analysis. They had to critically analyse Parliament's use of language against other sources of meaning, including commitments to rights. Proportionality review has allowed courts not only to determine whether or not a government decision was lawful, and, by extension, to rule on which decision they thought ought to have been taken in the first place. In one example, judges determined who should be the winners and losers of a policy. The 2014 case at the High Court is notable in particular for the fact that the government did not consider it worth appealing against the ruling.[80] In order to try and save money, the government had sought limitations on legal aid via the *Legal Aid, Sentencing and Punishment of Offenders Act 2012*. Specifically, they used a statutory instrument (a form of secondary legislation) to remove the right of those without citizenship to civil legal aid. But, it was ruled that there was no power for the government to deny access

[78] [1999] 3 All ER 400.

[79] Ibid at 412.

[80] *R(Public Law Project) v. Secretary of State for Justice (Office of the Children's Commissioner intervening)* [2014] EWHC 2365 (Admin).

to aid for those without "sufficient connection to the UK". The government's aim was not only to save money, but also to frustrate claims from asylum seekers and immigrants relying on legal services. Such a multi-faceted policy was not determinatively mandated by the 2012 Act, and therefore the court struck down the statutory instrument. As Moses LJ put it:

> Of course, it might have been possible to draft primary legislation which has the broader ambition of cutting the cost of legal aid by permitting the Lord Chancellor to adopt criteria irrespective of need. But it is clear to me that the statute has neither such overriding ambition nor purpose. It does precisely what the Government announced it was intended to do, namely, to allocate civil legal aid to those in the greatest need. It would be startling if the statute contained the power to introduce secondary legislation with a wider purpose in precise contradiction to the public announcements of government.[81]

It is very unusual for UK courts to impose a specific set of requirements for policy implementation. A rare counter example is a case where the High Court determined the meaning of "subsistence" in line with past practice and against the preferences of the government.[82] The British Government were enforcing the EU Parliament and Council Directive 2011/36/EU on preventing and combating trafficking in human beings. The Directive was indeterminately worded, with Recital 18 stating that the "assistance and support provided [to a trafficked individual] should include at least a minimum set of measures that are necessary to enable the victim to recover" and "assistance and support measures… shall include at least standards of living capable of ensuring victims' subsistence". The government set up a contract to provide subsistence services with the Salvation Army to the tune of £65 per week. The government then unilaterally changed the terms of this contract to £37.75 per week. At judicial review, the contract change was reversed because there has been no evidence for a change in circumstance justifying the unilateral contractual provision. This was despite the fact that, according to Mr. Justice Mostyn, there was substantial indeterminacy in the law:

[81] Ibid at 45.

[82] *R (K) v. Secretary of State for the Home Department* 8 Nov 2018 [2018] EWHC 2951 (Admin).

> ... 'subsistence' when used in these Directives is a heavily nuanced concept capable of different meanings in different contexts. It does not necessarily mean in the Trafficking Directive that subsistence is that minimal sum necessary to stave off destitution.[83]

The overall picture is that substantive intervention by courts into policy is unusual. Indeed, the degree to which judges were making policy is clearly disputable. Perhaps a more accurate description would be that judges are holding the government to standards loosely set out by Parliament. The "subsistence" contract is a case in point. Judges did not determine the amount that ought to be provided by the Salvation Army, they just stopped the government from reneging on a contract. Whilst for some this may appear to be activism of a kind, for others it would appear to be nothing more than straightforward contract law. Regardless of how these different behaviours are labelled, the key point is that judges have the opportunity to make a range of policy impactful rulings because of the increased indeterminacy in law.

Conclusion

Of the 2.5 million words of criminal justice legislation analysed for this chapter, 1.3 million were enacted after the millennium. Amongst these words were at least (according to the computer program) 104,299 indeterminate parts of speech—adjectives, adverbs, conditional conjunctions, indeterminate modal verbs, and enabling verbs. 101,549 such indeterminacies had been enacted across the preceding five decades, of which, only 1.4% were enacted in the 1950s. The upside is that UK criminal justice legislation has changed both in quantity and clarity since the war. These findings complement evidence from Chapter Four of consistently increasing indeterminacies across the entire gamut of policy domains.

The effects of this on judicial power could not holistically be explained by legal realist or positivist theories—because positive law has changed so much. What even is the positive law is very much open to contestation with textual sources being considered alongside new subtexts, shifting contexts, and new global intertextual analysis. That judges have the capacity to utilise transtextual and metatextual analysis to resolve these indeterminacies is unsurprising from the wide interpretive spaces

[83] Ibid at 25.

yielded by Parliament. Indeed, relative to other democracies, the British Parliament bears an extraordinary responsibility for determining social meaning. In the absence of codified constitutional law, all that is legal is ultimately Westminster's responsibility. As Lord Diplock famously stated in *Duport Steels Ltd and others v Sirs and others*[84]:

> Parliament makes the laws, the judiciary interpret them... Where the meaning of the statutory words is plain and unambiguous it is not for the judges to invent fancied ambiguities as an excuse for failing to give effect to its plain meaning because they themselves consider that the consequences of doing so would be inexpedient, or even unjust or immoral.

Parliament has left space for judicialisation. And, Parliament, as with all other modern democracies, is a conduit for increasingly diversified civic power. The consequences of which are heightened degrees of policy ambition, conflict, and ambivalence. As the UK grapples with globalisation, for example, it has struggled with sometimes incompatible demands for a flexible labour market and demands for tight immigration. This has focussed critical attention on human rights instruments, in particular, as unattenuated tools for judicial power. Such claims are simply not credible, however. The *Human Rights Act*, most notably, does not enable judges to disregard Parliament or the government. By global standards—as we will see in coming chapters—it retains far more power for politicians that it gives to judges. In line with Lord Diplock's point, only explicit instructions from Parliament that the HRA may be disregarded will suffice, because it itself is another Act of Parliament. Parliament may issue such disregarding instructions at any time. This was done with the *Communications Act 2003* so as to ban political advertising on radio and television. Judicialisation in the UK is not a consequence of judicial fiat, but legislative complexity and indeterminacy.

[84] [1980] 1 All ER 529 at 541.

References

Blom-Cooper, Louis, Brian Dickson, and Gavin Drewry. 2009. *The Judicial House of Lords*. Oxford: Oxford University Press.

Calabresi, Guido. 1982. *A Common Law for the Age of Statutes*. Cambridge, MA: Harvard University Press.

Craig, Paul. 1998. Ultra Vires and the Foundations of Judicial Review. *The Cambridge Law Journal* 57 (1): 63–90.

Dicey, Albert V. 1915. *The Law of the Constitution*, 8th ed. London: Macmillan.

Dworkin, Ronald. 1986. *Law's Empire*. London: Fontana.

Elliott, Mark. 2000. The Ultra Vires Doctrine in a Constitutional Setting: Still the Central Principle of Administrative Law. In *Judicial Review and the Constitution*, ed. Christopher Forsyth. London: Hart Publishing.

Ewing, Keith. 2010. *Bonfire of the Liberties*. Oxford: Oxford University Press.

Feldman, David. 2004. *English Public Law*. Oxford: Oxford University Press.

Forsyth, Christopher. 2000. *Judicial Review and the Constitution*. London: Hart Publishing.

Griffith, John. 1977. *The Politics of the Judiciary*. Manchester: Manchester University Press.

Haas, Ernst B. 1958. *The Uniting of Europe: Political, Social, and Economic Forces 1950–1957*. Stanford: Stanford University Press.

Hodder-Williams, Richard. 1997. Six Notions of 'Political' and the United States Supreme Court. *British Journal of Political Science* 22 (1): 1–20.

Lasswell, Harold D. 1936. *Politics: Who Gets What, When, How*. New York: Whittlesey House.

Lee, Simon. 1994. *"Law and the Constitution" in Anthony Seldon and Dennis Kavanagh, The Major Effect*. London: Macmillan.

Loveland, Ian. 2006. *Constitutional Law, Administrative Law and Human Rights: A Critical Introduction*, 4th ed. Oxford: Oxford University Press.

Oliver, Dawn. 2000. Is the Ultra Vires Rule the Basis of Judicial Review? In *Judicial Review and the Constitution*, ed. Christopher Forsyth. London: Hart Publishing.

Ormerod, David, and Karl Laird. 2015. *Smith and Hogan's Criminal Law*. Oxford: Oxford University Press.

Seaward, Paul, and Paul Silk. 2003. The House of Commons. In *The British Constitution in the Twentieth-Century*, ed. Vernon Bogdanor. Oxford: British Academy.

Stevens, Robert. 2005. *The English Judges: Their Role in the Changing Constitution*. Oxford: Hart Publishing.

Strøm, Kaare, Wolfgang C. Müller, and Torbjörn Bergman. 2003. *Delegation and Accountability in Parliamentary Democracies*. Oxford: Oxford University Press.

Voeten, Erik. 2008. The Impartiality of International Judges: Evidence from the European Court of Human Rights. *American Political Science Review* 102 (4): 417–433.

Volcansek, Mary L., and John J. Stack Jr. 2011. *Courts and Terrorism: Nine Nations Balance Rights and Security*. Cambridge: Cambridge University Press.

Williams, Matthew. 2017. The Grammar of Politics: A Brief History of Legislative Language in Britain. *Political Quarterly* 88 (2): 248–257.

Williams, Matthew. 2018. *How Language Works in Politics: The Impact of Indeterminate Legislation on Policy*. Bristol: Bristol University Press.

CHAPTER 6

Federalism and Party Polarisation in the US

Before the US Civil War, just two pieces of federal law were invalidated by judicial review. These cases were settled over fifty years apart, with *Marbury v. Madison* in 1803,[1] and *Dred Scott v. Sandford* in 1857.[2] There were other antebellum instances of judicial review that did not invalidate federal legislation but were instead applied against executive decisions or state laws.[3] It would be reasonable, nonetheless, to conclude that judicial review was an exceptional power, utilised only infrequently in the union's early years (Schwartz 1993; Graber 2006; Whittington 2015). Since 1960, by contrast, the US Supreme Court has nullified in whole or in part an average of eight state or federal laws per year. This makes for a total of 482 nullifications in sixty years.[4] And, the Supreme Court is just the tip of a judicial iceberg, with thirteen federal Courts of Appeal,

[1] 5 U.S. 137 (1803).

[2] 60 U.S. 393 (1857).

[3] For example, *Hylton v. United States*, 3 U.S. 171 (1796), was the first ever case utilising judicial review by the US Supreme Court. A tax on carriages was ruled not to be a direct tax, and therefore not to be apportioned amongst the states. And in *Ware v. Hylton*, 3 U.S. 199 (1796) the Supreme Court first invalidated a state law. Specifically, a Virginia statute clashed with the Treaty of Paris and was nullified under the Supremacy Clause.

[4] https://law.justia.com/constitution/us/acts-of-congress-held-unconstitutional.html accessed on 7th June 2021.

M. Williams, *Judges and the Language of Law*,
https://doi.org/10.1007/978-3-030-91495-0_6

ninety-four District Courts, more specialist courts of original jurisdiction (such as the US Tax Court), as well as similarly complex judicial systems for each of the fifty states.

The task of this chapter, therefore, is to explain the policy influence of US judges. Why do American judges—and especially those on federal courts—intervene more frequently in matters of "mega-politics" (Hirschl 2004)? In regards to America, this is a well-travelled academic path. Studies of judicial politics in the US vastly outnumber the output for any of the other countries covered by this book. Saying something fresh on the subject will involve utilising political science, legal theory, computer science, and literary theory. As with the other countries surveyed, machine reading millions of words of federal law offers new insights into the changing determinacy of authoritative language. Degenrification of criminal laws and rules will be shown to fit the patterns raised in Chapter Four of linguistic instability across all policy spaces. This chapter specifically offers a computer-assisted analysis of the Federal Criminal Code since the 1940s. There is evidence of indeterminacy in American statecraft that, as with the UK, signifies policy complexity and ambivalence. This indeterminacy as to what is lawful will be settled by judges through reconciliation of loose constitutional language and increasingly loose legislative languages. The chapter therefore considers evidence that judicialisation of federal judges was consequent on the state of law they have had to interpret. Whilst there is also striking evidence of politicisation, the narrative that judges pushed unilaterally for policy "activism" will be nuanced by the findings presented. To introduce these themes, the chapter will proceed by reiterating core definitions, followed by consideration of the macro-social context, through to the meso-level uses of language, and finally to the micro-level judicial decisions.

Well known Supreme Court cases (celebrated and maligned with equal fervour) frame this debate. These include *Brown v. Board* where judges ruled to desegregate schools[5]; or *Roe v. Wade* which ruled against blanket abortion controls within the first trimester[6]; or *Bush v. Gore* that halted the recount of contested ballots in the 2000 Presidential election.[7] These cases had significant policy consequences, and have thereby propelled a

[5] *Brown v. Board of Education of Topeka*, 347 U.S. 483 (1954).

[6] *Roe v. Wade*, 410 U.S. 113 (1973).

[7] *Bush v. Gore*, 531 U.S. 98 (2000).

narrative of "activism" (Lindquist and Cross 2009). Such activism is difficult to define, but broadly entails the application of constitutional and other jurisprudential principles to strike down existing laws, or create new rules of law. Activist rulings can pre-empt, forestall, or accelerate legislative or executive action. As such, a typical riposte from those advocating for judicial restraint is that social problems ought to be left to legislatures, and courts ought to occupy themselves with purely legal problems. This chapter will demonstrate that court activism is a response to legal problems. Furthermore, the substance of activist rulings is almost never counter-majoritarian on a national scale. The interests countered tend to be confined to discrete regional or sectoral cleavages. This is in part why few judicial rulings are overruled in the US (Klarman 1996; Vanberg 2001). Albeit other reasons the federal courts are rarely overruled include their co-equal status to Congress and the Presidency, as well as the cumbersome mechanics of constitutional amendment. Nonetheless, school desegregation and abortion reform are examples of judicial policy power that vindicated rather than violated elite and public opinion across the nation, even if both rulings were vocally opposed in specific communities.

And, central to this book's thesis, both school desegregation and abortion reform rulings turned on the interpretation of constitutional and legislative indeterminacies. There were, in short, legal problems in need of judicial remedy. It is not sufficient to describe *Brown* or *Roe* as mere policy making from the bench enabled, in both cases, by Fourteenth Amendment latitude. The judges were using institutional norms to resolve a legal landscape that was anything but normal. Ironically, therefore, activism can be a device of institutional conservatism, even if it yields what some may describe as social progress. Starting with *Brown* as an example, there were conjoined appeals from several states, but most famously was that brought against the Topeka Board of Education in Kansas. Parents in Topeka appealed with support of the NAACP to the federal District Court.[8] Oliver Brown's daughter Linda, for one, had been barred from attending her local elementary school, and was forced to ride the bus to a distant school. The Browns sought, but were denied, the enjoined enforcement of a permissive Kansan statute—Chapters 72–1724 of the General Statutes of Kansas, 1949:

[8] 98 F. Supp. 797 (D. Kan. 1951).

> The board of education shall have power to... make all necessary rules for the government of the schools of such city under its charge and control and of the board... to organize and maintain separate schools for the education of white and colored children... no discrimination on account of color shall be made in high schools except as provided herein.

The board of education enjoyed wide discretion to "make all necessary rules". Albeit the board could not racially discriminate, except under a licence to segregate "as provided herein". The law was therefore indeterminate as regards what policies could or should be pursued, but it was clear that a conceptual distinction in law between discrimination and separation could be made. The Browns appealed to the Supreme Court, where Chief Justice Earl Warren wrote a unanimous opinion that separate could not mean equal. The precedent of *Plessy v. Ferguson*[9] applied by the District Court was practically (but not explicitly) overruled. In going against this precedent, Warren interpreted the Kansan statute against the Fourteenth Amendment's Equal Protection Clause:

> ... nor shall any State... deny to any person within its jurisdiction the equal protection of the laws.

There is little doubt that Warren and other Justices (notably Hugo Black) wanted this policy outcome. They controlled their docket and were ideologically committed to ending segregation. Black even went so far as to lament his fellow Justice Felix Frankfurter's inclusion of the elastic phrase "with all deliberate speed" in *Brown II* (Woodward and Armstrong 1979).[10] States opposed to desegregation simply chose to define what "deliberate speed" meant, to their toe-dragging advantage. Hence, discursive indeterminacy from judges creates the same latitude as indeterminacy from legislatures. But, if Warren and Black wanted to kill segregation then the question begging is "why then?". Why did it take until 1954, if the Equal Protection Clause was so permissive?

Motive is never sufficient to explain behaviour. Opportunity and means are required as well. The Court had to wait for an appropriate case, and *Brown* was just that. There was the human interest story of a little girl being forced to ride a bus when she could have attended a local school.

[9] 163 U.S. 537 (1896).

[10] 349 U.S. 294.

There were also Brandeis briefs used in the case, containing social science data to flesh out the impact of segregation across society. But, at root, courts are institutionally vulnerable, and have to play a game or risk being delegitimised and overruled. Courts are expected to settle disputes as to the law. The Kansas Legislature helped generate a legal dispute with their 1949 legislation. The law was simultaneously indeterminate as to its scope and applicability, whilst being strangely determinate on a conceptual point as to whether or not separation and discrimination were distinct. This admixture of confusion and clarity was almost perfect as an access point for a Fourteenth Amendment interpretation.

Added to which, the court was hardly deviating from its common law powers in reviewing precedents in *Brown*. Given the strong expectation of *stare decisis*, there was a distinct road to *Brown* charted in a series of precedents that chipped away at *Plessy* (Brenner and Spaeth 1995). In the 1938 case of *Missouri ex rel Gaines v. Canada*,[11] for starters, the Supreme Court quashed a policy of paying black students to leave the state for law school. Then in 1944, the case of *Shelley v. Kraemer* scrapped restrictive covenants that discriminated on race.[12] These were covenants added to contracts, such as property deeds, that attempted to block house sales to black people. Penultimately, in *Sweatt v. Painter* the court in 1950 rejected a submission that the Texan "law school for negroes" was of equal status to University of Texas Law School.[13] These three cases were heard by three different Chief Justices, all of whom preceded Earl Warren's accession in 1953. It is understandable that the Warren Court is celebrated, and castigated, for its landmark decisions, but this distorts the more complex history of slow degradation to segregation in law, in policy, and in sociology that began well before Warren's tenure on the court. It would be similarly ahistorical to argue that the Warren Court issued a final word on segregation. And, in more general terms, the Court is never truly definitive on any policy matter. For segregation, the judiciary spent decades working out details, including fights over busing as a means to speed up integration. As recently as 2007, the Supreme Court

[11] 305 U.S. 337 (1938).

[12] 334 U.S. 1 (1948).

[13] 339 U.S. 629 (1950).

ruled that there was no "compelling state interest" in assigning school places by race.[14]

The key insight of this and all other chapters is that regardless of motive, opportunities for judicial intervention in policy are proliferating because the law is increasingly difficult to determine. Judges are hence drawn into policy conflict, and they are not simply muscling their way in. Justice Harry Blackmun stated as much in his opinion for *Roe v. Wade*.[15] The case turned on interpretation of Article 1196 of the Texan Penal Code, first drafted in 1854. The law criminalised abortions, save for "medical advice for the purpose of saving the life of the mother". A doctor intervened on behalf of Jane Roe (real name Norma McCorvey), because he was facing two indictments for aiding in terminations. As Blackmun paraphrased:

> He [James Hubert Hallford] described conditions of patients who came to him seeking abortions, and he claimed that for many cases he, as a physician, was unable to determine whether they fell within or outside the exception recognized by Article 1196. He alleged that, as a consequence, the statutes were vague and uncertain, in violation of the Fourteenth Amendment, and that they violated his own and his patients' rights to privacy in the doctor-patient relationship and his own right to practice medicine.

It has been lamented that Blackmun was moved by the legal vulnerability of physicians, when perhaps he should have been more focussed on women. As a father of three daughters, there is recorded evidence, in addition to the opinion itself, that women were in his sympathies (Woodward and Armstrong 1979, 200–212). But, Blackmun had to find a legal basis for the Court's ruling. He found it in the Texan statute that rendered the powers of physicians so precariously defined. It would be fair to note that, as traders in language, lawyers and judges would face little difficulty in finding or imagining indeterminacies in law where there are none for a casual reader. Harder to deny, however, will be the evidence presented below that laws increasingly lack stable patterns of linguistic construction. This degenrification in law coincides with an increased policy role

[14] *Parents Involved in Community Schools v. Seattle School District No. 1*, 551 U.S. 701 (2007).

[15] 410 U.S. 113 (1973).

for judges. It is likely, indeed, that legal instabilities and judicialisation are causally linked and not just temporally coincident. But the liberal expansionism of private rights against state power (as seen in *Brown* or *Roe*) has been nonlinear, despite secular increases in legislative indeterminacy. For example, there were 92 uses of the Fourteenth Amendment to strike down laws by the Supreme Court in the two decades from the 1960s to the 1970s. There were just 56 such rulings in the three decades from the 1980s up to the 2020s.[16] These decades covered the Rehnquist and Roberts Courts which were indeed noted for their more restrained ideologies and methodologies as compared, most notably, to the Warren Court of the 1950s and 1960s.

Restrained interpretations of the constitution are still consequential for policy-making, however. A famous example from the Rehnquist Court is *United States v. Lopez*[17]—the first major ruling since the 1930s to restrict application of the Commerce Clause. The case concerned Alfonso Lopez Jr., who, in his 12th grade of school, brought a concealed handgun to class. This was in contravention of a federal statute banning "any individual knowingly to possess a firearm at a place that [he] knows... is a school zone".[18] This statute had to be interpreted against the constitutional powers for Congress to impose such policy on states, including, in this case, Texas:

> [The Congress shall have Power]... To regulate Commerce with foreign Nations, and among the several States, and with the Indian Tribes.[19]

Five conservative Justices found the Commerce Clause could not be stretched to apply to gun control. Four more liberal-minded Justices saw education as an essential prerequisite of interstate commerce. But, they lost this particular argument. The *Gun-Free School Zones Act* of 1990 (cited above) is, on its face, comprehensible. It made an offence of possessing a firearm within 1000 feet of a school. It is anchored to a possibly contentious double scienter component "*knowingly* possess... at a place [*known* to be a] school". But such *mens rea* complications would

[16] https://law.justia.com/constitution/us/acts-of-congress-held-unconstitutional.html accessed on 7th June 2021.

[17] 514 U.S. 549 (1995).

[18] 18 U. S. C. § 922(q)(I)(A).

[19] Article I, Section 8, Clause 3.

be for juries to determine. The key point is that legislative activity stimulated a judicial response, and just as in *Brown* and *Roe*, the court in *Lopez* said "no, you cannot do that" to a legislature. It just so happened that saying no to Congress in this instance thwarted what was seen as progressive, whereas saying no to states in *Brown* and *Roe* were seen to advance progressivism. Ironically, therefore, in these cases spoken of as ideologically oppositional, all three emerged from a similar state-emasculating stable.

It would be anachronistic nonsense to suggest that indeterminate legislation is entirely new, or that the Commerce Clause was not variably interpreted in the past. The historiographical claim made here is one by degrees, rather than of kind. There are simply more laws enacted, with less stable linguistic construction, offering greater opportunities for judicial latitude in interpretation. Hence why we see the number of appeals to the Supreme Court is consistently high—despite the more restrained contemporary justices—at around 7000 per year.[20] And we see demand for civil rights and criminal lawyers has expanded rapidly.[21] The sociolinguistic forces that pushed this market for legal services were not created by judges. Indeed, as an admittedly extreme illustration, within just three days in April 2021 there were no fewer than twenty-eight new abortion laws enacted by state legislatures, in the hope that they would generate lawsuits to overrule *Roe v Wade* on appeal.[22] These laws were designed to reach the desks of new conservative leaning Associate Justices Neil Gorsuch, Brett Kavanaugh, and Amy Coney Barrett. Such provocations to judicialise emphasise how reactive (not active) judges' political influence is.

And indeed we can observe the counterfactual, where judges denied themselves a policy shaping role when asked to interpret determinable laws. *Lopez* could be an example where the Commerce Clause was narrowly constructed to knock down a straightforward gun control statute. But, in that case, the court still invalidated a federal law. A true counterfactual would be where the government won a case by calling for a

[20] https://www.uscourts.gov/about-federal-courts/educational-resources/about-educational-outreach/activity-resources/supreme-1 accessed on 18th June 2021.

[21] https://lawyers.laws101.com/top-10-legal-practice-areas-in-demand-in-2020/ accessed on 18th June 2021.

[22] https://www.guttmacher.org/article/2021/04/2021-track-become-most-devastating-antiabortion-state-legislative-session-decades accessed on 17th June 2021.

close textual reading of their own legislation. An example of this could be *National Federation of Independent Business v. Sebelius*.[23] This case held enormous political significance as a legal challenge to the *Patient Protection and Affordable Care Act 2010*—better known as Obamacare. It was assumed that with a 5–4 majority of Republican-appointed Justices, that Obamacare would either be gutted or swept aside. In fact, it was Chief Justice Roberts (appointed by George W. Bush) who came to save the law from either fate. John Roberts hinted at his ideological misgivings in oral argument and in his opinion. He suggested that the individual mandate, whereby everyone was legally obliged to obtain health insurance could be analogised to a government mandate to buy and eat broccoli:

> Everyone will likely participate in the markets for food, clothing, transportation, shelter, or energy; that does not authorize Congress to direct them to purchase particular products in those or other markets today... According to the Government, upholding the individual mandate would not justify mandatory purchases of items such as cars or broccoli.[24]

The legislation in Roberts's sights was 26 U.S. Code § 5000A:

> (a) Requirement to maintain minimum essential coverage
> An applicable individual shall for each month beginning after 2013 ensure that the individual, and any dependent of the individual who is an applicable individual, is covered under minimum essential coverage for such month.

By the standards of 2010, this was a straightforwardly constructed piece of statute law, and the intent of Congress is easy to discern. Justices Scalia, Kennedy, Thomas, and Alito nonetheless dissented by arguing (as in *Lopez*) that the Commerce Clause could not undergird any such congressional mandate. Roberts agreed, but argued instead that Congress could use its taxing power, because anyone who refused to obtain insurance must make a "responsibility payment"[25] to the Internal Revenue Service.[26] Not everything was spared, however. An attempt to expand

[23] 567 U.S. 519 (2012).

[24] Ibid. at page 27.

[25] 26 U. S. C. §5000A(b)(1).

[26] 26 U. S. C. §§5000A(c), (g)(1).

the scope and generosity of Medicaid was severed from the Act by judicial ruling. Even in supporting this ultimately doomed expansion, Justice Ginsberg acknowledged that the Medicaid Act contains "hundreds" of provisions, conditions, and beneficiaries.[27] This complexity likely increased the law's vulnerability to attack by a norm-conserving judiciary that defaults to saying "no, you cannot do that" to legislators and executives.

As with the other countries studied here, the US has increasingly dispersed power. The pluralism of public opinion has created ambivalences in policy and law. More peculiar to the US is its origin as a reluctant state. Where English courts derived their original authority from an all-powerful monarchy, the US adopted this common law heritage, but added in a scepticism for statecraft. Federal courts are mandated by a constitutional authority which has, from the beginning, been defensive as to its right to exist. Hence why judicial review by federal courts most typically adopts a state-effacing posture, in line with principles of individual liberty. When courts pass down a momentous ruling, it is most likely to be a somewhat ironic assertion by a state organ that the state ought to recede. Such assertions shape agendas, but rarely determine policy contents. In line with Lukes's dimensions of power, the US courts are most likely to adopt the agenda-setting second dimension, therefore, rather than the more policy-generative first dimension (Lukes 1974). And, quite apart from this being in line with American history and ideology, it is a sensible decisional strategy for the judges, assuming they wish to maintain or enhance their legitimacy amidst a plurality of demographic, regional, sectoral, and material cleavages. In the words of Alexander Bickel, the judiciary is in policy shaping terms, "the least dangerous branch" (Bickel 1986).

And yet, the extent of diversity in America renders phrases such as "American history and ideology" as analytically useless. Reconciling the demands of a diverse populace is nothing new, and has been a challenge since the country's foundation. The anti-federalist "Brutus" who goaded Alexander Hamilton in the New York Journal put it in these prescient terms:

> The territory of the United States is of vast extent; it now contains near three millions of souls, and is capable of containing much more than ten times that number. Is it practicable for a country, so large and so numerous

[27] 567 U.S. 519 (2012) at page 49.

> as they will soon become, to elect a representation, that will speak their sentiments, without their becoming so numerous as to be incapable of transacting public business? It certainly is not.[28]

By asking how a country "will speak their sentiments", Brutus captures the difficulty of obtaining a logic of communication in a continent-sized polity. The founding fathers' solution, famously, was to make compromises in institutional design and ideological coherence, for the sake of agreement. And, the motivation to agree was an external security threat, not a shared vision (Riker 1964). The most notorious compromise came with regard to slavery. In addition to which, the constitution contained underdetermined powers for the new federal government, framed by multiple veto points to limit the likely extent of policy change. Important ambiguities include the "Elastic Clause", wherein Congress is empowered to, *inter alia*, regulate interstate commerce so far as is deemed "necessary and proper". These two adjectives and a conjunction are at the root of almost all litigation brought against federal spending policies. The Bill of Rights of 1791 appended tighter limitations on government, and was as such an insurance policy, allowing states to ratify the constitution. These first ten amendments have in their substance and language contributed to roaring court battles on matters from free speech and censorship; to prayer in schools; to gun ownership; to criminal procedure; to due process; to the death penalty; and to states' rights.

Besides some ambiguities in commission, the US constitution is also recognised for its taciturn ambiguities by omission. A pertinent omission from the text was with regards to judicial review itself. Article III makes no explicit mention of a power for courts to determine the legality of executive and legislative actions. A power of judicial review was, however, unquestionably known to the founding fathers, being another import from English law. Indeed, judicial review had been explicitly referenced, and used, in the original thirteen colonies decades prior to the Revolutionary War (Corwin 1910). Any claim that Chief Justice John Marshall somehow invented judicial review by using it for the first time is therefore unsustainable. His opinion in *Marbury v. Madison* was in fact paradoxical in so far as it recognised a power of judicial review, by limiting the powers of the judiciary. Specifically, Section 13 of the *Judiciary Act 1789*

[28] https://archive.csac.history.wisc.edu/Brutus_II.pdf accessed on 19th July 2021.

was declared unconstitutional, because it expanded court powers beyond that which was possible by Article III.

The case brought by William Marbury against James Madison was also an early instance of a court ruling amidst overt attempts to politicise justice. Marbury had been appointed a Justice of the Peace by out-going President John Adams the night before his rival Thomas Jefferson's inauguration as the first "Democratic-Republican" President. James Madison, as Jefferson's Secretary of State, tried to block the appointment. Marbury appealed directly to the Supreme Court for a writ of mandamus to force through his appointment. The Court had been granted original jurisdiction for such writs by Congress in the *Judiciary Act*. John Marshall—another Adams appointee—ruled that changing the Court's original jurisdiction by ordinary statute was unconstitutional, as an amendment was needed (Graber 1998). Marbury deserved the writ, it was stated, but he should not have been able to appeal directly to the Supreme Court for it. Marbury never took up his post, but Jefferson still felt aggrieved and complained:

> The Constitution is a mere thing of wax in the hands of the judiciary, which they may twist and shape into any form they please.[29]

Jefferson made this early complaint against court activism. This was consistent with him being a fierce early advocate of states' rights, which remains a primary fault line in US court battles. Where the US sustains demographic, material, and ideological cleavages, these are reinforced by geographic cleavages of states (especially those in the South and Midwest) against the federal government. These vertical separations of power include not only the states and territories, but also 574 federally recognised Native American Nations. Hence the anti-government effect of many famous Supreme Court rulings cohered federal rules of law, sometimes at the expense of state sovereignty. The "least dangerous branch" can indeed be dangerous to those seeking to deviate from what nine DC-based justices interpret as constitutional (McGuire and Stimson 2004). Despite complaints against this dominance of states, the right for federal courts to prioritise centre over periphery comes from unusually

[29] https://press-pubs.uchicago.edu/founders/documents/a1_8_18s16.html accessed on 26th January 2021.

plain constitutional language, laid out in the Supremacy Clause (Article IV.2):

> This Constitution, and the Laws of the United States which shall be made in Pursuance thereof; and all Treaties made, or which shall be made, under the Authority of the United States, shall be the supreme Law of the Land; and the Judges in every State shall be bound thereby, any thing in the Constitution or Laws of any State to the Contrary notwithstanding.

By a subsequent common law decision, federal supremacy also entailed the incorporation of federal rights against state governments. This incorporation of federal rights (analysed further below) has made up for the vast majority of top-tier judicial review cases since the war. As a starting point, 81% of laws invalidated by the Supreme Court between 1960 and 2020 were state and local, not federal. Although, fully 70% of these state constraining cases came in the 1960s and 1970s, before the Rehnquist Court eased off federal enforcement against states. Nonetheless, 92% of Supreme Court civil rights cases that led to invalidation of laws came against the states. And, 79% of criminal cases that were invalidated were against states as well. The federal government only wins out in quantitative terms over states with regard to invalidations in the following areas of law: advertising; communications; Federal Indian Law; food and drugs; intellectual property; immigration; labour; pensions and benefits; and veterans.[30]

The compound effects of extraordinary social diversity, continental scale, and institutional fragmentation are high degrees of policy stability, punctuated by infrequent but sometimes extreme policy change opportunities. Relative to the other countries studied here, the cleavages of US politics are deep and reinforcing, the opposing networks better resourced and organised, and institutions are a mixture of winner-takes-all with veto players. All of which is described by a more commonly applied metaphor of polarisation. As analysed in previous chapters, judicial power is a function of this democratic dispersal, where increased agency to citizens in the forms of money, and other resources, feeds back into litigation. A litigious culture, in particular with regards to public law, describes a citizenry that

[30] All data https://constitution.congress.gov/resources/unconstitutional-laws/ accessed on 20th June 2021.

is conscious of its rights, conscious of government fallibility, and materially able to act. Of course, many American citizens, as with citizens of the other countries analysed, lack access to justice. But American politics also has efficient mechanisms for organising contentious politics through multiple access points, including the courts (Tarrow 2013). Meaning that even the poor and disenfranchised can have their grievances utilised to fight for policy change or conservation. A more straightforward way of putting this point is that American politics gives little to the losers. For want of losers' consent for policy change or stasis, the power of courts provides an alternative grievance resolution mechanism (Anderson et al. 2005).

Besides these demand side pressures for public law, there have been supply side responses (Clayton 2002). For example, judges yielded to political pressure brought by Franklin Roosevelt's New Deal to ditch the so-called Lochner era. Named for the 1905 decision of *Lochner v. New York*,[31] it was an era typified by the Supreme Court striking down interventionist social policies, including in the eponymous case a limit to working times. President Roosevelt was so frustrated by the judges' minimalist ideology that he threatened to create new justices and "pack" the court. The sitting justices spared themselves an influx of new colleagues by yielding to social policy expansion, and, specifically, a minimum wage law, in *West Coast Hotel Co. v. Parrish*.[32] Known as a "switch in time that saved nine [justices]", the *West Coast* decision is a clear example of the courts reacting to political context, rather than shaping it. But in other supply-side matters, the courts were in the driving seat. The Supreme Court has substantial control of its docket, and only around 2% of the 7000 annual *certiorari* requests are granted hearing. Also, the Court has shown itself able and willing to adapt its rules of standing and mootness. In *Roe v. Wade*, for example, the case was moot by the time it had reached the Supreme Court, because the child had been born. The court nonetheless heard the case and issued an advisory opinion. There has also been a more relaxed attitude to the issuance of *amicus curiae* briefs and Brandeis briefs. These briefs focus not only on legal technicalities, but also provide wider social and political commentary to flesh out legal decisions and their likely consequences.

[31] 198 U.S. 45 (1905).

[32] 300 U.S. 379 (1937).

These demand and supply side forces that propelled public law coincided (and were in part caused) by a post-war "Rights Revolution", and a "new politics" of contention in the 1960s and 1970s (Epp 1998). The overall consequence was that legal texts were less amenable to "black letter" strict constructions, as Sir William Blackstone may have preferred (Temple 2019). Under conditions of disaggregated power and institutional fragmentation, rules of law become less authoritative and more contestable. In other words, a text of law, on its face, is distinguished with some vehemence according to differential context, different readings of subtext, and will require utilisation of creative interpretation to render a coherently shared meaning. Not only are extant legal texts opened up to new interpretations, but democratic pluralism also yields indeterminacies in legislation. These textual indeterminacies are both symptomatic of, and further contributors to, policy dissensus. A logic of communication is demanded of from the judiciary, because no other state organ would be trusted to have sufficient independence to settle it. But, of course, the independence of the judiciary is itself brought under suspicion, especially when court battles are used to resolve a political crisis. An important example of this would be *Bush v. Gore*,[33] where the Supreme Court Justices voted in line with the party of their appointing Presidents to decide the case (Segal and Spaeth 2002). The 5–4 decision to block a recount of contested ballots effectively handed the presidential election victory to George W. Bush.

Despite the intense interest in Supreme Court appointments, however, data from all cases heard since 1946 show that unanimous decisions are more not less likely now than they were in the past.[34] This suggests that correlating case outcomes solely on the basis of the Justices' appointing president will not yield predictive power (Maltzman et al. 2000). In the 1990s, 41% of the 1023 cases heard at the Supreme Court were unanimous. Whereas, from the 1940s to 1970s this unanimity proportion never exceeded 24%. Since the millennium, 37% of cases (577 cases) were unanimous, whilst just 22% of cases (355 cases) were 5–4 split decisions. And, unanimity was achieved even amongst the most politically charged

[33] 531 U.S. 98 (2000).

[34] Washington University Law Supreme Court Database: http://scdb.wustl.edu/data.php accessed on 22nd June 2021.

cases, being those heard against sitting Presidents—*US v. Nixon*,[35] and *Clinton v. Jones*.[36] The case against President Nixon is especially interesting for the insights it offers as to modern judicial methods. There were four Nixon appointed Justices that joined the unanimous and single-authored judgement against the President, including the opinion's author and Chief Justice, Warren Burger.[37] The ruling enforced a *subpoena*, and compelled Nixon to turn over taped conversations from the White House with regard to the Watergate break-in. Nixon resigned the presidency just sixteen days after the Supreme Court ruling.

In passing judgement, the Justices created in common law a new legal concept of presidential privilege. It was an idea pushed by Nixon's counsel, but it had no mention in Article II of the Constitution. The Justices ruled, nonetheless, that this privilege was limited, and the President could not claim a blanket exemption from criminal investigation whilst in office. At its core, once again, the case turned on constructing indeterminate rules of law. At least, that is how the Justices presented their determination of the case. Regardless of their true motivations, the Justices were, and Justices consistently have been, keen to demonstratively play the game of legal interpretation. As such, it does not much matter whether indeterminacies in law solely and directly caused political or policy interventions from the bench, they at least facilitate and justify such interventions. In *US v. Nixon*, everything hinged on the Federal Rules of Criminal Procedure. The Special Prosecutor had filed a motion under rule 17(c) for a subpoena *duces tecum*. Rule 17(c) states that (indeterminacies highlighted):

> A subpoena *may also* command the person to whom it is directed to produce the books, papers, documents *or other* objects designated therein. The court on motion *made promptly may* quash *or* modify the subpoena *if* compliance would be *unreasonable or oppressive*.

It was not typical for the Supreme Court to construct rule 17(c). The rule was bread and butter for trial courts, rather than the apex appellate court. Nonetheless, there was precedent for its interpretation at the Supreme

[35] 418 U.S. 683 (1974).

[36] 520 U.S. 681 (1997).

[37] Also appointed by Nixon but willing to rule against him was Harry Blackmun, Lewis F. Powell Jr., and William Rehnquist.

Court in a case which turned on the two adjectives and a conjunction in "unreasonable or oppressive". In the 1951 case of *Bowman Dairy Co. v. United States*,[38] it had been established that a subpoena would not be unreasonable or oppressive, provided it was not being used for a fishing expedition, where prosecutors had no idea what they may find. This was not the case with the Nixon tapes. From a deeper jurisprudential perspective, counsel for the President was seeking to oust judges from what he saw as an internal matter for the executive branch. In other words, the threat was to the rule of law itself, and its capacity to constrain all government officials, including the President.

There is therefore institutional competition over determining and defining away indeterminacies of law and sociology (Bauman 1991). In Nixon's case, the Supreme Court won a battle, but conceded that there were some unwritten privileges for the presidency to be found in the constitution. When set in a highly diverse, ideologically split, and continent-sized country, there ought to be little surprise that law is post positive. Meaning that the text of laws is never likely to be the true end of a legal dispute, because its positive meaning will always be contestable. It just so happens that we have uncovered evidence that these texts are not only capable of subjective reimagining, but are objectively unstable as regards their failing to sustain norms of semantics and construction. What becomes striking in this context is how tentatively the federal courts intervene in politics and policy. Ambivalence in legal texts offers opportunities for judges to pursue policy goals and claim to be doing so legitimately. But a more sensible strategy for policy-oriented judges is to be norm-conserving and to reconcile context and text according to existing principles of linguistic construction (Vanberg 2001). Whether judges are aiming to avoid being distinguished or overruled in their decisions, or whether they are seeking to ensure the longevity of judicial authority, the power of judges resides not in overtly stretching meanings, but in offering legal solutions that are derivative and rarely generative.

In public relations, the courts also downplay their power. This is utterly predictable, but is not entirely disingenuous. In 2018, for example, Chief Justice Roberts declared that "We do not have Obama judges or

[38] 341 U.S. 214 (1951).

Trump judges, Bush judges or Clinton judges".[39] He was probably in part fatigued by assumptions that his and his fellow Justices' behaviour was predictable from their appointing Presidents. But the usually taciturn jurist was defending the judiciary from targeted attacks. President Trump had elicited the comment after he lambasted an "Obama judge" for a unfavourable decision. Of course, the three Trump appointed Justices have in common a generalised conservatism, but they, like all other Justices, are capable of independent mindedness. They did nothing, for example, to support *certiorari* appeals from states seeking to litigate the 2020 election. In T*exas v. Pennsylvania*, for example, the former state tried to sue the latter state for perceived electoral irregularities that allegedly delivered a Biden victory in 2020.[40] And President Biden himself is no stranger to politicised justice. He was central to a nomination battle of such intensity that it yielded a neologism—borking—meaning an obstructionist campaign against a nominee for high office. Robert Bork had been blocked by the Senate for appointment to the Supreme Court, and, as Chair of the Judiciary Committee, Joe Biden had overseen this strict originalist's rejection. As President, his threats to pack the court to thirteen members with the *Judiciary Act 2021* demonstrated further that judges and justice continue to be weaponised by both parties.

Judges are not incentivised to lean into this political fray. John Roberts hence denied the existence of "Obama judges", because he does not want his or his Court's independence to be questioned. The continued authority of the judiciary depends on at least a perception of impartiality. As such, their methods of constructing political language are demonstratively norm-conserving. Whether the judges are in fact preserving norms by striking down law, or creating new legal ligatures, judges take great pains through diligent opinion writing to be seen to be playing the game of law, not politics. There are, therefore, consistent and coherent rules of statutory construction, that give benefits of any doubt to accountable policymakers. As the Tenth Circuit Court of Appeal put it in *United States v. Day*:

> When reviewing a statute alleged to be vague, courts must indulge a presumption that it is constitutional, and the statute must be upheld unless

[39] https://eu.usatoday.com/story/news/politics/2018/11/21/john-roberts-trump-statement/2080266002/ accessed on 15th May 2021.

[40] 592 U.S. ___ (2020).

> the court is satisfied beyond all reasonable doubt that the legislature went beyond the confines of the Constitution.[41]

The "beyond all reasonable doubt" formula is sometimes mathematically described as a 99% certainty that, in this usage, statute laws are constitutional. This is a cautious formula for courts to abide by, given inducements for them to be more political. Indeed, judges will work for legislators by refining "overbroad" statute law into a narrower, and thereby more workable, construction.[42] When it comes to state laws, federal appeals courts are especially reluctant to strike anything down before a state appeal court has had its say.[43] Federal courts will intervene if a statute is identified as "void for vagueness".[44] The test for this is whether a statute is so vague that an average citizen will fail to understand it, or if key terms are left undefined. This still leaves wide discretion for courts to arrogate to themselves the thoughts of an average citizen. But there is evidence that courts are in fact managing increased legislative indeterminacy, with scant reason or evidence that courts systematically abuse indeterminacies in pursuit of personal policy goals. This will be explored further below with regard to criminal justice. The void for vagueness doctrine in that context requires that:

> …a penal statute define the criminal offense with sufficient definiteness that ordinary people can understand what conduct is prohibited and in a manner that does not encourage arbitrary and discriminatory enforcement.[45]

We now turn to analyse the extent to which penal legislation has obtained sufficient definiteness.

[41] 223 F.3d 1225, 1228 (10th Cir.2000).

[42] See, notably, *Dirks v. SEC*, 802 F.2d 1468, 1471 (D.C.Cir.1986).

[43] See *Harman v. Forssenius*, 380 U.S. 528, 535, 85 S.Ct. 1177, 1182, 14 L.Ed.2d 50 (1965).

[44] First established in *Connally v. General Construction Co.*, 269 U.S. 385 (1926).

[45] *Kolender v. Lawson*, 461 U.S. 352, 357, 103 S.Ct. 1855, 75 L.Ed.2d 903 (1983).

Empirical—Textual Changes

The so-called culture wars in America have played out through reinforcing geographic, demographic, and institutional cleavages. Dissensus is of course nothing new to American politics. If anything disagreement was a foundational presumption of post-revolutionary statecraft. Exemplary to this is the US Senate, which was designed to thwart rather than facilitate policy change. Nonetheless, increased population growth, increased wealth, the distribution of power, and the strategic behaviour of parties have deepened the polarisation of politics. Given this policy environment, it is perhaps surprising that any laws are enacted at all, let alone laws whose content is underdetermined. Surely, we would expect no laws, or tightly constructed policy bargains as consequences of polarisation.

But what does the evidence say? Research from Sarah Binder showed that around one quarter of all major agenda items was legislated on by Congress in a typical year (Binder 2003). That leaves three quarters of legislation that fails to pass and acts predominantly as "messaging bills" targeted at voters. Other fates for bills include being put on the proverbial shelf until unified government or exogenous shocks make it viable. Descriptive statistics in Chapter Four revealed that the one quarter of all agenda items enacted accounts for an average of 1.6 million words per annum. The linguistic volatility of this language was the lowest of all five counties studied, with the US presenting a platykurtic distribution for the ten years of available data. Hence, of those laws enacted, the language has been stable. But, taking in a longer view reveals different patterns. Judges will similarly assess legislative language over the long term, so as to assess connections between rules of law, norms, and the facts of specific cases.

There is complete data available for federal criminal justice legislation dating back to the 1940s. Over this longer time frame, it is possible to observe substantial changes in legislative language. Also, criminal justice enjoys greater bipartisan support than other policy spaces. As such, we can expect limited disruption to the enactment of criminal legislation enabling wide discretion for federal agencies and law enforcement officers. In empowering agents of the state, the legislative language can be expected to be underdetermined, with the deliberate intention of it being adaptable to shifting contexts and agent discretion. Besides these general propositions, we can also expect an increased enactment of laws targeted at newly emergent, or increasingly common offences—such as cyber-crime and international terrorism.

It is important to note that the drafting process of federal bills is, by comparison to the other countries studied in this book, non-bureaucratic. This means that individual members of Congress have substantially greater chance of adding language to a Bill as compared to their foreign counterparts. There is therefore a greater likelihood of authorial pluralism, which will in turn lead to a diversity of writing styles. This is not to say that the federal bureaucracy has no role in drafting. The Department of Justice can and does draft bills on matters of criminal justice for the consideration of Congress. But any member of the House and Senate may also draft bills for the consideration of their peers. Any such drafts will be scrutinised and likely changed substantially on the path to enactment. In particular, bills will be reviewed by specialised committees and subcommittees that may amend a bill's drafting to obtain general policy change, sectoral advantage, or harmonisation with other rules of law. Specifically, interested entities will include the House Judiciary Committee and its subcommittee on Crime, Terrorism and Homeland Security. For the Senate, it is the Senate Judiciary Committee's subcommittee on Criminal Justice and Counterterrorism that takes a lead. Committees commonly control a bill's access to the floor, and thereby exert a prominent veto power. Other players, including the President, federal agencies, and lobbying organisations will push for bills to be altered or released for floor debate. This process of drafting is more reliant on individuals than institutions when compared to the other countries studied. The consequences of which lie at two extremes, the first being a lack of policy change, and the second being rapid and radical change. Criminal justice is open to the latter, and thereby is more likely subject to degenrification of legislative linguistics.

Table 6.1 describes the quantities of current federal criminal justice legislation enacted by decade. Unlike other chapters, these figures describe the currently enforced criminal code and the temporal origins of its contents. We cannot definitively conclude from these data that a certain decade saw more or less enactment of law than another. We can conclude how much a specific decade contributed to the criminal code as it stands at the time of writing. This is due to a lack of historical data on criminal legislation, other than the current United States Code. Nonetheless, we can infer certain patterns in legislative output, and we can compare the styles of language used for older and newer contributions to the code. Lawmakers in the 1990s, for example, contributed substantially to the present code.

Table 6.1 Descriptive statistics

Decade	*Sum of sections*	*Sum of word length*
1940s	64	5320
1950s	7	989
1960s	15	1716
1970s	35	8909
1980s	120	24,419
1990s	530	105,957
2000s	288	122,664
2010s	189	163,949
Average statute	22	7749
Standard deviation	50	13,319
Minimum	1 (Various)	23 (1958)
Maximum	350 (1994)	69,504 (2018)
Total	1248	433,923

The 1970s began with President Nixon's push for "law and order", which, in spite of it being a period of divided government, saw the contribution of relatively large quantities of law. The 1990s saw a compendious criminal justice law enacted in 1994 under a unified period of President Clinton's administration. The *Violent Crime Control and Law Enforcement Act* of 1994 had its Senate version authored by the then Delaware Senator, Joe Biden. The 1994 Crime Bill is exemplary of the claim that bipartisan criminal reforms tend to empower law enforcement through underdetermined language. The loose definition of civil disorders illustrates the point (machine read indeterminacies highlighted):

> (a) (1) Whoever teaches *or* demonstrates to *any other* person the use, application, *or* making of *any* firearm *or* explosive *or* ***incendiary*** device, *or* technique *capable* of causing injury *or* death to persons, knowing *or* having reason to know *or* intending that the same will be *unlawfully* employed for use in, *or* in furtherance of, a *civil* disorder which *may* in *any* way *or* degree obstruct, delay, *or adversely* affect commerce *or* the movement of *any* article *or* commodity... Shall be fined under this title *or* imprisoned not more than five years, *or* both.[46]

[46] 18 U.S. Code § 231.

Heading into the twenty-first century, there has been a contribution of fewer sections to the code, but of substantially greater average word length. Politics since the millennium has continued to be markedly polarised, but matters including counter-terrorism and drug control hold relative bipartisan support (Mayhew 2005). Given the vastly greater length of recently enacted sections of the code, it is not surprising that these contain more indeterminate parts of speech. This is confirmed by Table 6.2, which describes a jump to over 81 indeterminate parts of speech per section in the 2010s. The key point, as described in Chapter Two is that increased word length does not equate to increased specificity, because there have been increases both to word length and to the incidence of indeterminate language.

Graphically, we can see from Figs. 6.1 and 6.2 the quantities and relative indeterminacies of those parts of the Criminal Code enacted after the 1990s. As can be seen, the vast majority of the extant Criminal Code—specifically, 90.5%—was enacted after the 1990s. Criminal justice appears to have bucked the trend of other more gridlocked policy spaces. The more recently enacted legislation is also longer and more indeterminately constructed by comparison to older, pre-1989, legislation.

The following example of recently enacted legislation includes a list of offences, but does so with reliance on adjectives conjoined with multiple conjunctions. It is with regards to "Acts of terrorism transcending national boundaries" which was first enacted in 1996 and amended multiple times up to 2015:

> (1) Offenses.—Whoever, involving conduct transcending *national* boundaries and in a circumstance described in subsection (b)– (A) kills, kidnaps, maims, commits an assault resulting in *serious bodily* injury, *or* assaults with a *dangerous* weapon *any* person within the United States; *or* (B) creates a *substantial* risk of *serious bodily* injury to *any* other person by destroying *or* damaging *any* structure, conveyance, *or other real or personal* property within the United States... shall be punished as prescribed in subsection (c).[47]

It is difficult to conclude that legislative language has changed in America, because it is possible that those remaining elements of the Code that were enacted from the 1940s to the 1980s are not representative of their times.

[47] 18 U.S. Code § 2332b.

Table 6.2 Indeterminate parts of speech per section of criminal justice legislation

Decade	*Average of adjectives/section*	*Average of conjunctions/section*	*Average of indeterminate modal verbs/section*	*Average of enabling verbs/section*	*Average of compound indeterminacies/section*
1940s	4.52	6.96	0.58	0.05	12.12
1950s	7.87	18.80	1.07	0.13	13.93
1960s	3.08	12.22	0.93	0.08	8.15
1970s	7.85	10.29	1.34	0.19	15.73
1980s	13.27	10.99	1.78	0.06	15.66
1990s	15.80	22.39	1.45	0.17	39.80
2000s	18.18	28.55	1.39	0.21	48.33
2010s	32.50	46.30	2.49	0.24	81.52
Averages year	15.55	23.03	1.53	0.16	31.33
Standard deviation	15.03	20.09	1.40	0.22	35.30
Min	0	2.00	0	0	0
Max	64.18	94.59	7.24	1.00	163.76 (2015)

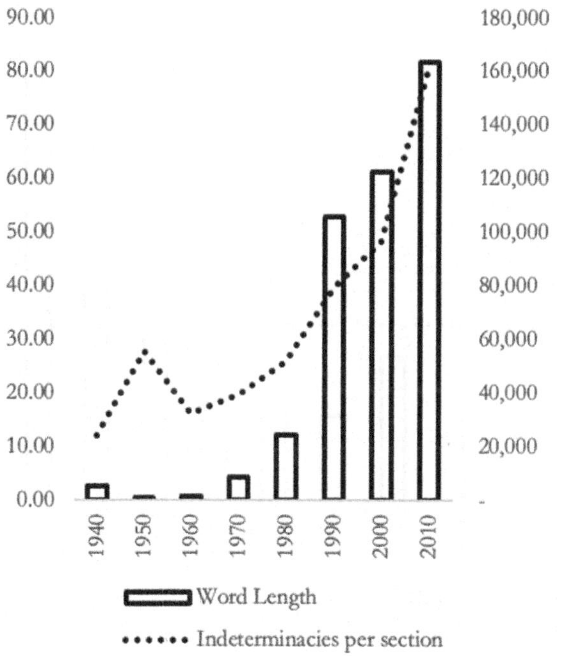

Fig. 6.1 Comparison of changes in indeterminacy (primary y-axis) and word length (secondary y-axis) in criminal justice legislation 1948–2020 (*Source* Author's creation)

However, there is evidence of substantial changes in linguistic norms since the 1990s, giving an inferential basis that legislative genre (as pertains to criminal justice) has been unstable. The next step is to see how changes may have affected the behaviour of judges tasked with interpreting such laws.

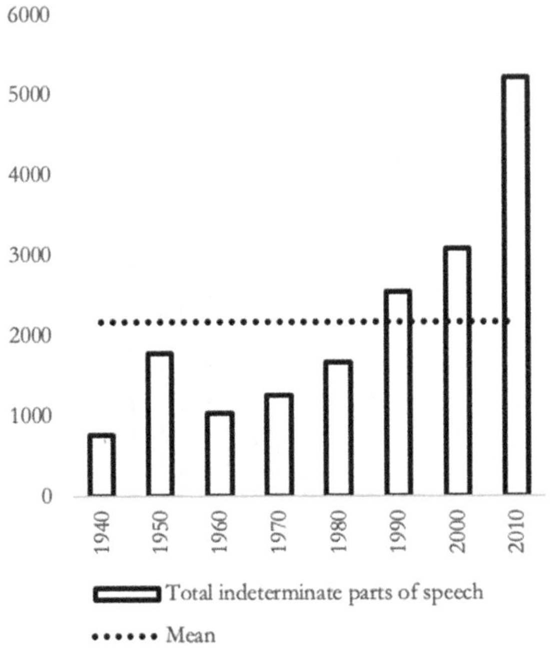

Fig. 6.2 Total indeterminacies (number of coded parts of speech) in all criminal justice legislation 1948–2020 (*Source* Author's creation)

Definitional—Subtextual Changes

In addition to broad policy discretion for law enforcement, judges themselves enjoy discretion derived from the constitution, statute, and common law to enforce laws and even to create new laws. Common law powers, in particular, allow judges to determine textual indeterminacies from a wide range of subtextual sources, including long past precedents, and their own understanding of contemporary norms, all conflated amidst the facts of a given case. The basic undergirding norms used to resolve textual indeterminacies are inclined to protect civic liberty from an overbearing state, unless and until individuals are denied their freedoms upon application of due process. There is, therefore, scope for judges to rein in law enforcement by referring to a dense and revered hinterland of criminal concepts, dating not only back to the American Revolutionary War, but to the English Civil War and even back to England's First Barons' War of 1215.

Magna Carta is still utilised in contemporary American jurisprudence to define away textual indeterminacies. It was used, for example, to resolve a dispute about expropriated raisins in 2015. In *Horne v. Department of Agriculture*,[48] it was ruled that the Fifth Amendment's Takings Clause applied to personal property and not just to real property:

> …nor shall private property be taken for public use, without just compensation.

Marvin Horne and other petitioners were raisin farmers in California. They were compelled under threat of a fine to surrender a portion of their annual crop to a government reserve scheme. This enabled the Department of Agriculture to control supply and donate surpluses. The Hornes were requested to turn over 47% of their crop, in return for which they received no compensation, just or otherwise. According to Chief Justice Roberts's majority opinion, this went against a foundational rule of law:

> The colonists brought the principles of Magna Carta with them to the New World, including that charter's protection against uncompensated takings of personal property. In 1641, for example, Massachusetts adopted its Body of Liberties, prohibiting 'mans Cattel or goods of what kinde soever' from being 'pressed or taken for any publique use or service, unlesse it be by warrant grounded upon some act of the generall Court, nor without such reasonable prices and hire as the ordinarie rates of the Countrie do afford.'[49]

The raisin reserve scheme was declared unconstitutional, and the interpretation of the Takings Clause was marginally reconfigured. This was a civil law matter. In criminal law, courts will also rely on historic sources of law to protect contemporary liberties. In defining the nature and extent of offences that would not have existed in thirteenth-century England, the judges must infer how long-standing principles could adapt to, as examples, a child exploitation enterprise or anti-abortion protests. Judges will interpret pertinent sources of law to solve such cases, not least of

[48] 576 U.S. ___ (2015).

[49] Ibid., p. 5.

which includes relevant congressional legislation. But for some particular crimes, Congress did not fully anticipate the actions that individuals might take. This means that governing statutes contain broad definitions of both crime and punishment, forcing judges to solve cases by themselves, adopting a pseudo-legislative role of defining what specific actions violate social mores.

In adopting this method, judges are unlikely to face disapproval if their definitions are in line with those advocated by the Government in its case submissions. More broadly, the likelihood of court deference to government counsel will increase where the punishment of crimes is supported by public opinion. A 2010 case heard by the United States Court of Appeals for the Eleventh Circuit is illustrative.[50] Four co-defendants were convicted of a series of child pornography offences that amounted to a "child exploitation enterprise". They appealed against their convictions, arguing that the guiding statute was unconstitutionally vague. The *Child Protection Act 2012* was so widely supported that the House passed it "under suspension of the rules" of normal procedure, and the Senate affirmed it unanimously. Under these conditions, it is possible that the statute left wide spaces for conceptual definition to be determined in context. Statutes that are difficult to pass typically have more determinate language, because lawmakers have already effectively litigated the meanings of vague terms. In this case, however, conceptual indeterminacy was not destructive of the convictions. The clause at issue was in § 2252A(g), wherein a child exploitation enterprise is defined as a "series of felony violations constituting three or more separate incidents". The defendants queried whether their actions were sufficiently separable to be described as in series. Assistant US Attorneys David L. Goldberg and Robert G. Davies, acting for the government, argued contrarily that the defendants had coordinated a group of 45 individuals in a sophisticated network for smuggling and distributing indecent images. The seriality of offences was established to the Court's satisfaction.

Other cases do not offer such a clear consensus of political or public opinions. *Scheidler v. National Organization for Women* was just such a case.[51] It was a high-profile fight over anti-abortion protests that had been jumping up and down the federal appellate hierarchy for two

[50] *United States v. Wayerski*, 624 F.3d 1342 (2010).

[51] 547 U.S. 9 (2006).

decades. The National Organization for Women ("NOW") filed a class action civil lawsuit in 1986 against Joseph Scheidler and his associates in the Pro-Life Action League (PLAL), and the Pro-Life Action Network (PLAN). PLAL and PLAN coordinated across states to, amongst other things, blockade abortion clinics, to harass patients and staff, and even to smash equipment, all of which was described by defendants as "Operation Rescue". NOW submitted a number of legal bases for their case, with claims for damage of property, aggravated by antitrust and racketeering claims. One of the most notable features of the case was an attempt by NOW to make a claim under the *Racketeer Influenced and Corrupt Organizations Act* (RICO) 1970. This legislation had been enacted to tackle organised crime, and, in particular, the mafia. Pertinent to the thesis here, § 1961 of RICO defines racketeering activities, with its primary subclause alone running to 754 words. The concept of racketeer influenced criminality is, hence, indeterminate, as the following excerpt demonstrates:

> (1) racketeering activity means (A) any act or threat involving murder, kidnapping, gambling, arson, robbery, bribery, extortion, dealing in obscene matter, or dealing in a controlled substance or listed chemical (as defined in section 102 of the Controlled Substances Act), which is chargeable under State law and punishable by imprisonment for more than one year; (B) any act which is indictable under any of the following provisions of title 18, United States Code…if the act indictable under such section of such Act was committed for the purpose of financial gain, or (G) any act that is indictable under any provision listed in section 2332b (g)(5)(B).

A successful RICO claim would have enabled NOW to treble any damages earned. A central question became whether the activities of anti-abortion protestors could be described as racketeering. The Supreme Court heard portions of the case on three occasions. In 1994, the court ruled on the narrow ground that an economic motive was not needed for a successful RICO claim, and thereby overruled on this point the Illinois District Court and Seventh Circuit Court.[52] In 2003, the court ruled that the activities of Operation Rescue did not amount to extortion, because property was not taken from abortion clinics.[53] Finally, and unanimously, in

[52] *National Organization for Women, Inc. v. Scheidler*, 510 U.S. 249 (1994).

[53] *Scheidler v. National Organization for Women*, 537 U.S. 393 (2003).

2006 the Supreme Court ruled in favour of Scheidler et al. Anti-abortion protests were not "racketeering influenced" nor extortive, and RICO could not be used for either damages or injunctive relief. The Supreme Court suggested that the viable grounding for NOW's case was the *Freedom of Access to Clinic Entrances Act* (FACE) 1994. By enacting this part way through the on-going saga, Congress was seen by the court as deciding against use of RICO for enterprises not typically associated with organised crime.

In managing textual indeterminacies, therefore, US courts may draw on a complex set of subtextual understandings and norms. Some sources of meaning are medieval, others are inferred from what Congress is or is not doing. When Congress overwhelmingly supported action against child pornographers, the subtext was clear that a common sense interpretation of seriality in offences was called for. When Congress specifically enacted legislation to manage anti-abortion protests, the subtext was that extant challenges based on extortion and racketeering were defunct. It is nonetheless difficult for judges to be deferential without controversy, because there is no single political authority to which deference may be given. The separations of power in both horizontal (federal) and vertical (state) plains make for complex determinations not only of meaning, but also of jurisdictional rectitude.

Systemic—Intertextual Changes

Whilst there is no single political authority, there is a single textual authority in the Constitution. The Supremacy Clause (Article VI.2) establishes this point without ambiguity. By monopolising constitutional interpretation, federal courts can become de facto, if not *de jure*, supreme over all political disputes. This point undergirds arguments made that juristocracy exists in America, and that courts engage in mega-politics (Hirschl 2004). The influence of courts is indeed enhanced by separations of power. With divided sovereignties, there are multiple institutional and ideological friction points, for which the designated resolution mechanisms are constitutional amendment or constitutional review (Stone Sweet 2012). The former is notoriously difficult, such that there have been only twenty-seven amendments in over 230 years. The twenty-seventh amendment took over 200 years to be ratified by the necessary three-fifths of states. Major proposed reforms—including the Equal Rights Amendment and Voting Rights Amendment—have been in consideration for decades without reaching fruition. This constitutional rigidity contributed substantially to violent breaching points, including no less than the Civil War. In the absence of efficient mechanisms for amendment, constitutional review is one of few legal mechanisms available to settle, at least partially, law and policy disputes.

Judges resolve intertextual inconsistencies between the Constitution and lower-order legal texts. It is little surprise that fights from abortion to the death penalty have thereby been judicialised as state and federal laws are interpreted relative to the Constitution. And, in terms of how this juridical behaviour is coordinated, the following schematic makes clear that the Supreme Court has the final say. Similar to Magna Carta, the United States has also inherited the centralised model of English Law. Indeed, just as the UK has retained only a husk of Magna Carta in its contemporary law, its legal hierarchy is less centralised today than the medieval model inherited and more holistically sustained by America. This makes for an interesting institutional ambivalence, with a juridical hierarchy derived from medieval kingship, set against popular institutions that were designed in opposition to monarchy and deference. A tension between elitism and populism is one of the original and most enduring cleavages in US politics.

In addition to courts being an institutional locus for informal constitutional amendment, indeterminacies in the constitution and legislation give judges wide interpretative spaces to perform this task. As argued previously, indeterminacies are indicative of political ambivalence. In the midst of ambivalences as to the form and content of rules, judges as umpires are of elevated importance. But in terms of the direction of causality, evidence presented in this and other chapters points resolutely to judges being more reactive to exogenous stimuli, rather than proactively expanding their influence. This section focusses on coordinative discourses between institutions of American government—both at the federal and state levels. Constitutional and legislative indeterminacies, in combination with the supremacy clause, compel judges to determine a balance of powers between federal entities, and between states and the federal government. Judges can effectively choose a balance of powers, provided it is acceptable to their fellow judges. Hence there have been a variety of federalism models, from more to less centralising. It is immaterial to discuss which of these different models was optimal, more important is the fact that such wide-ranging interpretations were possible in the first place (Fig. 6.3).

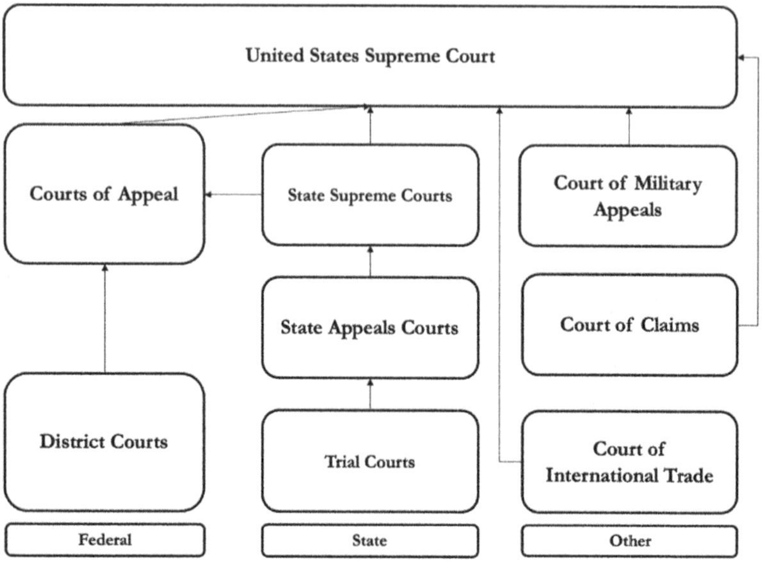

Fig. 6.3 US courts schematic
(*Source* Author's creation)

None of which is to conclude that the courts have untrammelled power. Courts are constrained by institutional and situational weaknesses. With federal courts as co-equal in stature to the executive and legislature, they must share authority and resources. In particular, the courts lack powers of sword, of purse, and even of personnel. Not only are federal judges chosen by the President and approved by the Senate, but even law clerks that work for these judges have to be paid for and approved by Congress. Technically, it is also possible for judges to be impeached. Although, only one Supreme Court Justice has ever faced this penalty, and Samuel Chase was acquitted on trial in the Senate. It is, in reality, very difficult to remove sitting judges, as exemplified by the striking case of founding father James Wilson, who spent two spells in debtors' prison whilst still serving on the highest court. It is nonetheless possible, despite the difficulties, for Congress and the President to collaborate against a judicial ruling. In the early case of *Chisholm v. Georgia*,[54] for example,

[54] 2 U.S. 419 (1793).

it was ruled that states do not have sovereign immunity on account of the newly ratified constitution. This meant that states could be sued by the citizens of other states. But this decision, along with a number of pending decisions, were voided by the rapid passing of the Constitution's eleventh amendment in 1795. The amendment demonstrated that even a rigid constitution could be overcome, albeit there were just fifteen states needed for the amendment at that time.

Of greater bearing than formal institutional inhibitions, are ideological and situational constraints. Judges are sensitive to public opinion. In the case of federal judges, they do not have to bend to public opinion for fear of losing an election.[55] The constraints against judicial overreach may thus be immaterial, but are nonetheless effective (Vanberg 2001). Judges cannot avoid the predicates of constitutional discourse, including individual liberties and states' rights. Judges risk losing their legitimacy in shaping discourses, if they are seen to be abandoning the role of independent referee, and becoming a player on the field. If judges utilised coordinative discourses that were unrecognisable to other power centres or to public opinion, they could lose the authority of their voice (Hart 1961). This reasoning is derived from evidence and shows up in an etymological reading of jurisdiction—judges as a mouthpiece of the law. Judges are powerful, not because they have money or muscle, but because they are recognised for their legitimate voice. If their words are perceived as sullied by politicking, their voice will be ignored. Judges can certainly provide leadership on coordinative discourses, but it would be inaccurate to say they control the creation and dissemination of authoritative communication between government institutions. Also, as stressed, they are reactive to others' uses of discourse, and they are empowered to correct what are perceived as errors. Their role is far less generative, and more conservative therefore. Judges may actively construct ligatures to resolve intertextual indeterminacies, but will do so according to recognisable standards.

An example of recognisable but nonetheless creative interpretation came early with *McCulloch v. Maryland*.[56] This 1819 case decided by the Supreme Court hinged on the elastic "necessary and proper" clause of

[55] Although, there are only seven states in which there is no public election of at least some judges: Delaware, Hawaii, Massachusetts, New Hampshire, New Jersey, Rhode Island, and Virginia. https://ballotpedia.org/Judicial_election_methods_by_state accessed on 30th June 2021.

[56] 17 U.S. (4 Wheat.) 316 (1819).

Article I. The Justices had to determine the extent of Congress's legislative power, where the Constitution had left that underdetermined. The case settled (for a time) a long-running practical dispute over federal power, the power to establish a national bank. It was a matter that had from the earliest days divided Federalists like Alexander Hamilton from the Democratic-Republicans like Thomas Jefferson. The state of Maryland became involved when it decided to tax the national bank. The Supreme Court ruled for the federal government, submitting that the "necessary and proper" clause created implied power that abetted the explicitly enumerated powers. Congress had enumerated powers to tax and spend, and a bank could be construed as a "necessary" instrument for the efficient administration of said powers. Also, given the Supremacy Clause, it was improper for a state to impede these implied and enumerated powers, especially as this was the second attempt to incorporate a national bank and was therefore not a new federal incursion. The court's constructive analysis of the adjective "necessary" is striking for its admixture of conservatism and creativity. The construction sought to conserve ordinary usage of the word, whilst enabling power by reading between the proverbial lines. Chief Justice John Marshall spoke for the court:

> Is it true, that this is the sense in which the word 'necessary' is always used? Does it always import an absolute physical necessity, so strong, that one thing to which another may be termed necessary, cannot exist without that other? We think it does not. If reference be had to its use, in the common affairs of the world, or in approved authors, we find that it frequently imports no more than that one thing is convenient, or useful, or essential to another.[57]

Marshall went on to anchor this flexible yet conservative construction in a philological theory:

> Such is the character of human language, that no word conveys to the mind, in all situations, one single definite idea; and nothing is more common than to use words in a figurative sense. Almost all compositions contain words, which, taken in a their rigorous sense, would convey a meaning different from that which is obviously intended... The word 'necessary' is of this description. It has not a fixed character, peculiar to itself.

[57] Ibid. at 413–414.

> It admits of all degrees of comparison; and is often connected with other words, which increase or diminish the impression the mind receives of the urgency it imports. A thing may be necessary, very necessary, absolutely or indispensably necessary. To no mind would the same idea be conveyed by these several phrases.

Marshall harboured undisguised Federalist sympathies, but his interpretation was in keeping with both ordinary usage (as understood by the court) and precedent. It was not, therefore, an especially stretched interpretation. Although, it was a ruling that helped stretch the Elastic Clause. It formed a jurisprudential foundation upon which later developments in federal power would be built. An example being the concept of incorporation, wherein federal rights were imposed on state governments. This further empowered federal judges to determine the validity of state laws, and was practiced in both *Brown* and *Roe*. The *McCulloch* ruling was, however, insufficient. In keeping with another theme of this book, major developments in judicial power took multiple iterations to become settled law. And, in addition to the sedimentation of legal precedents, there was also a need for political consensus supporting federal leadership. In the US case, this came with the Civil War and enactment of the Fourteenth Amendment. Prior to the Civil War, in the case of B*arron v. Baltimore*,[58] Marshall and the Supreme Court ruled that the Bill of Rights could not be brought to bear against state governments. The due process and equal protection clauses effectively overturned this ruling.

The first unequivocal act of incorporation came with the 1925 case of *Gitlow v. New York*.[59] Benjamin Gitlow had been convicted under New York state law for sedition by publishing a socialist manifesto. The Supreme Court upheld his conviction, and ruled that the Fourteenth Amendment made the federal government responsible for administering the Bill of Rights amongst the states. In this case it was the First Amendment right to freedom of expression that was incorporated. Important acts of incorporation have included with regards to the Fourth Amendment protections against "unreasonable searches and seizures" in *Mapp v. Ohio*.[60] Fifth and Sixth Amendments protections against self-incrimination and rights to due process were incorporated by the Warren

[58] 32 U.S. 243 (1833).

[59] 268 U.S. 652 (1925).

[60] 367 U.S. 643 (1961).

Court in *Gideon v. Wainwright*,[61] and *Miranda v. Arizona*.[62] Notably, incorporation was not extended to the Second Amendment right to bear arms in *United States v. Cruikshank*.[63] Although, incorporation of the second amendment was finally achieved but in order to reverse gun control measures in *District of Columbia v. Heller*[64] and *McDonald v. City of Chicago*.[65] What all of these acts of incorporation have in common is that they are examples of judges pulling back the state from interfering in citizens' lives. With regard to the First, Fourth, Fifth, and Sixth Amendments their results tend to be celebrated by political progressives. But it is conservatives that tend to take solace from incorporation of a right to bear arms against the states. What must be recognised, however, is that despite the contemporary framing of these policy positions, the judicial ideology of minimising state interference is broadly consistent across the gamut.

There is, nonetheless, a prominent counter example to the incorporation doctrine—it does not apply to Native American Nations. The power of the United States Supreme Court in regards to these nations is therefore, again, typified by negativity, insofar as it can say what Congress and the states cannot do, but has a very limited active presence in policy. Rulings under John Marshall in the 1820s and 1830s confirmed a concept of "Tribal Sovereignty".[66] And, the post-Civil War case of *Talton v. Mayes*,[67] ensured that incorporation via the Fourteenth Amendment would not impede this sovereignty. Although, this was later caveated by *Lone Wolf v. Hitchcock* in which it was ruled that Congress could, if it so wished, unilaterally breach treaty obligations to these nations.[68] And, despite a negative power for the courts, this does not mean that it lacks impact. In the 2020 case of *McGirt v. Oklahoma*,[69] for example,

[61] 372 U.S. 335 (1963).

[62] 384 U.S. 436 (1966).

[63] 92 U.S. 542 (1876).

[64] 554 U.S. 570 (2008).

[65] 561 U.S. 742 (2010).

[66] *Johnson v. M'Intosh*, 21 U.S. (8 Wheat.) 543 (1823); *Cherokee Nation v. Georgia*, 30 U.S. (5 Pet.) 1 (1831); *Worcester v. Georgia*, 31 U.S. (6 Pet.) 515 (1832).

[67] 163 U.S. 376 (1896).

[68] 187 U.S. 553 (1903).

[69] 591 U.S. ___ (2020).

the Supreme Court denied the state of Oklahoma jurisdiction to prosecute crimes committed by Native Americans in the lands reserved for the Creek Nation. In his majority opinion, Justice Gorsuch submitted a tight interpretation of the plainly worded 1885 *Major Crimes Act:*

> (a) Any Indian who commits against the person or property of another Indian or other person any of the following offenses...[including the sexual offences for which McGirt was indicted] shall be subject to the same law and penalties as all other persons committing any of the above offenses, within the exclusive jurisdiction of the United States.[70]

What the avowed literalist Gorsuch could not find was an explicit ceding of Tribal Sovereignty by either the Nation themselves, or by unilateral imposition from Congress:

> Missing in all this, however, is a statute evincing anything like the 'present and total surrender of all tribal interests' in the affected lands. Without doubt, in 1832 the Creek 'cede[d]' their original homelands east of the Mississippi for a reservation promised in what is now Oklahoma... And in 1866, they 'cede[d] and convey[ed]' a portion of that reservation to the United States... But because there exists no equivalent law terminating what remained, the Creek Reservation survived allotment.[71]

Chief Justice Roberts pointed out the policy consequences of the majority's ruling, but did so in geopolitical and not explicitly legal terms.

> Not only does the Court discover a Creek reservation that spans three million acres and includes most of the city of Tulsa, but the Court's reasoning portends that there are four more such reservations in Oklahoma. The rediscovered reservations encompass the entire eastern half of the State – 19 million acres that are home to 1.8 million people, only 10%–15% of whom are Indians.[72]

This case encapsulates the paradoxical tension between conservatism and creativity in coordinative discourses. Judges must determine how language has been used by a variety of actors, and explain how it should

[70] 18 U.S. Code § 1153.

[71] 591 U.S. ___ (2020) at page 10.

[72] Ibid., at page 1.

best be used going forward. For the most part, the ideological and institutional forces operating on judges are more negative than genetic—in that judges tend to describe what is not possible rather than what is possible. This commitment to negative liberty is not universal, however, and in certain contexts judges defer to political will.

Prudential–Contextual Changes

It is necessary to consider when and why federal judges refuse to intervene in policy disputes. In some instances, there will be no substantial case to be heard against a policy that is clearly within the "four corners of law". But, as seen with preceding cases, it is rare that constitutional and subordinate laws neatly nest within each other. The four corners of law may—as Ian Loveland (2006, 504) put it—not resemble a neat geometric vessel but an indeterminate mess. Reasons for judges deferring in favour of a politician's determination include legal incapacity and strategic prudence. Judges may simply acknowledge an asymmetry of capacity, competence, or collective legitimacy to strike down legislative or regulatory determinations of law. Courts will, notably, lack the contextual data often needed to reify legal concepts appropriately.

A noted, and much used, precedent of such deference is the 1984 case of *Chevron v. NRDC*.[73] The case established "Chevron deference", wherein courts defer to a federal agency's construction of Congressional statute. Specifically, the case turned on whether the Environmental Protection Agency (EPA) had correctly construed a congressional ambiguity. Congress had amended the *Clean Air Act* to enable the regulation of any "stationary source" of air pollution. The question became whether a stationary source would mean individual device contributing to pollution, or whether all devices in a plant ought to be "bubbled" together. Under the latter interpretation used by the EPA, it would be easier to deny permits to polluting factories, even if they had cleaned up individual (un-bubbled) sources of pollution. The Court of Appeals ruled in favour of Chevron.[74] Because the concept of stationary source was not "squarely

[73] *Chevron U.S.A., Inc. v. Natural Resources Defense Council, Inc.*, 467 U.S. 837 (1984).

[74] *Natural Resources Defense Council, Inc. v. Gorsuch*, 222 U.S.App.D.C. 268 (1982).

addressed in the legislative history"[75] and was "at best contradictory".[76] Precedent, therefore, compelled a conclusion that the bubble concept was inappropriate for measures to improve air quality. But the Supreme Court reversed this decision and deferred to the EPA's approach. In the majority opinion of that court, Justice Stevens explained the deference:

> The basic legal error of the Court of Appeals was to adopt a static judicial definition of the term 'stationary source' when it had decided that Congress itself had not commanded that definition... If... the court determines Congress has not directly addressed the precise question at issue, the court does not simply impose its own construction on the statute, as would be necessary in the absence of an administrative interpretation. Rather, if the statute is silent or ambiguous with respect to the specific issue, the question for the court is whether the agency's answer is based on a permissible construction of the statute.[77]

In this particular case it was felt that the EPA's construction was permissible, and likely based on greater contextual knowledge of the policy environment. Beyond lacking perceived capacity to interpret context, as in the *Chevron* case, judges will also engage in strategic deference. This is where they choose not to interfere with a congressional or presidential construction of the law, for fear of retribution. It is difficult to operationalise the differences between strategic and authentic adjudication, but some indicators can be discerned. A relatively clear indication of strategic behaviour comes when judges disavow their own past rulings. Overturning or distinguishing precedent is a major step for judges to take and is not taken lightly in common law jurisdictions. The consequences will be that all extant decisions and behaviours derived from precedent are thrown into doubt. All lower courts take their marching orders from superior courts, which in changing precedent will be changing rules of law. The example of *West Coast*, wherein a "switch in time saved nine", was discussed above. Another New Deal case where the Supreme Court moved away from its precedent and towards the President's position was

[75] Ibid., at page 273.

[76] Ibid., at page 276.

[77] *Chevron U.S.A., Inc. v. Natural Resources Defense Council, Inc.*, 467 U.S. 837 (1984), at pages 466–7.

National Labor Relations Board v. Jones and Laughlin Steel Corporation.[78] In the preceding Lochner Era, the Supreme Court had imposed a narrow construction on the Interstate Commerce Clause in order to strike down federal macroeconomic interventions. Franklin Roosevelt openly threatened the court and elicited a major change in direction. In this particular case it was ruled that a federal agency could sanction companies that discriminated against unionised workers. Justices expanded the clause's construction to mean that Congress may regulate any activity with a "close and substantial relationship" to interstate commerce. They reached this loose construction not on their own volition, but in response to extraordinary external pressure.

Other cases of strategic deference have been predicated on there being a preferred mechanism of dispute resolution. For example, in *Schlesinger v. Holtzman*,[79] the Supreme Court refused to halt the US Air Force bombings of Cambodia in 1973. They did so firstly because there was ruled to be no judicial oversight of the Commander in Chief Clause in this context. And, because Congress was itself defunding the bombing campaign as the case progressed through the courts. Congress and the Presidency were the rightful determiners of war powers, it was decided. Making this a strategic decision for the judges was the fact that a lower court ruling to stay the bombing was ignored by the military, suggesting that any similar ruling by the Supreme Court would similarly be unsuccessful. Also, the litigant was Elizabeth Holtzman, a Democratic Congresswoman from New York, making the case overtly politicised. William O. Douglas, an outspoken anti-war Justice had unilaterally ordered a stay of the bombing during a court recess. All eight other Justices convened by phone to overrule him (Woodward and Armstrong 1979, 167–180). Besides these strategic considerations, the Constitution's war powers are relatively determinable. There were questions as to whether Congress should have declared war formally against Vietnam and Cambodia, but once military action is engaged, the Constitution explicitly empowers authority in the President, as per Article II.2:

[78] 301 U.S. 1 (1937).

[79] 414 U.S. 1321 (1973).

> The President shall be Commander in Chief of the Army and Navy of the United States, and of the Militia of the several States, when called into the actual Service of the United States...

There is some ambiguity in that last clause, as to when and by whom the union is "called into... actual Service". The case against the Cambodia bombings was that there had not been a lawful process for its initiation. But, in the instance case, the Court decided it had neither the material capacity, nor the legal power to interfere. In other politically sensitive disputes, the Supreme Court came close to sustained intervention, only to defer to federal and state policies. Death penalty jurisprudence exemplifies this. The Court came close to rendering all executions as unconstitutional violations of the Eighth Amendment's "cruel and unusual punishments" clause. In the 1972 case of *Furman v. Georgia*,[80] it was ruled that the death penalty was imposed arbitrarily and inconsistently. This was because those executed were vastly more likely to be poor, uneducated, and black. This unequal application of the law violated the Due Process and Equal Protection clauses of the Fourteenth Amendment. And, Justice Potter Stewart pointed out in conference that the practice was literally "unusual", in that capital crimes were not systematically met with capital punishments (Woodward and Armstrong 1979, 492–497). The ruling stopped all federal and state executions for four years.

In the interim, states enacted new capital punishment statutes in direct response to *Furman*. Several were found to be acceptable, by imposing consistently applied and risk assessed applications of capital punishments.[81] Other state death penalty laws were voided by the Supreme Court, typically for being mandatory punishments for specified crimes, and therefore arbitrary.[82] The crucial ruling, however, was in a highly unusual case. Gary Mark Gilmore demanded that he be executed for two murders. The Supreme Court had the power to stay his execution when deciding the turning point cases heard together in *Gregg v. Georgia*.[83] Judges had set out what was needed for constitutional executions in *Furman* and state legislatures had developed the required legislation.

[80] 408 U.S. 238 (1972).

[81] *Proffitt v. Florida*, 428 U.S. 242 (1976); *Jurek v. Texas*, 428 U.S. 262 (1976).

[82] *Woodson v. North Carolina*, 428 U.S. 280 (1976); *Roberts v. Louisiana*, 428 U.S. 325 (1976).

[83] 428 U.S. 153 (1976).

Nobody had been executed in nearly ten years when Gilmore was killed by firing squad in 1977. By not striking out all executions, however, the Supreme Court has continued to have its docket loaded with *habeas corpus* petitions from death row inmates, and has had to rule on a range of specific matters, such as which lethal concoctions may be used and whether alternative methods of execution have to be available.[84] Death penalty cases combine elements of both judicial deference to contextual knowledge, and strategic acceptance of political will. It is therefore necessary to ascertain when and why judges are willing to stand up to politicians and say "no, you cannot do that".

Influence-Seeking—Transtextual Changes

In the next section we will assess when court decisions adapt and create wholly new law. For this section, we are focussed on courts invalidating extant laws. For judges to invalidate a text, there must be a coincidence of factors. These factors funnel down from macro to micro levels. At a macro-social level, there needs to be conspicuous ambivalence as to the rectitude of policy. Sustained political dissensus, with no viable coalition to resolve it, is a necessary first step. Absent this ambivalence, there would likely be political action to determine rules of law, and there would not be a dispute for judges to resolve. At the meso-level, there then needs to be indeterminacies in legislative texts, as well as intertextual discrepancies with constitutional law. These incompatible discourses will encourage the analysis of transtextuality that gives meaning to the law. This analysis will be developed by lawyers, by academics, by lobbyists, by politicians, and by other interested parties. It will then be litigated by application to a specific case. At the micro-level, a court judgement to invalidate a legal text will depend on such a decision being highly unlikely to be overruled.

We have considered the case of *Lopez*, where federal legislation to limit guns in and around schools was struck down. In the subsequent case of *Printz v. United States*,[85] the Supreme Court invalidated federally imposed background checks on gun owners. Gun-control has long been a divisive issue in American politics, rendering the policy space riddled with

[84] *Baze v. Rees*, 553 U.S. 35 (2008); *Glossip v. Gross*, 576 U.S. ___ (2015); *Bucklew v. Precythe*, 587 U.S. ___ (2019).

[85] 521 U.S. 898 (1997).

ambivalence and textual indeterminacies. Amongst the textual sources of dispute are construction of the Second Amendment's "militia" clause, whether the amendment is incorporated to the states, and whether the federal government can order state law enforcement agents. Jay Printz and Richard Mack brought a constitutional case against the 1993 *Brady Handgun Violence Prevention Act*. Their lawyers proposed a transtextual analysis as preferable to sections of the Act that forced state law enforcement to implement federal background checks. They contended a violation of the Tenth Amendment's separation of sovereignties between federal and state governments. The Supreme Court agreed, and excised the offending sections. But they did not gut the entire legislative scheme, and stressed that voluntary background checks were still possible, even if mandatory checks could not be imposed from Washington.

That case saw a 5–4 split of more conservative against more liberal justices. It was seen by some as a straightforwardly ideological decision, therefore. But, such a conclusion underestimates the textual conflict that enabled a conservative interpretation of gun laws that would not, in all likelihood, be overruled or distinguished. Also, the decision was markedly liberal in ethos, even if not ascribing to that term's interpretation in popular American usage. An even more recent gun case was also decided 5–4, but with a majority that surprised court observers. The 2018 ruling of *United States v. Davis* saw two Trump-appointed conservatives on opposing sides.[86] In this case, a piece of long-standing criminal law was declared unconstitutional on account of vagueness. The defendants—Maurice Davis and Andre Glover—were charged with a number of robberies. A jury found them guilty on all points, including for conspiracy to commit a felony with a firearm. The definition of their crime was captured in a residual clause that embellished an elements clause, but did so indeterminately. In it, a "crime of violence" is defined as:

> ...that [which] by its nature, involves a substantial risk that physical force against the person or property of another may be used in the course of committing the offense.[87]

There is social and political ambivalence as to how serious crimes of violence can be managed. Not ambivalence that serious crimes should be

[86] 588 U.S. ___ (2019).

[87] 18 U. S. C. §924(c).

tackled, but how. How crimes are to be defined and prosecuted, and how punishments are to be enforced are controversial matters that dig into first-order debates on fairness versus security. Indeed, a degree of desperation from Congress to act in a manner that could tackle serious crimes can explain the broad and non-specific language of this residual clause. It was ruled by the majority that a categorical construction was needed, such that a "crime of violence" could be defined without inferring its meaning solely from case facts. It was decided that a category definition was not available, and the residual clause therefore failed as a rule of law. As per Justice Gorsuch:

> In our constitutional order, a vague law is no law at all. Only the people's elected representatives in Congress have the power to write new federal criminal laws. And when Congress exercises that power, it has to write statutes that give ordinary people fair warning about what the law demands of them. Vague laws transgress both of those constitutional requirements... When Congress passes a vague law, the role of courts under our Constitution is not to fashion a new, clearer law to take its place, but to treat the law as a nullity and invite Congress to try again.[88]

The defendants did not have all of their convictions quashed. Their convictions for armed robbery remained intact, as these were set out in a more determinable elements clause. Only on a narrow ground of conspiracy to commit a residual crime were their convictions nullified. The case therefore contains the steps expected prior to a court nullification—social and political dissensus on fairness versus security; indeterminate legislation; and case facts where a moderate opinion was available to excise the offending section without pulling down an entire legal house of cards. Justice Gorsuch wrote the majority opinion that invalidated this subsection of law. He was joined by stalwart liberal Justices Ginsberg, Breyer, Sotomayor, and Kagan. He was opposed by all remaining conservative Justices, with the primary dissent authored by his fellow Trump-appointee, Justice Kavanaugh. These two most junior justices will have been assigned their writing tasks by the most senior justices (Ginsberg for Gorsuch, Roberts for Kavanaugh). That Ruth Bader Ginsberg gave the case to Neil Gorsuch is telling evidence that justices are not automata whose decision algorithms are fixed at appointment. It also

[88] 588 U.S. ___ (2019) page 4.

demonstrates that despite narratives of polarisation, specific policy and legal disputes rarely conform to either purely liberal or conservative principles. This gun crime case is a murky admixture of traditional small-state constitutionalism, with concern for security.

Policy-Oriented—Metatextual Changes

We can explain when judges excise laws as attempts to make a more coherent rules of law. But how can we explain more classic examples of activism, where judges do not justify their behaviour on grounds of conservation, but make new legal and policy frameworks? In a case like *Roe v. Wade*,[89] for example, the Supreme Court recognised a right to privacy that was not explicitly set out in the Constitution. Such cases are not solely text dependent, but extend beyond textual limitations in interpreting social and political facts. The rulings are therefore metatextual and often derive from a critical analysis of legislative texts. A description of one such method in US jurisprudence is substantive due process. It bears many of the hallmarks of European rationality or proportionality review. Courts first determine whether a right exists, if not in law, then in long-standing social practice. If a right is considered to exist and be of fundamental importance, the courts then apply a "strict scrutiny" review of whether transgressive legislation can be justified. The judges determine whether there is a legitimate government interest in interfering with a right, and, if not, they invalidate the law and recognise the unenumerated right. A right to privacy, for example, does not exist textually, but it was considered as presumptively extant, given civil society protections that are enumerated.

Substantive due process moves away from procedural due process. The latter is concerned not with what the law is, but how it is implemented. The basis of substantive judicial review is for the most part founded on close readings of the Fifth and Fourteenth Amendments. The Fifth Amendment's due process clause revived Magna Carta in stating that no one may "be deprived of life, liberty, or property, without due process of law". This clause has two core interpretations. The first interpretation states a condition that life, liberty, and property may only legitimately be deprived if recognised processes are followed. A second interpretation

[89] 410 U.S. 113 (1973).

asks what counts as law. If the concept of law is realist or textualist, then only that which can positively be identified in the "black letter" of law books is legal. Other concepts of law take a wider view, that law includes that which is recognised as customary, or inferred from other rules of law. This latter conception underpinned the founding of common law, wherein the wisdom of judges and communities recognised communal practices as informing law, in addition to that which was written down by lawmakers. Ultimately law under this conception includes both positively enacted legislation as well as customary understandings of fairness and justice. The priority is that rules maintain peace and order. Such rules will typically be consistent with each other and customarily recognised principles of social order. It is less material whether the rules are categorically enumerated by sovereign entities.

Substantive due process is therefore anything but new. It is closer to a pre-democratic form of adjudication. It is, however, not necessarily undemocratic. Judges reviewing the substance of laws may stop majorities from attacking minority rights, but, sovereign will has long been disregarded as monopolising notions of fairness and justice. Might, in other words, is not always right. Majorities may be tempted to enfeeble minorities, rendering their future participation in civic institutions as impaired or impossible. Court rulings against majorities may therefore protect democracy. Celebrated English cases of judicial law making were widely known by America's founders. These include, notably, 1610's *Dr Bonham's Case*, where Sir Edward Coke ruled against the College of Physicians by using common law to challenge Parliament's sovereignty. Substantive due process is, in this vein, fundamentally liberating, as it strips back majoritarian encroachments and builds a "black letter" scaffold of law around minority rights. It is law that imposes limits on law. It often entails the enumeration of rights that are not explicitly laid out in any constitution, legislation, or regulation. Given that judges have no accountability for their law making, such behaviour is understandably controversial, especially given that they may be opposing powerful sovereign institutions.

Judges utilising such methods are described as legislating rather than adjudicating. In fact, the strict separation of adjudicatory and legislative modes of linguistic construction is a modern notion (Vile 1998). Earlier conceptions of law did not draw sharp distinctions between law making and adjudication. These were two sides of the same coin, as modes of reflecting and consolidating social norms. It was post-revolutionary separations of power that conceived of a disjunction of governmental roles. It was also ideologically desirable for the Founding Fathers to distinguish their separations of power from the power-combining "High Court of Parliament", as it was sometimes known in medieval England (Goldsworthy 2004). Ironically, the US republican ideology of dividing sovereignty between institutions has affected notions of popular sovereignty. Institutions are always imperfect at representing social norms and values, but it is institutions that are allocated power in the US Constitution. There is, of course, recognition of "We The People" in the preamble and in the Bill of Rights. But this adds to constitutional ambivalence as to whether powers are separated amongst institutions, or ultimately held by the people. The main constitutional text pushes a variant of republican ideology that favours institutional power and accountability. Somewhat at odds to this, the preamble and Bill of Rights add democratic theory, and regard institutions as derivative of popular will.

In common law rule making, judges attempt to recognise popular and communal will. It is indeed an "attempt", and will not infrequently fail on account of judges lacking proximity to the people. But judges will rarely attempt a ruling that so clearly deviates from popular will as to be distinguished or overruled. Even though it is difficult to overrule the Supreme Court, this does not mean that its justices are insensitive to popular opinion. Indeed, this can help explain why judicial "activism" in the US often conspicuously lacks progressive credentials. In recognising social norms, judges will be biased in favour of regular practices. Such social practices become regularised through structures of power. The conspicuously powerless of American society rarely benefit from judicial activism. *Brown v. Board* is a clear counter example of the powerless benefiting from judicial action. But then even that case recognised the practices of most school boards throughout the country (Klarman 1996). The Warren Court did not create the movement for desegregation, and whilst their ruling marked a major psychological victory, it did little to materially improve the circumstances of African American children.

In short, what is described as activist is, again, notably conservative. It conserves that which is widely considered to be customary. It is rarely generative of a new policy order. Consistent with this analysis, criminal law is rarely a site of policy innovations from federal judges. We have seen the incorporation of the Bill of Rights to states, but this did not see courts create new rights, but rather decide that constitutional rights pertained universally. There are interesting examples where courts updated criminal laws and practices, but these adopted such modest approaches that they hardly suggest of judicial overreach. A particularly important precedent in this regard is *Trop v. Dulles*.[90] In it, the Warren Court took note of "evolving standards of decency" to reach their determination. They were asked whether a deserting soldier could be stripped by the government of his citizenship. The government based their case on clear statutory language:

> [a citizen] shall lose his nationality [for] deserting the military or naval forces of the United States in time of war, provided he is convicted thereof by court martial and as a result of such conviction is dismissed or dishonorably discharged from the service,[91]

In 1944, Albert Trop had snuck out of a military base in Morocco whilst serving as a private. With a friend, he tried to make his way to Casablanca, but without food or warm clothing he gave himself up within just twenty-four hours. He was convicted of desertion by court martial and punished with three years hard labour, forfeiture of pay, and a dishonourable discharge. As a naturalised US citizen, he met the conditions for losing his nationality. When he applied for a passport he was therefore denied it and rendered stateless. Chief Justice Warren used the Eighth Amendment protections against cruel and unusual punishments to rule that denaturalisation was a harsh punishment that was inconsistent with contemporary "standards of decency":

> This Court has had little occasion to give precise content to the Eighth Amendment, and, in an enlightened democracy such as ours, this is not surprising. But when the Court was confronted with a punishment of 12 years in irons at hard and painful labor imposed for the crime of falsifying public records, it did not hesitate to declare that the penalty was cruel in its excessiveness and unusual in its character. *Weems v. United States*, 217 U. S. 349. The Court recognized in that case that the words of the Amendment

[90] 356 U.S. 86 (1958).

[91] § 401(g) *Nationality Act* 1940, amended 1944.

> are not precise, and that their scope is not static. The Amendment must draw its meaning from the evolving standards of decency that mark the progress of a maturing society.[92]

Trop had already been through years of hard labour without pay. It was not as if the Supreme Court was somehow letting him off with a slapped wrist. The Supreme Court was, it is true, going directly against a piece of determinate congressional law. And, in doing so, they were arrogating to themselves a capacity to recognise contemporary standards of decency of which Congress was presumably ignorant. This case presents tensions in variants of republican ideology—between institutionalist and civic versions. It is likely that the justices assumed a substantial change in opinion in 1958, as compared to when the law was drafted during a major conflict. Whilst there would have been little public or political appetite for desertion in 1944 when Congress enacted its law, standards of decency will have evolved quite rapidly post-war. Indeed, the 1940 *Nationality Act* and its 1944 amendment were incorporating an even earlier 1865 Civil War provision. The judges dug in to the statutory record to find that the provision on denaturalisation had been incorporated by Congress with no debate. The implication being that Congress was deficient in its responsibility to use power within reasonable limits. It is not the task of this chapter to legitimise the judges' decision, but to explain how it came about. Denaturalisation was, statistically speaking, an unusual punishment. Imposing it on someone who had already been punished for a twenty-four hour desertion could be described as cruel. There was sufficient linguistic and ideological indeterminacy for the judges to be called on to make a determination.

Given the evidence of growing linguistic indeterminacies, why are judges not constantly making new laws? It is because they must, as discussed in the previous section, wait for an alignment of macro-social, meso-linguistic and micro-level case facts. Linguistic indeterminacy is necessary but insufficient to explain judicial law making. Furthermore, moving beyond a negative ruling to stop policy towards a positive description of policy by judges is more risk-laden. For this policy generative power, judges must be sure that their ruling conforms to the interests of powerful allies. If the ruling deviates from what is desired by a nexus of political and economic elites, then it will not be enforced. It can be,

[92] 356 U.S. 86 (1958) at pages 100–1.

therefore, that the justices are merely facilitating a change in the law that was evidently desired by powerful policy-makers, but, for whatever reason, could not easily be enacted. Again, therefore, judicial creativity in law is both modest in ambition and norm-conserving rather than truly innovative.

An example is the 1897 case of *Allgeyer v. Louisiana*.[93] The Supreme Court ruled in this case that "liberty" in the Fourteenth Amendment included freedom of contract. This was an economically as opposed to socially liberal adjudication. It was also an act of negative liberality. It did not create a right to, but a freedom from interference. In this case, E. Allgeyer & Company used a New York based insurance company to cover international shipments of cotton from the port of New Orleans. Under Louisiana law, however, it was an offence to use out-of-state insurers, for which the punishment was a fine. The intent of the law was to combat fraud. At trial, a local court ruled in favour of Allgeyer, and the Supreme Court confirmed a broader interpretation of liberty was necessary. The unanimous ruling adopted an *obiter dictum* from Justice Bradley's dissent in the *Slaughterhouse Cases* of 1872.

> ... by the fourteenth amendment... citizenship of the United States is the primary citizenship in this country... The States have not now, if they ever had, any power to restrict their citizenship to any classes or persons. A citizen of the United States has a perfect constitutional right to go to and reside in any State he chooses, and to claim citizenship therein, and an equality of rights with every other citizen, and the whole power of the nation is pledged to sustain him in that right... And when the spirit of lawlessness, mob violence, and sectional hate can be so completely repressed as to give full practical effect to this right, we shall be a happier nation, and a more prosperous one, than we now are.[94]

Recognising inter-state freedom of contract was not progressive radicalism. It recognised in law a practice pursued in almost every state, and aligned with the interests of commercial and political elites. The court was pushing against an open door. A more recent and more controversial example of economic liberalising came in the 2005 case of *Kelo v. City*

[93] 165 U.S. 578 (1897).

[94] 83 U.S. 36 (1872) at pages 82 and 83.

of New London.[95] This case did not protect rights, but enabled power. Along with other citizens of New London, Connecticut, Susette Kelo had her property forcibly purchased under eminent domain powers. She sued the city, claiming that her rights under the Fifth Amendment's Public Use Clause were violated. Under that clause, private property may be taken for "public use". The city wanted to redevelop the land on which Kelo and others were living. Specifically, they wanted to develop a business park for the Pfizer Corporation. The question then became whether "public use" could be read as "public purpose". The proposed redevelopment was not primarily intended to be used by the public, but would have benefits to the local community in terms of an improved tax base and new job opportunities. The court ruled in favour of the city, citing a trend in precedents to render the Public Use Clause as allowing expropriation for public purposes. Justice Thomas, an avowed textualist and originalist, excoriated the judgement in his dissent:

> ...the Court replaces the Public Use Clause with a '[P]ublic [P]urpose' Clause.. (or perhaps the 'Diverse and Always Evolving Needs of Society' Clause... This deferential shift in phraseology enables the Court to hold, against all common sense, that a costly urban-renewal project whose stated purpose is a vague promise of new jobs and increased tax revenue, but which is also suspiciously agreeable to the Pfizer Corporation, is for a 'public use.'... Today's decision is simply the latest in a string of our cases construing the Public Use Clause to be a virtual nullity, without the slightest nod to its original meaning.

Why the court had so strayed was obvious to Justice Thomas, as he laid out in a preamble to the above comments:

> Long ago, William Blackstone wrote that 'the law of the land ... postpone[s] even public necessity to the sacred and inviolable rights of private property.'

If the ruling can be described using any ideological label, it would be neoliberal. The court was adapting the word "use" to a sense of "utility". This economistic reading of the Fifth Amendment is not an errant deviation from public policy priorities. The court's ruling, activist as it may be

[95] 545 U.S. 469 (2005).

described, was economically liberal, and therefore in keeping with extant social norms. Justice Thomas was aiming to protect the weak and vulnerable from eminent domain. Justice Kennedy writing a concurrent opinion with the majority, set out how public use could practically be determined. As occurred in the *Allgeyer* ruling, he delegated the task to lower courts to think through the legitimacy and rationality of redevelopment works on a case-by-case basis. This delegating of authority is not consistent with narratives of federal courts as seeking to arrogate policy power. But, as a postscript, the redevelopment never went ahead in New London as Pfizer made other plans.

Another example of metatextual interpretation enabling a freedom to act was with regard to same sex marriage. The major ruling on this—*Obergefell v. Hodges*[96]—identified this new right in the Fourteenth Amendment. Cases from Kentucky, Michigan, Ohio, and Tennessee were all consolidated in the Supreme Court hearing. In all cases, lower courts had found in favour of the couples and against the State governments. Cases included individuals having their out-of-state marriages unrecognised, to having a death certificate fail to acknowledge the deceased's marital status. The Court ruled 5–4 that marriage is and always was a fundamental right that could not be abridged by State governments. They noted disparities between eleven States and the District of Columbia where same sex marriage was recognised, against all other States and Territories where it was not. This, it was ruled, created unequal treatment. Again, the task here is not to argue whether the ruling was correct in law or policy, but to explain how the judges could, to put it bluntly, get away with it. As Chief Justice Roberts put it in his dissent:

> Whether same-sex marriage is a good idea should be of no concern to us. Under the Constitution, judges have power to say what the law is, not what it should be… Although the policy arguments for extending marriage to same-sex couples may be compelling, the legal arguments for requiring such an extension are not… Understand well what this dissent is about: It is not about whether, in my judgment, the institution of marriage should be changed to include same-sex couples. It is instead about whether, in our democratic republic, that decision should rest with the people acting

[96] 576 U.S. 644 (2015).

> through their elected representatives, or with five lawyers who happen to hold commissions authorizing them to resolve legal disputes according to law. The Constitution leaves no doubt about the answer.

However, contrary to Roberts's position, there is doubt on this jurisdictional question. Article III.2 of the Constitution states that:

> The judicial Power shall extend to all Cases, in Law and Equity, arising under this Constitution, the Laws of the United States, and Treaties made, or which shall be made, under their Authority.

A modicum of doubt comes with "Law and Equity". Roberts's judgement is that only law is within the judicial purview. But what is law and equity? Equity branched off English common law before making its way to America. It is concerned with questions of fairness and justice, and which today is focussed on distributions of wealth and property. Equity is law, but its rules of law are predominantly judge-made, rather legislative. The *Obergefell* case was not an equity matter, but reference to equity in the constitution is a reminder of the wide discretion afforded to judges in America from their common law inheritance. As with other examples of judicial policy intervention, they were pushing against an open doorway. Due to Federal recognition, State legislation, and Supreme Court rulings, same-sex marriage was legal in 32 states and the District of Columbia before *Obergefell*. The Supreme Court had contributed to this rising tide of acceptance. In a landmark case, Section 3 of the *Defence of Marriage Act 2003* was declared unconstitutional in so far as it defined "spouse" and "marriage" in Federal law as excluding same-sex marriage. This decision had a basis in equity, when the estate of a deceased spouse in New York was charged Federal taxes because their spousal status was not federally recognised. This, it was ruled, violated the Fifth Amendment's Due Process Clause.[97] In another instance, standing was refused to a group who wanted to maintain a same-sex marriage ban in California, when that State's own government disavowed it.[98] In the cases of five other States, the Supreme Court did not even grant certiorari to aggrieved

[97] *United States v. Windsor*, 570 U.S. 744 (2013).

[98] *Hollingsworth v. Perry*, 570 U.S. 693 (2013).

groups as they were not harmed by same-sex marriage, beyond their moral disapproval.[99]

Importantly for *Obergefell*, the Federal Government was pushing for recognition of same-sex marriage. And it had been obtained for the majority of Americans in most States. This of course does not mean it was a settled issue at law, but that there was unlikely to be sustained political resistance to the court's ruling. Whilst the decision's legal rectitude was and is debatable, it was linguistically, politically, and institutionally possible. The crucial swing vote in *Obergefell* was Justice Kennedy's. In his opinion, Kennedy outlined the dynamism of constitutional law, and the essential liberality of Supreme Court "activism":

> The dynamic of our constitutional system is that individuals need not await legislative action before asserting a fundamental right. The Nation's courts are open to injured individuals who come to them to vindicate their own direct, personal stake in our basic charter. An individual can invoke a right to constitutional protection when he or she is harmed, even if the broader public disagrees and even if the legislature refuses to act.

Conclusions

Given its institutional and sociological complexity, it is almost unavoidable that US politics is post positive. In short, there are few incontrovertibly positive rules of law. All law is in a state of becoming or receding as a speech act. Policy bargains struck loosely by legislators will encourage logomachy in court. The response of judges has been to persuade institutions and citizens that their interpretations of law accord most closely to a logic of communication. The central aim of this book is to explain how such opportunities for linguistic intervention by judges have increased. The increased enactment of indeterminate statute law (in both federal and state legislatures), set alongside an indeterminate constitutional text, has generated friction points that have been exploited by increasingly empowered citizens, by lobby groups, by parties, by individual politicians, and, not least, by judges themselves.

However, relative to the other countries studied in this book, the US also has a culture of rights consciousness, and scepticism of bureaucratic

[99] https://www.theatlantic.com/politics/archive/2014/10/supreme-court-quietly-allows-same-sex-marriage-in-5-states/381129/ accessed 8th July 2021.

solutions to problems. This ideological commitment to individualism empowers courts and judges to make rulings without fear of favour, even when there is a strong risk of their being overruled. The thesis of this book has been that increased judicialisation is a function of indeterminacies in law with opportunities for judges to intervene without being overruled. The implication being that judges are cautious when expanding their policy influence. There are of course examples that counter this general trend. A noted example is *Texas v. Johnson*,[100] where the Supreme Court struck down a Texan statute that banned the burning of American flags. The court did so by describing flag desecration as protected expression under the First Amendment. By extension of the ruling, bans on flag burning were obliterated in forty-eight of the fifty states. The ruling did not tear into particularly indeterminate language:

> No person shall publicly mutilate, deface, defile, defy, trample upon, or by word or act cast contempt upon any such flag, standard, color, ensign or shield.[101]

Nor did the ruling rely on public or elite opinion to be sustained. Congress jumped to overrule the Supreme Court by means of the *Flag Protection Act 1989*. In riposte, the Supreme Court then invalidated that new statute in *United States v. Eichman*.[102] The independence of courts was again demonstrated in a series of cases that chipped away at executive discretion during the post-9/11 War on Terror. In *Rasul v. Bush*, for example, it was ruled that federal courts could determine whether non-American inmates at Guantanamo Bay had been lawfully imprisoned.[103] It was later ruled that any US citizens detained as "enemy combatants" held their due process rights intact.[104] The Supreme Court even took the unusual step of relying on international law, when invalidating

[100] 491 U.S. 39.

[101] *Uniform Flag Act 1917*, Section 3, from which most state legislation, including Texas's, was derived.

[102] 496 U.S. 310.

[103] 542 U.S. 466.

[104] *Hamdi v. Rumsfeld*, 542 U.S. 507.

military commissions at Guantanamo for breaching the Geneva Convention.[105] These and other cases can and have been cited as evidence of an out-of-control, imperial judiciary. Note, in particular, this dictum from Justice Scalia whilst dissenting from the 1992 abortion ruling of *Planned Parenthood v. Casey*:

> The Imperial Judiciary lives. It is instructive to compare this Nietzschean vision of us unelected, life tenured judges--leading a Volk who will be 'tested by following,' and whose very 'belief in themselves' is mystically bound up in their 'understanding' of a Court that 'speak[s] before all others for their constitutional ideals'--with the somewhat more modest role envisioned for these lawyers by the Founders.[106]

This near hysterical reaction to the majority opinion raises more questions than it answers. Of course we may find isolated examples of federal courts stretching interpretations of law, and in ways that seem to accord with the Justices' own morality and ideology. But how are we to explain the gradual accretion of judicial power over decades? Simply arguing that the judges wanted more power flies in the face of many self-negating examples to the contrary. The notion of an Imperial Judiciary cannot explain their failure to intervene in the Cambodia bombings, or "Chevron deference", or the "switch in time that saved nine". Theories of judicial activism ignore counter examples, over-emphasise individual motive, and underplay the means and opportunities for judicialisation.

Lawyers partake in linguistic arbitrage. If there are opportunities for judicialisation, it is because lawyers are trading in language that takes policy influence from government and gives it to courts. The most sustained method for judicialisation is not by a conspiracy of individuals, but structural forces that enable, justify, and even reward judicial policy incursions. This mechanism can be seen from indeterminacies in contemporary statute law, set alongside the loose and state-constraining language of US constitutional law. An irony in Scalia's dictum is that for him the judges were being imperious by removing state interference. No imperium exists that rescinds power.

[105] *Hamdan v. Rumsfeld*, 548 U.S. 557.

[106] 505 U.S. 833 at pages 25–6.

References

Anderson, Christopher J., André Blais, Shaun Bowler, Todd Donovan, and Ola Listhaug. 2005. *Losers' Consent: Elections and Democratic Legitimacy*. Oxford: Oxford University Press.

Bauman, Zygmunt. 1991. *Modernity and Ambivalence*. Cambridge: Polity Press.

Bickel, Alexander M. 1986. *The Least Dangerous Branch*. New Haven: Yale University Press.

Binder, Sarah A. 2003. *Stalemate: Causes and Consequences of Legislative Gridlock*. Washington, DC: Brookings Institution Press.

Brenner, Saul., and Harold J. Spaeth. 1995. *Stare indecisis: The alteration of precedent on the US supreme court*. Cambridge: Cambridge University Press.

Clayton, Cornell W. 2002. The Supply and Demand Sides of Judicial Policy-Making (or, Why Be so Positive about the Judicialization of Politics). *Law and Contemporary Problems* 65 (3): 69–88.

Corwin, Edward S. 1910. The Establishment of Judicial Review. *Michigan Law Review* 9 (2): 102–125.

Epp, Charles. 1998. *The Rights Revolution: Lawyers, Activists and Supreme Courts in Comparative Perspective*. Chicago: University of Chicago Press.

Goldsworthy, Jeffrey. 2004. *The Sovereignty of Parliament*. Oxford: Oxford University Press.

Graber, Mark A. 1998. Federalist or Friend of Adams: The Marshall Court and Party Politics. *Studies in American Political Development* 12: 229–266.

Graber, Mark A. 2006. *Dred Scott and the Problem of Constitutional Evil*. Cambridge: Cambridge University Press.

Hart, H.L.A. 1961. *The Concept of the Law*. Oxford: Clarendon.

Hirschl, Ran. 2004. *Towards Juristocracy: The Origins and Consequences of the New Constitutionalism*. Cambridge, MA: Harvard University Press.

Klarman, Michael. 1996. Rethinking the Civil Rights and Civil Liberties Revolutions. *Virginia Law Review* 82 (1): 1–67.

Lindquist, Stefanie A., and Frank B. Cross. 2009. *Measuring Judicial Activism*. Oxford: Oxford University Press.

Loveland, Ian. 2006. *Constitutional Law, Administrative Law and Human Rights: A Critical Introduction*, 4th ed. Oxford: Oxford University Press.

Lukes, Steven. 1974. *Power: A Radical View*. Basingstoke: Macmillan.

Maltzman, Forrest, James F. Spriggs, and Paul J. Wahlbeck. 2000. *Crafting Law on the Supreme Court: The Collegial Game*. Cambridge: Cambridge University Press.

Mayhew, David R. 2005. *Divided We Govern: Party Control, Lawmaking, and Investigations, 1946–2002*. New Haven, CT: Yale University Press.

McGuire, Kevin T., and James A. Stimson. 2004. The Least Dangerous Branch Revisited: New Evidence on Supreme Court Responsiveness to Public Preferences. *The Journal of Politics* 66 (4): 1018–1035.

Riker, William H. 1964. *Federalism: Origin, Operation, Significance*. Boston: Little Brown.

Schwartz, Bernard. 1993. *A History of the Supreme Court*. Oxford: Oxford University Press.

Segal, Jeffrey, A., and Harold Spaeth. 2002. *The Supreme Court and the Attitudinal Model Revisited*. Cambridge: Cambridge University Press.

Stone Sweet, Alec. 2012. Constitutional Courts. In *The Oxford Handbook of Comparative Constitutional Law*, ed. Michel Rosenfeld and András Sajó. Oxford: Oxford University Press.

Tarrow, Sidney. 2013. *The Language of Contention: Revolutions in Words, 1688–2012*. Cambridge: Cambridge University Press.

Temple, Kathryn. 2019. *Loving Justice: Legal Emotions in William Blackstone's England*. New York: New York University Press.

Vanberg, Georg. 2001. Legislative-Judicial Relations: A Game-Theoretic Approach to Constitutional Review. *American Journal of Political Science* 45 (2): 346–361.

Vile, Maurice. 1998. *Constitutionalism and the Separation of Powers*, 2nd ed. Indianapolis: Liberty Fund.

Whittington, Keith E. 2015. The Power of Judicial Review. In *The Oxford Handbook of the U.S. Constitution*, ed. Mark Tushnet, Mark A. Graber, and Sanford Levinson. Oxford: Oxford University Press.

Woodward, Bob, and Scott Armstrong. 1979. *The Brethren: Inside the Supreme Court*. New York: Simon and Schuster.

CHAPTER 7

Mixed Legal Systems with Human Rights Reform in Canada

A central proposition of this book is that indeterminate legislation can be interpreted in multiple, often excludable, ways. The text can be reified by subtext, inter-textual comparison, context, transtext, and metatext. Governments are incentivised to enact legislation that opens interpretative spaces as an efficient solution to complex multipolar policy-making. Judges, by contrast, will be instructed by litigants to delimit legislative language down to more bipolar renderings (lawful/unlawful, proportionate/disproportionate, reasonable/unreasonable). This constraining interpretative mode is encouraged by zero-sum adversarial litigation. Put simply, one side's interpretation of the law must exclude another's. Policy pathways are thereby closed down via adjudication, often to the chagrin of governments who are then faced with either having to re-legislate, or accept that certain options are off the table.

In this chapter, we move to examine the Canadian experience with adjudication. It offers a rich example of rapidly developing judicial power. Since the 1982 patriation of Canada's constitution from the UK, and simultaneous enactment of a Charter of Rights and Freedoms, federal judges have taken on substantial policy powers. Judges are now central policy players, whether by wading into sensitive interprovincial and intertterritorial disputes, or even determining the substance of laws on fiery

M. Williams, *Judges and the Language of Law*,
https://doi.org/10.1007/978-3-030-91495-0_7

topics, including abortion,[1] and assisted suicide.[2] Compared to its US counterpart, Canada's Supreme Court is distinguished as a "judicial supremacy" exemplar. Indeed, it has even fewer institutional constraints than its cousin court to the south. Canada operates a variant Westminster Model democracy, with no federal separations of policy powers, save for the courts. And those courts have access to a modern (by international standards) and expansively worded Charter of Rights. The charter can be used to invalidate legislation, in a country whose constitution is all but impossible to amend formally. This makes for a concentration of policy power in the federal government, and with few constraining influences from the House of Commons or Senate, it is the courts that monopolise counter-majoritarian capacity in Ottawa.

Another source of extraordinary institutional power for the Canadian Supreme Court is its capacity to rule on abstract policy references. The federal Cabinet is entitled under the *Supreme Court Act* to refer questions to these appellate judges. By this mechanism, the Supreme Court takes on a function akin to the French Conseil constitutionnel as a "third legislative chamber" (Stone 1992). Although this mechanism has been used far less frequently in Ottawa than in Paris, it has managed hot-button issues ranging from inflation-busting economics,[3] to delegitimising unilateral secession by Québec,[4] to controls on genetic testing.[5] In addition to all of this, we have also seen in Chapter 4 that Canadian legislation presents similar evidence of degenerative linguistic norms to France, the UK, and the US. Canada is therefore a valuable case study both in terms of its substantial variation on the independent variable (legislative determinacy) and dependent variable (judicialisation of politics).

As compared to other jurisdictions, however, there is somewhat less digital legislation available for machine reading analysis. For this chapter on criminal law, amendments to the Canadian Criminal Code from 2003 to 2020 will be analysed. This is a narrower temporal range than was possible for the other nations under study for this book. It still accounts

[1] *R. v. Morgentaler*, 1988 CanLII 90 (SCC), [1988] 1 SCR 30.

[2] *Carter v. Canada (AG)*, 2015 SCC 5.

[3] *Reference Re Anti-Inflation Act*, [1976] 2 SCR 373.

[4] *Reference Re Secession of Québec*, [1998] 2 SCR 217.

[5] *Reference re Genetic Non-Discrimination Act*, 2020 SCC 17 (CanLII).

for 35,367,053 words of law, and there is evidence of degenrification in language, even within this relatively narrow timeframe. But, to compensate for a relative lack of legislative data, this chapter will also assess how the Canadian Parliament manages interpretative doubt before its legislative bargains are promulgated. Specifically, different bill drafts from the 42nd Parliament are analysed to see how the House of Commons and Senate amended government bills sent to it by the federal Cabinet. This allows us to ascertain the degree to which legislators are moved to constrain or expand interpretative spaces in legislative language.

The 42nd Parliament (3 December 2015 to 11 September 2019) was dominated by a resurgent Liberal Party. Justin Trudeau's Liberals won 184 seats, the largest share obtained since the Progressive Conservatives in 1984. Despite a comfortable House majority, there was no official Liberal caucus in the Senate, with it having been disbanded by Trudeau in 2014. With a Liberal-dominated House and politically rudderless Senate, it could be expected that the Federal Government faced little pressure to amend its Bills, either substantively or linguistically. And yet, there is evidence of significant linguistic changes through the parliamentary process. But what we do not observe are legislators regressing legislative language to the mean. In other words, rather than arresting the degenrification of legislation, lawmakers were complicit. The reasoning for this we will explore in detail below, but of interest are indeterminacies added (according to evidence from House of Commons Journals) to empower individuals, communities, and the provinces/territories of Canada through looser language. The consequence will be empowerment not only of those stakeholders, but also judges when disputed interpretations of legal language make their way to court.

In some instances, Parliament deliberately empowered courts to determine the scope of crimes and the extent of punishments. Bill C-84 amended the criminal code to criminalise bestiality and other animal rights abuses. The government bill as presented at first reading was transformed in its passage through Parliament, and in particular during the standing committee stage in the House of Commons. By Royal Assent, the law had moved from an average of five to over eight indeterminate parts of speech per section. At first reading, the government's draft of clause one read as follows (emphases added):

> 1 Section 160 of the Criminal Code is amended by adding the following after subsection (3): (4) In this section, bestiality means *any* contact, for a *sexual* purpose, with an animal.

After a hearing of the House Standing Committee on Justice and Human Rights, the clause was transformed with the following additions:

> The court *may*, in addition to *any other* sentence that it *may* impose under *any* of subsections (1) to (3),
> (a) *make* an order prohibiting the accused from owning, having the custody *or* control of *or* residing in the *same* premises as an animal during *any* period that the court considers *appropriate but*, in the case of a second *or* subsequent offence, for a minimum of five years; *and*
> (b) on application of the Attorney General *or* on its own motion, order that the accused pay to a person *or* an organization that has taken care of an animal as a result of the commission of the offence the *reasonable* costs that the person *or* organization incurred in respect of the animal, *if* the costs are *readily* [adverb] *ascertainable*.
> (6) Sections 740 to 741.2 apply, with *any* modifications that the circumstances require, to orders *made* under paragraph (4)(b).

Italicised parts of speech open the text to variable contextual determinations. The Commons Committee opened up interpretative space in the Bill with the explicit intention that judges fill it. More controversial are those laws where courts were not named recipients of powers, but obtained power nonetheless. In addition to the degenrification of legislative language that has been observed in Canada, there are also sources of power for courts, and institutional friction points that call for these powers to be used. For one thing, Canada presents a case of asymmetric federalism, wherein provinces and territories do not have equal rights and privileges. Québec and the Indigenous Territories (the Northwest Territories, Nunavut, and Yukon) have more linguistic and cultural powers than the nine anglophone-dominant provinces. There are also mixed civil and common law systems, as Québec maintains the French codified system of law and courts. These complex institutional and socio-cultural divergences are nonetheless pulled together (sometimes reluctantly) by a powerful federal Parliament and courts. The courts mediate closely between linguistic, cultural, and regional cleavages. By law, three of the nine Supreme Court Justices must be Québécois. As a matter of convention, Ontario takes another three seats on the highest bench, as Canada's most-populace province. The remaining three seats then tend to be shared by the Western and Atlantic provinces. Canada is the only state considered in this book to have multi-ethnic and multi-lingual institutions, as all laws and legal decisions are transliterated bilingually. Whilst the UK presents an example of a multinational state with considerable ethnic diversity, as well as targeted use of Welsh, Canada to a greater extent than any other country surveyed here has made allowances for difference within its political frameworks.

This makes it all the more important to note how centralising the Supreme Court can be. Both in the senses of federalising policy from the periphery to the metropole, and in the ideological sense of disseminating the presumed liberal and capitalistic sensibilities of a literally and figuratively remote elite in Ottawa (Hutchinson 2017). Another unusual feature of the Canadian court, relative to its peers presented in this volume, is the lack of transparency as to appointments. Despite attempted reforms and some tinkerings around the margin, appointments to the federal bench are still dominated by the Minister of Justice and Prime Minister making direct recommendations to the Governor General. Opacity of appointments had been uncontroversial, when it was another institutional inheritance from the UK. But then the decision was made in 1982 to bring constitutional review into a common law system with a Westminster-style Parliament. This was a major deviation from the British model, and has made for policy-influential judges. One irony to note is that it was the British Parliament that technically created this constitutional review power for Canada, as part of its imperial *coup de grâce*. Indeed, it was at the Palace of Westminster that British lawmakers yielded powers to Canadian judges that are yet to conceded to British judges.

Connections to London therefore ceased only recently. Patriation was delayed for the most part because of disagreements between provinces (especially Québec) on how federal power would be organised after powers were brought to Ottawa. Prior to patriation, the highest appeal court for Canada was the Judicial Committee of the Privy Council, based in London, and made up of British Law Lords. Appeals from Canada to this court were scrapped from 1949, but not before that imperial court handed down major tools to Canadian judges for expansive interpretations of law. The JCPC's phlegmatic attitude to judicialised politics was typical of its common law methods. And, specifically, in a 1929 ruling, it fixed in precedent that Canadian law is a "living tree", capable of growing under judicial pruning. In this "Persons Case", the Law Lords overruled the only nominally Supreme Court of Canada and confirmed that, being persons, women were eligible to take seats in the Senate.[6] Where it had been common to interpret "persons" to mean men in nineteenth-century legislation, this interpretative norm was rejected in favour of an interpretation more in keeping with social subtext.

Only after 1949 was the Canadian Supreme Court supreme in fact and not only in name. The court nonetheless remained relatively toothless until the 1980s. With the Canadian Bill of Rights, enacted in 1960, there were protections for citizens from excessive federal incursions into their "life, liberty, and security of the person". But this instrument went little further than the common law Bill of Rights that had osmotically penetrated from England's 1689 enactment of that name. And, the Canadian Bill had nothing to say on provincial or territorial infractions of rights. The Canadian *Human Rights Act* of 1977 similarly protected citizens from discriminatory laws and practices, but only within a federal purview. There were two institutional reforms that truly created the modern potential for Canada's Supreme Court to reach beyond federal and into provincial law. The first came in 1975, when appeals as of right to the Court were abolished. This meant the Court could control its docket and choose to rule on those cases of greatest moment. The second was, as telegraphed, the patriation of law and creation of a Charter of Rights and Freedoms under the *Constitution Act 1982*. The rights laid down are a fairly standard list of fundamental freedoms (section 2), democratic rights (sections 3–5), legal rights (sections 7–14), and equal protection (section 15). More *sui generic* are sections 16–23, covering linguistic rights and education of minority languages.

Quantitatively, changes to court activity were substantial after 1982. There are now around twenty Charter-based complaints heard at the Supreme Court every year, of which a third are upheld. On average, 3.4 federal or provincial statutes are wholly or partially struck down annually. Under the Bill of Rights, by contrast, there were just thirty-four cases heard in the twenty-two years from 1960 to 1982. Of these, just five went in favour of the weaker litigant, and in only one case was a solitary section of an Act invalidated (Kelly and Manfredi 2010). But, the

[6] *Edwards v. Canada (AG)* [1930] A.C. 124, 1929 UKPC 86.

Charter does not unconditionally empower judges. Section 1 opens space for democratic dominance of individual rights:

> The Canadian Charter of Rights and Freedoms guarantees the rights and freedoms set out in it subject only to such reasonable limits prescribed by law as can be demonstrably justified in a free and democratic society.

This construction is akin to the European Convention on Human Rights, with its demarcated "margin of appreciation" wherein rights apply "except such as is in accordance with the law and is necessary in a democratic society". The adjectival and adverbial indeterminacies of "reasonable" and "demonstrably justified" in section 1 have themselves been subjects of litigation. In a case from Manitoba, the Supreme Court ruled that there were protections to free expression that could be used to defend prostitution and bawdy houses. And yet, legislative breeches of section 2 (freedom of expression) could be justified under section 1, and the laws were spared from invalidation.[7] Of even greater potential significance is section 33, the "notwithstanding clause":

> Parliament or the legislature of a province may expressly declare in an Act of Parliament or of the legislature, as the case may be, that the Act or a provision thereof shall operate notwithstanding a provision included in section 2 or sections 7 to 15 of this Charter.

This is something of a nuclear option to assert politicians' dominance of policy. It has never been used by the federal government, and has only been used by Québec to judge-proof a law on signs, mandating they be solely in French. The law had been invalidated by the Supreme Court, so was re-enacted with section 33 armour.[8] Québec had also repealed all of its pre-Charter legislation in 1982 and re-enacted it with section 33 provisions included. The province had not agreed to patriation or the Charter on terms set by the federal government, so had sought to minimise its impact. Nonetheless, it is federal judges that have determined

[7] *Reference re ss. 193 and 195.1(1)(C) of the criminal code (Man.)*, 1990 CanLII 105 (SCC), [1990] 1 SCR 1123.

[8] *Ford v. Québec (Attorney General)*, [1988] 2 SCR 712.

the limitations on section 33, ruling, for instance, that it cannot be used retroactively, only prospectively.[9]

Sections 1 and 33 of the Charter claw back enough power for lawmakers, such that analogising the Canadian and US supreme courts is unhelpful (Martin 2003; Morton and Knopff 2019). The Canadian Parliament has substantially more capacity to recover policy powers from judges than does the US Congress, or state capitols. It just so happens that the Canadian Parliament rarely does try to claw anything back from judges. Indeed, a compelling theory speaks to both a potential for, and practice of, substantial dialogue between judges and legislators in Canada (Hogg and Bushell 1997). Unlike in the US where constitutional review is more typically monologic, it is possible for the branches of Canadian government to coordinate their discourses. Dialogue is only possible with mutually respecting discussants. The provisions of sections 1 and 33 ensure that courts neither offer zero resistance to lawmakers nor become heedlessly over-active. Dialogue compels moderated behaviour, on both sides.

And, it is the mechanisms by which communicative and coordinative discourses develop, and are disseminated, that is the primary interest of this book. As with previous chapters, we will progress by interrogating core elements of textual interpretation—from changes to text, to uses of subtext, to inter-textuality, to shifting context, to transtext, to metatext. Again, the thesis of this book leads to expectations that policy influence from judges is derivative of indeterminacies in legislation. Regardless of the tools created by docket control and the Charter, Canadian judges are not incentivised to expand their powers and influence, unless it is in reaction to a conspicuous indeterminacy in law. As ever, the empirical focus here will be criminal justice legislation, which in Canada is codified under C-46. And, as with the other countries surveyed, judges are grappling with legislative degenrification in this Code.

Empirical—Textual Changes

With regard to changes in legislative text, let us begin by describing quantitative changes. Figure 7.1 details the annual legislative output (measured in words) for the Canadian Parliament from 2001 to 2019. The figure

[9] *Irwin Toy Ltd. v. Québec (Attorney General)*, [1989] 1 SCR 927.

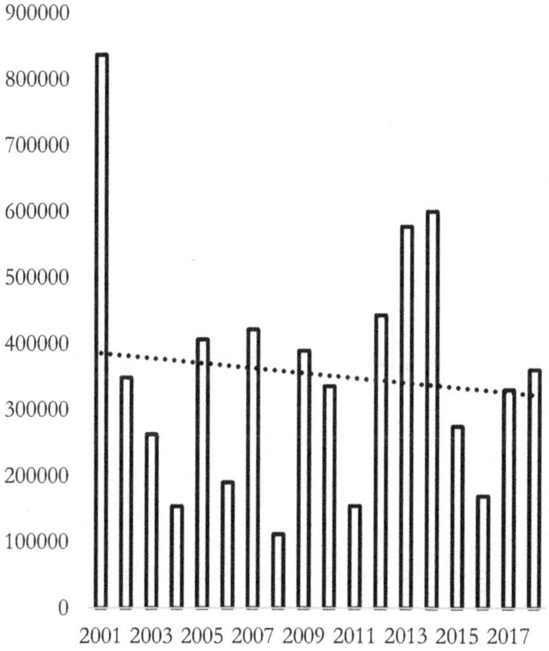

Fig. 7.1 Legislative output (number of words enacted), 2001–2019 (*Source* Author's creation)

shows that excluding a peak in 2001 of 837,211 enacted words, the Canadian Parliament submits between 200,000 and 600,000 words of law per year for Royal Assent. Output typically dips in election years (2004, 2006, 2008, 2011, 2015, 2019), although 2019 outlies this pattern. The 42nd Parliament (2015–2019) enacted less than its immediate predecessor, but is roughly comparable in activity to the 38–40th Parliaments (2004–2011).

Turning specifically to criminal laws, there were 109 separate amendments made to C-46 between 2003 and 2020. Many of these were fairly minor changes in terms of word length, but, with 109 versions of the Code to compare, we have a total dataset of 35,367,053 words. Table 7.1 describes changes to the language of Code iterations. Even if Parliament's quantitative output has been unpredictable since the millennium's turn, there has been a secular upswing in legislative indeterminacy in C-46:

Table 7.1 Indeterminate parts of speech per section of criminal code, 2003–2020

Year	*Average of adjectives/section*	*Average of conjunctions/section*	*Average of indeterminate modal verbs/section*	*Average of enabling verbs/section*	*Average of compound indeterminacies/section*
2003	11.99	17.72	2.06	0.36	32.12
2004	12.11	17.99	2.08	0.37	32.55
2005	12.48	18.46	2.14	0.39	33.47
2006	12.73	18.86	2.16	0.41	34.16
2007	12.76	18.93	2.16	0.41	34.26
2008	13.02	19.32	2.18	0.41	34.93
2009	13.28	19.63	2.21	0.42	35.55
2010	13.36	19.74	2.22	0.42	35.74
2011	13.66	20.09	2.26	0.44	36.45
2012	13.80	20.27	2.29	0.46	36.82
2013	13.90	20.38	2.29	0.46	37.04
2014	14.16	20.60	2.30	0.47	37.52
2015	14.61	21.11	2.38	0.49	38.59
2016	15.21	21.67	2.46	0.51	39.84
2017	15.27	21.73	2.46	0.51	39.97
2018	15.48	21.92	2.50	0.53	40.43
2019	15.60	21.56	2.48	0.54	40.18
2020	16.03	21.61	2.49	0.56	40.69
Average	13.86	20.09	2.28	0.45	36.68
St. deviation	1.23	1.31	0.14	0.06	2.72
Minimum	11.99 (2003)	17.72 (2003)	2.06 (2003)	0.36 (2003)	32.12 (2003)
Maximum	16.03 (2020)	21.92 (2018)	2.50 (2018)	0.56 (2020)	40.69 (2020)

Focusing specifically on compound indeterminacies per section, Fig. 7.2 describes a gradual increase:

Even across a relatively short time frame, there were demonstrable changes in legislative indeterminacy. Considering that these data constitute the universal available set, there is no requirement of declaring confidence intervals. We can have, as close as is ever possible in academia, complete confidence that the observed pattern presents reality. Where there were just over 30 indeterminacies per section of the Code in 2001, there were over 40 per section by 2020.

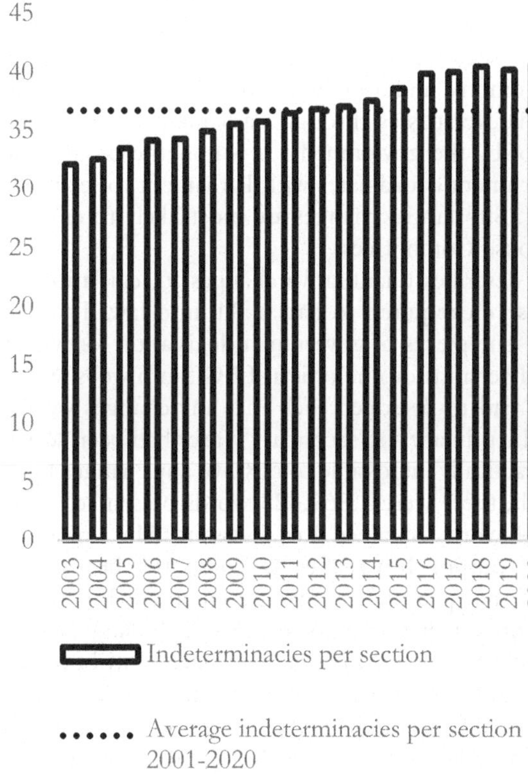

Fig. 7.2 Legislative indeterminacy (parts of speech per section), 2001–2020 (*Source* Author's creation)

Focusing further on the 42nd Parliament, we can see how a Westminster-style Parliament, dominated by a single party, dealt with language through the law making process. The 2015 election was comfortably won by The Liberals. They secured 184 of 338 Commons seats. It marked the largest increase in seat share for any party in Canadian history. The appointed Senate had, as mentioned, no party majority and had seen the Liberal caucus officially disbanded. The expectation is that Parliament could do little to affect the legislative language desired by government. Therefore, the language of Bills will closely match the final Acts of Parliament. The exception to this rule is expected where legislators in fact increase indeterminacy in legislative language. They will do so either to further empower their co-partisan government or in order to create more sectoral powers for citizens. With party control of the House of Commons, and a limited Senate role in creating or amending legislation, whatever passes through Parliament is almost guaranteed to be approved of by the government. It is nonetheless interesting to note how the government coordinates with Parliament to secure an acceptable legislative text. Substantial changes are most likely to emerge from close scrutiny in House Committees.

Figure 7.3 describes quantitative changes to legislation at four major stages of the seven required to pass a Bill into law. The data presented cover all forty-one pieces of government legislation for which there were four published versions on the official LEGISinfo website.

This graph had to be scaled such that any changes would be observable. If both the primary and secondary y-axes had been scaled from zero, it would be practically impossible to observe any changes by eye. In terms of word length, there were 1,361,325 words presented at First Reading, and 1,377,704 words obtained Royal Assent. This amounts to a paltry 1.2% change in output. It was after the committee hearings of the House when most of the quantitative changes emerged, but these amount to just 20,000 words, which is still just 1.5% of the linguistic output. Only between one and two words in every 100 were contributed by the House of Commons working (at least in theory) independently of the government. Whilst word length tipped up a tiny amount, the number of clauses dipped, meaning that each section at Royal Assent was on average longer than it had been at first reading. The number of clauses decreased most markedly after Third Reading and before Royal Assent, meaning that it was in part as a consequence of Senate amendments. But, again, these changes amounted to a tiny proportion of just 0.3%.

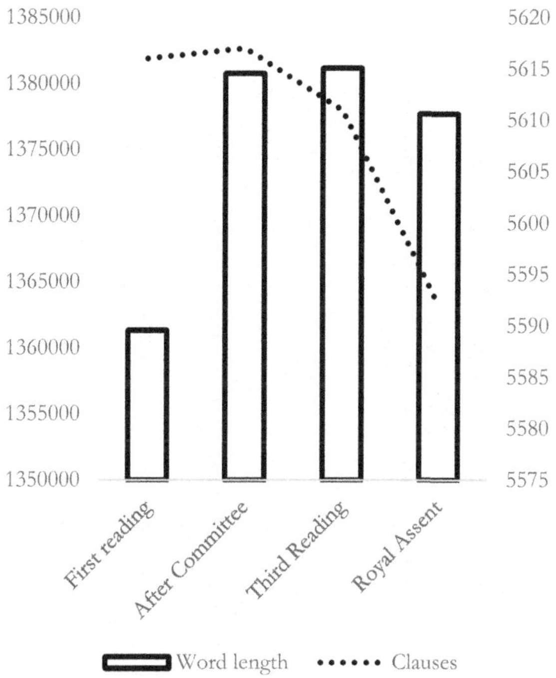

Fig. 7.3 Number of words (primary *y*-axis) ad clauses (secondary *y*-axis) agreed to at four legislative stages, 42nd Parliament (*Source* Author's creation)

Modest changes to the quantity of words belie substantial changes to the indeterminacy of language. Table 7.2 describes changes to the per section compound indeterminacies of legislative language:

From Table 7.2, we can see that laws became more indeterminate through the parliamentary process. On average, per section indeterminacy grew by 8% from First Reading to Royal Assent. Standard deviations are wide, and medians are lower than means, both of which suggest that there are a relatively small number of laws that changed substantially and skewed results. For example, the maximum change came for C-93, a law on cannabis possession. It had 5.11 indeterminate parts of speech per section at First Reading, and this proportion had more than doubled to 13.78 parts of speech per section at Royal Assent. The vast majority of these linguistic changes came after the House Committee stage, which saw a 161% increase in indeterminacies per section from First Reading.

Table 7.2 Indeterminate parts of speech per section agreed to at four legislative stages, 42nd Parliament

	Indeterminacy at first reading	*Increase in indeterminacy first to second reading*	*Change in indeterminacy second to third reading*	*Change in indeterminacy third reading to royal assent*	*Indeterminacy at royal assent*
Average	19.64	+1.04	+0.04	+0.29	21.01
St. deviation	10.80	+1.55	+0.17	+1.18	10.42
Minimum	5.00 (C-84 On Bestiality)	−0.01 (C-37 Controlled Drugs)	−0.26 (C-69 Energy regulation)	−4.17 (C-29 Budget)	8.25 (C-84 On Bestiality)
Median	16.18 (C-45 Cannabis decriminalisation)	+0.41 (C-51 Amend Crim Code)	0.00 (29 of 41 Bills were unchanged)	0.00 (18 of 41 Bills were unchanged)	17.86 (C-76 Election reform)
Maximum	53.20 (C-69 Energy regulation)	+8.22 (C-93 Cannabis possession)	+0.78 (C-7 Labour regulation)	+4.96 (C-6 Citizenship)	55.32 (C-69 Energy regulation)

n = 41 Government Bills introduced to the House, 2015–19

As will be seen below, the increased indeterminacies came in the form of conditional limitations in that law, designed to protect the vulnerable. The Senate (described in column 3) was associated with just one-fifth of changes to legislative language from First Reading to Royal Assent. The most substantial senatorial alterations were to C-6 (on citizenship) and C-29 (on budgeting). C-29 was the only Bill that saw major cuts in its indeterminate language. This was because the Senate stripped out a portion of the bill that would have empowered the government at the expense of provinces and territories. Despite the outlying examples of C-29 and C-93, it is interesting to observe how and why parliamentarians are moved to adapt legislative language, typically in a more conditional, context-dependent, and ultimately indeterminate manner. Also notable is how substantially the Canadian Government secured its preferred linguistic constructions with a House of Commons majority. Therefore, legislative degenerification must predominantly be attributed to the government and the power-concentrating Westminster model.

Definitional—Subtextual Changes

A rule of law will only be followed if it can be understood. Incomprehensible laws breed dispute, and empower judges to wade in and define away the confusion. Not only are judges compelled to determine the meanings of law, there is reason to argue that incomprehensible legislation is not even law at all. This very point was made in a 1992 Supreme Court case, that turned on how the adverb "unduly" was to be defined.[10] Twelve pharmacists from Halifax, Nova Scotia, were indicted for "conspiracy to prevent or lessen competition unduly". They had been running something of a cartel in Halifax and were thereby facing punishment. The case turned on whether it was possible to identify intent to conspire if the offence was so vaguely described. Indeterminate law is described in Canadian case law by the separate but conjoined concepts of vagueness and overbreadth (Sharpe 1987). The Nova Scotia Supreme Court, Trial Division, quashed the indictments, citing a breach of section 7 of the Charter:

[10] *R. v. Nova Scotia Pharmaceutical Society*, 1992 CanLII 72 (SCC), [1992] 2 SCR 606.

> Everyone has the right to life, liberty and security of the person and the right not to be deprived thereof except in accordance with the principles of fundamental justice.

The Crown appealed, ultimately leading to a case heard by the Supreme Court, which reinstated the indictments. There was no breach of fundamental justice inherent in this use of "unduly". And, in reaching this conclusion, the judges set parameters for determining what counts as indeterminacy. Gonthier J summarised past precedent in these terms:

> The doctrine of vagueness can be summed up in one proposition: a law will be found unconstitutionally vague if it so lacks in precision as not to give sufficient guidance for legal debate – that is, for reaching a conclusion as to its meaning by reasoned analysis applying legal criteria.[11]

This incapacity to sustain legal debate has two separate but related effects. It undermines citizens' ability to foresee the consequences of their actions (vagueness), and it opens up excessive discretion for law enforcement (overbreadth). Gonthier J elaborated a five-point method for determining away indeterminacies in a 1995 case[12]:

> a court must determine the meaning of the impugned provision having regard for: (i) purpose; (ii) subject matter and nature of the impugned provision; (iii) societal values; (iv) related legislative provisions; and (v) prior judicial interpretations of the provision. All the while a court must have regard, in particular, for the second proposition referred to in Nova Scotia Pharmaceutical Society: the need to provide fair notice and to limit prosecutorial discretion.

Given evidence of rising numbers of noun-qualifying adjectives and adverbs in law, and, given Gonthier J identified courts as the key agents of change ("a court must determine"), we can expect an association of increased legislative indeterminacy with increased judicial "activism". In judging the Nova Scotia pharmacists, the Supreme Court approvingly cited an earlier dictum of that tribunal:

[11] *R. v. Nova Scotia Pharmaceutical Society*, 1992 CanLII 72 (SCC), [1992] 2 SCR 606 at p. 643.

[12] *Ontario v. Canadian Pacific Ltd.*, 1995 CanLII 112 (SCC), [1995] 2 SCR 1031 p. 1070.

> Absolute precision in the law exists rarely, if at all. The question is whether the legislature has provided an intelligible standard according to which the judiciary must do its work. The task of interpreting how that standard applies in particular instances might always be characterized as having a discretionary element, because the standard can never specify all the instances in which it applies. On the other hand, where there is no intelligible standard and where the legislature has given a plenary discretion to do whatever seems best in a wide set of circumstances, there is no 'limit prescribed by law'.[13]

The Charter did not create this need for courts to determine limits prescribed by law. It did enhance the judicial toolkit, and it coincided with growing demand for clarification of what the legislature intended. Prior to the Charter, there were common law methods of statutory construction that guided judicial determinations. In a 1962 case, for example, the adjective "undue" was the subject of litigation. The Supreme Court was asked whether D.H. Lawrence's *Lady Chatterley's Lover* was obscene insofar as it utilised "undue exploitation" of sex. At trial, and then on first appeal, the novel was declared obscene and a seller's prosecution upheld. Four judges of the Supreme Court backed this judgement, but a five-judge majority went against their colleagues and overturned the prosecution.

> The phrase 'undue exploitation' is aimed at excessive emphasis on the theme of sex for a base purpose. Measured by the internal necessities of the novel, there was no such undue exploitation. There was no more emphasis on the theme of sex than was required in the treatment of such a serious work of fiction. No matter whether 'undue exploitation' is to be measured by the internal necessities of the novel itself or by offence against community standards, this novel does not offend.[14]

Whether defining "undue" in 1962 or "unduly" in 1992, the Supreme Court was gifted this reifying power through legislative indeterminacy. We can now turn to consider how parliamentarians contributed to these definitional requirements during the 42nd Parliament. The linguistic patterns

[13] *Irwin Toy Ltd. v. Québec (Attorney General)*, 1989 CanLII 87 (SCC), [1989] 1 SCR 927 p. 983.

[14] Brody, Dansky, Rubin v. The Queen, 1962 CanLII 80 (SCC), [1962] SCR 681, p. 682.

in successful backbencher and senatorial amendments included indeterminacies to expand rights of vulnerable citizens and widen discretion for provincial and territorial governments. More specifically, where legislation sought to empower individuals, communities, or provinces/territories, its conditional language (*if/and/or* conjunctions) increased through the passage of a bill. Based on previous research in the UK, conditional language widens discretion for those gifted powers in law (Williams 2017). As such, where a law gifts new rights or protections to individuals, then conditionality allows these rights to be more widely applied. As an example, this subclause was added at the House Committee hearing for Bill C-14 on assisted dying:

> (i) *if* the person has *difficulty* communicating, take *all necessary* measures to provide a *reliable* means by which the person *may* understand the information that is provided to them *and* communicate their decision.

Committee members wished to protect vulnerable citizens who may struggle to express their decision to live or die. Including this "if" subclause allowed for more varied and textured interpretations of the text. This sophistication of language has clear policy benefits. As ever, the intent here is not to disparage the degenrification of language, but to catalogue it, and point out its significance to judicial discretion. Judges may yet be called upon to determine "if… all necessary measures" were taken in a case.

In only rare instances did Parliament cut out conditional language that was to the government's benefit. With a stable majority in the Commons, and a fragmented party system in the Senate, very few such attempted amendments were successful. Indeed, the only notable case of Parliament reducing linguistic indeterminacy was Bill C-29, pertaining to the 2016 Federal Budget. More typically the House "respectfully declined" to follow senatorial amendments. Illustrative of more standard inter-chamber dialogue was Bill C-37, on drug reform. The bill sought to establish safe and clean areas for addicts to take otherwise illegal drugs. Out of a 17,000-word bill, fifty words were amended through the parliamentary process. All of the amendments (including the successful fifty words) were suggested by the Senate Standing Committee on Legal and Constitutional Affairs. They sought three amendments but secured only one:

> 56.2 A person who is responsible for the *direct* supervision, at a supervised consumption site, of the consumption of *controlled* substances, *may* offer a person using the site *alternative pharmaceutical* therapy before that person consumes a *controlled* substance that is obtained in a manner not authorized under this Act.

Whilst the Commons accepted the broad thrust of this insertion, they toned down the original Senate construction relying on "shall…" offer alternative pharmaceuticals to "may…" so offer, hence further increasing linguistic indeterminacy. When rejecting another proposed Senate amendment (to have citizen advisory committees for approving drug consumption sites), the government spokesperson explained the decision as follows:

> While such committees could be seen as a way to maintain an open and ongoing dialogue with the surrounding community, it also represents a level of citizen oversight and influence that is not in place for any other health care service… By including a process that could further add to the stigmatization faced by people who use drugs, this amendment runs against the intent and the spirit of Bill C-37. For this reason, our government respectfully disagrees with the second amendment.[15]

Bill C-37 was typical. Parliamentarians made policy-insubstantial changes, that added linguistic indeterminacies so as to empower individuals and communities. These changes modestly took powers away from Federal officials and gifted them to the private sphere, and then to judges when mediating disputes.

Systemic—Intertextual Changes

Having considered the development of communicative discourse—from state to civil society—we now turn to coordinative discourse between state institutions. How are discrepancies between courts and between different authoritative texts resolved when indeterminacies of law arise? The answer is hierarchically, and therefore not strictly according to federalism. In other words, the courts structure is centralised in Ottawa, overseen by the

[15] Mr. Joël Lightbound (Parliamentary Secretary to the Minister of Health, Lib.) Canada, Parliament, House of Commons Debates, 42nd Parl, 1st Sess, Vol. 148, No. 176 (12 May 2017) at 1005.

dominant Supreme Court. Whilst this is typical of a federated union, more unusual is the leadership capacity of central government over provincial jurisprudence. Not only do the federal courts have a final say over interpretations of provincial law, but the Prime Minister and Minister of Justice appoint judges to provincial courts, as well as appointing to provincial branches of Federal courts. As per section 96 of the *Constitution Act*:

> 96 The Governor General shall appoint the Judges of the Superior, District, and County Courts in each Province, except those of the Courts of Probate in Nova Scotia and New Brunswick.

There are separate section 92 courts to which provincial Attorneys General make appointments, but substantially more power is exercised by section 96 courts, and section 101 courts, which include the Supreme Court. Added to which is the relative lack of transparency in judicial appointments, with there having been only modest reforms to the Prime Minister's powers to populate the senior benches. Despite the significant policy and law making autonomy enjoyed by Canada's provinces and territories, in regard to jurisprudence, the constitutional set-up is only quasi-federal. The following courts schematic, Fig. 7.4 describes this pyramidal structure:
As discussed, the Canadian judicial hierarchy had, prior to 1949, culminated with the Judicial Committee of the Privy Council. This court was based in Whitehall's Cabinet Office (since 2009 in Middlesex Guildhall), at the heart of London. The Supreme Court's supremacy was more than just nominal after appeals to London ceased. And yet, as also discussed, the Supreme Court did not take a leadership role in jurisprudence until patriation, the Charter, and in response to increasingly indeterminate federal and provincial legislation. Before the 1982 patination of Canadian constitutional law, the Supreme Court used the Bill of Rights infrequently and sparingly to coordinate jurisprudence. As an example, in 1963 the Supreme Court ruled the Bill of Rights was merely declaratory, meaning it could only describe freedoms that had demonstrably existed when the Bill was enacted in 1960. As such, the courts felt compelled to uphold convictions for operating a bowling alley on a Sunday.[16] This somewhat self-effacing dictum did not conform to the "living tree" principle of the

[16] *Robertson and Rosetanni v. The Queen*, 1963 CanLII 17 (SCC), [1963] SCR 651.

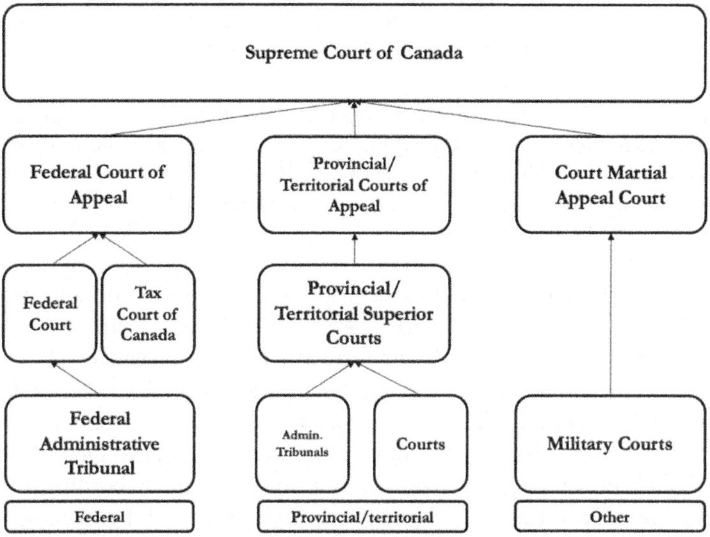

Fig. 7.4 Canadian courts schematic (*Source* Author's creation)

Persons Case considered above, and was later distinguished under Charter jurisprudence. Notably, in the 1984 case of *Hunter v. Southam Inc*,[17] the Supreme Court rekindled its powers of purposive interpretation. Judge Brian Dickson is most often quoted from this case, very shortly before his elevation to the Chief Justiceship. In the quote he responds to a highly indeterminate adjective:

> It is clear that the meaning of 'unreasonable' cannot be determined by recourse to a dictionary, nor for that matter, by reference to the rules of statutory construction. The task of expounding a constitution is crucially different from that of construing a statute. A statute defines present rights and obligations. It is easily enacted and as easily repealed. A constitution, by contrast, is drafted with an eye to the future... It must, therefore, be capable of growth and development over time to meet new social, political and historical realities often unimagined by its framers. The judiciary is the guardian of the constitution and must, in interpreting its provisions, bear these considerations in mind.[18]

[17] [1984] 2 SCR 145.

[18] Ibid., p. 155.

Reinforcing this dictum of purposive construction, L'Heureuz-Dubé J summarised the jurisprudential awakening of the Court in these terms:

> The Charter does not purport to confer new freedoms. It gives a constitutional guarantee to the old freedoms and, in so doing, it protects them... However, it is now incontrovertible that the Charter, in order to be capable of adapting to the social conditions and problems of the present and the future, must be given a purposive and expansive interpretation.[19]

We can now better see why Québec opposed patriation and adoption of the Charter. That province had more to lose from a centralising legal instrument than did the predominantly anglophone provinces. A striking example came in the 1989 case of *Tremblay v. Daigle*.[20] A cohabiting couple had separated when the appellant was eighteen weeks pregnant. Her partner succeeded in obtaining an injunction from the Québec Superior Court, preventing her from having an abortion. According to that court, the foetus was a human being and protected by section 1 of the Québec Charter of Human Rights and Freedoms. The Canadian Supreme Court not only set aside the injunction, it also ruled that there was no "right to life" protection for foetuses in the Québécois Charter. Although Québec had opposed the patriation of Canada's constitution, the Supreme Court even had a hand in overturning this objection. In *Reference Re Resolution to amend the Constitution*,[21] the court determined that it would be constitutional to patriate the constitution. More specifically, the court ruled that despite an unwritten convention in favour of provincial consent for constitutional amendments, there was no legal check against the federal government acting unilaterally to amend the constitution.

However, it must be noted that prominent voices within the Federal Government represent provincial and territorial interests. Looking to evidence of law makers' behaviour in the 42nd Parliament, the Senate was particularly motivated to protect regional privileges, such as maintaining

[19] *Committee for the Commonwealth of Canada v. Canada*, 1991 CanLII 119 (SCC), [1991] 1 SCR 139.

[20] 1989 CanLII 33 (SCC), [1989] 2 SCR 530.

[21] [1981] 1 SCR 753.

independent legal rights. For example, Bill C-16 sought amendments to the Canadian *Human Rights Act*, by including "gender identity or expression" as protected from discrimination, and to recognise it as an aggravating circumstance in criminal sentencing. This bill was subject to an unusually high number of divisions, as Senators sought delays to bake in localised protections. There were particular concerns expressed that C-16 would supplant provincial rights, practices, and case law. In New Brunswick and Yukon, for example, there were existing guidelines on gender identity discrimination that their senators wanted to safeguard. But, the Federal Government secured its bill, unchanged, through the Senate. This demonstrated the relative weakness of that chamber in revising legislation when faced with a stable Commons majority and a sufficient number of supportive senators. Under these circumstances, the federalising trend of policy and law is unstoppable. Even if the centralising of policy could be counteracted on a local level, the leadership capacity of the Federal Courts ensures that human rights laws retain a high degree of national coherence.

Prudential–Contextual Changes

This begs the question of how institutional constraints on judicial power operate. Under what circumstances will senior judges refuse to expand legal policy, regardless of an opportunity to do so via interstitial interpretation? As discussed above, judges can be barred from legislative oversight using the section 33 "notwithstanding clause" of the Charter. And, more in line with the other countries surveyed for this book, Canadian judges demure from an intervention if they lack the democratic capacity, or the technical competency to rule. It can be difficult to identify *ex ante* when exactly judges will lack capacity or competence, but they will seek to avoid being overruled and delegitimised. As such, the courts are most likely to defer to political actors on polycentric policy problems, especially those bearing significant financial implications, and for which there is an overwhelming public opinion in favour of political leadership. In other words, judges will not interfere when they are poorly placed to determine the most politically sensitive interpretation of a fluid context. The prime examples of this would include national security and counterterrorism.

But, consistent with other federated democracies, there are still questions with regard to which politicians Canadian judges defer to. Questions concerning national security and counterterrorism are monopolised by central governments, but criminal justice more broadly is decentralised in most democracies, Canada included. If there is a clash between provincial and federal authorities, on whose side will the judges fall? The answer is, as telegraphed above, that the path of lesser institutional resistance is towards the centralisation of legal and public policies. Whilst the constitution secures autonomy for the provinces and territories of Canada, it was a constitution that had been patriated by the Federal Government, and abutted by federal rights protection in the Charter. Added to which is the other fact mentioned above, that federal courts dominate the judicial hierarchy, and many provincial judges are appointed from Ottawa. All of which tends to point the force of institutional gravity towards the centre, especially in cases where there is doubt as to the reconciliation of legal text with context.

An important example, segueing from the previous discussion of Québec autonomy, came with a privacy case in 2020.[22] The Canadian Parliament had enacted legislation that banned any requirement to genetically test an individual as a condition for obtaining a contract, good, or service. Such tests had been used on occasion to predict an individual's risk of disease or likelihood of transmitting illnesses. Besides a few enumerated exceptions, Parliament attached custodial punishments to the use of such tests. A reference was then made by the Québec government to their provincial Court of Appeal. It was not accepted by the government in Québec City that the Federal Parliament had jurisdiction to criminalise genetic testing. The Court of Appeal agreed, and ruled that offending sections of the legislation were inoperable. The Canadian Coalition for Genetic Fairness then appealed to the Canadian Supreme Court, contending that the proposed legislation touched on intersecting matters of human rights, privacy, equality, and access to services, all of which were overseen centrally, not regionally. The most senior judges agreed, albeit with four dissenters, including the Chief Justice and one other Québec-trained jurist. The judgement set out in the following terms how courts determine whether an act of Parliament is *ultra vires*:

> To determine whether a law falls within the authority of Parliament or a provincial legislature, a court must first characterize the law and then, based on that characterization, classify the law by reference to the federal and provincial heads of power under the Constitution.

[22] *Reference re Genetic Non-Discrimination Act*, 2020 SCC 17 (CanLII).

As the Canadian Constitution is derivative of the Westminster model, via the 1867 *Canada Act*, federal and provincial powers are not symmetrical when it comes to such multifaceted policy problems. Even in more understandably centralised policy spaces, the courts yield significant discretion to Parliament, self-consciously limiting their own powers of oversight, and hence forestalling any accusations of them being anti-democratic. This is particularly noticeable in cases pertaining to public safety where appellants claim "overbreadth" in legislative language. Although, the picture is nuanced. In a 1992 case, for example, the courts struck out a subsection of the criminal code that they felt established a "standardless sweep" power for courts to order pre-trial detention of suspects.[23] The over broad language at issue here allowed suspects to be detained if it was deemed necessary in the "public interest". The Supreme Court was here constraining both Parliament and the judiciary. This *Morales* precedent did not stay intact for long, however, before being distinguished.

In the same year, 1992, the case of *R. v. Farinacci* reached the Ontario Court of Appeal.[24] The judges were again asked, based on *Morales,* to interpret public interest narrowly. The specific request was to read down statutory language that denied bail to those appealing convictions. Given that public interest here was to be served post-trial, not pre-trial, the Attorney General of Canada intervened in support of the Crown and *Morales* was distinguished in these terms:

> The respondent [the Crown] submits, alternatively, that in the post-conviction context the 'public interest' criterion is not unconstitutionally vague and that if it is impermissibly vague, such vagueness is a reasonable limit within s. 1 of the Charter.

Morales was invoked again in 1994 in a free speech case. In the case of *R. v. Keegstra* at the Alberta Court of Appeal,[25] Mr. Keegstra appealed his convictions for promoting hate. As a teacher of social studies, he had given anti-Semitic lectures to his students. He was convicted for promoting hatred, but successfully appealed in 1988.[26] The Crown then

[23] *R. v. Morales*, 1992 CanLII 53 (SCC), [1992] 3 SCR 711.

[24] 1992 CanLII 1136 (ON CA).

[25] 1994 ABCA 293.

[26] *R. v. Keegstra* (1988) 1988 ABCA 234 (CanLII), 87 A.R. 177.

appealed and had the conviction reinstated by the Supreme Court,[27] although that court ordered a rehearing at the Albertan Court of Appeal on matters of provincial law. Whilst his case moved around the country, the *Morales* ruling then appeared to give Mr. Keegstra a new basis for challenging his conviction. The court was asked to consider the following, given the *Morales* precedent:

> Are words such as 'public interest', 'public benefit', 'religious subject', 'race', 'religion', 'ethnic origin', and 'hate' void for vagueness under section 7 of the Charter?

The Albertan court used the Supreme Court's reasoning against Keegstra, that even if the language was vague or over broad, it could stand as a justifiable "minimal impairment" of Charter rights. This minimal impairment doctrine forms part of the so-called *Oakes* test, named for a 1986 precedent.[28] The test allows courts to determine limitations on Charter rights, based on any "pressing and substantial objective" that can be "demonstrably justified in a free and democratic society".

This vaguely framed test allows courts to turn a blind eye to legislative vagueness. But only when political sensitivities demand it. As mentioned, the archetypically sensitive matter is national security, and, in particular, counterterrorism. An example is the Supreme Court case of *R. v. Khawaja*.[29] Mr. Khawaja was, by his own admission, obsessed with Osama Bin Laden and Al-Qaeda. In pursuit of these obsessions, he became a terrorist puppet-master. He attended a training camp in Pakistan; he sent material and immaterial resources to a cell in London for a bombing campaign; he engineered a remote detonator; he recruited money handlers; and he encouraged a young supporter to conduct a suicide mission to Israel. Seven charges were brought against him. But at trial he was able to convince the court that the "motive clause" violated freedoms of religion and expression safeguarded by section 2 of the Charter. This clause is highly indeterminate:

> Terrorist activity means… (b) an act *or* omission, in *or* outside Canada, (i) that is committed (A) in *whole or* in part for a *political*, *religious or*

[27] *R. v. Keegstra* (1990), 1990 CanLII 24 (SCC), 61 C.C.C. (3d) 1.

[28] *R v. Oakes* [1986] 1 SCR 103.

[29] 2012 SCC 69 (CanLII), [2012] 3 SCR 555.

> *ideological* purpose, objective *or* cause, *and* (B) in *whole or* in part with the intention of intimidating the public, *or* a segment of the public, with regard to its security, including its *economic* security.

The law on counterterrorism relies, in all countries, on both vague conceptual language and broad discretionary empowerment of state agents. Although Mr. Khawaja had convinced the trial judge that the motive clause would have a chilling effect on self-expression, the Crown appealed and won at the Federal Court of Appeal. By reinstating the terror motive, the offences carried a substantially heavier punishment—up from ten to twenty-four years of imprisonment. The Supreme Court confirmed its junior's ruling. It also refused to concede that punishing anyone who "participates in or contributes to, directly or indirectly, any activity of a terrorist group" is overly broad language. In most other contexts, this language would be overly broad, but judges nonetheless know what they cannot know when it comes to politics.

Influence-Seeking—Transtextual Changes

None of which allows us to conclude that Canadian judges will entirely deny their jurisdiction in counterterrorism law and policy. Indeed, judges will develop transtextual analyses around indeterminate counterterrorism legislation. This is in order to determine its proper execution, even if they demur from striking down the overall substance of policy. This influential behaviour by courts is better described as light pruning of law, than lopping from the bench. It nonetheless is an instance of judges affecting policy agendas. As such, this is the second face of power as described by Steven Lukes (1974). It is not originative power, but reactive and nonetheless influential.

A specific example of judges overseeing the execution of counterterrorism policy was *Suresh v. Canada*.[30] Mr. Suresh was a member of, and money raiser for, the Liberation Tigers of Tamil Eelam. Also known as the Tamil Tigers, they are a suspected terrorist organisation in Sri Lanka.

[30] *Suresh v. Canada (Minister of Citizenship and Immigration)*, 2002 SCC 1 (CanLII), [2002] 1 SCR 3.

A deportation order was made by the government on advice of the Canadian Security Intelligence Service. In law, Mr. Suresh was deported under s. 53(1)(b) *Immigration Act*, as he was considered to be a "danger to the security of Canada". A crucial procedural step in his deportation was a memorandum from an immigration officer confirming the danger posed by Mr. Suresh. The basis of his appeal was that he had not seen this memorandum, nor was he able to respond to it before deportation proceedings were commenced. At trial and on first appeal, his claims that this was procedurally unreasonable and that the law was unconstitutionally vague were both dismissed. However, the Supreme Court accepted that there had been improprieties in the mode of his deportation, and that he was entitled to a re-hearing. They did not, however, agree that section 7 of the Charter invalidated the indeterminately worded deportation powers of the *Immigration Act*. This is therefore an example of judges influencing the execution of policy, without altering its substance.

Judges will exert influence over the substance of law, but can do so by editing it down or excising words without creating new law. This negative power is typical of statutory construction in common law jurisdictions. It is most often indeterminate language that is "read down" in order to reconcile statutory language with wider linguistic norms. If statutory language appears to deviate from the Charter, as an example, this can encourage judges to read down that which offends, but otherwise apply the statute in full. A disturbing example came at the turn of the millennium in the case of a brutal murder.[31] A woman's body had been found with multiple stab wounds, including an attempted decapitation. Understandably this led to generalised concern that a dangerous killer was on the loose. An individual was charged with first degree murder, and he applied for bail before the trial could begin. A bail judge ruled that detaining the suspect before trial was not required for public safety nor for preventing the suspect from escaping, but more broadly "to maintain confidence in the administration of justice". A habeas corpus writ was denied, as was an appeal to the Court of Appeal. The Supreme Court similarly refused to countenance bail for the individual, but did concede that portions of the statutory scheme were unconstitutional. Specifically they decided to edit out powers from the Criminal Code wherein bail could be denied "on any other just cause being shown". This was ruled to

[31] *R. v. Hall*, 2002 SCC 64 (CanLII), [2002] 3 SCR 309.

be inconsistent with section 11 of the Charter, that an individual was "not to be denied reasonable bail without just cause". A majority of the judges also ruled that it went against the presumption of innocence in criminal justice. In this particular instance, senior judges were constraining the discretion of their own judicial brethren. Albeit, it also demonstrates the court's willingness to influence the administration of justice via the reconfiguration of legislative language.

More generally, there is a thesis that Canadian judges are positionally liberal, if not sometimes also partisan Liberals (Hutchinson 2017). Evidence for such a thesis would be systematic constraining of public policy powers, and thereby framing policy agendas in more deregulating and often capitalistic orientations. Specifically, this thesis predicts a tougher ride for more social democratic policies in court, as compared to more liberalising measures. Such rulings from court could be ascribed not only to the personal preferences of the judges, but also the liberal base of Canadian constitutionalism in general, and the Charter in particular. These are amongst the most controversial aspects of judicialised politics, where a court strikes down the popularly mandated policies of a legislature. For the most part this has not elicited complaints from the Federal Government, which is dominated by Liberal and Conservative politicians. It has, however, created substantially more resentment from the provinces, and in particular Québec. But, as stressed throughout this book, such an argument is motivationally incomplete. Superior court judges may be institutionally protected when overruling a regional legislature, but it is nonetheless suboptimal for the judiciary and rule of law to be delegitimised in the periphery. Judges will not be incentivised, therefore, just to march after their policy preferences. They will need a specific stimulus to justify intervening. The stimulus, in many cases, will be conspicuous indeterminacies in law.

One particular case raises these issues with fascinating complication. The case of *Gosselin v. Québec* was a class action suit brought by a Québecois citizen against her government.[32] The appellant sought $389 million (plus interest) in backpay. The Québec government had introduced a policy in 1984 to provide welfare assistance of substantially greater generosity to those aged over thirty as compared to those

[32] *Gosselin v. Québec (AG)* [2002] 4 SCR 429, 2002 SCC 84.

under thirty. It was claimed that this violated section 7 of the Charter's protection of "life, liberty and security", in particular by rendering the claimant economically insecure. Section 7 had in prior jurisprudence been restricted to the administration of justice, and whether or not life or liberty was being deprived through procedural irregularities. Nonetheless, a philosophical argument was raised that this section imposed positive obligations on the state to empower citizens, and was not simply a negative dictum that state institutions ought to stay out of the way. As per Chief Justice McLachlin:

> Thus far, the jurisprudence does not suggest that s. 7 places positive obligations on the state. Rather, s. 7 has been interpreted as restricting the state's ability to deprive people of their right to life, liberty and security of the person. Such a deprivation does not exist here and the circumstances of this case do not warrant a novel application of s. 7 as the basis for a positive state obligation to guarantee adequate living standards.

Although the Supreme Court ultimately supported the Québec government and dismissed the class action, they also admitted the case for hearing. This suggests the senior judges were at least open to the possibility that section 7 could be used beyond the administration of justice, and could even indicate positive obligations for the state. They were shaping the agenda for future lawsuits to interrogate provincial and territorial legislation. And yet, predictably enough for some commentators, the judges opted in this case for a state-constraining resolution to the dispute. So on the one hand the court admitted that there was standing for provincial citizens to make claims in federal court against policy substance, whilst on the other hand the guiding principle of Canadian constitutionalism would be resolutely liberal. In a case just two years later coming out of British Columbia, the Supreme Court ruled that "non-core medically necessary treatments" could not enjoy Charter-protected funding.[33] Again, the Supreme Court had the capacity to interrogate provincial legislation and policy, but did not overrule on the basis of liberal constitutionalism. None of which is meant as a criticism. This is not a moral case, but an empirical catalogue of how and why judges intervene in policy disputes.

[33] *Auton (Guardian ad litem of) v. British Columbia (AG)*, [2004] 3 SCR 657, 2004 SCC 78.

Of course, it would be excessively broad to conclude that liberality is the sole base of the Canadian policy superstructure. There is ambivalence between the principles of liberality and regulation when it comes to public policy in Canada, even from Liberal governments. This, as discussed in previous chapters, is a common source of both indeterminacy in legislation and degenrification through time. We can see this in the 42nd Parliament as it legislated to liberalise Canadian cannabis laws. That Parliament not only decriminalised consumption and possession of cannabis, it also amended rules on criminal records kept for past cannabis misdemeanours. This amounted to a mass pardoning. The government bill (C-93) provided for free-of-charge and efficient record suspensions. But, the suspensions were not automatic, and individuals had to apply. This thereby insured a degree of regulatory oversight to this deregulation. This is not a flat contradiction, but it does evince a degree of bureaucratised liberality. The House of Commons reacted by adding further indeterminacies to the bill before Royal Assent. They were particularly keen to ensure that vulnerable applicants would not find the process onerously bureaucratic. As such they added the following language to the bill:

> ...*if* the applicant is not able to obtain documents that would provide evidence that the conditions... are met, the applicant *may* submit a *sworn* statement *or solemn* declaration that explains the *reasonable* efforts made by the applicant to obtain the documents, *and* the reasons why they could not be obtained, including because they were lost *or* destroyed.

This could not be categorised as ambivalent in the sense of not knowing the principles at work. Rather this is epistemic ambivalence, as to how the policy will best be implemented amidst a variety of possibilities. All of which is justifiable in democratic theory and practice, but also creates wide interpretive spaces for judges.

Policy-Oriented—Metatextual Changes

It is not merely policy ambivalence with indeterminacies in language that elicits judicialisation. Judges will also react to arbitrariness in law and policy. This is the very opposite of ambivalence. It is an excess of certainty, leading to inflexibility of concepts and approaches. Legislative text may be determinable, but interpreted as unjust and incoherent as regards wider rules of law. This can encourage courts to develop a metatext rendering, wherein the legislative text is embellished and reformed by reference to constitutional and common law norms. This differs from the preceding discussion of determining text according to transtext, in that judges create new law, and do not merely reproduce existing norms. This is very much the most controversial aspect of judicial politics, wherein judges appear to be creating policy and not just determining its legality.

An important illustration is the decriminalisation of abortion in Canada. In 1975, Dr. Henry Morgentaler had his appeal against conviction dismissed by the Supreme Court.[34] He had been charged with procuring a miscarriage in violation of the Criminal Code. A jury had acquitted him, on grounds of common law necessity. The Court of Appeal reversed the acquittal and ordered a trial judge to pass sentence. The senior appeal courts rejected his necessity defence in common law, as well as his reliance on the Bill of Rights and a statutory defence. Then in 1988, the same Dr. Morgentaler, with other appellants, was again pleading at the Supreme Court.[35] He had again been acquitted by a jury for procuring miscarriages, and again this had been put aside by the Court of Appeal. This time the Supreme Court had the Charter and section 2 jurisprudence. Section 2 calls for defence of "life, liberty and security". This was the tip of the spear used for reversing precedent:

> State interference with bodily integrity and serious state-imposed psychological stress, at least in the criminal law context, constitutes a breach of security of the person. Section 251 [criminalising abortion in all but a highly regulated set of exceptions] clearly interferes with a woman's physical and bodily integrity. Forcing a woman, by threat of criminal sanction, to carry a foetus to term unless she meets certain criteria unrelated to her own priorities and aspirations, is a profound interference.[36]

But, interestingly, the Charter was not the only basis of declaring section 251 of the Criminal Code as void. Also implicated were principles of fundamental justice. These principles were in essence procedural, but

[34] *Morgentaler v. The Queen*, 1975 CanLII 8 (SCC), [1976] 1 SCR 616.

[35] *R. v. Morgentaler*, 1988 CanLII 90 (SCC), [1988] 1 SCR 30.

[36] Ibid., page 32.

with profound substantive implications. The argument was that Parliament had established a regime for obtaining abortions that was so flawed in its practicalities and procedures, that it barely existed in fact.

> Any infringement of the right to life, liberty and security of the person must comport with the principles of fundamental justice. These principles are to be found in the basic tenets of our legal system. One of the basic tenets of our system of criminal justice is that when Parliament creates a defence to a criminal charge, the defence should not be illusory or so difficult to attain as to be practically illusory.[37]

Most tellingly, the judges concluded that infringing a woman's right to choose in the manner achieved by section 251 constituted a violation of "basic tenets" of Canadian law. And yet the very same section 251 had, only thirteen years previously, been the basis for convicting the same appellant for the same behaviour. So, how can a case of judges making abortion laws be reconciled with this book's argument? The central thesis here is that judges are reactive to churning adaptations in legal language. They are not proactive policy-makers, but reactive and institutionally conservative. There are two defences. Firstly, the thesis was only ever presented as offering probabilistic insights, not deterministic laws of judicial behaviour. As such, the rising incidence of judicialisation is not merely coincident but causally connected to the rising quantity and altered determinability of legislation. There will nonetheless be cases where legislative indeterminacy is not the precursor to judicialisation. However, secondly, it is important to consider the rule of law holistically. Whilst individual cases may be somewhat difficult to situate within a theory of linguistic evolution, individual cases will contribute to on-going coordinative and communicative discourses, within and beyond the judiciary. Whilst it is tempting to isolate individual cases as appearing to be evidence of unconstrained judicial activism, every case is connected. Singular cases therefore need to be considered as part of a much longer story of judges developing tools in response to institutional deformation, and that when these tools are available they can be used to resolve cases in a more proactive, seemingly engineering, approach.

Also, it would be wrong to conclude that legislative indeterminacy had no bearing on the abortion case. Notably, the word "health" in s 251(4)

[37] Ibid., page 33.

was undefined, meaning there were inadequate guidelines to establish "therapeutic abortion committees" tasked with protecting health, be it mental or physical health. Of course, such indeterminacy can be perceived rather than real. Some may well counter that misunderstanding can be manufactured, and used to justify the unjustifiable intervention of a court into policy. But, again, we need to establish the causal mechanism and incentives for judges to intercede in policy. In Dr. Morgentaler's case, the senior judges were reinstating a jury decision, were adapting new human rights law to extant precedent, and could in 1988 see a breach of fundamental justice that was somehow obscured in 1975. This final element—in recognising the injustice of law—was connected to changing public attitudes on abortion. The judges were unlikely to be overruled by politicians as they could refer to jury decisions and sense the way the wind was blowing. The moral question is whether judges should be pre-empting political action and assessing public mood in this way. That moral question is not tackled here. The aim is to establish empirical developments in law through time. The difference between 1975 and 1988 was not simply in perception and public opinion, there had also been major changes to law that could shield a judicial incursion.

The concept of fundamental justice is itself indeterminate and relative to perspective. Another controversial case where this vague judicial dictum clashed with a vague legislative dictum came with regard to human trafficking in 2015.[38] Appeals were brought by four individuals, charged under section 117 of the *Immigration and Refugee Protection Act 2001*, for their attempt to "organize, induce, aid or abet" illegal immigration to Canada. The four were in fact crew members of a vessel carrying seventy-six undocumented asylum seekers fleeing war in Sri Lanka. They were picked up off Vancouver Island, and the four appellants were arrested for their part in a for-profit smuggling operation. They contended that section 117 was unconstitutionally vague, but, interestingly, not as it applied to them.[39] Section 117 states as follows:

> 117. (1) No person shall *knowingly* organize, induce, aid *or* abet the coming into Canada of one *or more* persons who are not in possession of a visa, passport *or other* document required by this Act.

[38] *R. v. Appulonappa*, 2015 SCC 59 (CanLII), [2015] 3 SCR 754.

[39] Ibid., para 10.

The four appellants accepted that they had been part of an operation charging \$25–35,000 per head for transport across the Pacific. But they also argued that section 117 was "overbroad", and an offence to fundamental justice because it threw too wide of a net around what ought to be a targeted policy. Notably, they pointed out that humanitarian interventions, such as from family members helping an undocumented migrant, would also fall foul of section 117, even though they had no profit motive. In what can perhaps be described as litigious philanthropy, the appellants were able to convince the Supreme Court that the law was unjust and unlawful, except as it affected themselves. The court agreed, and not only relied on fundamental justice to rule section 117 as unconstitutionally overbroad, but even used the official record of Parliament's proceedings to suggest that the legislative text could not be said to represent the legislature's will. The judges were therefore criticising the legislation, and yet realising the intent of the legislature. Such behaviour could be described as arrogating to the judiciary legislative responsibilities. That is as may be, but the trigger for and justification of such a ruling was a conspicuous interpretative space between legislative language and constitutionalism.

One of the most often cited examples of judicial overreach is a case concerning private health insurance in Québec.[40] Although not a criminal case, it would be analytically incomplete not to mention this case, given how much attention it brings. George Zeliotis had waited over a year for hip replacement under Québec's public health plan. In provincial legislation, it was impossible to obtain private treatment, where a public option was available. Dr. Jacques Chaoulli—the physician caring for Mr. Zeliotis—convinced the Canadian Supreme Court that Québec's health care monopoly and its long waiting lists constituted breaches of rights to life, liberty and security of person, and was an affront to principles of fundamental justice. The case was hugely controversial, as it amounted to a federal reworking of provincial legislation. In this instance, the legislative language was neither vague nor overbroad:

> No insurer may enter into or maintain an insurance contract that includes coverage for the cost of an insured service furnished to a resident.[41]

[40] *Chaoulli v. Québec (AG)* [2005] 1 SCR 791, 2005 SCC 35.

[41] *Hospital Insurance Act*, CQLR c A-28.

Again, to explain the ruling in this case, we need to observe the ratcheting effect of compound legislative and constitutional indeterminacies through iterated rulings. Taken on its own, the ruling in *Chaoulli* is barely comprehensible. If we go back to the preceding decades of Charter jurisprudence, however, we see a trail of juridical breadcrumbs that leads to this striking down of provincial health legislation. The business-friendly ruling was not particularly surprising given the common law and liberal foundations of Canadian constitutionalism, as well as the post-1982 development in section 7 interpretations of "life, liberty and security".

Besides taking on legislative functions, the Canadian courts have even taken on executive roles. In the case of *Doucet-Boudreau*,[42] a trial judge in Nova Scotia ruled that the province needed to apply "best efforts" to provide French-language education. The judge even set specific dates by which policy reforms had to be achieved and intended to oversee their implementation. The Nova Scotian Court of Appeal ruled this to be an excessive intrusion into executive discretion. However, the Canadian Supreme Court granted the judge this oversight power, justifying it under section 24 of the Charter, as pertains to remedies. According to the judges:

> A purposive approach to remedies in a Charter context requires that both the purpose of the right being protected and the purpose of the remedies provision be promoted. To do so, courts must issue effective, responsive remedies that guarantee full and meaningful protection of Charter rights and freedoms.

This was an unprecedented expansion of the Charter, beyond purposive interpretation of its provisions to purposive interpretation of its implementation. In this particular instance, the indeterminacy justifying judicial incursion was constitutional rather than legislative. The text of section 24(1) of the Charter allowed for an expansive interpretation:

> Anyone whose rights *or* freedoms, as guaranteed by this Charter, have been infringed *or* denied *may* apply to a court of *competent* jurisdiction to obtain *such* remedy as the court considers *appropriate* and *just* in the circumstances.

[42] *Doucet-Boudreau v. Nova Scotia (Minister of Education)*, 2003 SCC 62 (CanLII), [2003] 3 SCR 3.

A common assumption of judicial activism theories is that legislatures and executives are spoken at by judges, not spoken with. But in this case, the aim was collaborative, with the judges intending to implement settled law. It is typical for remedies to come with a degree of judicial oversight. Whether it is incarceration, levying a fine, paying costs, or amending legislation, the courts will keep an eye on implementation, utilising the threat of contempt of court proceedings to ensure compliance. A striking example of judges ruling that legislation needed to be amended was with regard to assisted suicide. In the 2015 case of *Carter v. Canada*, the Supreme Court struck down portions of the Criminal Code that denied a competent adult a right to commit suicide with assistance.[43] This ruling was suspended for a year, to give Parliament the time to legislate away the perceived inconsistency between the Charter and the Criminal Code. This is an example of dialogue theory, albeit the conversation was very much initiated and led by judges with the politicians reacting.

The legislative reaction came with Bill C-14 in the 42nd Parliament. Unusually, this bill was substantially amended by Parliament. It was also nearly twice as indeterminate in its language as compared to the average government bill. Sixteen amendments were included by the reviewing House Committee. These amendments added further safeguards, focussed in particular on potential problems in communication. For example, the Committee added the following:

> (i) *if* the person has difficulty communicating, take *all necessary* measures to provide a *reliable* means by which the person *may* understand the information that is provided to them *and* communicate their decision.

Of course, communication is the recurring theme of this book. Aspiring to tailored communication between the state and particular citizens, the House of Commons included further indeterminacies to the bill, but not without justification. Indeed, the Committee went so far as to amend the bill's preamble, so as to capture their desire to treat differently that which is different:

> Whereas the Government of Canada recognizes that in the living conditions of Canadians, there are diverse circumstances and that different

[43] *Carter v. Canada (AG)*, 2015 SCC 5.

> groups have unique needs, it commits to working with provinces, territories and civil society to facilitate access to palliative and end-of-life care, care and services for individuals living with Alzheimer's and dementia, appropriate mental health supports and services and culturally and spiritually appropriate end-of-life care for Indigenous patients.

This altered preamble captures the ambivalence of contemporary policy. Whilst "ambivalence" can be interpreted as lackadaisical or uncaring, in this instance there is no basis for such a conclusion. Instead, the ambivalence is with regard to policy finality. Lawmakers recognised something had to be done, but they were clearly not sure what would be the best thing to do in every circumstance. In legislating this ambivalence, they have left open wide space for judges to use discretion to determine law.

Conclusion

Canadian courts have extensive policy influence and power, even by North American standards. The centralisation of human rights law gives federal courts wide capacity to interpret provincial and territorial policies. The Charter, specifically, leaves no doubts as to its applicability against sub-national politics. By comparison, the US Constitution had to be incorporated by judges against the states through a near century-long series of precedents. The Canadian approach happened practically overnight when the UK Parliament legislated for a new and patriated Constitution. As mentioned, it is stunningly ironic that the British Parliament laid down such a robust charter of rights to be applied throughout its former Dominion, where its own Human Rights Act is vastly weaker in the face of government power.

There is clearly a before-Charter and post-Charter divergence in public law power for the courts. Judicialisation was also, of course, stimulated more generally by patriation and the unquestioned supremacy of Canada's Supreme Court after 1982. Patriation was less immediately relevant to judicial power than the Charter, because appeals to London had ceased in 1949. Nonetheless, patriation has created both psychological and mechanical effects for federal court dominance. In a notorious case under the Constitution Act, the Supreme Court even influenced judicial salaries. Sections 99 and 100 of the Constitution guarantee judges secure tenure and salaries, respectively. The Charter of Right and Freedoms abutted these provisions in section 11(d) with a guarantee to citizens of access to "independent and impartial tribunals". In a 1997 case, the Supreme Court effectively created a new bureaucratic mechanism to administer pay for judges.[44] There were to be judicial compensation commissions whose recommendations could only be rejected by government. But—and herein came the controversy—any government rejections would be open to judicial review. The ruling seemed to be in breach of the separation of powers, by enabling judges to be judge in their own cause, as well as everyone else's.

But, judicial strength is a function of state strength. Strong judges have been deliberately empowered by democracies to avoid social disorder and insecurity. In addition to which, there has developed an informal expansion in judicial power, consequent on the informal (as in not led by constitutional amendment) expansion of state bureaucracy. Confining the growing demands from a diverse citizenry into determinable language has proven impossible. As such, we have seen steadily rising indeterminacies in criminal law, with highly indeterminate constitutional and human rights protections. There are simply wider interpretative spaces for judges to fill. However, we have not found evidence of judges using mere casuistry to pretend that these indeterminacies exist. As Justice Lamer (as he was then) put it in response to laws on prostitution in Manitoba:

> In my opinion, one of the first characteristics of a reasonable limit prescribed by law is that it should be expressed in terms sufficiently clear to permit a determination of where and what the limit is. A limit which is vague, ambiguous, uncertain, or subject to discretionary determination is, by that fact alone, an unreasonable limit. If a citizen cannot know with tolerable certainty the extent to which the exercise of a guaranteed freedom may be restrained, he is likely to be deterred from conduct which is, in fact, lawful and not prohibited. Uncertainty and vagueness are constitutional vices when they are used to restrain constitutionally protected rights and freedoms. While there can never be absolute certainty, a limitation of a guaranteed right must be such as to allow a very high degree of predictability to the legal consequences.[45]

[44] *Reference re Remuneration of Judges of the Provincial Court* [P.E.I] 1997.

[45] *Reference re ss. 193 and 195.1(1)(C) of the criminal code (Man.)*, 1990 CanLII 105 (SCC), [1990] 1 SCR 1123, pp. 1156–1157.

References

Hogg, Peter W., and Allison A. Bushell. 1997. The Charter Dialogue between Courts and Legislatures (Or Perhaps the Charter of Rights Isn't Such a Bad Thing after All). *Osgoode Hall LJ* 35: 75.

Hutchinson, Allan. 2017. The Politics of Constitutional Law: A Critical Approach. In *The Oxford Handbook of the Canadian Constitution*, ed. Peter Oliver, Patrick Macklem, and Nathalie Des Rosiers. Oxford: Oxford University Press.

Kelly, James B. and Christopher P. Manfredi. 2010. Courts. In *The Oxford Handbook of Canadian Politics*, ed. John C. Courtney and David E. Smith. Oxford: Oxford University Press.

Lukes, Steven. 1974. *Power: A Radical View*. Basingstoke: Macmillan.

Martin, Robert. 2003. *The Most Dangerous Branch: How the Supreme Court of Canada Has Undermined Our Law and Our Democracy*. Montreal: McGill-Queen's University Press.

Morton, F.L., and Rainer Knopff. 2019. *The Charter Revolution and the Court Party*. Toronto: University of Toronto.

Sharpe, Robert J. 1987. *Charter Litigation*. Toronto: Butterworths.

Stone, Alec. 1992. Where Judicial Politics Are Legislative Politics: The French Constitutional Council. *West European Politics* 15 (3): 29–49.

Williams, Matthew. 2017. Legislative Language and Judicial Politics: The Effects of Changing Parliamentary Language on UK Immigration Disputes. *British Journal of Politics and IR* 19 (3): 592–608.

CHAPTER 8

Executive Dominance with Decentralisation in France

The book's central question asks why judges have increasingly made and enforced public policy, sometimes at the expense of their own governments. France ought to be perfect for probing and observing counterfactuals. Considering its history, culture, and institutions, we might expect almost never to observe either government losses or major policy changes come about in French court rulings. Ever since Napoleon laid down his eponymous legal code, judges were supposed to keep away from policy. A conspicuous aim of codification was to tighten the Emperor's personal grip on public affairs, thereby rendering judges (and all other bureaucrats) little more than unimaginative technicians (Jones 1856). The enterprise was supported by republican ideology, affirming a shared destiny for all citizens. Public policies were to be administered from Paris to the peripheries, never the other way around. Also helpful in ensuring court quiescence was France's tradition of social conservatism, captured in the party system, and described by republican norms, such as secularism, or *Laïcité*. This conservatism, in turn, is ironically juxtaposed to a radical and highly flexible constitutionalism, with (on paper at least) near untrammelled parliamentary supremacy. In short, the French state was designed to be adaptable, but adaptable according to political visionaries, rather than the dead hand of constitutionalism, and certainly not the creative intuition of judges.

M. Williams, *Judges and the Language of Law*,
https://doi.org/10.1007/978-3-030-91495-0_8

How are we to explain the increased number of policy impactful court rulings in France therefore? The bases of French court power today include widened jurisdiction for the courts relative to their 1958 founding conditions; increased accessibility for minority parties and individual citizens; broadened jurisprudence of "fundamental principles"; increased resort to European Union courts; and enhanced remedies for litigants. Explanations for these institutional and normative changes must be drawn in part from peculiarly French experiences. Long-term peculiarities include the burgeoning power of administrative law, overseen by the Cour d'Etat, during the Third (1870–1940) and Fourth Republics (1946–1958). This was an exigency of wars and post-war recoveries, and was in part redolent of French republican ideology. The state expansion is epitomised by post-war *dirigisme*. Also, concerning French geopolitics, was its founding membership of the European Coal and Steel Community, latterly the European Union. This pan-continental and supranational entity altered both the institutional and normative logics of French justice. With regard to its internal domestic politics, of importance to judicialisation has been the "hyper-presidentialism" of near cultish concentration on the individual occupant of the Élysée Palace. Ever since the literal and figurative giant, General de Gaulle, created the Fifth Republic (Hazareesingh 2012), French politics has largely danced to the tune of one man at a time (Wenzel 2016). But this of course has come with consequences for political unity and policy stability. Most notably have been schisms on the right of France's party system, in particular under Presidents Pompidou, d'Estaing, Chirac, and even the centrist Macron.[1] There have been two relatively brief periods of Socialist Party control (under Presidents Mitterand and Hollande) that were robustly opposed by establishment stake holders, including in the courts. There has even been decentralisation of the great dirigiste state under Gaston Defferre's late 1980s reforms (Unger 2011).

With fragmentation to institutions, splits amongst elites, cleaved ideologies, and destabilised norms of French politics, we can see the roots of policy ambivalence and legislative indeterminacy that drove a global

[1] Although Macron himself is not leading a nominally conservative group, his *La République En Marche!* party is most directly courting votes and influence from the Republicans and the National Front.

trend towards state expansion and judicialisation (Tate and Vallinder 1995). The courts have policy power—whether by banning the erection of new cockfighting gallodromes[2]; or protecting suspected terrorists online[3]; or even going so far as to declare a tax rise as unconstitutional.[4] Even the rudiments of democratic competition were subjected to judicial oversight—from regulating elections (Brouard 2016) to even imprisoning former President Sarkozy for campaign finance irregularities.[5]

An example will help root the book's theory. The Conseil constitutionnel—France's constitutional review court—"was seized" (*a été saisi*) on 3rd September 2013. It was so seized by the Supreme Court—the Cour de cassation—to adjudicate on tax matters for local authorities.[6] Specifically, the dispute concerned how local taxes on outdoor advertising would be collected. This seemingly banal dispute in fact provides an excellent description of this book's central contention—that policy and legal indeterminacies have judicialised politics. The case was brought by Boulanger, a chain of electrical stores, contesting provisions in *The Modernisation of the Economy Law* (Loi n° 2008-776). This was a signature supply-side reform of President Nicolas Sarkozy and his Finance Minister Christine Legarde. They had sought to reform taxes and regulations for France's small and medium size industries, with the backdrop of a global financial crisis. Adding flexibility to labour laws and increasing working hours was no mean feat against the legendary inflexibility of France's trade unions. That the legislation contained indeterminate elisions and omissions is perhaps not surprising therefore. But ideas not figuratively litigated in the legislature will encourage literal litigation in court.

[2] ECLI: FR: CC: 2015: 2015.477.QPC.

[3] ECLI:FR:CC:2017:2017.682.QPC.

[4] ECLI:FR:CC:2013:2013.685.DC.

[5] https://www.lemonde.fr/idees/article/2021/03/02/nicolas-sarkozy-dans-le-piege-de-la-surenchere_6071673_3232.html *"A chaque fois qu'il s'est trouvé acculé juridiquement, l'ex-président de la République a cherché à galvaniser ses troupes contre les juges, ce qui était une façon de se réarmer politiquement. Aujourd'hui, il récolte la monnaie de sa pièce."* "Whenever he [Sarkozy] found himself in a legal corner, the former President of the Republic sought to galvanize his troops against the judges, which was a way of rearming himself politically. Today, he is collecting reaping what he sowed," accessed 3 August 2021.

[6] FR: CC: 2013: 2013.351.QPC.

Also crucial to this case is the fact that private citizens were even able to be party to it This was a novel development, brought about in 2008. In another attempted modernisation of the French state, President Sarkozy had promised in his 2007 election to improve accessibility to the Conseil constitutionnel. In Article 61 of the Constitution, it was made possible for citizens to pursue a posteriori (concrete) constitutional review for the first time. Citizens were entitled to raise a question prioritaire de constitutionalité (QPC). Specifically, from 2010 onwards, it was possible for citizens to contest the constitutionality of promulgated legislation, all the way up to France's constitutional court. Previously, only a priori (abstract) review of a law was possible during its parliamentary consideration. And, only institutional representatives of the French state had enjoyed standing to these proceedings—including at least sixty members of the National Assembly, sixty Senators, the Prime Minister; or the Presidents of the Republic, Assembly and Senate as individuals.

Hence, Boulanger found that they were empowered by the Sarkozy administration to contest a signature policy of the Sarkozy administration. Judges certainly didn't take an axe to the law, as they merely questioned how tax on outdoor advertising was to be collected. But, relevant here, is how Boulanger encouraged the court abrogation. They contended that the French state was not sufficiently clear in its use of language:

> 13...the disregard by the legislator of its own jurisdiction can be invoked... in the event that this disregard in itself affects a right or a freedom guaranteed by the Constitution;
>
> 14... it follows that, when defining an imposition [tax], the legislator must determine its modalities of recovery, which include the rules governing control, recovery, litigation, guarantees and penalties applicable to this imposition;
>
> 15. Considering that the lack of determination of the modalities of recovery of an imposition affects the right to an effective remedy guaranteed by article 16 of the Declaration [of the Rights of Man and the Citizen] of 1789.

The court was encouraged into a politically impactful intervention by indeterminacies of legislative will. As with the other countries studied in this book, changes to judicial power in France came with both pace and intensity. Exemplary are cases of constitutional review. There were just over three such cases heard at the Conseil constitutionnel, per year, prior to 1974 (Brouard 2016). Most of these were automatic referrals of organic laws, as required under article 46 of the Constitution. Others still were referrals by Prime Ministers to frustrate legislative majorities during a time of splintered party politics. But, after 1975, over three quarters of Conseil cases dealt with ordinary laws, not institution-altering organic laws. It is now the case that more than one in every six pieces of ordinary legislation (14.7%) is subject to partial or complete veto in court. This is three times the interventionist rate of the German Federal Constitutional Court (Gallagher et al. 2011). It is an extraordinary rate of judicialisation, leading Alec Stone Sweet to describe the Conseil as a "third legislative chamber" (Stone 1992).

Explaining this emergent tricameralism of Assembly, Senate and Conseil often (and helpfully) proceeds by highlighting way markers of 1971, 1974, and 2008 (Brouard 2016). In 1971, the Conseil decided it could use "fundamental principles" of French constitutionalism, specifically the Declaration of the Rights of Man and the Citizen in 1789, as well as the preambles to the Third and Fourth Republican constitutions. None of the sources of law were explicitly provided in the Fifth Republican constitution as bases for Conseil rulings. The court was identifying for itself, albeit not without good reason, what fundamental principles breathe life into French constitutionalism. This was achieved in Decision 71–44 in just 598 words. The case had been brought by President of the Senate, Alain Poher.[7] Poher was a centrist politician, and was reacting to legislative moves from Georges Pompidou's Gaullists. The challenged law had been approved by the National Assembly and was being deliberated in the Senate. The law sought to amend a 1901 law on freedom of association, and a 1936 law on private militias:

> 2. Considering that, among the fundamental principles recognized by the laws of the Republic and solemnly reaffirmed by the preamble of the Constitution, the principle of freedom of association should be stored.[8]

[7] He also served twice as interim President of the Republic.

[8] ECLI:FR:CC:1971:71.44.DC.

The Conseil set out some extra-textual sources of meaning ("fundamental principles"), beyond the Fifth Republic Constitution. It also reached beyond the legislative text to resolve a suit brought by disgruntled politicians. Hence, the notion that the Conseil was a "third legislative chamber". It is an apt description of this instance, where the Conseil deliberated on a bill before it was promulgated and whilst it was being considered in the Senate.

Changes in 1974 and 2008 were both initiated by constitutional amendment. The 1974 reform allowed suit to be initiated by sixty members of the National Assembly or sixty Senators, where previously only the three Presidents (of the Republic, of the Assembly, or of the Senate) were able to initiate proceedings at the Conseil. Fairly predictably, the 1974 reform encouraged minority parties to call on the Conseil to rule on the constitutionality of draft legislation, either with an authentic belief in its aberration from rules of law or with a strategic intent to frustrate governments. Given that sixty members of the National Assembly is only a little over 10% of that body's membership, it does not take much to pull together a quorum of litigants.

A notable test case shortly after the 1974 reform came in response to the 1975 "Veil Law".[9] This legislation, also known as the *Voluntary Interruption of Pregnancy Act*, decriminalised abortion. It was named after Simone Veil, the Bill's champion. In an attempt to prevent decriminalisation, a group of 81 other Deputies (79 men and two women) brought a case claiming incompatibility between the proposed law and international treaties protecting life. The court in this instance demurred from intervening, claiming it had no authority to overrule domestic legislation against international laws. In doing so it described the constitutional language on its own jurisdiction as determinate, even if that language referring to the supremacy of treaties was capable of multiple contextual reinterpretations (emphases added):

> 4. Considering, in fact, that the decisions taken pursuant to Article 61 of the Constitution [on jurisdiction of the Conseil] are of *absolute and definitive character*...

[9] ECLI:FR:CC:1975:74.54.DC.

> On the contrary, the superiority of the treaties on the laws, the principle of which is posed in Article 55, presents a character *at the same time relative and contingent*, holding, on the one hand, to what it is limited to the scope of the treaty and, on the other hand, that it is subordinated to a condition of reciprocity whose realisation may vary according to the behaviour of the Treaty and the time when the respect should be appreciated this condition;

This "definitive" perspective on jurisdiction weakened, particularly in the face of Europeanisation. In May 1975—four months after the Veil ruling—the Cour de cassation ruled that it could overturn domestic legislation that contradicted international treaties, stating that Article 55 of the Constitution obliged as much with regard to the Treaty of Rome.[10] The case was far less ethically fraught than that concerning abortion, dealing as it did with imports of instant coffee from The Netherlands. But it recognised the primacy of EEC (now EU) laws, as asserted by the European Court of Justice (now CJEU) in their 1964 ruling of *Flaminio Costa v. E.N.E.L.*[11] The Conseil d'Etat ruled along similar lines in a 1989 case determining the rights of French overseas territories to participate in European Parliament elections.[12] Although, this decision struck out legislation that pre-dated France's treaty commitments. The Conseil constitutionnel joined the party in 2013, effectively reversing its "Veil Law" decision on jurisdiction, not that precedence is as important in civil law jurisdictions as it is in common law. Nonetheless, the Conseil referred a case to the CJEU for a preliminary ruling, thereby acknowledging the European courts and treaties as capable of dominating domestic constitutional law (Millet and Perlo 2015).[13]

A key change from the 1975 *Veil case* to the 2013 decision was the 2008 reform and introduction of questions prioritaire de constitutionalité (QPC). The 2013 case was an example of QPC. The primary litigant was a Monsieur F, subject to a European Arrest Warrant, and seeking guidance as to whether it was constitutional to be deported to an EU member state to face punishment. Mr F was seeking interpretation of domestic legislation (Articles 695-11 to 695-51 of the Code of Criminal Procedure) that had been promulgated in 2004. In other words, this was a

[10] Cour de cassation—Chambre mixte N° de pourvoi: 73–13.556.

[11] ECLI:EU:C:1964:66.

[12] ECLI:FR:CEASS:1989:108,243.19891020.

[13] ECLI:FR:CC:2013:2013.314P.QPC.

litigant bringing a personal case about domestic legislation that had been promulgated. This capacity for a citizen to bring suit marks a transformative difference in how the French court system operates now as compared to before the 2008 reform came into force in 2010. It is no longer simply the case that abstract review of law not yet promulgated is led by institutional representatives of the French state. Constitutional review has been opened up to citizens and for concrete and not just abstract review.

Another Europeanisation angle to explore is with regard to the continent's two notable rights instruments—the European Convention on Human Rights (administered by the non-EU Council of Europe), and the EU Charter of Fundamental Rights (administered by the CJEU). Adherence to these instruments of law is obliged by France's membership of the European Union, but the instruments themselves drew heavily from French political culture. A notable friction point, however, between French civic liberties and international human rights has come through commitment to *Laïcité*. This secularist principle forms Article 1 of the constitution, telegraphing the post-revolutionary importance of separating church from state. This commitment to secularism has nonetheless created public policy conflict, especially with regard to France's Muslim population. A prominent example was legislation banning face coverings in public (Loi n° 2010-1192). Whilst the law prohibited any facial occlusion—including motorcycle helmets—the law was intended as a "Burqa Ban". In the case of *S.A.S. v. France*,[14] a young woman took the French government to the European Court of Human Rights claiming infringements of her rights to private life, freedoms of thought and religion, and freedom from discrimination. The Court declared its misgivings, but upheld the law. Such deference to France's "living together" regulation was not shared by the United Nations, which invoked the International Covenant on Civil and Political Rights to declare the French state as having transgressed religious freedom. But without any enforcement mechanism, this had no effect. Nonetheless, transgression of international human rights laws and norms remains exceptional in France (Davis and Taithe 2011).

Thus far we have traced a typical macroscopic narrative of widening accessibility to court remedies. Another important element of the story are players of the game, not just the institutional rules. Louis Favoreu,

[14] Application no. 43835/11.

for one, emphasised a micro-level analysis, noting pioneering jurists in his work on French constitutionalism. Indeed, he would become one such pioneer, as his academic work obtained the rare distinction of shaping that which was being observed (Favoreu et al. 2005). More broadly, politicians keeping a grip on judicial appointments is a consistent theme of French constitutionalism. This is in keeping with republican ideology, and a concomitant desire for accountability of justice. At the Conseil constitutionnel, notably, one-third of its nine permanent members is replaced every three years. Each of the three Presidents (of the Republic, of the National Assembly, and of the Senate) has one appointment apiece. Given the dominance of these three institutions by centre-right politicians since 1958, the court has similarly been assumed to bear conservative inclinations. Periods of Socialist government, or inter-party *cohabitation*, never fully lustrated the justice system of its conservative-appointed personnel.

This has encouraged theories of naked politicking from judges. In a 2010 case, most famously, the Conseil declared as unconstitutional a 75% super-tax on the wealthy that had been a centrepiece of François Hollande's bid for the presidency.[15] This was a DC case (*Contrôle de constitutionnalité des lois ordinaires, lois organiques, des traités, des règlements des Assemblées*), not a QPC case. It was therefore brought to the court pre-promulgation by disgruntled Deputies and Senators. Indeed, vastly more than the needed quorum of sixty litigants were mustered in opposition to the tax (149 Deputies, 118 Senators). They submitted that the tax was unconstitutional on account of being unequal, even if that is perhaps the point of a variable-rate tax:

> 68. Considering that, according to the Deputies and the requesting Senators, this exceptional contribution, added to the maximum marginal rate of income tax provided for in Article 3 of the Finance Law for 2013, as well as to the exceptional contribution on high incomes and social security contributions, will result in a global taxation at the rate of 75% and therefore has a confiscatory character; that this exceptional contribution would also undermine the principle of equality before tax arising from Article 13 of the Declaration of 1789, by retaining as the tax unit natural persons and not the tax household, by not providing for capping or reduction mechanism and not taking into account family expenses.

[15] ECLI:FR:CC:2012:2012.662.DC.

These legalistic arguments could not expel the whiff of political interference from judges, not least from the perspective of tax reform advocates. The tax was eventually declared constitutional the following year,[16] but President Hollande then shortly dropped what had by then become a policy millstone.[17] Part of the 2008 constitutional reform also gave Parliament a power of veto over any judicial appointment. And, similar to the process utilised by the US Senate for giving its "advice and consent", nominees for French judgeships must now be scrutinised by a standing commission of the National Assembly and Senate.

A legal realist, or an attitudinalist analysis of court decisions—such as is more common to the US—might reveal that French judges are no more than politicians in disguise, whose decisions are pursuant to personal attitudes (Segal and Spaeth 2002). There is much to commend this micro-foundational theory of adjudication. But, drawing generalised models of behaviour from totemic cases is problematic. As with the attitudinal model in the US, so too in France it underestimates the significance of macro, and, as is the contribution of this book, meso-level constraints on judicial agency. Whilst judges of course will either consciously or unconsciously be swayed by their attitudes, there is not a clear path for them to be in direct pursuit of these attitudes. For example, in a DC case of 2013, the Conseil was called upon by 327 Senators and Deputies to declare same-sex marriage legislation as unconstitutional.[18] Clearly the legislators felt there was a decent chance that the then ten members of the Conseil (including former President d'Estaing *ex officio*) would not countenance the progressive measure. And yet, barring some inconsequential reservations, the court gave its blessing to the radical change in marriage laws. If judges are becoming more politically active, it is because opportunities for such activism are being made available. In short, judges cannot easily take power, but they may have it thrust upon them.

True to the model of this book, French politics has undergone a transformation in the genre of its legal language. This degenrified logic of communication not only implicates problem-solving, but also encourages more holistic assessment of what in fact are state norms and practices.

[16] ECLI:FR:CC:2013:2013.685.DC.

[17] https://www.reuters.com/article/us-france-supertax-idUSKBN0K11CC20141223, accessed 17 March 2021.

[18] Decision No. 2013-669 DC of 17 May 2013.

Whilst much of this reimagining of state priorities and operations has assuredly been led under political mandate—from Parliament and the President—much of the confusion around concepts of law and statecraft have been left underdetermined in legislation. This meso-level dynamism operates between macro-level shifts in post-war society, and micro-level changes in citizen behaviour. Changes to legislative language are not only symptomatic of changes to an expanded state, but have also triggered citizens to dispute interpretations of new legal forms. This builds on Stone Sweet's model of judicialisation that traces feed-back between rising dyadic disputes between citizens, and the triadic development of norms by judges (Stone Sweet 2000). This book is adding theoretical and empirical dimensions: that the triggering of disputes between dyads and the empowerment of judges to step in as neutral third parties have both been consequential of forces external to this feedback loop. This external force is degenrified legislative norms, and difficulties faced by politicians in communicating a new normal of legal language (Hart 1961).

As with all of the country case studies, this chapter will focus on criminal justice legislation. Specifically, the focus lays on enactments under the Fifth Republic (1958–). For the most part, therefore, we will be drawing observations on legislative reforms to the Droit pénal of 1994, which updated the Napoleonic criminal code of 1810. All available legislation pertaining to criminal justice from 1958 to 2020 was analysed, making for a total data set of 4,013,365 words, 18,504 articles, within 439 laws. The six-point Hodder-Williams (1997) typology will be re-employed to describe increased indeterminacies in legislative text, followed by consideration of these effects on subtext, inter-textuality, context, transtext, and metatext. The first four consider how text is adapted conservatively via a logic of appropriateness. The final two categories describe where norm conserving is considered impossible and a new logic of communication is developed.

Empirical—Textual Changes

First we must test for textual changes in French criminal justice legislation. Let us assess the increased quantity of criminal justice legislation, before turning to its changing qualities. Table 8.1 describes changes to legislative output from the start of the Fifth Republic in 1958, up to 2020.

In terms of word length, the legislative output of the 1950s cannot usefully be compared to other decades, as the Fifth Republic was inaugurated with only fifteen months of that decade left. The 1960s therefore offers a more useful baseline. Of the 4,000,000 words of criminal legislation enacted under the Fifth Republic, just 1% came in the 1960s, whereas 50% was enacted in the 2010s. Nonetheless, whilst quantity has implications for legislative degenrification, it is the quality of language and not just its quantity that is under scrutiny for this book. Changes in language are described in Table 8.2.

The most indeterminate law was the Loi n° 2011-884 with 102 indeterminate parts of speech per article. It pertains to the French overseas departments of Guiana and Martinique. Figures 8.1 and 8.2 describe these changes graphically.

There is evidence of increases in noun or verb qualifiers per article of criminal legislation as a function of time. The rate of change accelerated after the millennium's turn. The effects of these changes on jurisprudence can now be assessed.

Table 8.1 Increased legislative output, 1958–2020

Decade	*Sum of articles*	*Sum of length*
1950s (Oct 1958–Dec 1959)	7	353
1960s	428	40,667
1970s	745	97,163
1980s	3453	414,732
1990s	2372	298,477
2000s	4553	1,070,775
2010s	6946	2,091,198
Average statute	42	9142
Standard deviation	52	15,124
Minimum	1 (Various)	14 (Loi n° 82-683)
Maximum	373 (Loi n° 92-1336)	133,254 (Loi n° 2014-366)
Total	18,504	4,013,365

Table 8.2 Increased legislative indeterminacy

Decade	*Average of adjectives/article*	*Average of conjunctions/article*	*Average of indeterminate modal verbs/article*	*Average of enabling verbs/article*	*Average of compound indeterminacies/article*
1950s	2.20	1.20	0.53	0.00	3.93
1960s	3.31	3.77	0.19	0.02	7.29
1970s	3.97	4.87	0.45	0.04	9.33
1980s	4.58	5.36	0.48	0.03	10.44
1990s	4.62	4.88	0.48	0.04	10.02
2000s	8.97	9.60	0.78	0.08	19.43
2010s	10.17	11.43	0.76	0.10	22.46
Averages statute	6.84	7.62	0.60	0.06	15.12
Standard deviation	5.80	6.12	0.61	0.10	12.01
Min	0	0	0	0	0 (Loi n° 82-683)
Max	45.76	50.43	5.76	1	102.43 (Loi n° 2011-884)

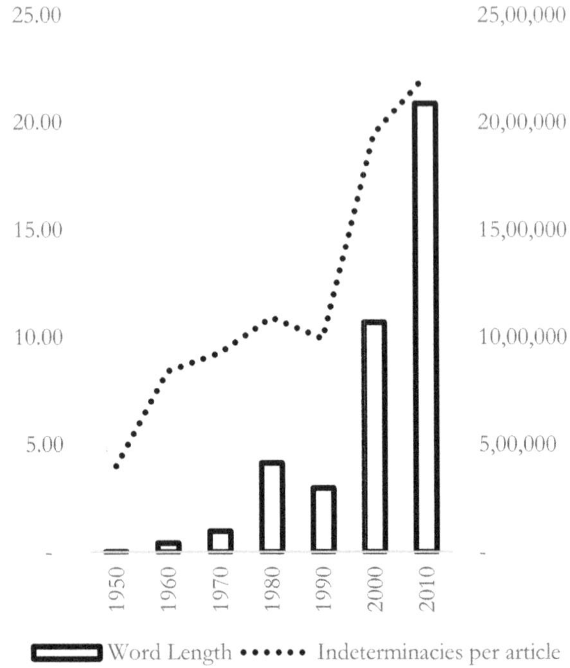

Fig. 8.1 Comparison of changes in indeterminacy (primary *y*-axis) and word length (secondary *y*-axis) in criminal justice legislation 1958–2020

Definitional—Subtextual Changes

In this section, we will work through specific examples of how the French courts have used existing laws and legal norms to provide a narrow construction of new legislative language. As a court deriving its jurisdiction from the Roman and Germanic traditions, the French courts do not lionise precedent as common law jurisdictions would. This is not to say that extant interpretations of law are meaningless, but that the subtext of indeterminate legislation is not determined by past interpretations, so much as by reversion to the original intent of laws as set out by authoritative sources. Similar to how common law judges look back to past decisions to define away new indeterminacies, their civil law counterparts will draw back to as close as possible a literal interpretation of the constitution or code to dispel interpretational conflicts. In the US, for one, this

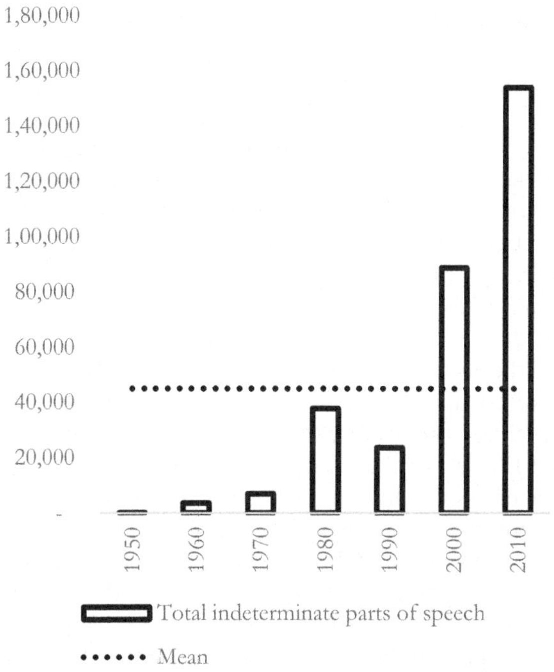

Fig. 8.2 Total indeterminacies (number of coded parts of speech) in all criminal justice legislation 1958–2020 (*Source* Author's creation)

approach to interpretation would be described as originalism, wherein indeterminacies in legal language are resolved as far as possible in line with evidence of the original intent of lawmakers.

To define is to constrain, and where definition is anchored to parliamentary supremacy, constitutional law or the civil code, it likely conserves the power structures that developed and relied on such interpretations. Hence definition with reference to extant laws will in most cases be to the advantage of the institutional litigant. An aspect of definition is to determine the hierarchy of laws when several sources of law appear to be in friction, or downright contradiction. The hierarchy of laws was especially important to determine amidst post-war degenrification and globalisation. In French politics, parliamentary supremacy is key. All else (including the 1789 Declaration of the Rights of Man and Citizen) is subordinate. The decision algorithm for French judges is therefore: if in doubt, defer to Parliament. Definition is a paradoxical power, in so far as it is a self-denying use of power. The judges are shutting down potential avenues for subtextual expansion of legal language, and deferring to other institutions.

Starting at the macro-level, confusion as to the hierarchy of laws has followed in the train of globalisation. French adherence to, in particular, the European Convention on Human Rights and the supremacy of European Union laws has complicated analysis of the domestic legal pecking order. If, for example, a piece of domestic legislation is in contradiction to convention rights or EU law, which is to prevail? How can such a contradiction be resolved in a norm conserving manner? We have already seen the long road taken by the Conseil in making a preliminary reference to the CJEU. The ECHR has similarly been integrated with the supremacy of Parliament. As a Treaty assented to by Parliament in 1974, the ECHR can be used to strike down domestic legislation in court. This is unusual amongst signatories, with only Luxembourg being the other example of a state whose courts can overrule domestic legislation using the convention.[19] In other countries, like the UK, there was a need for special legislation to empower the courts with a modest capability of applying the Convention against domestic legislation. France is not a frequent human rights offender, having received only ten rulings of partial violations in 2020 out of 538 applications to the European Court in Strasbourg.[20] The most common ground for ruling against the French state by the European Court is on the basis of Article 6—the rights to a fair trial. This is the basis for over 60% of cases lost by the French state.[21]

Given French courts have the capacity to overrule parliamentary legislation using the Convention, there is enormous potential for judges to expand the subtextual understandings of indeterminate legislation. But, there has not yet been a case where the Convention was used to strike down a piece of domestic legislation. Rather, the courts typically integrate Convention norms with domestic legislation. A particularly complex case example presents the confluence of a wicked social problem, Convention rights, and legislative indeterminacy. This case, at the Cour de cassation,

[19] https://www.corteidh.or.cr/tablas/28469-1.pdf, accessed 23 March 2021.

[20] https://www.echr.coe.int/Documents/CP_France_ENG.pdf, accessed 23 March 2021.

[21] https://www.echr.coe.int/Documents/Facts_Figures_France_ENG.pdf, accessed 23 March 2021.

pertained to domestic violence administered by a man against his wife and children.[22] The Civil Code, and amending legislation (notably Loi n° 2019-1480), empowered judges to make protection orders if (per Article 515-11) "there are serious reasons to consider as likely the commission of the alleged acts of violence and considering the dangers to which the victim or one or more children are exposed".

There are few more paradoxically authoritarian-cum-liberating state powers than the removal of children from dangerous parents. The Cour d'appel was ruled to have absolved itself, wrongly, of this power by the superior court. In doing so, the Cour de cassation invoked not only breaches of legislation on the part of its junior partner, but also called forth ECHR Articles 2 (right to life), 3 (protection from torture), and 14 (protection from discrimination). This is a striking intertextual interpretation of legislation, given that French courts admit oral evidence but do not rely on counsel submission in forming their judgements. In a common law court, by contrast, the court would only be permitted to include in the official court judgement—*ratio decidendi*—those laws that had been cited by counsel. The French Supreme Court therefore invoked the Convention without officially needing to, as they were able to resolve the case purely on domestic grounds. What we see therefore is an example of the courts providing coherence between domestic and international interpretive norms, in order to maximise certainty in legislation, that, for good reason, is indeterminate as to the "serious reasons" that are "likely" to count for child protection.

Besides these adjectival sources of conceptual indeterminacy (*serious* and *likely*), there has also been a substantial rise in conjunctive indeterminacy (if, and, or). These conjunctions, coupled with vastly longer sentences, increase the likelihood of complex legislative conditions with multiple forking paths—as in if *x*, or *y*, apply resolution *a* and *b*, or *c*. A real-world example is this from article L. 752-6 of the Commercial Code, as amended by Loi n° 2018-1021 (indeterminacies highlighted with italics):

> on the animation *and economic* development of the city centre of the settlement municipality, *neighbouring* municipalities *and* the *public* establishment of *inter-municipal* cooperation with its own taxation of which

[22] Cour de cassation chambre civile 1 Audience publique du jeudi 13 février 2020 N° de pourvoi: 19-22,192.

> the settlement municipality is a member, as well as on employment, based in particular on *demographic* trends, the vacancy rate *and* the supply of *commercial* square metres already existing in the *relevant* catchment area.

This confusing and very long sentence was the subject of QPC litigation in March 2020.[23] The Conseil ruled this legislation to be in conformity with the Constitution. A key question here is, why they would do that. What incentives are in place for judges to take highly indeterminate language and assert its conformity with extant constitutional laws? Surely this was a prime opportunity for the courts to assert their own interpretational preferences, given that the language opened several exclusive constructions. The indeterminacy itself could be argued to be unconstitutional, quite apart from the substance of this law. Inaccessibility is recognised as a legitimate cause of action in appellate jurisprudence.

The way the courts resolved this case was to distil a legal principle that can help define away the indeterminacies in law. The principle was, as is typical in a legal case, a balance between the public interest and private liberties. Specifically, the legislation was intended to authorise new commercial ventures, provided they were to revitalise city centres. According to the complainants, this overbearing bureaucracy came at the expense of free enterprise, as is protected by the constitution. The basic norm of French jurisprudence is, as mentioned, the supremacy of Parliament. It is not in the interests of the courts, nor individual judges, to overtly infringe this basic norm. To do so would encourage legislators to curtail the judges' powers further.

Given that France does not have co-equal branches of government, the judiciary is unambiguously subordinated to the legislature. As such, the judges are in a substantially more vulnerable position than their American counterparts. If they are to use the Constitution to strike down legislation, it needs to be because doing so would further the basic norm of French jurisprudence. For example, we can imagine a case where legislation seeks to curtail the power of future parliamentary majorities. Assuming no Parliament can bind its successors, this would seem to be a straightforward basis for judicial intervention. Alternatively, judges may be tempted to exploit divisions within the legislative majority, such as was

[23] ECLI:FR:CC:2020:2019.830.QPC.

observed over the tax dispute outlined above. What judges are not incentivised to do is abrogate the powers of the legislature. As the judges put it demurely in this particular case:

> 5. It is open to the legislator to bring to the freedom of enterprise, which derives from Article 4 of the Declaration of the Rights of Man and the Citizen of 1789, limitations related to constitutional requirements or justified by the general interest, provided that this does not result in disproportionately affecting the objective pursued.

An interpretation of the indeterminate language was made that supported the powers behind that language. A final case example will demonstrate that defining away indeterminacies in law can be norm conserving without being socially conservative. In many instances, the barrage of legislation is aiming to progress a role for the state in regulating erstwhile private affairs. A caricature of judges as old aged and out of touch cannot, therefore, easily square with their duty to implement reams of new progressive legislation. The example is a QPC litigation brought to the Conseil in 2015, disputing the state's authority to ban the setting up of a cockfighting Gallodrome.[24]

It is an interesting case not only for its subject matter, but because it demonstrated how a QPC route to constitutional litigation was used by citizens to contest well-established legislation. Specifically, a 1960s era animal cruelty law (Loi n° 61 690) was being challenged fifty years after its enactment. It was only with QPC that private litigants were able to make such constitutional challenges to the Conseil. The legislation ensured that cruelty to animals would be punished by imprisonment or a fine, with exceptions made for bullfighting and cockfighting where "an unbroken local tradition... can be established". The claimants wished to set up a new venue for cockfighting, in line with what they saw as an unbroken local tradition. They were not given regulatory approval to do so, and claimed that such restrictions were not meted out on newly established bullfighting rings. Invoking Article 6 of the 1789 Declaration of the Rights of Man and the Citizen, the claimants pleaded unequal, and hence unconstitutional, treatment. To resolve the case, the Conseil declared Parliament's authority as undiluted. They even went so far as to enquire into the preparatory materials for the Bill, in order to resolve

[24] ECLI: FR: CC: 2015: 2015.477.QPC.

indeterminacies in its language. This is similar to what the UK House of Lords had done in the case of *Pepper v. Hart*,[25] where judges used Hansard to establish what parliamentarians had said as a way to determine the legislative will. The point being that the Conseil not only deferred to the principle of parliamentary supremacy, they sought out evidence for what the legislature thought to make up for a lack of clarity in the legislation. Where there was a benefit of the doubt, it went here to Parliament.

Systemic—Intertextual Changes

Parliament caps the French legal hierarchy, even if Presidents tend to receive a disproportionate degree of praise and blame for policy. That is, Parliament dominates in all domestic matters not pertaining to EU law. Whilst the constitution can be used to nullify parliamentary legislation, the constitution can be amended with greater ease than, say, its American counterpart. The constitutional text has been amended twenty-four times since 1958. And, the constitution itself has been completely overhauled not only within five different republics since 1789, but through a total of 15 different constitutional instruments, including both republican and imperial establishments. French political culture is a superstructure upon a base of popular sovereignty, therefore. There is little of the fetishisation of dusty constitutional texts, as might be observed in other countries.

As such, with regard to intertextual means of interpreting indeterminate laws, the presumption is that Parliament is in charge, and new legislation trumps older wisdom. Although, France is often to be found in a paradoxical space between revolutionary institutional churn on one hand, and social and normative conservatism on the other. The role of courts and judges is to implement laws as if civil servants, not to make laws (unless it is the Conseil being called upon to act as a "third legislative chamber"). Indeed, judges in France are effectively bureaucrats, trained as postgraduates as the École Nationale de la Magistrature (ENM—National School for the Judiciary), in Bourdeaux. Unlike the Inns of Court in London, legal education is closely regulated by the French state, producing a *magistrat* cadre of prosecutors and judges. The upshot is that whilst judges have independence in their rulings, they are

[25] [1992] UKHL 3.

institutionally dependent on the state to an extent that would be unrecognisable in any common law jurisdiction. And, as with the bureaucracy, the judiciary is not in a leadership position, nor occupies a separated and adversarial posture relative to political branches of government. In regard to legal development, courts provide advisory and supportive services to politicians.

With little institutional capacity for leadership, it is unsurprising that there have not been celebrated juridical leaders in France of lasting repute, in the vein of a Lord Denning or a Chief Justice Earl Warren. Even within the courts structure there is no singular apex, save for Parliament itself. There are separations of the administrative, private, and criminal law courts with few avenues for inter-jurisdictional coordination. By contrast, the UK Supreme Court is a tribunal of general jurisdiction, technically capable of hearing any matter pertaining to law, from abatement to young offenders. The Conseil only hears matters pertaining to the constitution, and is not the Supreme Court, as the Cour de cassation occupies an apex position in civil and criminal matters. There are in fact four apex courts, one of which The *Tribunal des conflits* mediates between the other three (Fig. 8.3).

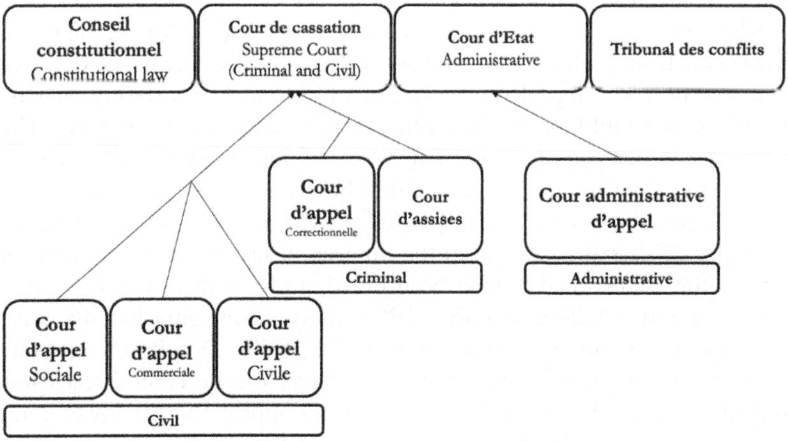

Fig. 8.3 French courts schematic (*Source* Author's creation)

Unlike in the UK, US and Canada, there is not a pyramidal court structure in France. The implications are that French courts lack the institutional capacity, in most matters, to coordinate a response to changing legal norms. There are appeals from lower to higher courts within the system, allowing for some regulation of legal norms from Paris to the peripheries. There has also been a substantially increased role for constitutional review, placing the Conseil in something closer to an overarching jurisdiction than hitherto. But, it remains the case the courts lack both the institutional capacity and individual incentives to pioneer solutions to legal indeterminacies. This is not to say that the courts are quiescent, as we will see later in the chapter, but that by comparison to the UK and the US, the French courts are less well-placed to fix legal degenrification unilaterally.

As is typical of appellate courts, the higher courts in France are more concerned with settling questions of law. Matters of fact are typically confirmed by lower courts, and, occasionally, a nine-person *jury populaire*. Complex overlapping laws pertaining to criminality call forth appeal judges to trace paths through the thicket. Standard clashes might include questions as to scope of jurisdiction, definition of crimes, or timing and the retroactivity of punishments. An upsetting case that contains these disputes pertained to incestuous paedophilia as committed by an elder brother on his siblings.[26] The accused was found guilty of rape and sentenced to seventeen years imprisonment, plus ten years of deprived civil liberties. He appealed on a point of cassation, contesting that his punishment should be for indecent assault rather than for rape. This claim was based on the fact that some of his offences had occurred before a change in the law in 1980. The claimant also contended that the alleged crimes were underspecified in the Cour d'assises ruling. So the Cour de cassation was given the unpleasant task of determining if the two young victims had indeed been raped, and whether, as the offences were committed before and after 1980, more severe punishments could be retroactively imposed on offences in the 1970s. Despite the claimant attempting various defences—including reliance on the 1789 Declaration, and the ECHR—he was not successful in his appeal and the lower court ruling was confirmed in its entirety by the appellate court. This case exemplifies a non-controversial expansion of state authority to regulate private

[26] Cour de cassation chambre criminelle Audience publique du mercredi 12 mars 2003 N° de pourvoi: 02-85,299.

actions. But, even in this utterly defensible enlargement of state power, there are various complex interpretations needed of incoherent rules of law. Higher courts work to create such coherence in the face of changing legal norms.

All judges in the democratic world are agents of state power. But in France judges are particularly institutionalised and socialised into bureaucratic norms. There is far less space, and there are far fewer incentives for creativity than would be the case in the common law. This extent of bureaucratic oversight of judicial power is most clearly exemplified in the professional education of lawyers as outlined above. In some common law jurisdictions there has been a conspicuous deprofessionalisation of legal services, but not so in France (Abel and Lewis 1988; Barak 2006). If a profession can be taken narrowly to be a marketable service where the training of future providers is overseen by current providers, the law was an archetypical profession, akin to medicine. Lawyers trained future lawyers, just as doctors trained future doctors. At least that was the case until universities and private companies muscled in to educate future lawyers in the UK. Although barristers are still required to be called as members of the bar in one of the four Inns of Court in London, the state has practically no role in this education, and other legal services now have diversified human resources. This deregulation of labour markets is coincident with entrepreneurialism in legal services. There are a greater array of choices for consumers of legal services, and heightened creativity in providing innovative legal solutions to otherwise intractable problems. As more and more firms, chambers, and individual practitioners push for changes in rules of law, it is not surprising that we see British judges more frequently making law from the bench.

The French state, by contrast, has kept a tight lid on both the legal profession and judicial training. In addition to a norm conserving network of judicial institutions, legal personnel in France are more closely socialised into patterns of thought and behaviour. A 2016 QPC case at the Conseil shook the branches of this sturdy tree.[27] Applicants sought a declaration of unconstitutionality for a 1971 law regulating the legal profession. The legislation laid a number of conditions on anyone wishing to practice as a lawyer, including the need of specific qualifications, and ordinary residence within France, French overseas territories, or the EEA.

[27] ECLI: FR: CC: 2016: 2016.551.QPC.

In keeping with the thesis of the book, the Conseil noted the claimants point that language in the legislation was unhelpfully non-specific in places, but the called for declaration was not made. The applicants' case was based on their perceived rights to pursue free enterprise, but the French legal profession has remained closed to wider diversity of practitioners.

Prudential—Contextual Changes

How are these practitioners trained to deal with novel contexts and indeterminate texts? In the preceding chapter on the British courts, the prudential section focussed on when and how judges defer to the greater fact-finding competence and capacity of political actors. Courts feel they know the legal texts, but are conscious of their limited capacity to ascertain social context. The consequences of this epistemic asymmetry were observed as benefits of doubt given to the government in public law litigation. The UK government enjoys a "margin of appreciation"[28] where it is perceived to know best how to interpret social facts pertaining to, for example, counterterrorism and similarly multifaceted "wicked problems".

French courts have similarly been observed to yield their government a margin of appreciation, acknowledging the asymmetries in both capacity and legitimacy to act on certain policy problems. We have already considered several examples where the courts refused submissions made against the government, and there are many more to choose from, with, for example, judges assisting in government-led efforts to stamp out holocaust denial,[29] or transposing tough new EU directives to tackle gang crime but offering the government a generous grace period to implement.[30] As with their British counterparts, French judges know what they do not know. They know, in particular, their limited capacity to determine social facts in a legitimate manner, and so they will prudentially yield to those better placed at doing so. The prudence here is in reference to the

[28] This is a term of art used by the European Court of Human Rights in its rulings. It applies when a democratically accountable government is considered better placed to make certain determinations of policy. Although it is derived from an international context, the margin of appreciation is in substance a judicial mode of policy deference common to domestic jurisprudence as well.

[29] Cour de cassation chambre criminelle Audience publique du mardi 27 mars 2018 N° de pourvoi: 17-82,637.

[30] ECLI:EN:CC:2014:2014.420. QPC.

delicate legitimacy of courts. As an unelected institution within a democratic system, courts must carefully assess when to rule against majority will (Vanberg 2001).

But there is nuance to these claims. Judicial restraint does not only favour the government. And, it is not counter-majoritarian to rule against the government, if the government itself is leveraging powers and resources so as to go against popular will. This means that a prudential decision can include those that constrain the government in favour of Parliament. This again is something observed in the UK, when, for example, the Supreme Court blocked use of Royal prerogative powers to prorogue Parliament for over a month in 2019. Sometimes when conserving norms and acting cautiously, judges constrain radical government decisions. As with the prorogation case in the UK, similarly in France a means of constraining the government is by imposing procedural rules. This is where the substance of a policy decision is not at issue, but the way it has been pursued is declared as procedurally improper. We will come on to when courts assess the substantive propriety of policy in the following sections on influence seeking and policy orientation. But, for now, when assessing a restraining judiciary, it is necessary to analyse how and why courts impose procedural norms, and how this can relate to indeterminacies in legislation.

As discussed, indeterminate legislation can enable multiple excludable interpretations of the same text. Governments are incentivised to stretch interpretations so as to maximise their policy influence on behalf of key stakeholders. This has implications for concrete review of government decisions taken. Of interest in France is also the capacity of its constitutional court to conduct abstract review, prior to a law being promulgated and used. How can indeterminate legislation encourage a court ruling against the government, prior to such law even being promulgated or used? To solve this, a distinction is needed between real-world and institutional contexts. Text must be interpreted according to real-world context when a law has been promulgated. But even before a law has been promulgated it must be understood relative to institutional norms. The context that courts use to understand texts in this instance is laid out in constitutional rules, organic laws, and law-making conventions. Indeterminacy emerges between the substance of the text and the procedures of law making. This is still relevant to a study of degenerating legislative norms, but here we are including the nuance of how legislative language can influence courts within and not just beyond the law-making process.

Here we can observe the courts working as a "third legislative chamber", but with an interest in procedures rather than the substance of policy. Judicialising the implementation of law is as old as law itself. Courts assessing government decisions for procedural impropriety is one of the oldest heads of judicial review in the English legal system, for example. Far more modern is the Conseil's capacity to interrogate legislation for improprieties whilst it is passing through Parliament. As discussed above, the court was empowered to review laws pre-promulgation by the Fifth Republican constitution.[31] And, these powers were expanded by a 1974 constitutional amendment allowing sixty members of the National Assembly or sixty Senators to be amongst the actors capable of bringing an intra-legislative case to the Conseil.

Particularly important for any government will be its finance bills. In the UK, losing a budget vote is taken as a loss of confidence in the government, who are then expected to resign. The French position is more complicated, given the Council of Ministers (Cabinet) and Prime Minister are institutionally separated from the President. They are often, but not necessarily, linked by party affiliation. If confidence is lost, the Prime Minister resigns, but the President need not (Article 50). Given the intimate role played by Presidents in shaping economic policies, they are in a sheltered political position relative to their Prime Ministers. But to avoid anything like the Fourth Republic's governmental instability, Michel Debré, when designing the Fifth Republic, raised the bar for securing no confidence in the government. Indeed, the Prime Minister was empowered under the Fifth Republic to use motions of confidence to threaten, under Article 49.3 of the constitution:

> The Prime Minister may, after deliberation by the Council of Ministers, make the passing of a Finance Bill or Social Security Financing Bill an issue of a vote of confidence before the National Assembly. In that event, the Bill shall be considered passed unless a resolution of no-confidence, tabled within the subsequent twenty-four hours, is carried as provided for in the foregoing paragraph. In addition, the Prime Minister may use the said procedure for one other Government or Private Members' Bill per session.

[31] The High Council of the Judiciary established by the Fourth Republic had few enumerated powers in just two short Articles (83 and 84) of the constitution.

In short, a Prime Minister can avoid a vote on legislation by threatening to collapse the government. In all of other democracies studied for this book, an affirmative vote in favour of legislation is always needed, even if, as can happen in Britain an appended motion of confidence strong arms support. In France, the mere threat of government collapse means that legislation need not be approved, but simply left alone to become authorised legislation by the passage of twenty-four hours. It is little surprise that some Prime Ministers have made substantial use of this facility. The record is currently held by Michel Rocard with twenty-eight applications. Despite this extraordinary capability, governments in the Fifth Republic must nonetheless contend with the courts, and, in particular, the tricameral role sometimes played by the Conseil. The court has been known to block financial provisions (as seen with the 75% tax) which would be unthinkable in other jurisdictions. But to avoid accusations of improper meddling in financial matters, courts typically externalise the charge of impropriety. The most legitimate means of challenging a budget is, in other words, not to say it is wrong in substance, but that it was improperly processed.

An early example of the court flexing its muscles, after a quiescent period in de Gaulle's shadow, came with a DC case in 1976. The President of the National Assembly seized the Conseil on this occasion, complaining that a budget measure was improperly shot through with social and political ambitions—including reform of the judiciary, and even the forced sterilisation of certain animals.[32] Such a wide remit was held by the Conseil to be well in excess of the Organic Law on Financial Legislation, which states that:

> No additional article, no amendment to a finance bill may be presented unless it tends to effectively abolish or reduce expenditure, to create or increase revenue or to ensure the control of public expenditure.

Whether or not the judges disapproved of the substantive attempts to reform their profession is not recorded in the efficient 671 words spent delivering their judgement. All that mattered was that the government was breaking the rules and could without any qualms be stopped and forced to rethink.

[32] No. 76–74.

A more recent, and more controversial judicial incursion came in response to the "Macron Law". Emmanuel Macron's now eponymous, and signature, legislation came whilst serving as Minister of the Economy, Industrial Renewal and Digital Affairs in the Valls government. It contained ambitious plans to reform labour and market regulations, including relaxations to Sunday working rules. Anticipating trouble in Parliament, Prime Minister Manuel Valls initiated the Article 49.3 procedure and left the bill to be voted down, rather than allowing it to be voted up. This initiated a DC case at the Conseil where Deputies, Senators, and MEPs attacked the law not on its substance, but on its irregularities of procession.[33] Here the indeterminacies were not in the face of the law, but the institutional context within which that law was to be made. Claimants, for instance, were able to convince the Conseil that a constitutionally mandated impact study was "insufficient", and mostly inoperative, because so much of the bill had been added as last-minute amendments.

In addition, there was indeterminacy between the face of the law and institutional rules. It was successfully claimed in court that the legislation was a fiscally reforming wolf, in social policy sheep's clothing. This is because there were powers to vary a levy that would help provide legal services around the country. The fact that monies could be raised or lowered by decree was considered a new fiscal power, and claimants convinced the judges that this should therefore have undergone the constitution's Article 47 procedure for new budgeting proposals. All proposed fiscal laws must be interrogated by the Cour des Comptes, a body somewhat akin to America's Congressional Budget Office. Interestingly, the court ruled that the "legislature has disregarded the scope of its jurisdiction" by setting up a regulatory agency with tax varying powers. Even though this was unambiguously a loss for the government, it was framed by the Conseil as legislative overreach. This was in the sense that Parliament was technically delegating its own powers to another agency. Contextual indeterminacies between institutional rules and the substance of a major reforming bill therefore empowered the courts to intervene. The courts did so by adopting a restrained rendering of context. Eventually the legislation was passed, but more obviously in accordance with legislative rules.

[33] ECLI: FR: CC: 2015: 2015.715.DC.

Influence-Seeking—Transtextual Changes

In the last section on assimilating text to context, we saw the Conseil operating in effect as a veto player (Tsebelis 2002). Where there was a disjunction between text and institutional context, the court was capable of striking down laws. In this section we will analyse further the negative power of courts. In some cases, an assimilation of text and context is achieved by courts identifying a transtext of legal concepts and theories. This allows indeterminacies on the face of law to be reconciled with more abstract principles of legality. This puts courts into a more influential position of not merely vetoing proposals, but shaping the development of future proposals. This is redolent of Steven Lukes's (1974) second face of power, where the powerful shape agendas, and determine what sorts of matters can or cannot be considered.

This may have a freezing effect, with restrictive Overton windows placed around policy domains by the courts. Law makers will be discouraged from even presenting laws that risk deviating from legal norms. A consequence of this was the Rocard memo of 1988. Similar to "The Judge Over Your Shoulder" memorandum that made its way around Whitehall during the Thatcher government, Michel Rocard warned policy-makers of the likely consequences in court of any norm-deviating policy. But, there is also a constructive possibility from this judicial behaviour. The courts can carve for themselves a degree of policy influence, where by identifying what is unacceptable they also help policymakers work out what would be acceptable. In highly controversial and conceptually indeterminate policy spaces, this judicial guidance can be of significant utility. For example, it can delimit policy ambiguity, and mitigate bureaucratic drift that might be consequent. Again, as is consistent with the thesis of this book, the judges expanded their role in establishing transtextual guidance as a response to increased indeterminacies in legislation.

An illustrative case tackled the extent to which legislation could regulate interactions between prisoners and the outside world.[34] Included were some uncontroversial restrictions on transmissions of money, objects, or illicit substances. But the legislation also included a blanket provision disallowing anyone "to communicate *by any means* with a detained person, except in the cases authorised by the regulations".

[34] ECLI:FR:CC:2017:2016.608.QPC.

Similar to the *Simms* case in the UK discussed previously, legislation was here attempting a prohibition on communication between prisoners and the outside world save for exceptions that would be determined solely by a regulator. This could risk a regulator becoming judge in its own cause. We can imagine a situation where the regulator blocks communication between prisoners and journalists, or even between prisoners and lawyers. A regulator may be incentivised to stop such communications from revealing a possible miscarriage of justice. In essence, the legislation was ruled by judges to be so broad in its scope that it shifted expectations as to what the state is by rights capable of in regard to its citizens. Whilst the state has a right to incarcerate individuals, it was argued, it is in excess of democratic authority that prisoners would only be permitted to communicate with the outside world via the very organisation that had imprisoned them. Whilst the legislation was not explicitly aimed at restricting access to lawyers, its potential breadth deviated from ideas of an accountable and constrained state. The Conseil therefore stripped the offending "by any means" subclause from the law, as it "disregarded the extent of [Parliament's] competence in conditions affecting… rights and freedom".

Here the court surgically removed from legislation an indeterminacy. They "read down" powers from the face of the law, in a manner similar to the editing capabilities of British courts under section 3 of the *Human Rights Act 1998*. Pruning was justified because the language exceeded Parliament's competence. Other justifications for reading down legislative language include where restrictions on civil liberties are deemed unnecessary, inappropriate, or disproportionate. These concepts can enable judges to interpose their own policy preferences. Notably, why would the courts be best placed to determine what is or is not necessary or appropriate in policy? These concepts are themselves indeterminate, and therefore capable of broad interpretation. But, as argued, the courts are not incentivised to overplay their hand. Evidence for judges using these concepts comes when they are constraining the legislature and executive, rather than aggrandising their own policy position. They are not actively expanding the courts' jurisdiction therefore, they are restraining the state. To illustrate this point is a case regarding access to online terrorist materials.[35] Some impugned legislation stated as follows (indeterminacies italicised):

> The act of *usually and* without *legitimate* reason consulting an *online public* communication service providing messages, images *or* representations either *directly* provoking the commission of *terrorist* acts *or* advocating *such* acts… a *legitimate* reason… constitutes consultation resulting from the *normal* exercise of a profession intended to inform the public, intervening in the context of *scientific* research *or* carried out in order to serve as *legal* evidence.

Claimants submitted that the scope of this language went beyond the principle of legality, because what would or would not be lawful was indeterminate. Put simply, they did not even know what the law was. The law to a non-trivial extent was unknowable to anyone except the government empowered with enforcing it. As the court put it:

> 15. Consequently, the contested provisions cause uncertainty as to the lawfulness of consulting certain communication services to the public online and, consequently, of using the internet to search for information.
> 16. It follows… that the contested provisions infringe on the exercise of the freedom of communication which is not necessary, appropriate and proportionate.

A further interesting point to note in this case is how the courts relied on *res judicata*—a matter that had already been adjudicated. This has echoes of common law adherence to precedent. Specifically, claimants reminded the Conseil that just two weeks prior to the legislation being enacted, the same judges had ruled against attempts to restrict freedom of communication. The courts are clearly exercising policy influence here, but there is no clear evidence that the judges were personally motivated to meddle with public policy. More sustainable is a claim that the courts were using existing concepts and principles of law (including constitutionalism and precedent) in order to make sense of new and indeterminate provisions.

[35] ECLI:FR:CC:2017:2017.682.QPC.

Another case of the court editing out indeterminate legislative language pertained to the intelligence services.[36] Here we have the opportunity to consider how the courts may intervene in the construction of state power, and not just in the restriction of civil liberties. A 2015 law sought to empower the intelligence services to monitor and control any communications transmitted on a Hertzian frequency. That would essentially allow the intelligence services to control all wireless communications. Given that the legislation had no explicit safeguards against intercepting or storing data, the courts felt that there was a manifest breach of the 1789 Declaration:

> 9. It follows from the above that, in the absence of appropriate guarantees, the contested provisions infringe a manifestly disproportionate attack on the right to respect for private life and the secrecy of correspondence resulting from article 2 of the Declaration of 1789.

There are a number of interesting transtextual points to be extracted from this example. First of all, the courts did not rely on any international or supranational legal instruments to reach this conclusion. A similar case in the UK would almost certainly have lent on article 8 ECHR and the right to respect for private and family life. The French court was able to utilise a domestic transtext in order to determine the meaning of text. Further, the rights instrument being relied on is significantly older than the ECHR. Indeed, the 1789 Declaration of the Rights of Man and the Citizen was promulgated fully 68 years before Heinrich Hertz was even born, let alone before he could give his name to wireless communication frequencies. And yet, the essential principle of protecting correspondence could be adapted to post-industrial technologies from a pre-industrial rights instrument. By developing transtextual analysis in this way, courts generate influence over the texts of future legislation. This gives them some policy power, but there is little reason or evidence to suggest that this influence is consistent with the personal views of individual judges.

[36] ECLI:FR:CC:2016:2016.590.QPC.

Policy-Oriented—Metatextual Changes

Somewhat more complicated to explain with regard to the theory of this book is when judges develop or suggest entirely new legislative language. It is consistent with judicial norms for courts to look to past interpretations of language to inform new interpretations. But we must explain when courts develop new norms. To solve this conundrum, we again must look to the substantial changes in legislative language since the Fifth Republic's founding. Courts will create new legislative language when merely editing out language is insufficient to resolve indeterminacies on the face of law. Creating legislative language can seem to be evidence of policy orientation from judges. It might, for example, be taken as evidence of judges moving law towards their own policy preferences. However, there are severe institutional and political constraints on the judges policy-making unilaterally. Courts will be incentivised only to make new legislative language in concert with other institutions of state, and, in particular, in concert with Parliament. The method is therefore multilateral and dialogic. Again, we can compare the situation to the policy-making behaviour of British courts. In the UK, judges will only "read in" new legislative language if (a) there is conspicuous indeterminacy to be resolved; (b) the language read in does not transform the substance of legislation but reconciles its operation with existing norms of law; and (c) if there exist mechanisms for Parliament to review and change the alterations made.

The first step to review is when courts move away from reading down language and start proposing alternative language for legislation. There is a grey area between judges editing out offending language, and suggesting fruitful alternatives. An illustrative example came in a 2016 case on punitive fines for tax evasion.[37] Legislative amendments were targeted at those using trusts and offshore assets to minimise tax liabilities. The Conseil ruled that newly created penalties were disproportionate, and spelt out their jurisdiction in such matters:

> If the need for the penalties attached to offenses falls within the discretion of the legislator, it is incumbent on the Conseil constitutionnel to ensure that there is no manifest disproportion between the offense and the penalty incurred. In addition, the principle of individualisation of penalties which

[37] ECLI:FR:CC:2017:2016.618.QPC.

> flows from article 8 of the 1789 Declaration implies that a fiscal fine can only be applied if the administration, under the supervision of the judge, has expressly imposed it. taking into account the circumstances specific to each species. However, it cannot prohibit the legislator from laying down rules ensuring an effective repression of the breach of tax obligations.

It is tempting to assume that individual judges or their associates might themselves be targeted by these tax provisions brought in by a Socialist administration. But there is no evidence that the judges were so motivated. Indeed, they make clear that a substantial problem with the law was that fines were not "expressly imposed". And, judges therefore offered assistance to Parliament in improving the law, by setting out what would be acceptable. Hence, this is an example of where reading down language meets reading in language:

> 8. By providing for a fine, the amount of which, not capped, is fixed in proportion to the goods or rights placed in the trust as well as the products which are capitalised in it, for a simple breach of a reporting obligation, even when the goods and rights placed in the trust have not been exempted from tax, the legislator has imposed a clearly disproportionate penalty to the gravity of the facts which he intended to repress.
>
> 9. Consequently, the words 'or, if higher, of an amount equal to 5% of the property or rights placed in the trust as well as of the products which are capitalized there'... must be declared contrary to the Constitution.

The line here between negation and generation of language is subtle, to be sure. The courts effectively instructed Parliament that the language used was unacceptable, but the basic policy intent was constitutional. In short, the court was suggesting Parliament go back and try again. A more explicit act of law making from the court came in a 2014 case concerning rent controls.[38] This being a DC case, the legislative language was yet to be promulgated and therefore the courts' suggested amendments had no effect until agreed to by Parliament and the President. In keeping with the Conseil's capacity to be a "third legislative chamber", it worked in concert with other state institutions to improve legal language. In this case, the court followed the complainant Deputies and Senators' wishes

[38] ECLI: FR: CC: 2014: 2014.691.DC.

by stripping out five uses of the adjective "exceptional" and two uses of the phrase "exceptional by nature and extent" from the legislation. And, besides this editing, the court also suggested changes in other parts of the Bill:

> HELD... the 2nd paragraph I of Article 6, the words 'based on the dispersion of rent levels observed by the local rents observatory' in the fifth paragraph of section I of Article 17 of the Law No. 89-462 of 6 July 1989 to improve tenancy relationships and amending law No. 86-1290 of 23 December 1986; consequently the seventh paragraph of section I of the same Article 17, the words 'cannot be fixed,' and the eighth paragraph, the words 'cannot be set at a higher amount' should be replaced by the words: 'is equal'.

These examples show the court not acting destructively, but constructively engaging with other state institutions to improve the language of legislation. But, in unusual cases, entire laws need to be excised. This of course will have major policy implications. The instigation for striking down entire laws has only occurred when those laws have been superseded by EU Directives. In these instances, the courts are implementing treaty obligations. It is typical in cases of supersession that the judges grant lawmakers sufficient time to domesticate EU provisions and replace any obsolete domestic regulations. This cooperative attitude can be observed from a 2014 case at the Conseil constitutionnel.[39] The judges declared that holding suspected criminals for ninety-six hours, as well as use of enhanced surveillance techniques, were no longer in accordance with EU law. And yet, they went on:

> 25. Considering... that the immediate repeal... would therefore have manifestly excessive consequences; that in order to allow the legislator to remedy the unconstitutionality of article 706-73 of the code of criminal procedure, it is necessary to postpone to September 1, 2015 the date of this repeal.

It is beyond question that judges are analysing and affecting the substance of policy. Lacking, however, is theory or evidence to implicate judicial attitudes in these policy-making modalities. There is substantially more

[39] ECLI:EN:CC:2014:2014.420. QPC.

reason and evidence, however, to connect indeterminacies in criminal law to a range of reparatory measures taken by judges in accordance with, and to the advancement of, essential principles of French law and constitutionalism. In keeping with the book's thesis, French judges have been judicialised, passively, by increased indeterminacies of legislative language.

Conclusion

As with all the other court systems studied, in France judges are bound by tight institutional constraints. The scope of their creativity and contributions to policy are limited to interpretative spaces opened by the legislature and by constitutional indeterminacy. With the rapid degenrification of French criminal justice legislation since the Fifth Republic's inauguration, there have been many more such opportunities for judicial policy intervention. Judicialisation has also been facilitated by constitutional innovations, empowering judges and litigants in constitutional review. Nonetheless, somewhat similar to the UK, the courts in France are legally subservient to a supreme parliament. Although, unlike the UK there are codified constitutional laws that can constrain these political bodies, and France continues to recognise the supremacy of EU law, in contradistinction to its neighbour.

Judges in France, as elsewhere in the democratic world, are institutionally weak. Such policy discretion as they enjoy is not of their own manufacture, but is yielded, intentionally or unintentionally, by political institutions. But, this idea of passivity can be taken too far. It would be inappropriate to conclude that French judges are constantly looking at the "politician over their shoulder".[40] They can and do rule without fear of favour in highly controversial policy domains. But, consistent with the thesis of this book, they engage when there is a legitimate opportunity to do so. And, such opportunities are textual not substantive. In other words, there needs to be some sort of indeterminacy in law to enable judges to intervene. There is no pretext to judicialisation. Everything is textual.

An example case from an exceptionally sensitive policy area was with regard to counterterrorism. France has suffered some appalling crimes against its citizens in recent years. The understandable policy response was

[40] A bastardisation of "The Judge over your shoulder" https://www.gov.uk/government/publications/judge-over-your-shoulder, accessed 28 September 2021.

to increase security measures and suspend the operation of civil liberties, where necessary. Determining the balance between liberality and security is ultimately a judicial matter. It is certainly not an easy balance to strike, but French judges did not shy away. In a 2017 QPC case, the Conseil was asked whether state of emergency powers were sufficiently determinate.[41] Under a 2016 statute (Loi n° 2016-987) local prefects could administer state of emergency zones, wherein identity checks, searches, and even arrest powers were all enhanced. The Conseil acknowledged that all such powers were time-limited to twenty-four hours, and restricted in space. The court also acknowledged Parliament's authority in managing public safety. But, the court also agreed with complainants that the law was couched in such general language as to be in breach of Articles 2 and 4 of the Declaration of the Rights of Man and of the Citizen of 1789:

> If it is open to the legislator to provide that the operations carried out in this context may not be linked to the behaviour of the person, the practice of these operations in a generalized and discretionary manner would be incompatible with the freedom to come and go and the right to privacy. By providing that these operations may be authorized anywhere in the areas where the state of emergency applies, the legislator has allowed their implementation without them being necessarily justified by specific circumstances.[42]

A notable development in French jurisprudence is that senior courts provide these sorts of detailed reasonings for their rulings. In the past, as a civil law jurisdiction, French judges were not required nor expected to justify their decisions and could merely point to an infraction in law (Robertson 2010). Court opinions are still markedly shorter than anything from the common law world, but they provide useful indications as to what the judges' justifications are (or purport to be) when making politically sensitive decisions. There are, of course, examples when the courts look and sound like they are legislating, not adjudicating. Take this excerpt from the ruling against a proposed 75% tax hike:

[41] ECLI:FR:CC:2017:2017.677.QPC.

[42] Ibid. at para 6.

> Considering that, in the case of the application of the maximum marginal tax rate, when the employer allocates company early retirement benefits for which article L. 137-10 of the social security code establishes a tax due by the employer at the rate of 50%, or when he allocates free shares or allocation of subscription options for which article L. 137-13 of the same code establishes a tax due by the employer to rate of 30%, the cumulative rate of withdrawals exceeds 75% of the amount corresponding to the compensation awarded...[43]

The court dived into policy technicalities throughout its ruling. All of this analysis built to a conclusion that the 75% tax rate was unequal, and did not in fact constitute a tax take of 75% because of various ancillary charges. Nonetheless, it is striking how French courts have gone from taciturnity to this degree of specific policy analysis. This is an example of the "third legislative chamber" intervening via a DC (pre-promulgation) case in line with the assumed policy preferences of the judges. However, another advantage of much longer recorded decisions from French courts is that we can obtain a more sophisticated understanding of their behaviour. Where the quick conclusion was that conservative judges overruled a tax increase, in fact, on twelve counts, impugned articles were declared to be in conformity with the constitution. As in, for example:

> Considering that the contested provisions relate solely to the company vehicle tax; that it appears from parliamentary proceedings that the legislator, in amending the tariff of this tax, intended to increase its performance; that it has moreover intended to encourage companies to renew their fleet with vehicles emitting fewer air pollutants; that by not subjecting private vehicles to these same provisions, the legislator has not ignored the principle of equality... it follows from the above that Article 30 must be declared constitutional.[44]

Although, overall, the court ruling was destructive of a major Socialist Party policy, it would be simplistic to suggest that the judges were insensitive to their relative lack of a policy mandate. Instead, the judges took care to describe how a tax rate of 75% would violate the equality provisions of the 1789 Declaration. Of course, the motive underlying this ruling is suspicious. But, as argued throughout this book, motive is less useful

[43] ECLI:FR:CC:2013:2013.685.DC at para 23.

[44] ECLI:FR:CC:2013:2013.685.DC at para 50–1.

in describing the overall trend towards judicialisation than is means and opportunity. To consider means and opportunity, we have to look outside the judiciary, not within it.

References

Abel, Richard, and P.S.C. Lewis. 1988. *Lawyers in Society: The Common Law World*. Berkley, CA: University of California Press.

Barak, Aharon. 2006. *The Judge in a Democracy*. Princeton, NJ: Princeton University Press.

Brouard, Sylvain. 2016. Constitutional Politics: The French Case and Theory-Building. In *The Oxford Handbook of French Politics*, ed. Robert Elgie, Emiliano Grossman, and Amy G. Mazur. Oxford: Oxford University Press.

Davis, Adam, and Bertrand Taithe. 2011. From the Purse and the Heart: Exploring Charity, Humanitarianism, and Human Rights in France. *French Historical Studies* 34 (3): 413–432.

Favoreu, Louis, Loïc Philip, and André Roux. 2005. *Le Conseil constitutionnel, 7e éd*. Paris: Presses Universitaires de France.

Gallagher, Michael, Michael Laver, and Peter Mair. 2011. *Representative Government in Modern Europe*, 5th ed. New York: McGraw-Hill.

Hart, H.L.A. 1961. *The Concept of the Law*. Oxford: Clarendon.

Hazareesingh, Sudhir. 2012. *In the Shadow of the General: Modern France and the Myth of De Gaulle*. Oxford: Oxford University Press.

Hodder-Williams, Richard. 1997. Six Notions of 'Political' and the United States Supreme Court. *British Journal of Political Science* 22 (1): 1–20.

Jones, Robert. 1856. *A History of the French Bar, Ancient and Modern: Comprising a Notice of the French Courts, Their Officers, Practitioners, etc., and of the System of Legal Education in France*. Philadelphia: T. & J.W. Johnson.

Lukes, Steven. 1974. *Power: A Radical View*. Basingstoke: Macmillan.

Millet, François-Xavier, and Nicoletta Perlo. 2015. The First Preliminary Reference of the French Constitutional Court to the CJEU: Révolution de Palais or Revolution in French Constitutional Law? *German Law Journal* 16: 1471–1490.

Robertson, David. 2010. *The Judge as Political Theorist: Contemporary Constitutional Review*. Princeton, NJ: Princeton University Press.

Segal, Jeffrey A., and Harold Spaeth. 2002. *The Supreme Court and the Attitudinal Model Revisited*. Cambridge: Cambridge University Press.

Stone, Alec. 1992. Where Judicial Politics are Legislative Politics: The French Constitutional Council. *West European Politics* 15 (3): 29–49.

Stone Sweet, Alec. 2000. *Governing with Judges: Constitutional Politics in Europe*. Oxford: Oxford University Press.

Tate, C. Neal, and Torbjorn Vallinder. 1995. *The Global Expansion of Judicial Power*. New York: New York University Press.

Tsebelis, George. 2002. *Veto Players: How Political Institutions Work*. Princeton, NJ: Princeton University Press.

Unger, Gérard. 2011. *Gaston Defferre*. Paris: Fayard.

Vanberg, Georg. 2001. Legislative-Judicial Relations: A Game-Theoretic Approach to Constitutional Review. *American Journal of Political Science* 45 (2): 346–361.

Wenzel, Nikolai G. 2016. Descartes, Rousseau, de Gaulle: France's Constitutional Waltz of Plebiscitarian Caesarism. *Journal Des Économistes Et Des Études Humaines* 22 (2): 191–211.

CHAPTER 9

The Burden of History, with the Promise of Philosophy in Germany

Chapter 4 presented evidence that German legal language is relatively stable, as compared to the other countries studied so far. Patterns in legislative language there are platykurtic—where variations in linguistic styles are bunched closer to the mean than would be expected with a normal distribution. There was also the lowest degree of skew amongst the five countries surveyed for this book. This means that outliers to normal patterns of linguistic use are not only rare, those outlying instances do not skew the overall distribution. In short, German legal language is norm-bound. There is at first blush no evidence for legislation that is degenrifying. There are, conversely, genericisms of German legal language that can be identified and have been sustained across the decades since Germany's Basic Law (Grundgesetz [GG]) was promulgated in 1949.

None of which should be surprising. Post-war German politics has been highly normative—both in a sense of guided by principle and in a sense of beholden to customary behaviour. Radicalism in German politics is long gone, replaced by consensus institutions, diversified party systems, power-sharing occasionally in grand coalitions, and long-tenured Chancellorships. Consensual and stable politics was not only pushed by Allied lustration of Nazism, but also came from rekindled pre-war principles of German statecraft (Murkens 2013). The roots of which stretch back at the very least to the enlightenment-defining deontology of Immanuel Kant. Protections of human dignity in the Basic Law are therefore baked in

M. Williams, *Judges and the Language of Law*,
https://doi.org/10.1007/978-3-030-91495-0_9

to the extent that they can under no circumstances (save revolution) be eclipsed or removed.

Institutions have likewise been designed with risk aversion in mind. Electoral rules lay thresholds of vote shares needed for parties to win Bundestag seats. These rules stipulate that at least 5% of the vote, or three single-member seats, are needed for parties to be admitted. Such rules would have stopped the National Socialists securing a Reichstag toehold in May 1928. The new rules are so tough that even the mainstream Free Democratic Party—long-standing coalition makers of post-war German governments—were shut out of the Bundestag from 2013 to 2017. Indeed, parties can and have been banned by court order. The Socialist Reich Party suffered this fate in 1952, followed in short order by the communist KPD in 1956. In word and in deed, German politics has elevated human dignity and "militant democracy" through stable institutions, policies, and political language (Loewenstein 1937; Capoccia 2013).

All of which leads to an expectation of inactivity in public law judges, bereft of substantial interpretational matters to keep them occupied. And yet, this is not what we see. German judges—particularly those on the Federal Constitutional Court (FCC—Bundesverfassungsgericht, BVerfG)—have been active participants in shaping policy. Perhaps most famously (or infamously) have been FCC interventions on the law of abortion. In 1974, the West German Criminal Code was amended in line with its East German neighbour. Abortions within the first twelve weeks of pregnancy were decriminalised. But the FCC set out how the law was to work, and gave the power to decide on abortions from women to doctors and medical advisory boards (Landfried 1994, 116). If an abortion went ahead despite this advice, the mother would be convicted of a criminal offence.[1] This was despite the fact that the German Parliament had deliberately sought to avoid criminalising abortion law within the first trimester. The court reached this decision by extending the right to life protections in Article 2 of the Basic Law to unborn foetuses. It was a socially conservative interpretation of life when compared to the *Roe v. Wade* judgement reached in the US two years previously.

Then, after reunification, the Bundestag sought to reconcile abortion laws in east and west. Abortion was again decriminalised in the

[1] BVerfG, Feb. 25, 1975, 39, 1.

first trimester, provided that women undertook discouraging counselling. The Court received constitutional complaints from no less an authority than Chancellor Kohl contesting the decriminalisation. They reaffirmed the essence of their 1975 decision—foetuses were protected by the Basic Law—but the judges conceded that Parliament had a right to manage abortions in the first trimester.[2] A reasonable theory could explain these decisions as derivative of the judges' own conservative attitudes. The sixteen members of the FCC's two senates are appointed by the Bundestag and Bundesrat, with political affiliation a central factor in a judge's viability for elevation. Given the post-war dominance of German politics by the centre-right Christian Democrats (CDU/CSU), the federal courts are also dominated by adherents of that party. It appeared in the abortion cases that judges were not reacting to exogenous stimuli in the social landscape, nor reacting to indeterminacies in legal language, but were actively shaping law in line with their personal views.

More recently, the FCC exerted itself even beyond Germany's borders. In a 2020 case, the court ruled that the Court of Justice of the European Union (CJEU) was operating *ultra vires* its authority.[3] The EU court had, according to the German court, ignored proportionality principles enshrined in the Treaty on European Union (Articles 5(1) and (4)). The CJEU had not sufficiently analysed the likely aims and effects of a mutualised debt instrument used by the Central Bank (ECB) to tackle the 2020 pandemic—known colloquially as Coronabonds. Given this procedural oversight, the FCC ruled that it was inconsistent with principles of German democracy to go along with the debt scheme. The scheme would have seen the German taxpayers as collateral, with southern and eastern European countries as primary beneficiaries. Not only was the FCC affecting monetary policy, which rarely enjoys judicial oversight, their decision had implications for the 500 million inhabitants of the EU.

Germany appears to offer an extreme case of judicial activism. In ruling on abortion and shared debt, the FCC judges seem very much to be "politicians in robes" (Vanberg 2005). And, famously, those red and white robes worn are so elaborate that the judges need help getting them on. But we need to take the long view, as ever in this book. Isolated cases, devoid of their wider contexts cannot establish a sound model of judicial

[2] BVerfG, May 28, 1993, 88 BVerfGE 203.

[3] BVerfG, May 5, 2020, 2 BvR 859/15.

behaviour (Pünder and Waldhoff 2014). If we look at first to quantity rather than the qualities of specific rulings, we see that successful constitutional complaints are highly unusual. From 1951 to 2020 there were 249,023 cases brought before the FCC. Fully 97% of these proceedings were constitutional complaints, with all other procedures (such as disputes between the Federal and Länder governments) occupying the remaining 3%. Of the constitutional complaints, just 2.3% were successful. Although this amounts to 5372 successful constitutional challenges, that is across nearly seventy years.[4] Put simply, the vast majority of complaints brought before the judges are rejected.

However, the abortion and Coronabond examples demonstrate that qualitative impact cannot be swept aside. These two instances undoubtedly describe the judges' capacity and willingness to exert policy power, and they were roundly criticised as a result (Landfried 1994; Kommers 1997). Does this mean that the judges simply implemented a policy decision in line with their preferences? The division of judges between Social Democrat and Christian Democrat appointees would certainly seem to suggest as much. Although, there is conspicuous indeterminacy in Article 2(2) of the Basic Law that was not clarified sufficiently by politicians (indeterminacies italicised):

> (2) *Every* person shall have the right to life *and physical* integrity. Freedom of the person shall be *inviolable*. These rights *may* be interfered with *only* pursuant to a law.

Settling the meaning of the determiner "Every" in conjunction with "person" was an interpretational problem that judges had to settle. That the judges may have settled this interpretative problem in line with their political preferences is perhaps unsurprising. Undeniable is the fact that the interpretative space was there to be filled. It was for lack of clarity that the judges defended their judgement on Coronabonds as well:

> 118 a) Where an ultra vires review or an identity review raises questions regarding the validity or interpretation of a measure taken by institutions, bodies, offices and agencies of the European Union, the Federal Constitutional Court, in principle, bases its review on the understanding and the

[4] "Jahresstatistik 2020" URL: https://www.bundesverfassungsgericht.de/DE/Verfahren/Jahresstatistiken/2020/statistik_2020_node.html Accessed 9 May 2021.

> assessment of such a measure as put forward by the CJEU. However, this no longer applies where the interpretation of the Treaties is simply not comprehensible and thus objectively arbitrary.[5]

There are again themes of indeterminacy of law mediating macro social dynamics and micro decision-making behaviour. Whilst German law has been relatively stable since the millennium, it has been significantly more volatile across the seventy years of democracy. Interestingly, Germany is not a case of degenrifying legislative norms, because of its contemporary stability. Germany is better described as a regenrified polity. There was substantial post-war volatility in institutional discourses which have settled into patterns only relatively recently. Notably, Germany experienced volatility not only in legislative language but also in higher-order constitutional language. The German Basic Law has been amended sixty times since its promulgation in 1949. This is substantially more frequently than any other country surveyed in this book. The story of post-war German politics can explain this movement from volatility towards stability. Notable sources of discursive discombobulation have been, *inter alia*, denazification, Europeanisation, remilitarisation, and reunification (see, for example, Wiegandt 1995). German politics has developed stability in its institutions and, hence, its logic of communication. German politics has been regenrified, but that was with the help of judges, using their power to settle a new normal (Hailbronner 2015). Judges have helped reimagine many of the dormant principles of the *Rechtsstaat*, from towering figures like Kant, Weber, and Kelsen. The foundation upon which post-war normality was built is, however, the *grundnorm*. This "basic norm" is laid out as Article 1 of the Basic Law. It is conspicuously influenced by Kantian ethics:

> (1) Human dignity shall be inviolable. To respect and protect it shall be the duty of all state authority.
> (2) The German people therefore acknowledge inviolable and inalienable human rights as the basis of every community, of peace and of justice in the world.
> (3) The following basic rights shall bind the legislature, the executive, and the judiciary as directly applicable law.

[5] BVerfG, May 5, 2020, 2 BvR 859/15.

Human dignity is the "inviolable and inalienable" foundation of German statecraft. And, as mentioned, the inalienability of this right is literal, not merely idiomatic. According to Article 79(3), the "eternity clause" (Ewigkeitsklausel), there is no means by which the basic principles of German law can be removed. The idea of empowering a specialist constitutional court to review all state actions in line with such foundational principle was advocated by Austrian jurist Hans Kelsen in 1920. The Kelsenian model spread through continental Europe, spurred by post-war revulsion at wartime abuses. Human rights were to be protected robustly, either through abstract or concrete review procedures.[6] Democracy itself was subordinated to individual human dignity, because of the horrifying consequences of Nazi populism. The red-robed judicial defenders of this basic norm were therefore deliberately gifted the power to constrain democracy where necessary (Castillo-Ortiz 2020).

In fact, two articles of the Basic Law are listed as unalterable, Article 1 and Article 20. The latter categorises Germany as a "democratic and social federal state". It goes on to acknowledge popular sovereignty, as "All state authority is derived from the people". There is clearly potential for tension in the inalienability of Article 1's individual protections, and Article 20's popular sovereignty. It is a tension familiar to all democracies, but, unlike in the other countries surveyed for this book, German constitutional review is tethered to immovable foundations. And, German judges were quite expansively empowered to rule on the rectitude of public policies:

> 93(1) The Federal Constitutional Court shall rule:
> 1. on the interpretation of this Basic Law in the event of disputes concerning the extent of the rights and duties of a supreme federal body or of other parties vested with rights of their own by this Basic Law or by the rules of procedure of a supreme federal body;
> 2. in the event of disagreements or doubts concerning the formal or substantive compatibility of federal law or Länd law with this Basic Law...

[6] The abstract review of pre-promulgated law was used for the infamous 1975 abortion decision outlined above. The concrete constitutional complaint, moreover, was used for the Coronabond case, and 97% of the FCC's caseload.

The roots of Germany's Basic Law can be traced to the city of Kaliningrad. Under its erstwhile name of Königsberg, it had been the home of Immanuel Kant. Therefore, the home of German legal principle is no longer even a part of Germany, but is an exclave and oblast of Russia. Similar to the now French city of Strasbourg, there are sites of extraordinary importance to the history of German philosophy and law that are not in Germany itself. This is of historic but of no practical significance. Contemporary German statecraft is rooted in rationalist considerations of the mind, and not so much concerned for lines on maps. And the deontology of Kantian principle contrasts in other striking ways with the more grounded and distributional justice typical of common law. Kantian ideas of human dignity offer a potentially deeper jurisprudential well from which to draw, as compared to common law natural justice and fairness. It therefore supports decisions that raise eyebrows outside of Germany. But none of this obviates the thesis of this book. Judges in Germany are active in policy-making in order to ascertain a logic of communication capable of reconciling divergent legal texts and political contexts.

A notably eyebrow raising ruling for foreign observers was that concerning the power to shoot down hijacked aircraft. Under a utilitarian calculus, the state would be within its rights to shoot down a hijacked aircraft, if there was a risk to it being used as a missile. Such ghastly considerations were made after the 9/11 attacks on New York City. The decision-making algorithm adopted by the UK was representative of worldwide policies—the head of government could authorise a hijacked aircraft to be shot down, so as to spare destruction on the ground. The simple calculation being that x lives on the plane were outweighed by the prospect of multiples of x losing their lives on the ground. This, it was ruled by the FCC, is not how the German *grundnorm* would guide counterterrorism policy (Youngs 2008).

The FCC received a constitutional complaint from some frequent flyers.[7] They contended that Section 14 of the *Air Safety Act* (Luftsicherheitsgesetz [LuftSiG]) was incompatible with Basic Law protections of inviolable human dignity (Art 1), and the rights to life and physical integrity (Art 2). The *Air Safety Act* empowered the Air Force, via the

[7] BVerfG, Feb. 15, 2006, 1 BvR 357/05.

Federal Minister of Defence, to "prevent the occurrence of a particularly serious accident". The legislation was cautious. It laid out several measures that fell short of destroying the aircraft, including forcibly diverting its course. The law also stressed that use of force could not be disproportionate to the objective, and must minimise harm to both stricken passengers and the wider public. But it also made clear that fighter pilots could "threaten the use of force of weapons or give warning shots", and "The Federal Minister of Defence *may generally* authorise… measures". Such wide discretion created the possibility that passengers on the plane may be used as a means to the end of avoiding a greater loss of life, as opposed to being an end in themselves. This instrumentalising of human beings is not compatible with their inviolable dignity, nor right to life, according to the judges:

> The complainants object directly to the aviation security law with the constitutional complaint because it allows the state to deliberately kill people who have not become perpetrators, but victims of a crime… The constitutional complaint is admissible. The complainants would be directly affected by the contested regulation in their fundamental rights. Since they frequently used aircraft for private and professional reasons, it is not only a theoretical possibility that they… could be affected.[8]

Such a judgement is barely conceivable in Britain or America. Not only was it a constitutional complaint against something that had not yet happened, but the ruling also refused to acknowledge that the state could legitimately threaten innocent lives under such circumstances. The ruling is therefore both procedurally and substantively unthinkable in a common law jurisdiction. But, in spite of these divergences, the German case conforms to the patterns offered in other chapters. There has in Germany, as elsewhere, been considerable volatility in official discourses caused by rapid social and technological changes being couched indeterminately in law. The consequent judicialisation of policy can therefore best be explained according to these exogenous stimuli acting on judges. What especially marks Germany out is the extent to which it was starting from a *tabula rasa* after the war. It had to build a recognisable genre of legalese, from scratch.

[8] Ibid., paras 35–36.

A foundational moment of this regenrification came with the 1957 *Elfes* judgement.[9] A constitutional complaint was brought before the FCC when a prominent critic of German militarisation and unification was denied a passport. Herr Elfes had vocally criticised the state both within and outside Germany. He sought an interpretation of the Basic Law that would acknowledge a right to leave the country. Article 11 deals with freedom of movement, and is couched in highly indeterminate language (indeterminacies italicised):

> (1) All Germans shall have the right to move *freely* throughout the federal territory. (2) This right *may* be restricted *only* by *or* pursuant to a law, *and only* in cases in which the absence of *adequate* means of support would result in a *particular* burden for the community, *or* in which *such* restriction is *necessary* to avert an *imminent* danger to the existence of the *free democratic basic* order of the Federation *or* of a Länd, to combat the danger of an epidemic, to respond to a *grave* accident *or natural* disaster, to protect *young* persons from *serious* neglect *or* to prevent crime.

The FFC rejected the complaint, holding that it was within the state's power to deny emigration. But, they also held that the "free development of one's personality" under Article 2 had to be broadly interpreted, as did the phrase "constitutional order" which "can only be understood as the general legal order".[10] The implications of this ruling being that the Basic Law is all-pervasive. It was not just relations with the state that could be regulated, but even private relations between citizens came under its purview. This was formally recognised with the 1958 FCC *Lüth* judgement.[11] To reach this maximalist interpretation in *Elfes*, the judges referred to records of the Parliamentary Council (Parlamentarischer Rat) that had written the Basic Law. They used this transtextual evidence to flesh out indeterminacies in the Basic Law text. A further *sui generic* feature of the German constitution thereby emerged from these cases—it is not formally a constitution at all. The "Basic Law" was deliberately not referred to as a constitution for West Germany, nor was it authored by a "constitutional assembly". This was so as to make clear that what had

[9] BVerfG, Jan. 16, 1957, 1 BvR 253/56.

[10] Ibid at para 17.

[11] BVerfG, Jan. 15, 1958, 1 BvR 400/51.

been established in Bonn would not be restricted to West Germany, and would have capacity to grow both in substance and in space.

Reunification was therefore a major driver of regenrification in German legal discourse. Where West Germany had by 1990 developed a holistic "constitutional order" after the war, the eastern DDR had a separate legal order with markedly fewer safeguards for human dignity (Jaggi 2016). The FCC was therefore called upon to cohere eastern and western norms through the Basic Law after reunification. A notable case of legal reconciliation came in 1996.[12] Four former officers of the DDR faced incarceration in the new Germany for their role in killing refugees attempting to flee from east to west. Even though their crimes had been committed under DDR law, they were ordered to be punished by the supreme criminal court of the Federal Republic—the *Bundesgerichtshof*. All four brought constitutional complaints to the FFC, arguing that they were being punished by retroactive application of Federal Republic laws to actions committed in a different time and context. Article 103(2) of the Basic Law forbids retroactive criminalisation. There were two options for public prosecutors therefore: (i) apply the Radbruch formula, or (ii) demonstrate that the officials had broken DDR laws. The Radbruch formula is an eponymous judicial algorithm suggested in an essay by Gustav Radbruch (Müller 1979). He argued that judges must misapply positive law if it is manifestly unjust and immoral. He was of course building this case in response to National Socialist crimes against humanity. These crimes had nominally been legal according to Nazi regulations, but were nonetheless barbarically unjust. The FFC judges chose not to use this formula, instead opting to assess breaches of DDR law, but punish under the much more lenient federal penal code.

The four individuals (three officers of the National Defence Council, and one border guard) had been responsible for seven grisly deaths. It was found that use of SM-70 antipersonnel mines, and refusals to obtain timely medical assistance for gunshot wounds, were in fact breaches of DDR law, even if both practices were far from unusual at the border. The four could therefore be convicted of breaking laws in force at the time the crimes were committed. But they were spared the punishments more typical of the East, which could include death. The FCC therefore

[12] BVerfG, Oct. 24, 1996, 2 BvR 1851/94.

confirmed the Federal Court of Justice decision to apply a milder western punishment for the eastern crime.[13]

This case brings together key themes of post-war judicial power in Germany—history, territory, and dignity. Judges were intentionally empowered by framers of the Basic Law to interpret an indeterminate set of ideals in a manner that would create a new normal. In specific regards to criminal laws—to which we will shortly turn—the heritage of Germany's Criminal Code (Strafgesetzbuch [StGB]) is, like the Basic Law, long and august. Owing much to von Feuerbach's Bavarian Criminal Code (Bayrisches Strafgesetzbuch), the modern StGB is resolutely grounded by reason and constraint (Herausgegeben von Koch et al. 2014). But, as we will see, it has been altered many times by indeterminate legislation, much of which has opened wide interpretative spaces for, in particular, the FFC to input Basic Law norms. And, as we will see, the Basic Law itself has been amended sixty times since its promulgation in 1949. In line with the thesis of this book, judges in Germany are best described as having been judicialised by state expansion and a concomitant indeterminacy in state communication. There is only sparse and incoherent evidence for an agency-based alternative theory, that judges took policy power to sate their own appetites.

Empirical—Textual Changes

Unlike with other country chapters for this book, this chapter will look not at changes to criminal legislation, but also textual changes in constitutional law. Given both the importance of constitutional review to the power of German judges and the relatively high degree of alteration in the Basic Law, it is important to track changing language in both higher and lower order legal texts. Starting with the Basic Law, Figs. 9.1 and 9.2 describe substantial changes in both word length and indeterminacy. In its 1949 debut iteration, the Basic Law was 13,406 words long, and had an average of 8.21 indeterminate parts of speech per article. By 2020 these statistics had changed to 27,386 words and 16.6 indeterminate parts of speech per article. That both word length and degree of indeterminacy

[13] BVerfG, Oct. 24, 1996, 2 BvR 1851/94, para 71(dd).

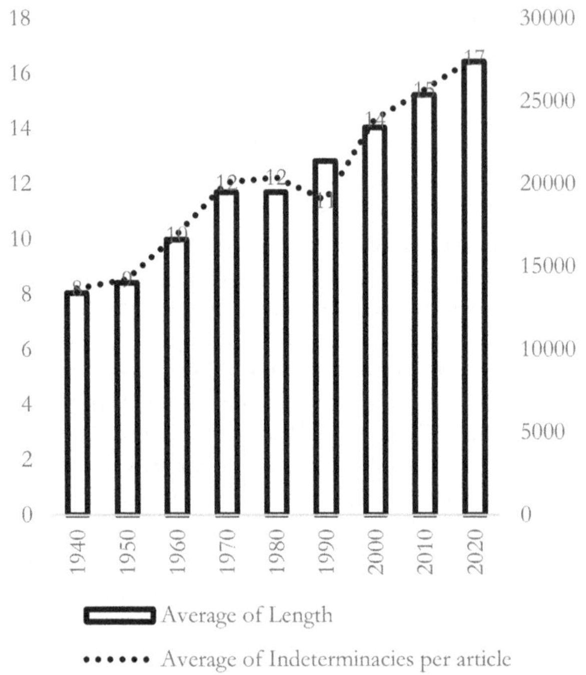

Fig. 9.1 Comparison of changes in indeterminacy (primary *y*-axis) and word length (secondary *y*-axis) in the Basic Law, 1949–2020 (*Source* Author's creation)

doubled in 70 years could be explained simply as the former driving the latter. As discussed in the opening chapters, increased word length often leads to increased indeterminacies per Article, simply because there are more words per Article. But this does not mean that the language is stable in genre. Doubling average Article length with double the indeterminate parts of speech means there has been a significant widening of interpretative space for judges.

The Basic Law can be amended by two-thirds majorities in both Bundestag and Bundesrat. As mentioned, Articles 1 and 20 cannot be removed on account of the "eternity clause". In addition to which, fundamental alterations to Articles 2–19 are also impossible. And yet, given the proportional electoral system used in Germany, it is notable

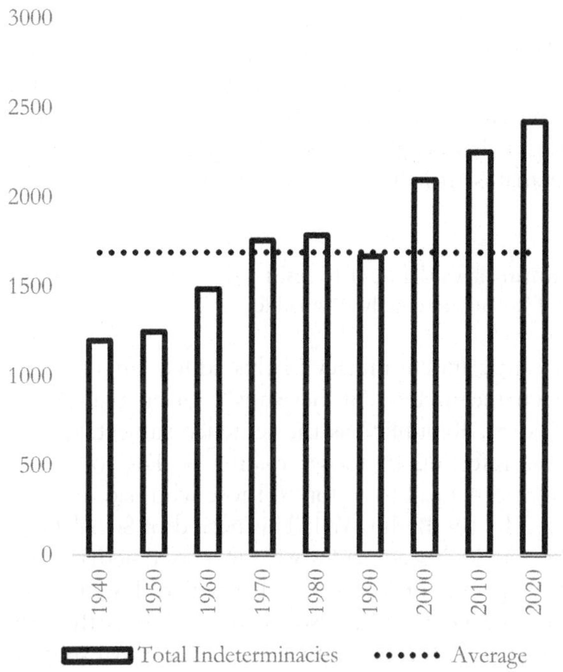

Fig. 9.2 Total indeterminacies (number of coded parts of speech) in the Basic Law, 1949–2020 (*Source* Author's creation)

how many times and to what substantial extents its Basic Law has been amended. Such inter-party consensus on the need for constitutional change is unique amongst the five nations surveyed for this book. Particularly notable were amendments in 1956 to establish a Bundeswehr and bring back conscription. After reunification in 1990 there were substantial amendments to better protect women's rights and the rights of disabled citizens. A decision was also made in these years after reunification not to create an entirely new constitution for a united Germany, and instead to integrate the old east into the Basic Law.

Figures 9.1 and 9.2 describe substantial changes in language occurring from the 1960s. This coincides with the first Social Democratic (SPD) governments (1969–1982) after a twenty year spell of CDU rule from

1949. The Basic Law grew by 25% in these years of SPD governance. An example addition made in 1968 was to the eternally protected Article 20. This amendment embellished but certainly did not remove the Article. In its origin form, Article 20 stated, *inter alia*, that "The Federal Republic of Germany is a democratic and social federal state" and that "All state authority emanates from the people". To this was added a new fourth paragraph:

> (4) All Germans have the right to resist anyone who undertakes to remove this order if no other remedy is possible.

There is very little indeterminacy in this added language, save for what may have been meant by "All Germans". Given that Article 20 opens with "The Federal Republic" as the sentence subject, it seems that "All Germans" was referring to those residing in East or West, and could therefore have been a call to action to those who had, in the 1960s, been newly enclosed by the Berlin Wall. This period of Social-Liberal coalition of the 1960s and 1970s coincides with increased activity from the FCC. The 1975 ruling on abortion was, in particular, described as a judge-led political brake ("politische Bremsfunktion").[14] It is this coincidence of progressive politics with conservative adjudication that suggested personal motivations lay behind judicial interpretations of law. However, a pattern of politically motivated rulings did not emerge even during the Brandt Chancellorship. And, the court would in the 1993 abortion ruling[15] and 1995 Crucifix decision[16] disappoint the longest ever tenured Chancellor, CDU's Helmut Kohl.

A more obvious pattern from which to explain increased judicial activity comes from secular increases in legal indeterminacy. Besides substantial changes in the Basic Law, there were also conspicuous changes to criminal law that obviated identification of normal or generic legislative language. Figures 9.3 and 9.4 summarise these changes across 70 years, through 103 pieces of legislation, and 1,440,856 words. Sampled were all pieces of legislation that made amendments, additions, or connections

[14] Hüter der Verfassung. Das BVerfG in der Geschichte der Bundesrepublik Deutschland Ulrich Herbert Freiburg, Samstagsuni, Dez. 2018.

[15] BVerfG, May 28, 1993, 88 BVerfGE 203.

[16] BVerfG, May 16, 1995, 1 BvR 1087/91.

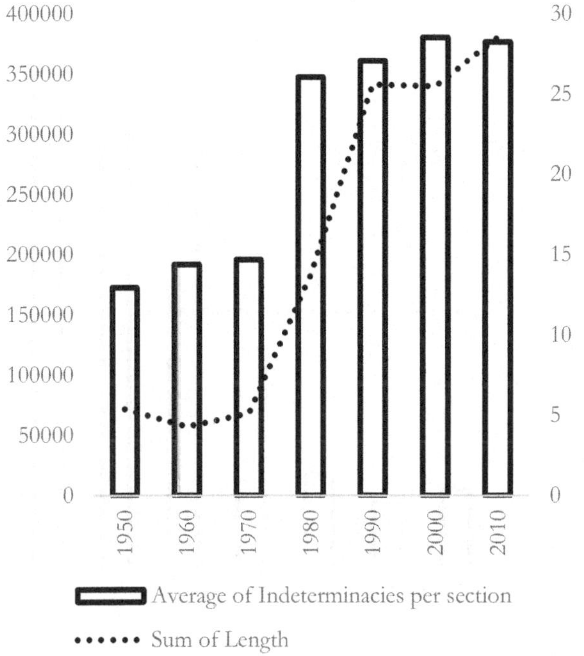

Fig. 9.3 Comparison of changes in indeterminacy (primary *y*-axis) and word length (secondary *y*-axis) in criminal justice legislation, 1950–2019 (*Source* Author's creation)

to the StGB criminal code. There was a conspicuous change to legislative language after the Social-Liberal era ended in 1982. The following sixteen years were dominated by Kohl's CDU who managed both reunification and post-Maastricht Europeanisation. These sixteen years accounted for the most substantial changes to norms of legislative language. The twenty-first century has then seen a levelling off and stabilisation of legislative genre, as described through all other German legislation by Chapter 4.

Despite greater consistency in the language of twenty-first century criminal legislation, Table 9.1 describes significant quantities of newly enacted legislation. Illustrative of this is the fact that the volume of new law enacted in the 2010s (380,649 words) was greater than the entire output of criminal laws enacted from the 1950s to the end of the 1980s.

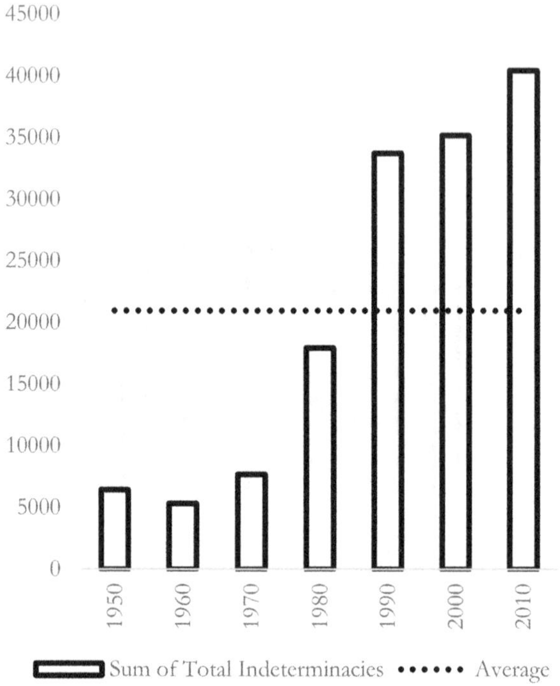

Fig. 9.4 Total indeterminacies (number of coded parts of speech) in criminal justice legislation, 1950–2019 (*Source* Author's creation)

Despite sharp increases to the quantities of legislation enacted after the 1990s, Table 9.2 reaffirms that the greatest changes to legislative language came a decade prior, in the 1980s, when average compound indeterminacies per section near doubled in ten years. Whilst it is not the aim of this chapter to explain these changes, we could hypothesise a correlation to the party system's right-ward shift after 1982, which was in turn derivative of global moves to New Right attitudes on criminality. Democratic states had expanded their powers post-war, so as to cater to citizen welfare. Many then moved in the 1980s to reimagine the seemingly lost civic and individual virtues of the pre-war era, somewhat counteracting the liberalising policies of the 1960s and 1970s.

As compared to the other countries surveyed, Germany has maintained a far greater degree of linguistic stability in its politics, despite the epochal

Table 9.1 Descriptive statistics

Decade	*Sum of sections*	*Sum of length*
1950s	566	71,446
1960s	336	56,972
1970s	467	67,879
1980s	705	182,775
1990s	1249	341,271
2000s	1183	339,864
2010s	1184	380,649
Average statute	55	13,989
Standard deviation	63	19,675
Minimum	2 (Verordnung zum Verzeichnis der Zuwiderhandlungen, die in das Aktennachweissystem für Zollzwecke aufgenommen werden sollen 2011 [FIDEVerzV])	162 (Gesetz zu dem Übereinkommen vom 26. Oktober 1979 über den physischen Schutz von Kernmaterial 1990 [AtSchÜbkG])
Maximum	359 (Kapitalanlagegesetzbuch 2013 [KAGB])	147,644 (Kapitalanlagegesetzbuch 2013 [KAGB])
Total	5690	1,440,856

changes to its post-war norms and political economy. Nonetheless, the increased volume of new legislation, taken with substantial Basic Law changes in the 1960s/70s and criminal law changes of the 1980s, have all given judges a formidable task of normalising textual indeterminacies into generic patterns.

Definitional—Subtextual Changes

A first and fundamental task for judges to perform in response to textual indeterminacy is to develop ligatures between laws and norms. This is particularly important in German jurisprudence, where all laws must be tethered to the *grundnorm*. Concretely, judges are required to define away textual uncertainties. In doing so they develop a coherent subtext that, like a dictionary, then forms an authoritative resource for resolving future textual confusion. The FCC does not have jurisdiction to define away indeterminacies in criminal legislation, as that would be done by the Federal Court of Justice. The FCC would also not determine the facts of

Table 9.2 Indeterminate parts of speech per section of criminal justice legislation

Decade	*Average of adjectives/section*	*Average of conjunctions/section*	*Average of indeterminate modal verbs/section*	*Average of enabling verbs/section*	*Average of compound indeterminacies/section*
1950s	6.99	5.50	0.44	0.03	12.95
1960s	7.95	5.97	0.39	0.07	14.38
1970s	8.30	6.05	0.29	0.03	14.67
1980s	14.03	11.11	0.78	0.13	26.05
1990s	14.40	11.82	0.73	0.13	27.08
2000s	15.28	11.96	1.17	0.12	28.53
2010s	14.89	12.23	1.03	0.11	28.26
Averages statute	13.26	10.59	0.83	0.10	24.79
Standard deviation	7.79	6.34	0.65	0.11	14.42
Min	0.80	1.00	0	0	1.80 (Gesetz zu dem Übereinkommen vom 26. Oktober 1979 über den physischen Schutz von Kernmaterial 1990 [AtSchÜbkG])
Max	43.81	35.88	3.07	0.62	81.54 (Gesetz über die Spende, Entnahme und Übertragung von Organen und Geweben 1997 [TPG])

a case, but would only offer its assessment of constitutional law. Nonetheless, it is possible that a lack of definition in criminal law, combined with complicated case facts, can contribute to a breach of fundamental rights. This then brings constitutional review to bear on an otherwise straightforward case of illegality. All of which was established in Judge Karl Heck's eponymous formula for when the FCC may intervene in ordinary legal disputes.[17]

An example is a 2021 case concerning "especially aggravated arson".[18] A drug dealer had been cornered by police in his grandparents' Munich apartment. He barricaded himself inside, grabbed a large kitchen knife, and started a fire to stop anyone entering the building. He was finally subdued by being shot in both legs by police. This finally allowed fire fighters to tackle a blaze that had spread to other apartments. Despite a litany of obvious crimes, there were substantial delays in setting a trial date. As such, the defendant was held in pre-trial detention for 13 months. He therefore complained to the FCC that his treatment amounted to a deprivation of liberty. The judges agreed and reprimanded the Bavarian authorities for their foot-dragging. One of the core reasons cited for on-going delays was the need for extensive investigations, so as to establish whether the fire could be described as "especially aggravated arson". To obtain a lengthier prison sentence, it was necessary to establish at trial if a breach of section 306b StGB had occurred:

> Especially aggravated arson. (1) Whoever, by committing arson within the meaning of section 306 or 306a, causes serious damage to another person's health or damage to a large number of people's health incurs a penalty of imprisonment...for a term of at least five years if... the offender... prevents the fire from being extinguished or makes extinguishing the fire more difficult.

Whether the defendant had caused "serious damage" and made "extinguishing the fire more difficult" had to be further investigated by the public prosecutor. The FCC judges recognised how adjectives in the legislation were responsible for procedural delays:

[17] BVerfG, June 10, 1964, 1 BvR 37/63.

[18] BVerfG, Feb. 3, 2021, 2 BvR 2128/20.

> The prosecution has not insignificant legal difficulties. The problem is whether the complainant can also be accused of especially serious arson... the follow-up investigations into the scope of damage are of considerable importance, because this legal question does not arise if essential components of the building had burned.[19]

The FCC did not in fact define away the indeterminacy here, rather they asserted the importance of procedural propriety and constitutional norms in the face of fuzzy legalese. Given the growing quantities of criminal legislation, and its increased indeterminacy after the 1980s, there are heightened risks that the sheer lack of clarity in law will itself constitute a breach of rights. There is only an incomplete rule of law if the law cannot readily be understood and used to guide action. An equal and opposite risk is that indefinite laws create indefinite public power. In other words, indeterminacies of law can, without careful management, lead to there being no discernible legal system, or to a perception that everything is legalised. The latter possibility could *in extremis* amount to totalitarianism, where the private sphere is unidentifiable and almost anything is capable of definition in law.

The *grundnorm* protection of human dignity, embellished by neo-Kantian ideas of a state-free "lifeworld", all set in the context of lived totalitarian experiences, have conspired to make for a liberal and restrained German state (Honneth and Joas 1991). Even as the quantities of law have increased and their determinacy decreased, judges were working to define, in the literal sense of to make finite what could otherwise be infinite. An interesting case that grappled with these themes is the *Tucholsky II* judgement of 1995.[20] There are strict criminal laws against publicly insulting individuals (see in particular section 185 StGB). This was intended to clamp down on the sort of hate speech that propelled National Socialism to power. But, criminalising insults could be a draconian state incursion into the private sphere. Ironically, in attempting to thwart totalitarianism, the state may be forced to behave as an authoritarian. These tensions came to a head in the *Tucholsky II* judgement as FCC judges had to determine whether four individuals deserved the prison time for publicly declaring that "Soldiers are murderers". *Soldaten sind Mörder* is a famous quote from Weimar journalist and pacifist Kurt

[19] Ibid., para 25.

[20] BVerfG, Oct. 10, 1995, 1 BvR 1476/91.

Tucholsky. The four defendants had been convicted by criminal courts of, amongst other things, putting stickers on cars with the offending quote. The judges had to determine a balance between freedom of expression (protected by Article 5 of the Basic Law) and the criminalisation of insults. This balancing act could in theory be aided by the relative clarity of Section 185 StGB:

> The insult will be punished with a prison sentence of up to one year or with a fine and, if the insult is committed publicly, in a meeting, by spreading a content or by means of an assault, with imprisonment of up to two years or with a fine.

If anything this language is plain to the extent of being arbitrary. Almost any insult could be criminalised, a point not lost of the judgs:

> §185 StGB does not describe a specific behaviour, but focuses on the extra-legal concept of insult. However, there is no social consensus on what should be understood by an insult. This uncertainty is all the more unbearable because this provision has a stop-gap function for missing state protection standards.

This poses a substantial challenge to the book's argument. In this case, indeterminacy was caused by laconic, not garrulous, legislation. However, as argued in the introductory chapters, whilst more words can provide more detail, when those words are qualifying parts of speech, they necessarily decontextualise meaning and must be reified by an agent (be it a citizen or a state actor). It may be that the law on insults is plain, but it has to cohere with Article 5 of the Basic Law, which uses qualifying parts of speech to empower citizens (indeterminacies italicised):

> (1) Every person shall have the right *freely* to express *and* disseminate his opinions in speech, writing *and* pictures *and* to inform himself without hindrance from *generally* accessible sources.

In the end, the judges resolved the case in favour of the defendants and quashed sentencing decisions of several Länd courts (Reutter 2020). They did so by defining "soldiers are murderers" as not being a targeted insult, but as a generalised pacifistic statement. The verdict was so unpopular that death threats were sent and the judges had to be put under police protection. The judges were already considered to have been politically active on account of their 1995 *Crucifix judgement*,[21] which had allowed schools to opt out of a Bavaria statute calling for the religious image to be present in classrooms (Campenhausen 1996). The senior judges faced criticism from politicians and the media for their liberality. But whichever decisions the judges had come to would have determined a power balance between state and citizen. They were forced into distributing power by indeterminate constitutional laws that sought to empower citizens, alongside criminal laws that sought to impose constraints. This legal tension was not created by the judges, but they were called on to resolve it.

Systemic–Intertextual Changes

How much scope is there for German judges to decide cases according to their own political attitudes? Judges are state trained bureaucrats, who must hold a relevant qualification for judicial office and excellent results in the Staatsexamen. Judges are therefore highly intelligent and their independence is institutionally protected. In addition to which, all Federal and Länd judges are appointed by politicians, with their party affiliations a crucial element in elevation to the highest judicial ranks. For example, on the FCC at the time of writing, there are seven CDU/CSU appointees (including President Stephen Harbarth), six SPD appointees (including Vice President Doris König), two Green appointees, and one FDP appointee. With intelligent, partisan, and institutionally independent judges, it would seem that their personal convictions are likely to affect their rulings. An often cited example was the clean split in opinion between CDU and SPD appointees over the 1975 abortion decision,[22] wherein the more conservative judges won the day (Landfried 1994).

Although there are protections for judicial independence and autonomy, there are also systems in place to insure against personal bias creeping into the adjudication processes. As the following schematic describes, there are layers to the federal judiciary, with five specialist trunks, and lines of accountability to enable judges to mark each other's homework. Reaching an intertextual consensus to resolve indeterminacy is ultimately overseen by the sixteen-person and bicameral FCC. That court ultimately works to reify the *grundnorm* in all cases brought before

[21] BVerfG, May 16, 1995, 1 BvR 1087/91.

[22] BVerfG, Feb. 25, 1975, 39, 1.

it. The FCC is not a supreme court of general jurisdiction, but any case from a specialist court can end up in front of its judges if a breach of fundamental rights is identified. In addition to which, the court, in keeping with its Kelsenian design, is capable of abstractly reviewing pre-promulgated laws if called to do so by other state organs (Fig. 9.5).

There are institutions and systems in place to develop a coherent (and therefore depersonalised) rule of law. These procedural safeguards operate from the micro-level on individual judges, all the way up to the global level where German judges act in concert with European courts. Starting at the micro-level, there is evidence of judges keeping their own house in order. For example, in a 2016 hearing, the FCC refused to grant leave for a constitutional complaint brought by one of their more junior

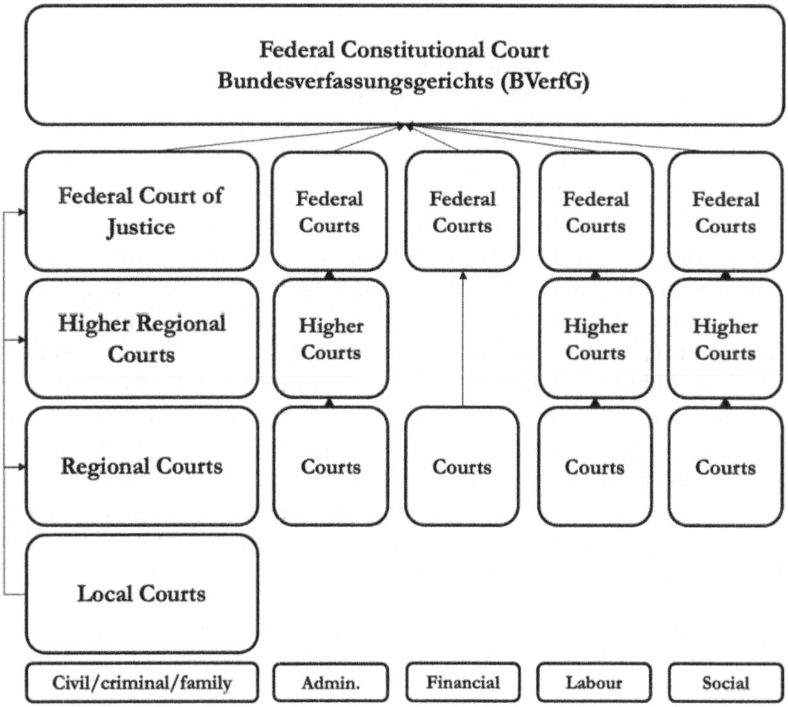

Fig. 9.5 German courts schematic
(*Source* Author's creation)

brethren.[23] A Local Court judge had been indicted for perverting the course of justice in seven of his decided cases. These cases were traffic offences, where the judge had summarily acquitted the defendants on the grounds that precise measurements of their offences were not provided by the prosecuting authorities. There was nonetheless sufficient evidence to prosecute, such that each decision was reversed by the Higher Regional Court. It was claimed that the judge held irrational grievances against the prosecuting authorities, and he was litigating these via the case docket. He counter-argued that judicial independence, as guaranteed by the Basic Law, allowed him unfettered discretion to dismiss the cases and reprimand the traffic authorities for their sloppy reporting. The Federal Court of Justice held, contrarily, that judicial independence was not unfettered, and did not constitute a fundamental right, but was rather an individual right and was subject to other rules of law.[24] Going out of his way to ignore statute law on grounds that he disapproved of other local officials was not constitutionally protected behaviour. The FCC agreed and refused to hear his constitutional complaint.

And the FCC has shown itself capable of monitoring its own membership. A clear risk of politicised appointments is that individual judges may have conspicuous policy views that they may then be called on to adjudicate. This can create a reasonable presumption of bias. For instance, in a 2018 case, the FCC refused to allow one of its own members to hear a constitutional complaint regarding assisted suicide.[25] Judge Peter Müller was a CDU member who had, prior to his judicial appointment, been Minister President of Saarland. In this executive office, he had literally made pulpit sermons against euthanasia and had even been credited with drafting the legislation to ban any business promotion of suicide. This legislation was enacted as section 217 StGB, and was the subject of a constitutional complaint. His fellow FCC judges reasonably felt that he would be viewed by parties to the complaint as biased, and he would therefore be replaced for the hearings. Ultimately, the FCC declared in 2020 that section 217 StGB was indeed unconstitutional.[26]

[23] BVerfG, July 14, 2016, 2 BvR 661/16.

[24] BGH, Feb. 24, 2016, 2 StR 533/15.

[25] BVerfG, Feb. 13, 2018, 2 BvR 651/16.

[26] BVerfG, Feb. 26, 2020, 2 BvR 2347/15, 2 BvR 651/16, 2 BvR 1261/16, 2 BvR 1593/16, 2 BvR 2354/16, 2 BvR 2527/16.

Moving up from micro-level review of individual behaviour, the courts also perform macroscopic oversight of whole institutions, both at Länd and Federal levels. This again is aimed at creating and sustaining norms of law. Critics may argue that it allows the courts to dominate and impose their will with the benefit of having a final say. Given the FCC has a further benefit of interpreting an (in part) unalterable Basic Law, they would seem to have both means and opportunity, so it merely becomes a question of whether they have the motive to act as the superior branch of government. As argued previously, there is not an unremitting motive for judges to play politics, but this is because they in fact do not have both method and opportunity fully open to them. In particular, courts lack the sufficient means for unquestioned dominance. Access to the senior courts is itself a matter of both statute law, and alterable elements of the Basic Law. If the court moves too far against another organ of government, they face a real risk of forever losing their institutional privileges. Indeed, the German *Rechtsstaat* is comprised of five separated power centres, capable of restraining each other—President, Bundestag, Bundesrat, Federal Government, and Federal Constitutional Court. It is also the norm that organs work collaboratively to constrain other organs. It would not, therefore, be the case that the FCC would, on its own, act against the judgement and interests of other organs of state without exposing its authority to question. For example, in the highly controversial abortion decision of 1975, it was opposition members of the Bundestag and the Free State of Bavaria, represented by its Minister President, that had petitioned the court in the first place.[27] Assuming that the courts are politically astute, they would not be so foolish as to act without allies that can ensure their sustained authority and legitimacy. The point being that when individual judges confront expanded state responsibilities couched by indeterminate laws, they do not have the capacity nor the motivation to behave entirely in accordance with their own interests. As such, theory and evidence would tend to suggest that the increased power of judges to undertake political decision-making is exogenous to the judiciary.

This does not however mean that judges seek to cultivate political alliances. Their authority derives in part from their independence, of course. Judges can and do therefore create trouble for other organs of

[27] BVerfG, Feb. 25, 1975, 39, 1.

state, without fear of how such behaviour may impact on future coalition building. An example is *Organstreit* litigation (disputes between state organs), with a notable case in 2017 before the FCC.[28] Green Party members of the Bundestag led the dispute against the Federal Government. They wanted information about the controversial railway upgrade "Stuttgart 21" that Deutsche Bahn AG was delivering overdue and overbudget. The Government had not answered parliamentary questions on the matter, nor had they given reasons for their taciturnity. Presumably this was because any answers given would have been embarrassing for the Government as sole shareholder in Deutsche Bahn. The FCC ruled—in spite of its majority of CDU appointees—that the CDU-led Government had breached the Bundestag's rights under the Basic Law by not answering questions.

Moving up another level—from national to supranational—the German FCC has upheld Basic Law principles even against EU policies. This is despite case law of the Court of Justice of the EU asserting the supremacy of EU laws over member states.[29] We have already encountered the Coronabond case, wherein the FCC ruled that the European Central Bank was operating *ultra vires* on account of its arbitrary debt policy.[30] This was not the first time the FCC had frustrated EU policies, however. In 2005, the FCC stalled an attempt to harmonise extradition throughout the bloc. In response to 9/11, there were attempts to make easier the movement of criminals between EU states via the European Arrest Warrant (Nohlen 2007). Crucial legislation within Germany was nonetheless declared unconstitutional when a suspected Al-Qaeda ring-leader brought a complaint to the FCC.[31] Another case that was unsuccessful, but nonetheless granted a hearing, was a complaint brought against the EU's "Banana Protocol".[32] The EU had granted Germany a licence to import 1.371 million tonnes of bananas per year. To ensure duty free importation, these bananas had to come from the EU or specified African, Caribbean and Pacific nations (ACP bananas). Third country bananas were subject to tight quotas, imports in excess of which were to

[28] BVerfG, Nov. 7, 2017, 2 BvE 2/11.

[29] *Flaminio Costa v. E.N.E.L.* ECLI:EU:C:1964:66.

[30] BVerfG, May 5, 2020, 2 BvR 859/15.

[31] BVerfG, July 18, 2005, 2 BvR 2236/04.

[32] BVerfG, June 7, 2000, 2 BvL 1/97.

be taxed steeply. A group of banana traders brought a complaint citing Article 23 of the Basic Law, which holds that EU laws must be compatible with fundamental German rights—including freedom to work and enjoy property.

That the FCC even heard this case suggests a willingness to keep EU courts under close scruitny. The European Arrest Warrant case was technically against the German Parliament, even if it frustrated EU policy. The Coronabond case was the most overt criticism of an EU institution. But even that case was not predicated on denial of EU supremacy. Instead it was in keeping with a 1993 ruling on the Maastricht Treaty, where the FCC accepted the supremacy of EU laws except where institutions acted beyond their mandate.[33] This decision was itself derivative of the "Solange II" ruling from 1986.[34] In that case, the FCC accepted that it would not review secondary legislation from the EU, under the assumption that it generally conforms to fundamental rights. As the judges put it in their Banana Protocol ruling, the EU was to be afforded a margin of appreciation by Solange II[35]:

> As long as the European Communities, in particular European case law, generally ensure effective protection of fundamental rights as against the sovereign powers of the Communities which is to be regarded as substantially similar to the protection of fundamental rights required unconditionally by the Basic Law, and in so far as they generally safeguard the essential content of fundamental rights, the Federal Constitutional Court will no longer exercise its jurisdiction to decide on the applicability of secondary Community legislation.

The FCC is happy with EU case law being both "generally" and "substantially" similar to domestic rights. And herein lies the key point. The German Constitutional Court is directed not by the individual whims of its sixteen judges, but rather by the coherent application of fundamental rights. The court has worked at regenrification of rights jurisprudence, both within and beyond Germany. This comes down to interpretations of coordinative discourses. Where EU institutions are generally or substantially sticking to the agreed script, the German courts will follow

[33] BVerfG, Oct. 12, 1993, 2 BvR 2134/92, 2159/92.

[34] BVerfG, Oct. 22, 1986, 2 BvR 197/83.

[35] BVerfG, June 7, 2000, 2 BvL 1/97 at para 59.

their lead. If anything, German courts are being particularly risk averse in seeking to maintain systemic coherence in rules of law, against the forbidding opposition of supranational institutions.

Prudential—Contextual Changes

One means by which German courts seek to obtain coherent rules of law is through specialisation. In common law jurisdictions it is typical to have generalised appellate courts, capable of reviewing all areas of law. Germany as noted above has five separate and specialist judicial branches. This could lead to intellectual silos and hence a failure to establish coordinative discourse between branches. The FCC is able to anchor specialised decisions back to the *grundnorm*, but is itself specialised in so far as it may only hear cases that pertain to fundamental rights. A crucial question to consider therefore is when and under what circumstances will the FCC choose to overrule their specialised juniors. This question must be answered to understand the potential power of Germany's constitutional court. Given both informational and capability asymmetries, the FCC must establish a balance between subsidiarity and control. But how do they do this?

There are at least two core components to an identifiable adjudication algorithm. First, the FCC establishes how new cases may or may not cohere with past decisions, and, second, they defer to lower courts and other authorities in establishing case facts. Rapidly changeable contexts are not well interpreted by the FCC. They are specialised in law, and working out what principles of law exist in abstraction. When it comes to reifying abstract principles to concrete reality, we see plenty of evidence of the FCC relying, prudentially, on other institutions and actors that are better placed at determining what actually happened. The FCC will only intervene in a factual assessment if they perceive the method of factual analysis to have deviated from past precedent. What we do not see is unambiguous evidence of judges taking every opportunity to exert their power. They are consistently relying on and deferring to other state actors.

To flesh out this claim, it is useful to focus on the interesting law on insults, mentioned above with regard to the *Soldaten sind Mörder* case. The case law on insults demonstrates the adjudication algorithm sketched so far. Judges must determine whether instructive precedents exist, and whether correct procedures for investigating facts have been followed. When it came to describing soldiers as murderers, the blanket nature of this condemnation is what made it allowable. By contrast, a 2020 case led to the criminal conviction of a young man for wearing an offensive sweater.[36] The man was participating in an anti-fascist protest against far right extremists in Göttingen. His sweater was emblazoned with "FCK BFE" meaning "Fuck Beweissicherungs und Festnahmeeinheit". The BFE is a specific police unit, and they were present to keep order at the clash of activists. Whilst other anti-police slogans such as "ACAB" ("All cops are bastards") and "FCK CPS" ("Fuck Cops") are considered sufficiently generalised to fall under freedom of expression laws, in this case it was felt the protester was being too targeted in his insults. He also demonstrated his intention to insult, as, when asked to remove or cover the offending slogan, he took off the sweater to reveal the very same inscription on a T-shirt. In their judgement, the FCC made clear the two strand algorithm—precedent and procedure for factual assessment—and deferred entirely to the Higher Regional Court's judgement on the case[37]:

> this violation of fundamental rights is justified. The interpretation and application of § 185 StGB, which restricts freedom of expression, primarily incumbent on the criminal courts, does not meet any constitutional concerns in the differentiated circumstances of the case. Failure to comply with the constitutional provisions for convictions under § 185 StGB following the principle of practical concordance (see summary BVerfG, decision of the 2nd Chamber of the First Senate of the 19th May 2020 - 1 BvR 2397/19 -, paragraphs 14 et seq.) and an exceedance of the technical assessment framework existing for the application of these conditions are not recognizable.[38]

So, when might the FCC decide that those powers "primarily incumbent on the criminal courts" should nonetheless be controlled? Again, an institutionalist algorithm predominates. If precedent and procedures for assessing case facts deviate from a lower court decision, then the FCC will intervene. In a 2020 ruling, the FCC[39] overruled the Landshut District

[36] BVerfG, Dec. 8, 2020, 1 BvR 842/19.

[37] Oberlandesgericht Braunschweig, Mar. 5, 2019, 1 Ss 77/18.

[38] BVerfG, Dec. 8, 2020, 1 BvR 842/19 at para 2.

[39] BVerfG, Oct. 16, 2020, 1 BvR 2805/19.

Court in regard to a perceived insult.[40] A German national had arrived at Munich airport with a colleague from outside the EU. The man waited with his colleague in the queue for non-EU entrants, but found that the process was, to his mind, unacceptably slow and probably in breach of rules. He therefore sought a name and address of someone so as to deliver a formal complaint. A couple of border officials were asked for this information, but hesitated, making him even more angry. He eventually snapped at one official and questioned, mockingly, if he was even able to understand basic German. Given that the remarks were this time targeted and were intended to disparage the border guard's intelligence, the complainant was charged with an offence. But his conviction was overturned. In doing so, the FCC cited several precedents that fleshed out the indeterminate statutory language around "insults":

> the fundamental right of expression as a prerequisite for a criminal conviction under § 185 StGB usually requires a balanced weighting of the impairments that threaten personal honour on the one hand and freedom of expression on the other (cf. BVerfGE 7, 198 <212>; 85, 1 <16>; 93, 266 <293>; stRspr). This fundamentally guided balance follows on from the open criteria and justifications of the Criminal Code, in particular the terms of 'insult' and the 'perception of legitimate interests' (cf. BVerfGE 12, 113 <124 ff. >; 90, 241 <248>; 93, 266 <290>)... The task of the Federal Constitutional Court is merely to check whether the specialised courts have sufficiently taken into account the importance and scope of the freedom of expression affected by the criminal penalty.

The FCC decided that in this particular case the passenger was agitated and lashing out. There was no evidence of premeditation to the insult, and given the conspicuous asymmetry of power between the border official and the immigrating pair, it was in many ways an exasperated expression from a position of weakness, rather than strength. It nonetheless shows how difficult it can be for the FCC to interpret an appropriate balance of rights and laws. It admitted it must only check the activities of specialised courts when compelled to do so in order to protect rights. By referring to past precedents, the court is delimiting its future discretion. Unlike in common law jurisdictions, there is no formal expectation that courts in Germany will conform to a doctrine of *stare decisis*. The fact nonetheless

[40] Amtsgericht Landshut, Nov. 11, 2019, 5 Ns 303 Js 3598/19.

that the judges are holding to a *jurisprudence constante* suggests they are delimiting and defining rules of law, as opposed to inventing new possibilities.

Influence-Seeking—Transtextual Changes

Of course, it would not be beyond the intelligence of senior judges to invent some casuistry that justifies basing a decision on cherry-picked precedents. But then why would judges deny themselves jurisdiction? By upholding fundamental rights, courts are restricting the state's capacity to influence future policy outcomes. Of course, denying jurisdiction can be just as politically consequential as asserting it. In ruling that an agitated passenger could not be convicted of an offence, the FCC added to protections for freedom of speech. Albeit, in doing so, they defined allowable speech, and state capacities to control it. They shaped the agendas by which policy-makers and bureaucrats frame viable choices. As discussed in previous chapters, this is well described by Steven Lukes's second dimension of power. By taking matters off the policy agenda, judges are undoubtedly exerting influence over policy that may be entirely unwelcome to other organs of state.

In denying the state a role, it could be claimed that judges are evincing their own liberal ideologies. A more impersonal, institutionalist, explanation for restricting state behaviour is to be found from an ideological transtext, against which indeterminate texts are rendered meaningful. In other words, judges are not acting for themselves in denying state power, rather the reconciliation of law to case facts is realised against the backdrop of a complex transtextual corpus stretching back to core state principles. Of course the transtext of constitutional law and principle does not determine specific case outcomes, and there is space for varying interpretations. But that is the ultimate point of this book. The political power of judges is derived from interpretative spaces found in increasing quantities of under-determined and indeterminate law. Why a judge decides is, in a longer historical perspective, not relevant. The fact that they can decide at all is the key mystery, and it is a mystery that is not readily solved by reference to individuated preferences.

Liberalism and individual dignity are baked into German statecraft, such that the default public policy is no policy at all. Liberalism is itself a contested conceptual label. It can be considered liberating for a state to protect individuals, or to secure communities. Balancing individual and communal rights is a familiar dilemma for apex courts the world over. This dilemma became especially pronounced post-war, when sensitivities to individual justice were, on occasion, set against the security and identity concerns of groups. Politicians had to walk this tightrope, and created ambivalent policies, textual ambiguities, and downright contradictions to be resolved in court. Again, judges did not create these opportunities, but were institutionally bound to manage them. Religion is a particularly common site of contestation between individual rights and group identities. The controversial 1995 *Crucifix decision*, mentioned above, is a clear example.[41] According to the Bavarian elementary school regulations:

> A cross must be placed in every classroom. Teachers and students are obliged to respect the religious feelings of everyone.[42]

Whilst this language is relatively free of indeterminate parts of speech, the first sentence could be said to contradict the second. In that, the placing of a cross may not be respectful of the feelings of everyone. Added to which, the concept of respect is undefined. At least that was the feeling of two claimants who brought complaints on behalf of their children. These children were being raised according to anthroposophical principles, and did not feel respected by the presence of a Christian symbol in their classroom. The FCC therefore had to decide a balance between states' rights and individual rights, seen through the Basic Law lens, specifically Article 4(1):

> (1) Freedom of faith and of conscience and freedom to profess a religious or philosophical creed shall be inviolable.

This language is also substantially below the average degree of indeterminacy as measured by the text-mining algorithm. As such, the FCC had to settle a dispute between two relatively determinate sources of law. In defence of the school regulations, it was claimed that Article 4 established a positive right to religious expression. It was further claimed from a practical perspective that this positive right did not affect the claimants in their negative right not to have their religion interfered with. The FCC

[41] BVerfG, May 16, 1995, 1 BvR 1087/91.

[42] VSO, June 21, 1983, (GVBl p. 597).

disagreed and overturned lower court decisions in the process. They based their decision on an alternative transtextual rendering of Article 4:

> The... view [of Bavarian authorities] is based on an unconstitutional change of meaning of the importance of the fundamental right of religious freedom. [Article 4] gives the individual citizen a right of defence against the state [and] is currently used for the protection of minorities. It is incompatible with this to claim that the establishment of symbols of the majority religion in state school premises is part of the positive religious freedom of a majority in the population.[43]

To the FCC, the undergirding principle of German law is that it protects individuals, and does not empower communities. Where there is any doubt, as in cases like this, the individual right is to prevail. This conclusion paid heed to historic uses of law as a majoritarian weapon against minorities. It was, nonetheless, a very controversial decision, not least because of its contestable enunciation of liberal and Kantian principles (Campenhausen 1996).

The FCC case law became yet more controversial in 2003 with a dispute over a teacher's right to wear a headscarf at work (see, for instance, Zellentin 2014).[44] The court annulled regulations in the state of Baden-Württemberg that forbade the wearing of religious symbols as a condition for civil service employment. The case bore superficial similarities to the Crucifix hearing. The court issue under dispute was state neutrality with regard to ideological and religious belief. Did liberal neutrality mean that the state had to enforce a level playing field, and ban all religious iconography from public spaces? It was contended that the headscarf is not straightforwardly a religious symbol, like a Crucifix, but signifies cultural and individual commitments to modesty. Furthermore, the concept of liberal neutrality does not mean that the state bans everything. That could indeed be an ironically totalitarian route to civic liberation. Rather, the state is obliged to "secure a space of activity" for individual and community identities.[45] It had not been sufficiently proven that a headscarf would influence the thinking of school children, given it

[43] BVerfG, May 16, 1995, 1 BvR 1087/91 at para 13.

[44] BVerfG, Sep. 24, 2003, 2 BvR 1436/02.

[45] Ibid at para 10.

was not used to proselytise. Also, the headscarf was not worn in realisation of a state regulation, whereas the Crucifix in Bavaria had been displayed in accordance with local laws. Nonetheless, the confusion and ambivalence felt by modern societies about the balance of individual and communal rights has fairly unsurprisingly yielded significant influence to the courts. Judges were nonetheless at pains to explain their ruling in regard to constitutional theory and past precedent:

> The relevant statements in the Crucifix decision of the Federal Constitutional Court are not transferable to the present case. While it was about a religious symbol, the installation of which is responsible for the state institution of school, the complainant as a fundamental rights holder is affected in her subjective right to freedom of belief. A restriction of the exercise of fundamental rights could only be considered in the case of unconditionally guaranteed fundamental rights in the event of concrete danger. This is missing; an alleged suggestive power of the headscarf and the alleged possibility of harmful psychological influence have not been proven.[46]

The supposedly harmful influences of cultural diversity have become politically salient in the twenty-first century. Security concerns over international terrorism, as well as domestic identity politics, have posed challenges to post-war individual rights ideals. Liberalism itself is under critical assessment in contemporary geopolitics. This has further encouraged a sense of ambivalence and confusion amongst policy-makers with regard to questions of state activism and restraint. Which, in turn, has yielded policy influence to judges. A 2020 case decided at the FCC is illustrative of on-going tensions.[47] The US Government's "9/11 Commission" report held, *inter alia*, that institutional silos between intelligence agencies thwarted coordinated counterterrorism. What was needed, therefore, was inter-agency data aggregation and sharing. Learning from these lessons, the German Government enacted the *Anti-Terror File Law* (Antiterrordateigesetz, ATDG) in 2006. This law created shared dossiers for police and intelligence agencies to use in coordinated investigations of domestic threats. This law had to be amended several times in order to comply with Basic Law protections of informational self-determination. But, even after

[46] Ibid at para 19.

[47] BVerfG, Nov. 10, 2020, 1 BvR 3214/15.

iterated improvements, sections of the law were still annulled by the FCC, including:

> (2) A participating federal authority may use the types of data stored in the file... insofar as this is necessary in the context of a specific individual case-related project for the prosecution of qualified crimes of international terrorism in individual cases, in order to clarify further contexts of the individual case.

The court ruled that separating data was necessary for its protection. In other words, the court wanted to maintain institutional silos. The policy intent of making use of available data in counter terrorism was to convert data gathered on innocent citizens into possibly actionable intelligence. The court was making state securitisation less efficient. Their incentives for doing so cannot easily be disparaged as bleeding heart liberality. There is clear protective language in Article 2 of the Basic Law to ensure individual personhood is not overwhelmed by state authority. As the judges made clear:

> ...the data thus obtained should remain in the area of constitutional protection and, in particular, should not be made available to the police authorities. Otherwise, the powers of intervention of the individual authorities will become digressive and the police will receive information that they would not have if only the legal provisions applicable to them were applied.[48]

A further practical question was whether the complainant had standing. Lawyers for the government claimed that even if there was a basis for the annulment, the complainant did not have a right to complain. Mr. S, as he is referred to in the court records, was an entirely innocent man who had not fallen victim to the law. Under a common law system, Mr. S would not have been granted a hearing. The FCC acknowledged that the complainant could "only show a specific probability of being affected by the storage to a limited extent".[49] But, they defined Mr. S's situation as representative of ordinary civic entitlement.

[48] Ibid at para 29.

[49] Ibid at para 37.

> The complainant, as an innocent citizen and through completely legal behaviour, can always come into the focus of the constitutional protection authorities and become the object of intelligence information procurement.[50]

In a fairly meaningless concession to the government, the judges rejected the constitutional complaint, but nonetheless annulled the offending legislation. They ordered that the government pay half the complainant's costs, because he had only won half of the case. And yet, all the court sought was an annulment, meaning that the policy influence was negative. More of an exertion of influence comes when courts say "Not this, but that…". That is, courts can, when annulling legislation, nonetheless establish criteria they would consider viable. This form of judgement comes closer to policy-making from the bench, albeit technically it is framing future policy agendas. The following section will delve further into cases where judges made identifiably new policy and did not just shape the policy framework for other actors. This next case example did not entail policy-making by judges, but left the legislature in no doubt as to what was expected of workable legislation.

A dispute was settled in 2020 by the FCC in favour of the complainants—journalists based in Germany and elsewhere in the EU.[51] The complaint was with regard to surveillance of telecommunications across borders. The Federal Intelligence Service (Bundesnachrichtendienst—BND) was authorised to collect cross-border communications in pursuit of internal security, and in support of international cooperation on counter terrorism. The complainants argued, successfully, that the powers of gathering data between German citizens and their contacts abroad would, in their circumstances, breach journalistic privacy and source confidentiality. The FCC went further still and held that fundamental rights in the Basic Law were to be applied outside of Germany's borders, and would extend to non-German nationals unless a clear danger was identified and verified by an authority other than the BND.[52] The sharing of data was in particular to be much more heavily regulated as a result of the ruling. Indeed, the court laid out detailed instructions on the acquisition and processing of sensitive intelligence data:

[50] Ibid at para 28.

[51] BVerfG, May 19, 2020, 1 BvR 2835/17.

[52] Ibid at para 165.

> the power to conduct strategic surveillance is an exceptional power that must be limited... the legislator must provide for the removal of telecommunications data of Germans and persons within Germany, limits to data that may be collected, the determination of specific surveillance purposes, the structuring of surveillance based on specifically determined measures, special requirements for the targeted surveillance of specific individuals, limits to traffic data retention, a framework governing data analysis, safeguards to protect confidential relationships of trust, the guaranteed protection of the core of private life and obligations to delete data.[53]

These enumerated conditions protect against a possibility of creeping securitisation. The ruling is consistent with post-war commitments to a restrained state, but it nonetheless entailed significant oversight by a court of core state functions (see, for example, Jestaedt et al. 2020). How can this kind of micromanagement be explained? The courts have the opportunity to participate in governance because of an elastic, and much altered Basic Law. This, coupled with under-specified intelligence regulations, gave judges the opportunity and motivation to intervene in policy. The policy itself was under-determined, and the broader transtextual norms of statecraft pointed to a default policy as being no policy at all.

Policy-Oriented—Metatextual Changes

The concept of informational self-determination was itself a judicial construct, derived by the FCC in their Census Ruling (*Volkszählungsurteil*) of 1983.[54] It is all very well explaining policy annulment of under-determined policy, but how can we explain judicial policy-making? In the Census Ruling, the judges weaved together Basic Law rights with analysis of how modern technologies and circumstances had reconfigured those rights. Comprehensive data collection from all citizens was not explicitly mentioned in the Basic Law, but was considered possible and desirable, so the judges had an opportunity to reimagine a new aspect of constitutionalism. They were reaching beyond the text of law and developing a new text that departed from past interpretations and rulings. Indeed, all lower courts and authorities (save for those in Hamburg) had

[53] Ibid at paras 166–7.

[54] BVerfG, Dec. 15, 1983, 1 BvR 209, 269, 362, 420, 440, 484/83.

ruled that a door-to-door census was entirely in keeping with the law. But the FCC strenously disagreed:

> under the conditions of modern information processing technologies... Anyone who cannot reasonably predict with sufficient certainty what information concerning him is known in certain areas of his social environment, and who cannot reasonably assess the knowledge of possible communication partners, can be significantly inhibited in their freedom to plan or decide on their own self-determination. A social order and a legal order that makes it possible would no longer be compatible with the right to informational self-determination, in which citizens can no longer know who knows what, when and on what occasion.

This ruling denied the Federal Government an open-ended power to collect citizens' data. The census went ahead, but with restrictions on what could be recorded and how it could be recorded. The key point is that, in this case, the courts developed new rights that had not explicitly existed before. They held that human dignity and freedom to develop a personality translated to the security of personal data. This decision created a scaffolding for new rights that went beyond simply restraining the state. The ruling created not only new powers, but even a new ideological framework, based on Michel Foucault's warnings against panopticism—the danger that observations of society will itself change society (Foucault 2008). In the words of the judges:

> Anyone who is unsure whether different behaviours are recorded at any time and stored, used or passed on as information will try not to be noticed by such behaviours. Anyone who expects, for example, that participation in an assembly or a citizens' initiative will be officially registered and that this can create risks, may be prevented from exercising their corresponding fundamental rights. (Art. 8, 9 GG)[55]

In their Census Ruling, the FCC generated not only new legal language, but they created new norms, they rooted these norms in rich social theory, and they even created cost implications for running a census. This seems conceptually beyond activism and ranging into policy interventionism. How can we explain it in accordance with a theory of judges reacting to linguistic uncertainty? The ruling seems far removed from positivist

[55] Ibid at para 146.

concerns with the letter of the law, and more motivated by concepts of justice.

However, the ruling is consistent with post-positivist theory. In fact, the ruling was surgical in its attention to language in the Census Act. Several sections were ruled to be compatible with the Basic Law, provided that extra safety regulations were employed. It was only a part of one section (section 9) on the use and sharing of data that was ruled to be void. In an earlier draft of this section, considered by the court, the legislature proposed a modest range of data that could only be shared with municipalities subject to tight conditions. In the final version, these conditions were diluted, allowing for indeterminate powers to share almost all data.[56] The court went so far as to analyse inter-party voting patterns on section 9 as it passed through the Bundestag.[57] This behaviour from judges is undoubtedly of political significance. But the aim is to understand and explain why the judges intervened in this way.

The evidence from their ruling suggests an opportunity to reconcile legislative and constitutional languages. Both sets of texts were sufficiently indeterminate to justify new textual ligatures. The judges could have deferred to the Bundestag to establish new legal language. And indeed they did defer on most points complained of, but not all. Absolute deference in a contested case could signal an acceptance of legal indeterminacy that would, if repeated, diminish further the determinacy of law and thereby undermine the authority of courts. It may have been that the judges were motivated by their own policy goals, but that is an untestable psychological hypothesis. What is observable is the fact that there was an opportunity for a judicial intervention in policy created by a lack of legal positivism. Put plainly, there was no discernible law on data sharing, especially in the contexts of social and technological changes. The concomitant absence of a coordinative logic of communication for institutions enabled the judges' decision. Their motivations to decide are of lesser importance than their opportunities to decide.

Whether or not the judges succeeded in optimally clarifying language is not at issue. They were, strictly speaking, acting within their powers in generating new legal language. FCC judges have, since the Republic's early years, developed and enforced norms of statecraft. In the *Lüth*

[56] Ibid at paras 82–3.

[57] Ibid at para 85.

judgement of 1958, notably, the court described fundamental rights as more than merely defensive against state intrusion.[58] The judges conceptualised a holistic "value system" centred on human personality, and argued it was the "expression of an objective order".[59] The concept of an objective order suggests the law is discovered rather than made by judges. In this particular case, the value system was identified in a complainant's right to call for a boycott. He was not seeking defence from the state, but defence against a private lawsuit designed to silence him. The lawsuit was brought by Veit Harlan, a Nazi propagandist who had made a new post-war film called "Immortal Lover". The complainant, a Hamburg Senator, argued that the release would bring Germany's film industry into disrepute. The question was whether he could be stopped from calling for a boycott. The judges interestingly contended in essence that the "objective order" of law meant that he could not be stopped. This was based on an assertion of objectivity, which challenges this book's overall thesis that positive law became increasingly unidentifiable post-war. But, crucially, the objective order was not described as being found in the past, rather as developing iteratively by a coalition of meaning-givers, including judges. The order may be more accurately described as inter-subjective, and post-positivist, rather than objective therefore. Law is not an object that all may perceive identically. Law is interpreted, but interpretations are subject to a variety of forces, ultimately centred on shared understandings of language. As was stated in the *Lüth* ruling:

> ...the Basic Law, which does not want to be a value-neutral order, has also established an objective value order in its fundamental rights section and that this precisely reflects a fundamental strengthening of the validity of fundamental rights. This value system, which finds its centre in the human personality and dignity unfolding freely within the social community, must be regarded as a basic constitutional decision for all areas of law; it receives guidelines and impulses through legislation, administration and case law. Of course, this also affects civil law; no civil law provision must conflict with it, each must be interpreted in its spirit.[60]

[58] BVerfG, Jan. 15, 1958, 1 BvR 400/51.

[59] Ibid at paras 25–6.

[60] Ibid loc cit.

Typically judges impose "order" in a fairly literal way—by preventing change, and asserting customary or normative propriety. By thus restraining other institutions, order in the sense of predictability can be conserved. Making new laws and norms from the bench seems the opposite of ordering behaviour. How can it ever be norm conserving to be novel? The answer is that norm conservation through restraint will be impossible when new disputes arise in new contexts. The norms of law therefore need to be reimagined if they are to survive novel circumstances. As Alec Stone Sweet argued (2000), there is a feedback wherein novel conditions create new disputes, these are settled by judges, and this in turn feeds into new disputed relationships. The space for judicial innovation comes not from context, but the under-determination of key texts. Constitutional concepts such as "human personality" develop according to new social contexts, and new interpretations thereby emerge. When context deviates from extant interpretations of text, it can be that no acceptable status quo position exists and judicial innovation becomes more defensible.

Predicting when disputes may lead to new interpretations of law by judges is almost impossibly difficult, because it is contingent on multiple necessary but insufficient factors. These include, but are not limited to: ideology; the state of law; an accretion of precedents; the complainants; the case facts; the coalition of opinion within the judiciary; public opinion; timing; and the likelihood of a political backlash. At a critical juncture, judges will be ideologically inclined and institutionally incentivised to create new protections for minorities, if these are conspicuously threatened by a change in context or a shift in political coalitions. Judges will be using powers of interpretation to ensure that disenfranchised groups have some capacity to self-determine in a threatening context. Given that many constitutional and legal contexts are indeterminate precisely because of an underpinning social ambivalence as to optimal policy, it is likely that a ruling protecting of minorities will obtain "losers' consent", as there are only ephemeral and unstable coalitions in favour of policies to disempower minorities (Anderson et al. 2005). This capacity to obtain losers' consent from the powerful in society means that judicial innovations will likely be shielded from overruling. An example FCC decision, building on the *Lüth* judgement, came when judges issued an injunction against Facebook, forcing the media giant to readmit a controversial user.[61] A right-wing party was campaigning for European Parliament elections by posting content about the supposed effects of immigration. Facebook decided that these posts veered into hate speech, so removed all of the content and froze the profile. The complainants pleaded their right to free expression under the Basic Law, which clearly had not anticipated social media when first promulgated. But, social and technological changes meant that free speech had to be reinterpreted in this novel context. Using the Basic Law to order a foreign company to act was a judicial innovation, but not likely one that would face sustained political opposition.

The Facebook case also highlights another spur to counter-majoritarian innovations from the bench. That case was brought by politicians, seeking to contest the procedures by which politics is transacted. The FCC will hear both concrete and abstract constitutional cases. The Facebook case was concretely fighting against a social media policy. In the next case example, 210 members of the Bundestag (35% of the total 598 members) brought an abstract case wherein there were no victims of the law, per se, but there was a general objection to how the law would discriminate if promulgated. Again, as with the Facebook case, this was a quick judgement brought in advance of the 2019 EP elections.[62] The complainants were left-wing members of *Die Linke*, and *Bündnis 90/Die Grünen* parties in the Bundestag. They managed to convince the FCC that individuals under state supervision, including those held in psychiatric facilities after having committed crimes, should be able to vote. This was not exactly a case that allowed prisoners to vote, but was a modest step removed from that. It was a politically significant ruling, and an innovative one at that. It grappled with questions of self-determination for those held in an uneasy limbo between absolute guilt predicated on malice, and criminality borne of incapacity. Such a decision would have been considered outrageous in the UK and US, where textual rules against criminals voting are highly determinate. In these countries, a political coalition against such judicial enfranchising would be likely. As such, the British courts sagely demurred when offered the opportunity to give votes to prisoners in *Hirst*.[63]

[61] BVerfG, May 22, 2019, 1 BvQ 42/19.

[62] BVerfG, Apr. 15, 2019, 2 BvQ 22/19.

[63] *Hirst v United Kingdom (No 2)* (2005) ECHR 681.

Innovation in the German courts depends on the same constellation of forces needed in the other countries studied—including ideology, sociology, and timing. What all the countries have in common is that these macroscopic forces tie into meso-level textual indeterminacies that either do or do not offer a propitious opportunity for judicialisation in a given case. Textual indeterminacy in constitutional or legislative sources indicate of ambivalence as to norms of law. Such ambivalence offers opportunities to those with little power in other institutions to press their claims in front of judges. Where ambivalence neither exists in ideology nor text, it will be highly unlikely for judges to press for innovative additions to the law. As considered in the sections above, the judiciary in Germany has been working towards negative liberty, by restraining actors and defining limits to criminal law. Judges are less likely to make entirely new potentialities in criminal justice. This could be seen with the FCC re-criminalising abortion, or blocking bans on private sector euthanasia. The courts are more attuned to saying what cannot be achieved using the Basic Law. And this feeds into a general observation held about the German courts. They are perceived as highly restrained. By international observers, however, the FCC is seen as activist, for determining whether planes may be shot down or if crucifixes can be hung in classrooms. Of course, this underscores the disutility of a concept like "activism", given it relies on subjectivity and moral approval of empirical acts. Nonetheless, judicial innovation in Germany has been audited in this chapter, and it has been shown to be tethered by textual indeterminacies which are themselves derivative of social and ideological changes since the war.

Conclusion

Judicialisation of German politics came as a consequence of the *Rechtsstaat's* post-war reassertion. It has been a successful reassertion. Legal normativity was attained in part by flexible and amended language in the Basic Law, as well as adaptative legislation. Since the millennium, Germany has attained the most stable genre of legislative language of any country studied in this book. This stability was attained after the potential disordering pressures of denazification, Europeanisation, remilitarisation, and reunification. The stability is itself a function of German political culture and its consensus-oriented institutions. Whether German politics is in some sense *too* stable remains a question to be answered elsewhere.

The intention here is to understand how and why judges rule against their own governments and other state agents.

As with the other countries studied, policy power for German judges is a direct reaction to indeterminate powers, duties, and licenses for government agents. The courts make finite what is, in language, under-defined. Germany, of course, has the most severe lived experiences of tyranny of the countries surveyed, and is hence unsurprisingly suspicious of powerful politicians using laws to authoritarian ends. The default, or basic (*grund*) norm of German politics is that individual dignity of citizens presupposes any state authority. The courts therefore act with power when defanging any state entity that may be threatening that basic norm. All else in the legal superstructure is connected to this base. Indeterminate laws are particularly troublesome, therefore, as they allow citizens scant opportunity to predict the lawfulness of their behaviour. Indeterminate laws tend to benefit those with institutional and material power. Such individuals, including state agents, have capacity to make post-legislative bargains on the meaningfulness of language. It is to the advantages of those with power to have their behaviour be unpredictable. But such mercuriality is a feature of arbitrary authoritarianism, and, as such, is sternly opposed by German courts in general, and the FCC in particular.

But, of course, indeterminate law is not the only trigger to judicialisation. Sometimes politicians simply twist, or even misuse, plainly stated laws. There is no evidence that a general rise in policy power for judges was led by governments breaking the law more often, but there are some disconnected examples of this happening. *Miller v. Prime Minister* was one such example from the UK when Boris Johnson was denied an extended prorogation of Parliament by court order. Somewhat similar were court cases in Germany brought against attempted dissolutions of the Bundestag (Lenz 1996). These early elections were obtained with "fake" motions of confidence in the Federal Chancellor. The relevant Basic Law provision, Article 68, is plainly worded, but both CDU (Kohl in 1982) and SPD (Schröder in 2005) Chancellors twisted it to their own advantages:

> (1) If a request by the Federal Chancellor to express confidence in him does not find the approval of the majority of the members of the Bundestag, the Federal President may dissolve the Bundestag within twenty-one days on the proposal of the Federal Chancellor. The right to dissolution expires as soon as the Bundestag elects another chancellor by a majority of its members.

In 1982, Helmut Kohl had become Chancellor following a constructive vote of no confidence against SPD's Helmut Schmidt. To secure a stronger Bundestag majority, Kohl wanted fresh elections, and called for a vote of confidence that he instructed his partisans to vote for. In the ensuing "fake" loss of confidence, President Karl Carstens felt compelled to order fresh elections. The subterfuge was clear for all to see, as Kohl had secured a new budget literally the day before supposedly losing confidence. The Federal Constitutional Court therefore received complaints from Members of the Bundestag. The President promised to resign if the "fake" vote was declared unconstitutional.[64] In the end, the court ruled that it was constitutional, and did so with a strict construction of Article 68. But, judges nonetheless carved themselves substantial influence in adjudicating on the legality of such moves:

> The objection that the Federal Chancellor did not ask a 'real' question of trust cannot be found in Art. 68 GG. This provision does not distinguish between 'real' and 'fake' questions of trust. The wording of Art. 68 GG, which regulates an important procedure and assigns important competences, must take a high priority. Even the history of its origin, if interpreted unbiasedly, speaks more in favour of the fact that the Parliamentary Council did not want to rule out the so-called fake question of trust.[65]

Gerhard Schröder also called a suspicious question of confidence in 2005, which again triggered an "organ dispute procedure" at the FCC. Again, the court ruled the move to be constitutional. And, again, the court set up a framework for better determining Article 68.[66] Judges approved the eponymous "Köhler formula", named for President Horst Köhler. The formula states that the Federal Chancellor's assessment of coalition stability was unambiguously to be preferred to anyone else's, even if a Chancellor was personally questioning confidence in that coalition. The court ruling offers a mixture of prudent passivity, with oversight (Castillo-Ortiz 2020). The judges did not want to become mired in the darker arts of electioneering. But, nor did they want the *Rechtsstaat* to become

[64] BVerfG, Feb. 16, 1983, 2 BvE 1, 2, 3, 4/83.

[65] Ibid at para 71.

[66] BVerfG, Aug. 25, 2005, 2 BvE 4/05.

sullied by political chicanery. Whilst their rulings endorsed the Chancellors' in both cases, they nonetheless heard the cases and established clearer guidelines as to the law of dissolution. The cases are important reminders to us that even plainly worded laws can be twisted to the advantage of the powerful. It is necessary, therefore, not to overstate the thesis that textual indeterminacies are required for interesting subtextual adaptations. Nonetheless, the degree of judicialisation in these cases was curtailed by the lack of indeterminacy in language. And, as a relevant postscript, Schröder's gamble failed, as he lost the 2005 elections to Angela Merkel.

References

Anderson, Christopher J., André Blais, Shaun Bowler, Todd Donovan, and Ola Listhaug. 2005. *Losers' Consent: Elections and Democratic Legitimacy*. Oxford: Oxford University Press.

Campenhausen, Axel Frhr. V. 1996. Zur Kruzifix-Entscheidung des Bundesverfassungsgerichts. *Archiv des öffentlichen Rechts* 121 (3): 448–464.

Capoccia, Giovanni. 2013. Militant Democracy: The Institutional Bases of Democratic Self-Preservation. *Annual Review of Law and Social Science* 9: 207–226.

Castillo-Ortiz, Pablo. 2020. The Dilemmas of Constitutional Courts and the Case for a New Design of Kelsenian Institutions. *Law and Philosophy* 39: 617–655.

Foucault, Michel. 2008. 'Panopticism' from 'Discipline and Punish: The Birth of the Prison'. *Race/Ethnicity: Multidisciplinary Global Contexts* 2 (1): 1–12.

Hailbronner, Michaela. 2015. *Tradition and Transformations: The Rise of German Constitutionalism*. Oxford: Oxford University Press.

Herausgegeben von Koch, Arnd., Michael Kubiciel, Martin Löhnig, and Michael Pawlik. 2014. *Feuerbachs Bayerisches Strafgesetzbuch: Die Geburt liberalen, modernen und rationalen Strafrechts*. Tübingen: Mohr Siebeck.

Honneth, Axel, and Hans Joas, eds. 1991. *Communicative Action: Essays on Jürgen Habermas's The Theory of Communicative Action*. Cambridge, M.A.: The MIT Press.

Jaggi, Stephan. 2016. *The 1989 Revolution in East Germany and Its Impact on Unified Germany's Constitutional Law The Forgotten Revolution?* Oxford: Nomos/Hart.

Jestaedt, Matthias, Oliver Lepsius, Christoph Möllers, and Christoph Schönberger. 2020. *The German Federal Constitutional Court: The court without limits*. Oxford: Oxford University Press.

Kommers, Donald P. 1997. *The Constitutional Jurisprudence of the Federal Republic of Germany*, 2nd ed. Durham, NC: Duke University Press.

Landfried, Christine. 1994. The Judicialization of Politics in Germany. *International Political Science Review* 15 (2): 113–124.

Lenz, Christofer. 1996. Die Wahlrechtsgleichheit und das Bundesverfassungsgericht. *Archiv Des Öffentlichen Rechts* 121 (3): 337–358.

Loewenstein, Karl. 1937. Militant Democracy and Fundamental Rights. *The American Political Science Review* 31 (3): 417–432.

Müller, Ingo. 1979. Gesetzliches Recht und übergesetzliches Unrecht: Gustav Radbruch und die Kontinuität der deutschen Staatsrechtslehre. *Leviathan (düsseldorf)* 7 (3): 308–338.

Murkens, Jo Eric Khushal. 2013. *From Empire to Union: Conceptions of German Constitutional Law Since 1871*. Oxford: Oxford University Press.

Nohlen, Nicolas. 2007. Germany: The European Arrest Warrant case. *International Journal of Constitutional Law* 6: 153–161.

Pünder, Hermann, and Christian Waldhoff, eds. 2014. *Debates in German Public Law*. Oxford: Hart.

Reutter, Werner. 2020. Subnational Constitutional Courts and Judicialization in Germany. *European Political Science*, 1–18.

Stone Sweet, Alec. 2000. *Governing with Judges: Constitutional Politics in Europe*. Oxford: Oxford University Press.

Vanberg, Georg. 2005. *The Politics of Constitutional Review in Germany*. Cambridge: Cambridge University Press.

Wiegandt, Manfred H. 1995. Germany's International Integration: The Rulings of the German Federal Constitutional Court on the Maastricht Treaty and the Out-of-Area Deployment of German Troops. *American University International Law Review* 10 (2): 889–916.

Youngs, Raymond. 2008. Germany: Shooting Down Aircraft and Analyzing Computer Data. *ICON* 6 (2): 331–348.

Zellentin, Alexa. 2014. Der philosophische Neutralitätsbegriff und die Kopftuchdebatte. *Archiv Für Rechts- Und Sozialphilosophie* 100 (3): 347–365.

CHAPTER 10

Conclusions

The book opened by setting out a mystery to be solved. A judicialisation of politics has been seen from an "expansion of the province of courts or the judges at the expense of the politicians and of the administrators" (Tate and Vallinder 1995). The aim was to understand this historical phenomenon across different democracies. There are a number of plausible (and non-excludable) explanations for judges obtaining more policy power. A somewhat glib summary could be as follows—some judges are born political, some seek out political power, and others have political power thrust upon them. Or, as James Gibson put it (1983, 9):

> In a nutshell, judges decisions are a function of what they prefer to do, tempered by what they think they ought to do, but constrained by what they perceive is feasible to do.

Judges cannot help but harbour policy preferences. The question is not whether these preferences affect adjudication, but how, to what extent, and with what implications. This book has made the case that judges' personal preferences are inadequate to explain a decades-long expansion of judicial power, such as has been seen across the world. Regardless of what individual judges may want from public policy, judiciaries remain dependent on other state institutions to implement their rulings. And, more importantly, judges need to maintain at least a perception of independence, or else their legitimacy to rule will be lost. As has been argued

M. Williams, *Judges and the Language of Law*,
https://doi.org/10.1007/978-3-030-91495-0_10

elsewhere, therefore, judges have attitudes, and will act strategically to vindicate those attitudes in their rulings (see, for example, Ferejohn and Weingast 1991). But, this book has sought to demonstrate that, beyond individual motives for policy change, judicialisation depends on means and opportunities, both of which predominately come from outside the judiciary.

In short, theories of judicialisation are most convincing when they appreciate the weaknesses of individual judges in regard to public policy. The circumstances of a global expansion in judicial power simply could not have been driven by judges alone. There must be complicity—be it conscious or unconscious—from political branches of government. And, besides these agents of change, more important still are the structural precursors to judicialisation. Stepping back to observe across seven decades, this book attempted to describe changes to the matrix of judicial policy power. These changes have included ambivalent ideologies that sought both to expand the state whilst protecting citizens; there have also been harmonising norms of international law; as well as newly empowered and better resourced litigants; and there has been a thriving market for public and administrative lawyers. The locus at which these forces converged was the language of contemporary law. The subtext and context of legal languages have undergone changes that would be expected from the passage of time, and changing constellations of power. There have also, as noted, been new global treaties and norms to allow for intertextual comparisons with domestic regulations. But, even more foundational than these changes have been changes to the textual indeterminacy of law.

The indeterminacies of modern law are symptomatic of social, ideological, and institutional indeterminacies. In some times and places there have been stable genericisms of legal language. This genre of legal linguistics describes a consistent "logic of communication" both within and beyond state institutions. Germany, for one, revived a stable *Rechtsstaat* after the swirling discombobulation of denazification, Europeanisation, remilitarisation, and reunification. The UK and France, by contrast have much more flexible legal linguistics that have enabled the reprogramming of state functions with efficiency. The consequence of this flexibility has nonetheless included a greater policy role for judges when interpreting these under-determined legislative bargains. By machine reading 60,556,672 words of legislation, and analysing 7469 country years, we have the longer perspective needed to situate modern judicial power in a story of communicative difficulties within and beyond states. There is a pretext to judicialisation, but the safest way for judges to justify expanding their powers is according to text, and that text is simply more difficult to interpret without dispute.

Of course, difficulties in interpreting laws are as old as law itself. And, trouble for judges in settling the consequent disputes is at least as ancient as the Book of Kings, when Solomon ruled that the baby should be cut in two. In all of the countries studied for this book, a tension between text and interpretation dates back to the earliest years. For example, one of the most notorious criminal trials in history took place in Salem, a town of what was then the Massachusetts Bay Colony. The Salem Witchcraft Trials saw hundreds charged with offences, nineteen people hanged, and one man stoned to death. Terrified citizens had justified these barbarous acts with extraordinarily indeterminate law that attempted to manage a policy problem:

> Be it enacted... That if any person or persons shall use, practice or Exercise any Invocation or Conjuration of any evil and wicked Spirit, Or shall consult, covenant with Entertain, Employ, feed or reward any evil and wicked Spirit to or for any intent or purpose... Or shall use, practice or Exercise any Witchcraft, Inchantment charm or Sorcery, whereby any person shall be killed, destroyed, wasted, consumed, pined or lamed in his or her body, or any part thereof, That then every such Offender or Offenders, their Aiders, Abetters, and Counsellors being of any the said Offences duly and lawfully convicted and attainted, shall suffer pains of death as a Felon or Felons.[1]

There is extensive use of noun and verb qualifying adjectives and adverbs here (such as "evil", and "wicked"), as well as complex conjunctive clauses ("Or shall use, practice or Exercise"). The result being that almost any act by any person could be interpreted as witchcraft. The very status of this text as a rule of law is thereby in question. The law likely failed as an act of communication and only became in any sense meaningful when used (Austin 1962). In other words, it was not a rule of law, but enabled arbitrary rule by powerful individuals. Care must be taken here

[1] (A Bill against Conjuration, Witchcraft and Dealing with Evil and Wicked Spirits) [December 14, 1692]. http://salem.lib.virginia.edu/n168.html, accessed on 19 July 2021.

to avoid anachronism. The language may have been perfectly cognizable to seventeenth-century New Englanders. Nonetheless, taking core sentence components (subject, object, and verb) and qualifying them or conjoining them creates interpretative space. These are timeless rules of grammar. In fact, very long sentences with multiple subordinating clauses were the norm in English statutory drafting before the twentieth century (Thring 1902). Nonetheless, of interest to this book have been changes to semantic and syntactic patterns in legislative language since democratisation. Of course laws were once used as tools for the powerful. Now, in theory, laws represent public priorities.

Although, perhaps another challenge posed by the Salem case to this book is with regard to the law's origins. In considering why indeterminate law is ever enacted, an explanation was that social and political indeterminacies are translated into under-determined legislative bargains. A specific description of this was policy ambivalence. And yet, the puritanical language hardly seems ambivalent. The Salem residents were if anything too eager to manage the problem of witchcraft. However, "ambivalence" has been used in this book according to its original construction—of there being multiple and simultaneous sources of valence. It is clear that the Salem law describes a willingness to act, so there was no ambivalence in the contemporary sense of being lackadaisical. The law does however betray the terror felt by these people and their incapacity to fix on a coherent solution. Everything is thrown into the legislative net here: "consult, covenant with Entertain, Employ, feed or reward". The people of Salem demanded solutions, but the law makers did not know what was optimal. There were multiple and simultaneous points of fear in need of legislative solution. The law's indeterminacy is at root derived from their not knowing what to do, and not really knowing the evil that they believed was oppressing them. They were striking out in all directions with indeterminate fury.

The Salem Trials are of course extreme examples. But there are some similarities to contemporary difficulties in enunciating policy complexity. Whether law makers are similarly driven by fear, as in counterterrorism, or the desire to please a diverse electorate, laws betray the sense of not knowing what text will fit an as yet unknown context. Over a century after the Salem Witchcraft Trials, Chief Justice John Marshall would offer one of the earliest and most famous interpretations of text designed to adapt to changing context. Indeed, it was just two adjectives and a conjunction in "necessary and proper". This "elastic clause" was litigated in *McCulloch v. Maryland* to determine what may be necessary for the federal government:

> Such is the character of human language, that no word conveys to the mind, in all situations, one single definite idea; and nothing is more common than to use words in a figurative sense. Almost all compositions contain words, which, taken in a their rigorous sense, would convey a meaning different from that which is obviously intended... The word 'necessary' is of this description. It has not a fixed character, peculiar to itself. It admits of all degrees of comparison; and is often connected with other words, which increase or diminish the impression the mind receives of the urgency it imports. A thing may be necessary, very necessary, absolutely or indispensably necessary. To no mind would the same idea be conveyed by these several phrases.[2]

Marshall's philological theory captures post-positivism (MacCormick 2005). In that, an interpretation is persuasive if it can be recognised as valid by language users (Hart 1961). But, by extension we may be tempted to conclude that all social demands (and hence all legislative language) are ambivalent as to the future. If future context is unknowable, then no text can hope to capture, restrain, or define it. Text can, nonetheless, be more or less meaningful on its face. Some laws are so tightly constructed as to be arbitrary and inflexible. Laws that define certain ages of capacity would fit this description. And, law at least has the conceit of determining future behaviour. Imagine a sport where the rules were considered so indeterminate that it was confusingly unplayable. There are distinctions drawn between more or less meaningful guides to lawfulness, or else there would be anarchy. But we have uncovered evidence of significant changes to the language of laws that have likely undermined any logic of communication (Schmidt 2008).

Starting with the superordinate sources of law, Chapter Three described significant changes to the language of constitutionalism. Offered there was a rudimentary taxonomy of constitutions according to their indeterminacy volumes, being the capacity each constitution has for reinterpretation without amendment. The "volume" was measured as the age of the constitution ('*x*'—measured in years since the first modern

[2] 17 U.S. (4 Wheat.) 316 (1819).

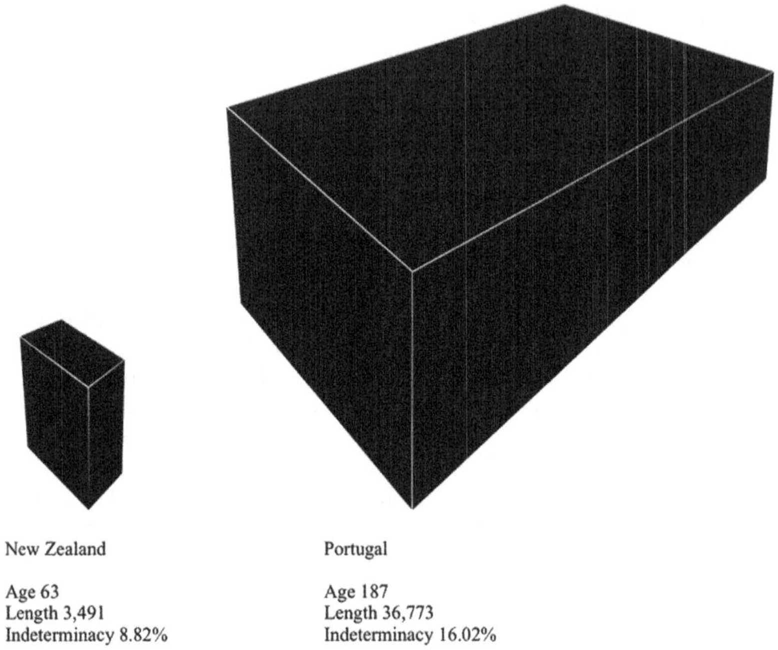

Fig. 10.1 Indeterminacy volumes of the New Zealand and the Portuguese Constitutions (*Source* Author's creation)

constitution of 1789), the word length ('*y*'), and the percentage of all words that are noun or verb qualifiers, conjunctions or indeterminate modal verbs ('*z*'). Younger constitutions ('*x*') are assumed to be more indeterminate because they are typically derivative of various international legal traditions, and have not established a settled subtext. Whereas, older constitutions retain greater coherence from a single nation's values (Horowitz 2002). These volumes can be compared figuratively, allowing us to visualise the interpretative space available (Lester and Piore 2004). In Fig. 10.1, for example, New Zealand is contrasted with Portugal:

Portugal's constitutional volume is markedly greater than New Zealand's. If we penetrate further, specific pairwise comparisons stand out. For instance, on equality before the law, New Zealand's constitution states (in Article 21):

> For the purposes of this Act, the prohibited grounds of discrimination are – ethnic or national origins.

And for Portugal, the construction states (in Article 13):

> No one shall be privileged, favoured, prejudiced, deprived of any right or exempted from any duty on the basis of ancestry, sex, race, language, place of origin, religion, political or ideological beliefs, education, economic situation, social circumstances or sexual orientation.

The differences in construction may be reductively described as between binary and analogue. In New Zealand, the copula verb "are" connects, in a binary fashion, the predicate (ethnic or national origins) to the subject (prohibited grounds of discrimination). The adjectives "ethnic" and "national" are nonetheless capable of multiple interpretations. In Portugal's version, a more analogue approach to categorisation is employed (Musolff 2004). It is not that "p things *are* q things" but a string of adjectives and conjunctions create the effect that "p-like *can* be construed as q-like". For instance, "no one shall be... favoured... on the basis of... social circumstances". Such a broadly worded protection against favourable treatment is comparatively indeterminate. The text lacks meaning until it is used in context by those with sufficient power to obtain extra-constitutional bargains.

Beneath the level of constitutions, there have also been significant changes in both the volume and determinacy of national legislation. In volumetric terms, there has been increased legislative output in all five of the countries studied. As a striking example, the UK's *Proceeds of Crime Act 2002* is, at 114,543 words, longer than the entire output of criminal legislation in that country from 1950–1970. And these changes in legislative quantity have of course been noticed by policy actors. Also documented by some have been changes to the relative determinacy of modern legislation. Indeed it was these qualitative assessments that encouraged the development of a machine reading algorithm to test the hypotheses rigorously and longitudinally. For instance, Pierre Mazeaud, the former President of the Conseil constitutionnel denounced indeterminate legislation where powers and duties were "unintelligible and inaccessible" to citizens. Sir Christopher Foster (2005, 340), a former British civil servant, made a connection between inaccessible language and judicial power:

> Worse legislation hands more power to judges because in practice they, rather than subsequent amending legislation, have the task of ironing out the incompleteness or ambiguities of laws and the inconsistencies between them.

Whether indeterminate law is necessarily "worse" depends on what it is to be used for. In the German *Mutzenbacher* decision, for example, a nuanced analysis was possible thanks to linguistic flexibility. Specifically it was ruled—in balancing freedom of expression against child protection—that pornography can be artistic, and art can be pornographic.[3] Such adaptability to changing expectations and contexts would be impossible with rigid and arbitrary legalese. Nonetheless, there are moral implications to the empirical findings of the book. These were summarised by the US Supreme Court in the 1972 case of *Grayned v. City of Rockford*.[4]

> Vague laws offend several important values. First, because we assume that man is free to steer between lawful and unlawful conduct, we insist that laws give the person of ordinary intelligence a reasonable opportunity to know what is prohibited, so that he may act accordingly… Second, if arbitrary and discriminatory enforcement is to be prevented, laws must provide explicit standards for those who apply them. A vague law impermissibly delegates basic policy matters to policemen, judges, and juries for resolution on an ad hoc and subjective basis, with the attendant dangers of arbitrary and discriminatory applications.

Interestingly, the Supreme Court felt that indeterminate law made arbitrary enforcement more, not less, likely, because it comes down to the whim of street-level bureaucrats. It was a point echoed by the Canadian Supreme Court in the 1990 case of *R. v. Keegstra*[5]:

> Given the vagueness of the prohibition… there is again a danger that the legislation may have a chilling effect on legitimate activities important to our society by subjecting innocent persons to constraints born out of a fear of the criminal process. Finally, the process by which the prohibition is effected – the criminal law – is the severest our society can impose

[3] BVerfG, Nov 3 1993, 1 BvR 402/87.

[4] 408 U.S. 104.

[5] CanLII 24 (SCC), [1990] 3 SCR 697.

> and is arguably unnecessary given the availability of alternate and more appropriate and effective remedies.

The crux of moral opposition to indeterminate law is that it implicates liberty. State officials can use linguistic confusion to determine lawfulness without accountability. They can thereby even degrade the concept of law as a guide to legitimate behaviour. At worst, indeterminate laws can be used as weapons for control. For instance, the US Code defines, and prohibits, the following:

> (1) 'torture' means an act committed by a person acting under the color of law specifically intended to inflict severe physical or mental pain or suffering.[6]

During the "War on Terror", John Yoo, as Deputy Assistant Attorney General, took the adjective "severe" to craft a defence for "enhanced interrogation techniques" (Rizzo 2014, 192). Practices such as putting detainees in stress positions, waterboarding them, and subjecting them to sexual degradation, were not, according to his memorandum, "severe". But, of course, it is important not to over generalise the moral implications of legislative indeterminacy. We have come across many instances in the preceding pages of laws attempting to capture public mood, and it simply being the case that the public mood is indeterminate. The fact that lawmakers seek to accommodate ambivalent priorities within a single text suggests that the inputs to democracy are at least reflected in its outputs (Easton 1965). Furthermore, we have seen instances where modern legislation attempts to define current practices, but in a more humane way than was achieved in customary law. This is particularly clear in common law jurisdictions, where centuries of legal accretion have been modernised with compendious, but no less well-intentioned, statutory schemes. For example, Lords Hughes and Toulson described the modernisation of joint enterprise murder in the 2018 UK Supreme Court case of *R v. Jogee*:

> There has indeed been a progressive move away from the historic tendency of the common law to presume as a matter of law that the 'natural and probable consequences' of a man's act were intended, culminating in England and Wales in its statutory removal by section 8 of the Criminal

[6] 8 U.S.C. §§ 2340–2340A.

> Justice Act 1967. Since then in England and Wales the foreseeability of the consequences has been a matter of evidence from which intention may be, but need not necessarily be, inferred.[7]

Statute law has in many instances replaced customary law, and even sought to regulate social habit. That these laws are often indeterminate is unsurprising given the messy complexities of democratic statecraft. And, indeed, lawmakers have taken steps to make laws otherwise more accessible. This book would have been impossible without the readily accessible digital copies of public laws. And, the socio-linguistics of law are adapting to a wider audience. In the past, the expected readership of legislation was a narrow practitioner elite. Modern laws are drafted with greater sensitivity to civic engagement. Laws are therefore more likely to be accompanied by explanatory notes, and other ancillary elements that describe why the law exists and where it came from (Butt and Castle 2001).

But none of this gets us away from the facts that there is more law that is of lesser determinacy. And, the consequences have included judicialisation. As Ronald Dworkin argued, the task of adjudication is so complex that even Hercules himself would struggle to balance the various sources of law to achieve the optimal resolution (Dworkin 1986). For H.L.A. Hart judges apply a "rule of recognition" that could be positively identified, and was not therefore a hermeneutic or inter-subjective interpretation of reality (Hart 1961). However, indeterminacies in legislation, and rapid changes in the patterns of legal language, make identifying rules of recognition more difficult. Due to the complexity and mercuriality of rules of law, the criteria of legal validity are persuasive rather than demonstrative (MacCormick 2005). Judicial behaviour may not be bound by purely objective rules, but it is nonetheless constrained by a logic of appropriateness (March and Olsen 1989). If judges simply failed to persuade audiences that their rulings accord with norms of law they would lose authority, which is their only policy resource. Deciding cases to advance personal preferences is difficult therefore. There are complex court hierarchies and multi-judge panels in place to minimise individuality.

But, of course, the widening interpretative spaces in legislation mean that judges have greater opportunities to push their own agendas. The

[7] [2016] UKSC 8 at para 73.

argument that judges rule according to norms of adjudication was fiercely rejected by Martin Shapiro (1983, 542):

> The Godfather of this jurisprudence of values is of course Dworkin, and Dworkin's work in turn is part of a far broader movement in moral and political philosophy. That movement rejects the notion that moral values are simply undebatable matters of personal preference such as 'I like vanilla.' The tendency of contemporary moral philosophy is toward showing that some ethical statements are clearly more true, or at least more appealing, satisfying, or persuasive than others so that morals is not simply a matter of individual preference or positing. Because this movement is also a reaction to utilitarianism it is sometimes called 'post consequentialist' ethics.

For Shapiro, and many others (for example, Waldron 2005), describing judicial review as rule-bound is impossible if those rules are made up by judges as they go. We would hardly describe a game as constrained by rules if the umpire was making up the rules during a match. However, the political weakness of courts means that judges are tightly bound by expectations. That these expectations are not neatly enumerated in a rulebook is just a consequence of the game's complexity. Hence, judicial norms are not puffed-up "ethical statements", but rather institutional requirements that are generally accepted. Judges cannot know for sure what these institutional norms require of them, but they will know the core principle and it is at the periphery that change happens (Hart 1961; Stone Sweet 2000). Therefore, we should not be so quick to throw away legal positivism. There are positively identifiable core principles of adjudication. There are also increasing opportunities to stretch interpretations across newly legislated policy problems, and via expansively worded statutes. But, sticking to game theory, if judges over stretch their weak position, they risk being overruled and having their voice delegitimised (Vanberg 2001).

Judicialisation is nonetheless highly controversial in most democracies. There are practitioners and observers of politics in the countries studied that blame judges for judicialising policy. Their assumption being that judges wanted power and took it. Such agency-based theories often present judges as anti-democratic and out-of-touch in their wokish liberality. In the UK, for one, came fierce rebukes against judges for ruling against the elected government. At the extreme end, examples included the "Enemies of the People" response to the *Miller v. Prime*

Minister judgement.[8] Other observers have called for reform to judicial power, including the UK's withdrawal from the European Convention on Human Rights and repeal of the *Human Rights Act 1998*.[9] And, as seen in the preceding pages, criticism of individuals judges for their "bad decisions" is common to all of the five jurisdictions analysed. Beyond the democracies studied, there are judges being fired in Poland, and courts being packed with partisans in Hungary.

Quis custodiet ipsos custodes? Who guards the guardians? When active, judges are contributing to an on-going dialogue between the legislature and the courts. If the courts' are considered to be wrong then legislators can come back with a rejoinder (Keck 2017). It is notable how rarely the courts are ever overruled by legislatures in the democracies examined.[10] What has instead happened is that governments complain about judges, but these complaints are not followed up by action to address the supposedly excessive interference. If the government truly suspected a ruling of devastating impropriety, then they should advise legislators to reverse it, or even petition for the impeachment of recidivist judges. And yet, removal of judges from their office is incredibly rare in the countries studied. No appeal judge in England and Wales, for example, has ever been impeached. Only two lower court judges have been, one of whom was caught smuggling whiskey from Guernsey to England.[11] Politicians are of course using courts as a whipping post. Judges are so institutionally weak that there are few repercussions to blaming them for policy failures.

Complaints of judicial activism are often predicated on its supposed insult to popular sovereignty. Put simply, a group of highly unrepresentative judges are overruling or restraining a popularly mandated government. But the real cause of judicialisation is the ambivalence of popular sovereignty and the confusing instructions delivered from legislatures. The restraints on popular sovereignty are not manufactured by

[8] https://www.dailymail.co.uk/news/article-3903436/Enemies-people-Fury-touch-judges-defied-17-4m-Brexit-voters-trigger-constitutional-crisis.html, accessed 11 March 2020.

[9] https://www.parliament.uk/business/lords/media-centre/house-of-lords-media-notices/2019/january-2019/human-rights-act-is-not-safe-after-brexit/, accessed 28 September 2021.

[10] Of all the declarations of incompatibility made there has never been an instance where Parliament ignored the judicial decision.

[11] https://www.judiciary.gov.uk/about-the-judiciary/the-judiciary-the-government-and-the-constitution/jud-acc-ind/judges-and-parliament/, accessed 28 September 2021.

judges, but are consequences of mass democracy and its "institutionalised uncertainty" (Alexander 2002). Albert Venn Dicey recognised fewer constraints on the pre-democratic, nineteenth-century Parliament that he observed. "Parliament", he said, "can do everything, but make a woman a man and a man a woman" (Potter 2015, 4). In other words, Parliament is all-powerful but must conform to the only constraint on her sovereignty: the law of the possible. In the same way that God could not make a triangle with four sides. Dicey was ultimately proved wrong as to what would be possible by section 1(1) of the *Gender Recognition Act 2004*:

> A person of either gender who is aged at least 18 may make an application for a gender recognition certificate on the basis of – (a) living in the other gender, or (b) having changed gender under the law of a country or territory outside the United Kingdom.

Parliament was able to make a woman a man and a man a woman. This would have been technically possible when Dicey wrote, but society was not prepared to accept it. The rule of law is hence a social, not natural phenomenon (Hart 1961). The only natural limits to the law are those imposed by the laws of physics and logic. Legislation cannot order things that go up must never come down. Nor could a law demand a conclusion precede its own predicate. Legislatures and societies have not created laws that defy physics, nor, for the most part, logic, but they nevertheless are more likely in the twenty-first century to create law that cannot be comprehended without creative interpretation.[12]

Additionally, confusion is why, for the most part, creative rulings from the court favour the weaker parties to litigation. The term "judicial activism" implies unrestrained energy, and even flippancy. But the very opposite is more often true. By denying a power and enhancing autonomy, the court is preventing what may be an act of disproportionate interference in the lives of individuals or groups. The goal of democratic power is to make citizens better off, but there will almost always be losers when power is used. The courts are simply trying to ensure the exercise of power is justified and in accordance with law, such as it can be

[12] Albeit it could be argued that retrospective law comes close to achieving this backwards reasoning. See Ewing (2010), 116–120.

understood. Contemporary court activism has been spurred by indeterminate governance from other branches. This is in turn dependent on atrophying institutional, ideological, and structural sources of coherence in public discourse. Activism is, in fact, reactive. Judges are incentivised to conserve institutional integrity through their rulings, not to up-end the system in pursuit of their favoured policies. Countries with very changeable legal genres present both the symptom and the cause of political indeterminacy.

Nonetheless, there are examples of court decisions that have damaged the authority of judges. It would be unsustainable to argue that judges always make appropriate judgements. The claim made is that judges are incentivised to be cautious, because they are so weak relative to other state organs. And yet, the self-reflective nature of judicial activism is perhaps its most controversial aspect. In other words, activism enlarges the procedural and substantive capabilities of the court itself. Active adjudication can also jar with judicial independence. Taking an active role suggests the judges change the conditions of the dispute. Some scholars would argue that judges hide their behaviour in the garb of constitutionalism and "appropriateness", when in fact they are acting in their own interests. A famous proponent of the view that judges were fundamentally undemocratic and biased was J.A.G. Griffith (1977). He used a class-based model, claiming that the ideological biases of individual judges are the only relevant variable in judicial politics. Judges are socially homogenous, he argued, and are subsumed by their class identity into protecting a public interest that is fundamentally bourgeois, by maintaining private property, minimising "moral danger", and generally supporting the interests of conservative political parties. The problem with this position is that it is fundamentally unverifiable, and is therefore not empirical political science. Also, judges in the countries studied have protected the interests of capitalism and a bourgeois state, because that was what the rules of law expected of them (Hutchinson 2017). Had judges sought to redistribute economic power from the bench, that would have been constitutionally indefensible. It is not the judges to blame for class antagonism in post-war democracy, it is the voters and politicians. Hence, if we want to assess changes in judicial behaviour we are better off looking outside the judiciary for the means and opportunities to change.

There have been a diverse set of justices with very different revealed preferences, hemmed by tight institutional constraints, deprived of material and infrastructural resources, most of whom have been moving the law in roughly the same direction. This direction has, despite fits and starts, been towards the liberalisation of the law, or, in other words, assuming that law is there to empower individuals and to rein in the state. This can be seen from court imposed limits to government or private power. This liberal momentum has been to the benefit of both gun owners and women choosing to terminate a pregnancy. In other words, the restraints imposed on power do not fit neatly into any party platforms and the judges' own personalities do not count as much as do the changed understandings of what it means to be a free citizen.

Added to which, it is a simple truth of collective decision-making that better and more durable decisions are made when some decision-makers have the ability to veto proposals. This is Arrow's paradox (1950). It will be familiar to anyone who has served on a large committee. It is only when the range of options of the committee is limited that effective decision-making can take place. Otherwise committee members will delay a decision interminably to secure a different outcome. The paradox is that collective decision-making only works when there are some decision-makers with dictatorial power, like the chair of a committee. Similarly, judges can limit the range of choices available, but this can make the choices taken more efficient and durable. Without judges managing indeterminacies in law, public policies would be less effective and more likely to serve a sectoral elite (Epstein et al. 2001).

But why should judges perform this dictatorial task of limiting the range of possible decisions? Why entrust the last remaining relic of pre democratic governance with such a sensitive task? It can be done by citizen participation, as Germany showed with consensus institutions reducing indeterminacies in law. There could even be citizen assemblies to resolve disputes, in a similar approach to that used by juries in criminal litigation. But it is the case that, for now, judges are the most efficient tool for repairing a logic of communication in modern democracies. Their task is technically complex and not widely appreciated. Few players like the referee, but they would not want to play without one. Judicialisation is, at root, extra-textual legalism. It is inferring new law from a range of textual and extra-textual sources. Judicialisation is the reification into text of untextual, under-textualised, or intertextual norms. It is triggered, but not solely caused by, indeterminacy in law. Indeterminacy also creates friction and victims who resort to litigation for satisfaction. There are, therefore, normative implications. Liberal democracy needs to be literal democracy. This is more than trite wordplay. The foundations of democracy are shared power through dialogue and debate. If the final communiqué of public discourse is indeterminate and inconsistent with expectations, it will likely represent and reinforce dysfunction in the democratic process. Either this communicative failure will be resolved by legislators, or it will end up in court.

References

Alexander, Gerard. 2002. Institutionalized Uncertainty, The Rule of Law, and The Sources of Democratic Stability. *Comparative Political Studies* 35 (10): 1145–1170.

Arrow, Kenneth. 1950. A Difficulty in the Concept of Social Welfare. *Journal of Political Economy* 58 (4): 328–346.

Austin, John L. 1962. *How to Do Things with Words*. Oxford: Clarendon Press.

Butt, Peter, and Richard Castle. 2001. *Modern Legal Drafting: A Guide to Using Clearer Language*. Cambridge: Cambridge University Press.

Dworkin, Ronald. 1986. *Law's Empire*. London: Fontana.

Easton, David. 1965. *A Framework for Political Analysis*. New Jersey: Prentice-Hall.

Epstein, Lee, Jack Knight, and Olga Shvestova. 2001. The Role of Constitutional Courts in the Establishment and Maintenance of Democratic Systems of Government. *Law & Society Review* 35 (1): 117–164.

Ewing, Keith. 2010. *Bonfire of the Liberties*. Oxford: Oxford University Press.

Ferejohn, John, and Barry Weingast. 1991. *Limitation of Statutes: Strategic Statutory Interpretation*. New York: Columbia Center for Law and Economic Studies.

Foster, Christopher D. 2005. *British Government in Crisis, or, the Third English Revolution*. Oxford: Hart Publishing.

Gibson, James L. 1983. From Simplisticity to Complexity: The Development of Theory in the Study of Judicial Behavior. *Political Behavior* 5 (1): 7–49.

Griffith, John. 1977. *The Politics of the Judiciary*. Manchester: Manchester University Press.

Hart, H.L.A. 1961. *The Concept of the Law*. Oxford: Clarendon.

Horowitz, Donald. L. 2002. Constitutional Design: Proposals versus Processes. In *The Architecture of Democracy: Constitutional Design, Conflict Management, and Democracy*, ed. Andrew Reynolds. Oxford: Oxford University Press.

Hutchinson, Allan. 2017. The politics of constitutional law: A critical approach. In *The Oxford Handbook of the Canadian Constitution*, ed. Peter Oliver, Patrick Macklem, and Nathalie Des Rosiers. Oxford: Oxford University Press.

Keck, Thomas M. 2017. The Relationship Between Courts and Legislatures. In *The Oxford Handbook of U.S. Judicial Behavior*, ed. Lee Epstein and Stefanie A. Lindquist. Oxford: Oxford University Press.

Lester, Richard, and Michael Piore. 2004. *Innovation: The Missing Dimension.* Cambridge, MA: Harvard University Press.

MacCormick, Neil. 2005. *Rhetoric and the Rule of Law: A Theory of Legal Reasoning*. Oxford: Oxford University Press.

March, James, and Johan Olsen. 1989. *Rediscovering Institutions: The Organisational Basis of Politics*. New York: The Free Press.

Musolff, Andreas. 2004. *Metaphor and Political Discourse: Analogical Reasoning in Debates About Europe*. Basingstoke: Palgrave Macmillan.

Potter, Harry. 2015. *Law, liberty and the constitution: A brief history of the common law*. Woodbridge, Suffolk: Boydell & Brewer.

Rizzo, John A. 2014. *Company Man: Thirty Years of Controversy and Crisis in the CIA*. New York: Scribner.

Schmidt, Vivien. 2008. Discursive Institutionalism: The Explanatory Power of Ideas and Discourse. *Annual Review of Political Science* 11: 303–326.

Shapiro, Martin. 1983. Recent Developments in Political Jurisprudence. *Political Research Quarterly* 36 (4): 541–548.

Stone Sweet, Alec. 2000. *Governing with Judges: Constitutional Politics in Europe*. Oxford: Oxford University Press.

Tate, C. Neal, and Torbjorn Vallinder. 1995. *The Global Expansion of Judicial Power*. New York: New York University Press.

Thring, Henry. 1902. *Practical Legislation: The Composition of Acts of Parliament and Business Documents*.London: John Murray.

Vanberg, Georg. 2001. Legislative-Judicial Relations: A Game-Theoretic Approach to Constitutional Review. *American Journal of Political Science* 45 (2): 346–361.

Waldron, Jeremy. 2005. The Core of the Case Against Judicial Review. *Yale Law Journal* 115: 1346–1407.

Cases

(continued)

M. Williams, *Judges and the Language of Law*,
https://doi.org/10.1007/978-3-030-91495-0

(continued)

(continued)

(continued)

(continued)

(continued)

(continued)

(continued)

(continued)

(continued)

(continued)

(continued)

Statutes

(continued)

(continued)

(continued)

(continued)

Index

M. Williams, *Judges and the Language of Law*,
https://doi.org/10.1007/978-3-030-91495-0

The manufacturer's authorised representative in the EU is Springer Nature Customer Service Centre GmbH, Europaplatz 3, 69115 Heidelberg, Germany. If you have any concerns regarding our products, please contact ProductSafety@springernature.com

Printed and bound by CPI Group (UK) Ltd, Croydon, CR0 4YY
30/09/2026
02225502-0017